6/628 - 710

W9-ACY-797

a.G. Cross

1988

Mama

CONISTON

CONISTON

BY

WINSTON CHURCHILL

AUTHOR OF "RICHARD CARVEL," "THE CRISIS,"
"THE CROSSING," ETC.

WITH ILLUSTRATIONS BY
FLORENCE SCOVEL SHINN

New York
THE MACMILLAN COMPANY
LONDON: MACMILLAN & CO., LTD.
1906

Norwood Press
J. S. Cushing & Co. — Berwick & Smith Co.
Norwood, Mass., U.S.A.

"We have been compelled to see what was weak in democracy as well as what was strong. We have begun obscurely to recognize that things do not go of themselves, and that popular government is not in itself a panacea, is no better than any other form except as the virtue and wisdom of the people make it so, and that when men undertake to do their own kingship, they enter upon the dangers and responsibilities as well as the privileges of the function. Above all, it looks as if we were on the way to be persuaded that no government can be carried on by declamation."

—JAMES RUSSELL LOWELL.

CONTENTS

BOOK I

LIST OF ILLUSTRATIONS

CONISTON

CONISTON

BOOK I

CHAPTER I

ON THE DANGERS OF CURIOSITY

FIRST I am to write a love-story of long ago, of a time some little while after General Jackson had got into the White House and had shown the world what a real democracy was. The Era of the first six Presidents had closed, and a new Era had begun. I am speaking of political Eras. Certain gentlemen, with a pious belief in democracy, but with a firmer determination to get on top, arose, — and got on top. So many of these gentlemen arose in the different states, and they were so clever, and they found so many chinks in the Constitution to crawl through and steal the people's chestnuts, that the Era may be called the Boss-Era. After the Boss came along certain Things without souls, but of many minds, and found more chinks in the Constitution: bigger chinks, for the Things were bigger, and they stole more chestnuts. But I am getting far ahead of my love-story — and of my book.

The reader is warned that this first love-story will, in a few chapters, come to an end: and not to a happy end — otherwise there would be no book. Lest he should throw the book away when he arrives at this page, it is only fair to tell him that there is another and a much longer love-story later on, if he will only continue to read, in which, it is hoped, he may not be disappointed.

The hills seem to leap up against the sky as I describe that region where Cynthia Ware was born, and the very old country names help to summon up the picture. Coniston Mountain, called by some the Blue Mountain, clad in Hercynian forests, ten good miles in length, north and south, with its notch road that winds over the saddle behind the withers of it. Coniston Water, that oozes out from under the loam in a hundred places on the eastern slope, gathers into a rushing stream to cleave the very granite, flows southward around the south end of Coniston Mountain, and having turned the mills at Brampton, idles through meadows westward in its own green valley until it comes to Harwich, where it works again and tumbles into a river. Brampton and Harwich are rivals, but Coniston Water gives of its power impartially to each. From the little farm clearings on the western slope of Coniston Mountain you can sweep the broad valley of a certain broad river where grew (and grow still) the giant pines that gave many a mast to King George's navy as tribute for the land. And beyond that river rises beautiful Farewell Mountain of many colors, now sapphire, now amethyst, its crest rimmed about at evening with saffron flame; and, beyond Farewell, the emerald billows of the western peaks catching the level light. A dozen little brooks are born high among the western spruces on Coniston to score deep, cool valleys in their way through Clovelly township to the broad river — valleys full of the music of the water and fresh with the odor of the ferns.

To this day the railroad has not reached Coniston Village — nay, nor Coniston Flat, four miles nearer Brampton. The village lies on its own little shelf under the forest-clad slope of the mountain, and in the midst of its dozen houses is the green triangle where the militia used to drill on June days. At one end of the triangle is the great pine mast that graced no frigate of George's, but flew the stars and stripes on many a liberty day. Across the road is Jonah Winch's store, with a platform so high that a man may step off his horse directly on to it; with its checker-paned windows, with its dark interior smelling of coffee and apples and molasses, yes, and of Endea rum — for this was before the days of the revivals.

How those checker-paned windows bring back the picture of that village green! The meeting-house has them, lantern-like, wide and high, in three sashes — white meeting-house, seat alike of government and religion, with its terraced steeple, with its classic porches north and south. Behind it is the long shed, and in front, rising out of the milkweed and the flowering thistle, the horse block of the first meeting-house, where many a pillion has left its burden in times agone. Honest Jock Hallowell built that second meeting-house — was, indeed, still building it at the time of which we write. He had hewn every beam and king post in it, and set every plate and slip. And Jock Hallowell is the man who, unwittingly, starts this chronicle.

At noon, on one of those madcap April days of that Coniston country, Jock descended from his work on the steeple to perceive the ungainly figure of Jethro Bass coming toward him across the green. Jethro was about thirty years of age, and he wore a coonskin cap even in those days, and trousers tucked into his boots. He carried his big head bent forward, a little to one side, and was not, at first sight, a prepossessing-looking person. As our story largely concerns him, and we must get started somehow, it may be well to fix a little attention on him.

"Heigho!" said Jock, rubbing his hands on his leather apron.

"H-how be you, Jock?" said Jethro, stopping.

"Heigho!" cried Jock, "what's this game of fox and geese you're a-playin' among the farmers?"

"C-callate to git the steeple done before frost?" inquired Jethro, without so much as a smile. "B-build it tight, Jock — b-build it tight."

"Guess he'll build his'n tight, whatever it is," said Jock, looking after him as Jethro made his way to the little tannery near by.

Let it be known that there was such a thing as social rank in Coniston; and something which, for the sake of an advantageous parallel, we may call an Established Church. Coniston was a Congregational town still, and the deacons and dignitaries of that church were likewise the pillars of the state. Not many years before the time of which we write actual disestablishment had occurred, when the town ceased — as a town — to pay the salary of Priest Ware, as the minister was called. The father of Jethro Bass, Nathan the currier, had once, in a youthful lapse, permitted a Baptist preacher to immerse him in Coniston Water. This had been the extent of Nathan's religion; Jethro had none at all, and was, for this and other reasons, somewhere near the bottom of the social scale.

"Fox and geese!" repeated Jock, with his eyes still on Jethro's retreating back. The builder of the meeting-house rubbed a great, brown arm, scratched his head, and turned and came face to face with Cynthia Ware, in a poke bonnet.

Contrast is a favorite trick of authors, and no greater contrast is to be had in Coniston than that between Cynthia Ware and Jethro Bass. In the first place, Cynthia was the minister's daughter, and twenty-one. I can summon her now under the great maples of the village street, a virginal figure, gray eyes that kindled the face shaded by the poke bonnet, and up you went above the clouds.

"What about fox and geese, Jock?" said Cynthia.

"Jethro Bass," said Jock, who, by reason of his capability, was a privileged character. "Mark my words, Cynthy, Jethro Bass is an all-fired sight smarter than folks in this town think he be. They don't take notice of him, because he don't say much, and stutters. He hain't be'n eddicated a great deal, but I wouldn't be afeard to warrant he'd make a racket in the world some of these days."

"Jock Hallowell!" cried Cynthia, the gray eyes beginning to dance, "I suppose you think Jethro's going to be President."

"All right," said Jock, "you can laugh. Ever talked with Jethro?"

"I've hardly spoken two words to him in my life," she

" As our story largely concerns him."

replied. And it was true, although the little white parsonage was scarce two hundred yards from the tannery house.

"Jethro's never ailed much," Jock remarked, having reference to Cynthia's proclivities for visiting the sick. "I've seed a good many different men in my time, and I tell you, Cynthy Ware, that Jethro's got a kind of power you don't often come acrost. Folks don't suspicion it."

In spite of herself, Cynthia was impressed by the ring of sincerity in the builder's voice. Now that she thought of it, there was rugged power in Jethro's face, especially when he took off the coonskin cap. She always nodded a greeting when she saw him in the tannery yard or on the road, and sometimes he nodded back, but oftener he had not appeared to see her. She had thought this failure to nod stupidity, but it might after all be abstraction.

"What makes you think he has ability?" she asked, picking flowers from a bunch of arbutus she held.

"He's rich, for one thing," said Jock. He had not intended a dissertation on Jethro Bass, but he felt bound to defend his statements.

"Rich!"

"Wal, he hain't poor. He's got as many as thirty mortgages round among the farmers — some on land, and some on cattle."

"How did he make the money?" demanded Cynthia, in surprise.

"Hides an' wool an' bark — turned 'em over an' swep' in. Gits a load, and Lyman Hull drives him down to Boston with that six-hoss team. Lyman gits drunk, Jethro keeps sober and saves."

Jock began to fashion some wooden pegs with his knife, for nails were scarce in those days. Still Cynthia lingered, picking flowers from the bunch.

"What did you mean by 'fox and geese,' Jock?" she said presently.

Jock laughed. He did not belong to the Establishment, but was a Universalist; politically he admired General

Jackson. "What'd you say if Jethro was Chairman of the next Board of Selectmen?" he demanded.

No wonder Cynthia gasped. Jethro Bass, Chairman of the Board, in the honored seat of Deacon Moses Hatch, the perquisite of the church in Coniston! The idea was heresy. As a matter of fact, Jock himself uttered it as a playful exaggeration. Certain nonconformist farmers, of whom there were not a few in the town, had come into Jonah Winch's store that morning; and Jabez Miller, who lived on the north slope, had taken away the breath of the orthodox by suggesting that Jethro Bass be nominated for town office. Jock Hallowell had paused once or twice on his work on the steeple to look across the tree-tops at Coniston shouldering the sky. He had been putting two and two together, and now he was merely making five out of it, instead of four. He remembered that Jethro Bass had for some years been journeying through the town, buying his hides and wool, and collecting the interest on his mortgages.

Cynthia would have liked to reprove Jock Hallowell, and tell him there were some subjects which should not be joked about. Jethro Bass, Chairman of the Board of Selectmen!

"Well, here comes young Moses, I do believe," said Jock, gathering his pegs into his apron and preparing to ascend once more. "Callated he'd spring up pretty soon."

"Jock, you do talk foolishly for a man who is able to build a church," said Cynthia, as she walked away. The young Moses referred to was Moses Hatch, Junior, son of the pillar of the Church and State, and it was an open secret that he was madly in love with Cynthia. Let it be said of him that he was a steady-going young man, and that he sighed for the moon.

"Moses," said the girl, when they came in sight of the elms that shaded the gable of the parsonage, "what do you think of Jethro Bass?"

"Jethro Bass!" exclaimed honest Moses, "whatever put him into your head, Cynthy?" Had she mentioned,

perhaps, any other young man in Coniston, Moses would
have been eaten with jealousy.

"Oh, Jock was joking about him.   What do you think
of him ?"

"Never thought one way or t'other," he answered.
"Jethro never had much to do with the boys.   He's always
in that tannery, or out buyin' of hides.   He does make
a sharp bargain when he buys a hide.   We always goes
shares on our'n."

Cynthia was not only the minister's daughter, — distinction enough, — her reputation for learning was spread
through the country roundabout, and at the age of twenty
she had had an offer to teach school in Harwich.   Once a
week in summer she went to Brampton, to the Social
library there, and sat at the feet of that Miss Lucretia
Penniman of whom Brampton has ever been so proud —
Lucretia Penniman, one of the first to sound the clarion
note for the intellectual independence of American women ;
who wrote the "Hymn to Coniston" ; who, to the awe of
her townspeople, went out into the great world and became editress of a famous woman's journal, and knew
Longfellow and Hawthorne and Bryant.   Miss Lucretia
it was who started the Brampton Social Library, and filled it
with such books as both sexes might read with profit.
Never was there a stricter index than hers.   Cynthia,
Miss Lucretia loved, and the training of that mind was
the pleasantest task of her life.

Curiosity as a factor has never, perhaps, been given its
proper weight by philosophers.   Besides being fatal to a
certain domestic animal, as an instigating force it has
brought joy and sorrow into the lives of men and women,
and made and marred careers.   And curiosity now laid
hold of Cynthia Ware.   Why in the world she should ever
have been curious about Jethro Bass is a mystery to many,
for the two of them were as far apart as the poles.   Cynthia,
of all people, took to watching the tanner's son, and listening to the brief colloquies he had with other men at Jonah
Winch's store, when she went there to buy things for
the parsonage ; and it seemed to her that Jock had not

"Moses was a steady-going young man."

been altogether wrong, and that there was in the man
an indefinable but very compelling force. And when a
woman begins to admit that a man has force, her curiosity
usually increases. On one or two of these occasions
Cynthia had been startled to find his eyes fixed upon her,
and though the feeling she had was closely akin to fear,
she found something distinctly pleasurable in it.

May came, and the pools dried up, the orchards were
pink and white, the birches and the maples were all yellow-
green on the mountain side against the dark pines, and
Cynthia was driving the minister's gig to Brampton.
Ahead of her, in the cañon made by the road between the
great woods, strode an uncouth but powerful figure—coonskin cap, homespun breeches tucked into boots, and all.
The gig slowed down, and Cynthia began to tremble with
that same delightful fear. She knew it must be wicked,
because she liked it so much. Unaccountable thing!
She felt all akin to the nature about her, and her blood
was coursing as the sap rushes through a tree. She would
not speak to him ; of that she was sure, and equally sure
that he would not speak to her. The horse was walking
now, and suddenly Jethro Bass faced around, and her
heart stood still.

"H-how be you, Cynthy?" he said.

"How do you do, Jethro?"

A thrush in the woods began to sing a hymn, and they
listened. After that a silence, save for the notes of answering birds quickened by the song, the minister's horse
nibbling at the bushes. Cynthia herself could not have
explained why she lingered. Suddenly he shot a question
at her.

"Where be you goin'?"

"To Brampton, to get Miss Lucretia to change this
book," and she held it up from her lap. It was a very
large book.

"Wh-what's it about?" he demanded.

"Napoleon Bonaparte."

"Who was he?"

"He was a very strong man. He began life poor and

unknown, and fought his way upward until he conquered
the world."

"C-conquered the world, did you say?   Conquered the
world?"

"Yes."

Jethro pondered.

"Guess there's somethin' wrong about that book —
somethin' wrong.   Conquer the United States?"

Cynthia smiled.   She herself did not realize that we
were not a part of the world, then.

" He conquered Europe, where all the kings and queens
are, and became a king himself — an emperor."

" I want to know!" said Jethro.   " You said he was a
poor boy?"

"Why don't you read the book, Jethro?" Cynthia answered.   " I am sure I can get Miss Lucretia to let you
have it."

" Don't know as I'd understand it," he demurred.

"I'll try to explain what you don't understand," said
Cynthia, and her heart gave a bound at the very idea.

" Will you?" he said, looking at her eagerly.   " Will
you?   You mean it?"

" Certainly," she answered, and blushed, not knowing
why.   "I — I must be going," and she gathered up the
reins.

" When will you give it to me?"

" I'll stop at the tannery when I come back from Brampton," she said, and drove on.   Once she gave a fleeting
glance over her shoulder, and he was still standing where
she had left him.

When she returned, in the yellow afternoon light that
flowed over wood and pasture, he came out of the tannery
door.   Jake Wheeler or Speedy Bates, the *journeyman*
tailoress, from whom little escaped, could not have said it
was by design — thought nothing, indeed, of that part
of it.

" As I live!" cried Speedy from the window to Aunt
Lucy Prescott in the bed, "if Cynthy ain't givin' him a
book as big as the Bible!"

Aunt Lucy hoped, first, that it was the Bible, and second, that Jethro would read it. Aunt Lucy, and Established Church Coniston in general, believed in snatching brands from the burning, and who so deft as Cynthia at this kind of snatching! So Cynthia herself was a hypocrite for once, and did not know it. At that time Jethro's sins were mostly of omission. As far as rum was concerned, he was a creature after Aunt Lucy's own heart, for he never touched it: true, gaunt Deacon Ira Perkins, tithing-man, had once chided him for breaking the Sabbath — shooting at a fox.

To return to the book. As long as he lived, Jethro looked back to the joy of the monumental task of mastering its contents. In his mind, Napoleon became a rough Yankee general; of the cities, villages, and fortress he formed as accurate a picture as a resident of Venice from Marco Polo's account of Tartary. Jethro had learned to read, after a fashion, to write, add, multiply, and divide. He knew that George Washington and certain barefooted companions had forced a proud Britain to her knees, and much of the warring in the book took color from Captain Timothy Prescott's stories of General Stark and his campaigns, heard at Jonah Winch's store. What Paris looked like, or Berlin, or the Hospice of St. Bernard — though imaged by a winter Coniston — troubled Jethro not at all; the thing that stuck in his mind was that Napoleon — for a considerable time, at least — compelled men to do his bidding. Constitutions crumble before the Strong. Not that Jethro philosophized about constitutions. Existing conditions presented themselves, and it occurred to him that there were crevices in the town system, and ways into power through the crevices for men clever enough to find them.

A week later, and in these same great woods on the way to Brampton, Cynthia overtook him once more. It was characteristic of him that he plunged at once into the subject uppermost in his mind.

"Not a very big place, this Corsica — not a very big place."

"A little island in the Mediterranean," said Cynthia.

"Hum.   Country folks, the Bonapartes — country folks?"

Cynthia laughed.

"I suppose you might call them so," she said.   "They were poor, and lived out of the world."

"He was a smart man.   But he found things goin' his way.   Didn't have to move 'em."

"Not at first," she admitted; "but he had to move mountains later.   How far have you read?"

"One thing that helped him," said Jethro, in indirect answer to this question, "he got a smart woman for his wife — a smart woman."

Cynthia looked down at the reins in her lap, and she felt again that wicked stirring within her, — incredible stirring of minister's daughter for tanner's son.   Coniston believes, and always will believe, that the social bars are strong enough.   So Cynthia looked down at the reins.

"Poor Josephine!" she said, "I always wish he had not cast her off."

"C-cast her off?" said Jethro.   "Cast her off!   Why did he do that?"

"After a while, when he got to be Emperor, he needed a wife who would be more useful to him.   Josephine had become a drag.   He cared more about getting on in the world than he did about his wife."

Jethro looked away contemplatively.

"Wa-wahn't the woman to blame any?" he said.

"Read the book, and you'll see," retorted Cynthia, flicking her horse, which started at all gaits down the road.   Jethro stood in his tracks, staring, but this time he did not see her face above the hood of the gig.   Presently he trudged on, head downward, pondering upon another problem than Napoleon's.   Cynthia, at length, arrived in Brampton Street, in a humor that puzzled the good Miss Lucretia sorely.

CHAPTER II

ON THE WISDOM OF CHARITY

THE sun had dropped behind the mountain, leaving Coniston in amethystine shadow, and the last bee had flown homeward from the apple blossoms in front of Aunt Lucy Prescott's window, before Cynthia returned. Aunt Lucy was Cynthia's grandmother, and eighty-nine years of age. Still she sat in her window beside the lilac bush, lost in memories of a stout, rosy lass who had followed a stalwart husband up a broad river into the wilderness some seventy years agone in Indian days — Weathersfield Massacre days. That lass was Aunt Lucy herself, and in just such a May had Timothy's axe rung through the Coniston forest and reared the log cabin, where six of her children were born. Likewise in review passed the lonely months when Timothy was fighting behind his rugged General Stark for that privilege more desirable to his kind than life — self-government. Timothy Prescott would pull the forelock to no man, would have such God-fearing persons as he chose make his laws for him.

Honest Captain Timothy and his Stark heroes, Aunt Lucy and her memories, have long gone to rest. Little did they dream of the nation we have lived to see, straining at her constitution like a great ship at anchor in a gale, with funnels belching forth smoke, and a new race of men thronging her decks for the mastery. Coniston is there still behind its mountain, with its rusty firelocks and its hillside graves.

Cynthia, driving back from Brampton in the gig, smiled at Aunt Lucy in the window, but she did not so much as glance at the tannery house farther on. The tannery

14

house, be it known, was the cottage where Jethro dwelt, and which had belonged to Nathan, his father ; and the tannery sheds were at some distance behind it, nearer Coniston Water. Cynthia did not glance at the tannery house, for a wave of orthodox indignation had swept over her : at any rate, we may call it so. In other words, she was angry with herself : pitied and scorned herself, if the truth be told, for her actions — an inevitable mood.

In front of the minister's barn under the elms on the hill Cynthia pulled the harness from the tired horse with an energy that betokened activity of mind. She was not one who shrank from self-knowledge, and the question put itself to her, " Whither was this matter tending ? " The fire that is in strong men has ever been a lure to women; and many, meaning to play with it, have been burnt thereby since the world began. But to turn the fire to some use, to make the world better for it or stronger for it, that were an achievement indeed! The horse munching his hay, Cynthia lingered as the light fainted above the ridge, with the thought that this might be woman's province, and Miss Lucretia Penniman might go on leading her women regiments to no avail. Nevertheless she was angry with Jethro, not because of what he had said, but because of what he *was*.

The next day is Sunday, and there is mild excitement in Coniston. For Jethro Bass, still with the coonskin cap, but in a brass-buttoned coat secretly purchased in Brampton, appeared at meeting ! It made no difference that he entered quietly, and sat in the rear slip, orthodox Coniston knew that he was behind them : good Mr. Ware knew it, and changed a little his prayers and sermon : Cynthia knew it, grew hot and cold by turns under her poke bonnet. Was he not her brand, and would she not get the credit of snatching him ? How willingly, then, would she have given up that credit to the many who coveted it — if it were a credit. Was Jethro at meeting for any religious purpose ?

Jethro's importance to Coniston lay in his soul, and that soul was numbered at present ninety and ninth.

"And sat in the rear slip."

When the meeting was over, Aunt Lucy Prescott hobbled out at an amazing pace to advise him to read chapter seven of Matthew, but he had vanished : via the horse sheds, if she had known it, and along Coniston Water to the house by the tannery, where he drew breath in a state of mind not to be depicted. He had gazed at the back of Cynthia's poke bonnet for two hours, but he had an uneasy feeling that he would have to pay a price.

The price was paid, in part, during the next six days. To do Jethro's importance absolute justice, he did inspire fear among his contemporaries, and young men and women did not say much to his face; what they did say gave them little satisfaction. Grim Deacon Ira stopped him as he was going to buy hides, and would have prayed over him if Jethro had waited; dear Aunt Lucy did pray, but in private. In six days orthodox Coniston came to the conclusion that this ninety and ninth soul were better left to her who had snatched it, Cynthia Ware.

As for Cynthia, nothing was farther from her mind. Unchristian as was the thought, if this thing she had awakened could only have been put back to sleep again, she would have thought herself happy. But would she have been happy? When Moses Hatch congratulated her, with more humor than sincerity, he received the greatest scare of his life. Yet in those days she welcomed Moses's society as she never had before ; and Coniston, including Moses himself, began thinking of a wedding.

Another Saturday came, and no Cynthia went to Brampton. Jethro may or may not have been on the road. Sunday, and there was Jethro on the back seat in the meeting-house : Sunday noon, over his frugal dinner, the minister mildly remonstrates with Cynthia for neglecting one who has shown signs of grace, citing certain failures of others of his congregation : Cynthia turns scarlet, leaving the minister puzzled and a little uneasy : Monday, Miss Lucretia Penniman, alarmed, comes to Coniston to inquire after Cynthia's health : Cynthia drives back with her as far as Four Corners, talking literature and the advancement of woman ; returns on foot, thinking of something

c

else, when she discerns a figure seated on a log by the
roadside, bent as in meditation. There was no going
back : the thing to do was to come on, as unconcernedly as
possible, not noticing anything, — which Cynthia did, —
not without a little inward palpitating and curiosity, for
which she hated herself and looked the sterner. The
figure unfolded itself, like a Jack from a box.

"You say the woman wahn't any to blame — wahn't any
to blame ? "

The poke bonnet turned away. The shoulders under it
began to shake, and presently the astonished Jethro heard
what seemed to be faint peals of laughter. Suddenly she
turned around to him, all trace of laughter gone.

"Why don't you read the book ? "

"So I am," said Jethro, "so I am. Hain't come to this
casting-off yet."

"And you didn't look ahead to find out ? " This with
scorn.

"Never heard of readin' a book in that fashion. I'll
come to it in time — g-guess it won't run away."

Cynthia stared at him, perhaps with a new interest at
this plodding determination. She was not quite sure that
she ought to stand talking to him a third time in these
woods, especially if the subject of conversation were not,
as Coniston thought, the salvation of his soul. But she
stayed. Here was a man who could be dealt with by no
known rules, who did not even deign to notice a week of
marked coldness.

"Jethro," she said, with a terrifying sternness, "I am
going to ask you a question, and you must answer me
truthfully."

"G-guess I won't find any trouble about that," said
Jethro, apparently not in the least terrified.

"I want you to tell me why you are going to meeting."

"To see you," said Jethro, promptly, "to see you."

"Don't you know that that is wrong ? "

"H-hadn't thought much about it," answered Jethro.

"Well, you should think about it. People don't go to
meeting to — to look at other people."

"Thought they *did*," said Jethro. "W-why do they wear their best clothes — why do they wear their best clothes?"

"To honor God," said Cynthia, with a shade lacking in the conviction, for she added hurriedly: "It isn't right for you to go to church to see — anybody. You go there to hear the Scriptures expounded, and to have your sins forgiven. Because I lent you that book, and you come to meeting, people think I'm converting you."

"So you be," replied Jethro, and this time it was he who smiled, "so you be."

Cynthia turned away, her lips pressed together. How to deal with such a man! Wondrous notes broke on the stillness, the thrush was singing his hymn again, only now it seemed a pæan. High in the azure a hawk wheeled, and floated.

"Couldn't you see I was very angry with you?"

"S-saw you was goin' with Moses Hatch more than common."

Cynthia drew breath sharply. This was audacity — and yet she liked it.

"I am very fond of Moses," she said quickly.

"You always was charitable, Cynthy," said he.

"Haven't I been charitable to you?" she retorted.

"G-guess it has be'n charity," said Jethro. He looked down at her solemnly, thoughtfully, no trace of anger in his face, turned, and without another word strode off in the direction of Coniston Flat.

He left a tumultuous Cynthia, amazement and repentance struggling with anger, which forbade her calling him back: pride in her answering to pride in him, and she rejoicing fiercely that he had pride. Had he but known it, every step he took away from her that evening was a step in advance, and she gloried in the fact that he did not once look back. As she walked toward Coniston, the thought came to her that she was rid of the thing she had stirred up, perhaps forever, and the thrush burst into his song once more.

*   *   *   *   *   *   *

That night, after Cynthia's candle had gone out, when the minister sat on his doorsteps looking at the glory of the moon on the mountain forest, he was startled by the sight of a figure slowly climbing toward him up the slope. A second glance told him that it was Jethro's. Vaguely troubled, he watched his approach ; for good Priest Ware, while able to obey one-half the scriptural injunction, had not the wisdom of the serpent, and women, as typified by Cynthia, were a continual puzzle to him. That very evening, Moses Hatch had called, had been received with more favor than usual, and suddenly packed off about his business. Seated in the moonlight, the minister wondered vaguely whether Jethro Bass were troubling the girl. And now Jethro stood before him, holding out a book. Rising, Mr. Ware bade him good evening, mildly and cordially.

"C-come to leave this book for Cynthy," said Jethro.

Mr. Ware took it, mechanically.

"Have you finished it ? " he asked kindly.

"All I want," replied Jethro, "all I want."

He turned, and went down the slope. Twice the words rose to the minister's lips to call him back, and were suppressed. Yet what to say to him if he came ? Mr. Ware sat down again, sadly, wondering why Jethro Bass should be so difficult to talk to.

The parsonage was of only one story, with a steep, sloping roof. On the left of the doorway was Cynthia's room, and the minister imagined he heard a faint, rustling noise at her window. Presently he arose, barred the door ; could be heard moving around in his room for a while, and after that all was silence save for the mournful crying of a whippoorwill in the woods. Then a door opened softly, a white vision stole into the little entry lighted by the fan-window above, seized the book and stole back. Had the minister been a prying man about his household, he would have noticed next day that Cynthia's candle was burned down to the socket. He saw nothing of the kind: he saw, in fact, that his daughter flitted about the house singing, and he went out into the sun to drop potatoes.

No sooner had he reached the barn than this singing ceased. But how was Mr. Ware to know that?

Twice Cynthia, during the week that followed, got half-way down the slope of the parsonage hill, the book under her arm, on her way to the tannery; twice went back, tears of humiliation and self-pity in her eyes at the thought that she should make advances to a man, and that man the tanner's son. Her household work done, a longing for further motion seized her, and she walked out under the maples of the village street. Let it be understood that Coniston *was* a village, by courtesy, and its shaded road a street. Suddenly, there was the tannery, Jethro standing in front of it, contemplative. Did he see her? Would he come to her? Cynthia, seized by a panic of shame, flew into Aunt Lucy Prescott's, sat through half an hour of torture while Aunt Lucy talked of redemption of sinners, during ten minutes of which Jethro stood, still contemplative. What tumult was in *his* breast, or whether there was any tumult, Cynthia knew not. He went into the tannery again, and though she saw him twice later in the week, he gave no sign of seeing her.

On Saturday Cynthia bought a new bonnet in Brampton; Sunday morning put it on, suddenly remembered that one went to church to honor God, and wore her old one; walked to meeting in a flutter of expectancy not to be denied, and would have looked around had that not been a cardinal sin in Coniston. No Jethro! General opinion (had she waited to hear it among the horse sheds or on the green), that Jethro's soul had slid back into the murky regions, from which it were folly for even Cynthia to try to drag it.

CHAPTER III

THE CLERK AND THE LOCKET

To prove that Jethro's soul had not slid back into the murky regions, and that it was still indulging in flights, it is necessary to follow him (for a very short space) to Boston. Jethro himself went in Lyman Hull's six-horse team with a load of his own merchandise — hides that he had tanned, and other country produce. And they did not go by the way of Truro Pass to the Capital, but took the state turnpike over the ranges, where you can see for miles and miles and miles on a clear summer day across the trembling floors of the forest tops to lonely sentinel mountains fourscore miles away,

No one takes the state turnpike nowadays except crazy tourists who are willing to risk their necks and their horses' legs for the sake of scenery. The tough little Morgans of that time, which kept their feet like cats, have all but disappeared, but there were places on that road where Lyman Hull put the shoes under his wheels for four miles at a stretch. He was not a companion many people would have chosen with whom to enjoy the beauties of such a trip, and nearly everybody in Coniston was afraid of him. Jethro Bass would sit silent on the seat for hours and it is a fact to be noted that when he told Lyman to do a thing, Lyman did it; not, perhaps, without cursing and grumbling. Lyman was a profane and wicked man — drover, farmer, trader, anything. He had a cider mill on his farm on the south slopes of Coniston which Mr. Ware had mentioned in his sermons, and which was the resort of the ungodly. The cider was not so good as Squire Northcutt's, but cheaper. Jethro was not afraid of Lyman, and he had a mortgage on the six-horse team, and on the farm and the cider mill.

After six days, Jethro and Lyman drove over Charlestown bridge and into the crooked streets of Boston, and at length arrived at a drover's hotel, or lodging-house that did not, we may be sure, front on Mount Vernon Street or face the Mall.   Lyman proceeded to get drunk, and Jethro to sell the hides and other merchandise which Lyman had hauled for him.

There was a young man in Boston, when Jethro arrived in Lyman Hull's team, named William Wetherell. By extraordinary circumstances he and another connected with him are to take no small part in this story, which is a sufficient excuse for his introduction.   His father had been a prosperous Portsmouth merchant in the West India trade, a man of many attainments, who had failed and died of a broken heart; and William, at two and twenty, was a clerk in the little jewellery shop of Mr. Judson in Cornhill.

William Wetherell had literary aspirations, and sat from morning till night behind the counter, reading and dreaming : dreaming that he was to be an Irving or a Walter Scott, and yet the sum total of his works in after years consisted of some letters to the *Newcastle Guardian*, and a beginning of the Town History of Coniston!

William had a contempt for the awkward young countryman who suddenly loomed up before him that summer's morning across the counter.   But a moment before the clerk had been in a place where he would fain have lingered — a city where blue waters flow swiftly between white palaces toward the sunrise.

> " And I have fitted up some chambers there
>   Looking toward the golden Eastern air,
>   And level with the living winds, which flow
>   Like waves above the living waves below."

Little did William Wetherell guess, when he glanced up at the intruder, that he was looking upon one of the forces of his own life! The countryman wore a blue swallow-tail coat (fashioned by the hand of Speedy

Bates), a neck-cloth, a coonskin cap, and his trousers were
tucked into rawhide boots. He did not seem a promising
customer for expensive jewellery, and the literary clerk
did not rise, but merely closed his book with his thumb
in it.

"S-sell things here," asked the countryman, "s-sell
things here?"

"Occasionally, when folks have money to buy them."

"My name's Jethro Bass," said the countryman, "Jethro
Bass from Coniston.   Ever hear of Coniston?"

Young Mr. Wetherell never had, but many years afterward he remembered his name, heaven knows why.
Jethro Bass! Perhaps it had a strange ring to it.

"F-folks told me to be careful," was Jethro's next
remark.   He did not look at the clerk, but kept his eyes
fixed on the things within the counter.

"Somebody ought to have come with you," said the
clerk, with a smile of superiority.

"D-don't know much about city ways."

"Well," said the clerk, beginning to be amused, "a man
has to keep his wits about him."

Even then Jethro spared him a look, but continued to
study the contents of the case.

"What can I do for you, Mr. Bass? We have some
really good things here.   For example, this Swiss watch,
which I will sell you cheap, for one hundred and fifty
dollars."

"One hundred and fifty dollars — er — one hundred
and fifty?"

Wetherell nodded.   Still the countryman did not look
up.

"F-folks told me to be careful," he repeated without a
smile.   He was looking at the lockets, and finally pointed
a large finger at one of them — the most expensive, by
the way.   "W-what d'ye get for that?" he asked.

"Twenty dollars," the clerk promptly replied.   Thirty
was nearer the price, but what did it matter.

"H-how much for that?" he said, pointing to another.
The clerk told him.   He inquired about them all, deliber-

ately repeating the sums, considering with so well-feigned an air of a purchaser that Mr. Wetherell began to take a real joy in the situation. For trade was slack in August, and diversion scarce. Finally he commanded that the case be put on the top of the counter, and Wetherell humored him. Whereupon he picked up the locket he had first chosen. It looked very delicate in his huge, rough hand, and Wetherell was surprised that the eyes of Mr. Bass had been caught by the most expensive, for it was far from being the showiest.

" T-twenty dollars ? " he asked.

" We may as well call it that," laughed Wetherell.

" It's not too good for Cynthy," he said.

" Nothing's too good for Cynthy," answered Mr. Wetherell, mockingly, little knowing how he might come to mean it.

Jethro Bass paid no attention to this speech. Pulling a great cowhide wallet from his pocket, still holding the locket in his hand, to the amazement of the clerk he counted out twenty dollars and laid them down.

" G-guess I'll take that one, g-guess I'll take that one," he said.

Then he looked at Mr. Wetherell for the first time.

" Hold ! " cried the clerk, more alarmed than he cared to show, " that's not the price. Did you think I could sell it for that price ? "

" W-wahn't that the price you fixed ? "

" You simpleton ! " retorted Wetherell, with a conviction now that he was calling him the wrong name. " Give me back the locket, and you shall have your money again."

" W-wahn't that the price you fixed ? "

" Yes, but — "

" G-guess I'll keep the locket — g-guess I'll keep the locket."

Wetherell looked at him aghast, and there was no doubt about his determination. With a sinking heart the clerk realized that he should have to make good to Mr. Judson the seven odd dollars of difference, and then he lost his head. Slipping round the counter to the door of the shop,

he turned the key, thrust it in his pocket, and faced Mr.
Bass again — from behind the counter.

"You don't leave this shop," cried the clerk, "until you
give me back that locket."

Jethro Bass turned.   A bench ran along the farther
wall, and there he planted himself without a word, while
the clerk stared at him, — with what feelings of uneasiness
I shall not attempt to describe, — for the customer was
plainly determined to wait until hunger should drive one
of them forth.   The minutes passed, and Wetherell began
to hate him.   Then some one tried the door, peered in
through the glass, perceived Jethro, shook the knob,
knocked violently, all to no purpose.   Jethro seemed lost
in a revery.

"This has gone far enough," said the clerk, trying to
keep his voice from shaking ; "it is beyond a joke.   Give
me back the locket."   And he tendered Jethro the money
again.

"W-wahn't that the price you fixed?" asked Jethro,
innocently.

Wetherell choked.   The man outside shook the door
again, and people on the sidewalk stopped, and presently
against the window-panes a sea of curious faces gazed
in upon them.   Mr. Bass's thoughts apparently were fixed
on Eternity — he looked neither at the people nor at
Wetherell.   And then, the crowd parting as for one in
authority, as in a bad dream the clerk saw his employer,
Mr. Judson, courteously pushing away the customer at the
door who would not be denied.   Another moment, and
Mr. Judson had gained admittance with his private key,
and stood on the threshold staring at clerk and customer.
Jethro gave no sign that the situation had changed.

"William," said Mr. Judson, in a dangerously quiet
voice, "perhaps you can explain this extraordinary state
of affairs."

"I can, sir," William cried.   "This gentleman" (the
word stuck in his throat), "this gentleman came in here
to examine lockets which I had no reason to believe he
would buy.   I admit my fault, sir.   He asked the price

"'It's not too good for Cynthy'"

of the most expensive, and I told him twenty dollars, merely for a jest, sir." William hesitated.

"Well?" said Mr. Judson.

"After pricing every locket in the case, he seized the first one, handed me twenty dollars, and now refuses to give it up, although he knows the price is twenty-seven."

"Then?"

"Then I locked the door, sir. He sat down there, and hasn't moved since."

Mr. Judson looked again at Mr. Bass, this time with unmistakable interest. The other customer began to laugh, and the crowd was pressing in, and Mr. Judson turned and shut the door in their faces. All this time Mr. Bass had not moved, not so much as to lift his head or shift one of his great cowhide boots.

"Well, sir," demanded Mr. Judson, "what have you to say?"

"N-nothin'. G-guess I'll keep the locket. I've paid for it — I've paid for it."

"And you are aware, my friend," said Mr. Judson, "that my clerk has given you the wrong price?"

"Guess that's his l-lookout." He still sat there, doggedly unconcerned.

A bull would have seemed more at home in a chinashop than Jethro Bass in a jewellery store. But Mr. Judson himself was a man out of the ordinary, and instead of getting angry he began to be more interested.

"Took you for a greenhorn, did he?" he remarked.

"F-folks told me to be careful — to be careful," said Mr. Bass.

Then Mr. Judson laughed. It was all the more disconcerting to William Wetherell, because his employer laughed rarely. He laid his hand on Jethro's shoulder.

"He might have spared himself the trouble, my young friend," he said. "You didn't expect to find a greenhorn *behind* a jewellery counter, did you?"

"S-surprised me some," said Jethro.

Mr. Judson laughed again, all the while looking at him.

"I am going to let you keep the locket," he said, "because it will teach my greenhorn a lesson. William, do you hear that?"

"Yes, sir," William said, and his face was very red.

Mr. Bass rose solemnly, apparently unmoved by his triumph in a somewhat remarkable transaction, and William long remembered how he towered over all of them. He held the locket out to Mr. Judson, who stared at it, astonished.

"What's this?" said that gentleman; "you don't want it?"

"Guess I'll have it marked," said Jethro, "ef it don't cost extry."

"Marked!" gasped Mr. Judson, "marked!"

"Ef it don't cost extry," Jethro repeated.

"Well, I'll—" exclaimed Mr. Judson, and suddenly recalled the fact that he was a church member. "What inscription do you wish put into it?" he asked, recovering himself with an effort.

Jethro thrust his hand into his pocket, and again the cowhide wallet came out. He tendered Mr. Judson a somewhat soiled piece of paper, and Mr. Judson read:—

"*Cynthy, from Jethro*"

"*Cynthy*," Mr. Judson repeated, in a tremulous voice, "*Cynthy*, not *Cynthia*."

"H-how is it written," said Jethro, leaning over it, "h-how is it written?"

"*Cynthy*," answered Mr. Judson, involuntarily.

"Then make it *Cynthy*—make it *Cynthy*."

"*Cynthy* it shall be," said Mr. Judson, with conviction.

"When'll you have it done?"

"To-night," replied Mr. Judson, with a twinkle in his eye, "to-night, as a special favor."

"What time—w-what time?"

"Seven o'clock, sir. May I send it to your hotel? The Tremont House, I suppose?"

"I—I'll call," said Jethro, so solemnly that Mr. Judson kept his laughter until he was gone.

From the door they watched him silently as he strode across the street and turned the corner. Then Mr. Judson turned. "That man will make his mark, William," he said; and added thoughtfully, "but whether for good or evil, I know not."

CHAPTER IV

ENTER A GREAT MAN, INCOGNITO

WHAT Cynthia may have thought or felt during Jethro's absence in Boston, and for some months thereafter, she kept to herself. Honest Moses Hatch pursued his courting untroubled, and never knew that he had a rival. Moses would as soon have questioned the seasons or the weather as Cynthia's changes of moods, — which were indeed the weather for him, and when storms came he sat with his back to them, waiting for the sunshine. He had long ceased proposing marriage, in the firm belief that Cynthia would set the day in her own good time. Thereby he was saved much suffering.

The summer flew on apace, for Coniston. Fragrant hay was cut on hillsides won from rock and forest, and Coniston Water sang a gentler melody — save when the clouds floated among the spruces on the mountain and the rain beat on the shingles. During the still days before the turn of the year, — days of bending fruit boughs, crab-apples glistening red in the soft sunlight, — rumor came from Brampton to wrinkle the forehead of Moses Hatch as he worked among his father's orchards.

The rumor was of a Mr. Isaac Dudley Worthington, a name destined to make much rumor before it was to be carved on the marble. Isaac D. Worthington, indeed, might by a stretch of the imagination be called the pioneer of all the genus to be known in the future as City Folks, who were, two generations later, to invade the country like a devouring army of locusts.

At that time a stranger in Brampton was enough to set the town agog. But a young man of three and twenty,

with an independent income of four hundred dollars a
year ! — or any income at all not derived from his own
labor — was unheard of.   It is said that when the stage
from over Truro Gap arrived in Brampton Street a
hundred eyes gazed at him unseen, from various ambushes,
and followed him up the walk to Silas Wheelock's, where
he was to board.   In half an hour Brampton knew the
essentials of Isaac Worthington's story, and Sam Price
was on his way with it to Coniston for distribution at
Jonah Winch's store.

Young Mr. Worthington was from Boston — no less ;
slim, pale, medium height, but with an alert look, and a
high-bridged nose.   But his clothes !   Sam Price's vocabu-
lary was insufficient here, they were cut in such a way,
and Mr. Worthington was downright distinguished-looking
under his gray beaver.   Why had he come to Brampton ?
demanded Deacon Ira Perkins.   Sam had saved this for
the last.   Young Mr. Worthington was threatened with
consumption, and had been sent to live with his distant
relative, Silas Wheelock.

The presence of a gentleman of leisure — although
threatened with consumption — became an all-absorbing
topic in two villages and three hamlets, and more than
one swain, hitherto successful, felt the wind blow colder.
But in a fortnight it was known that a petticoat did not
make Isaac Worthington even turn his head.   Curiosity
centred on Silas Wheelock's barn, where Mr. Worthington had fitted up a shop, and presently various strange
models of contrivances began to take shape there.   What
these were, Silas himself knew not ; and the gentleman of
leisure was, alas ! close-mouthed.   When he was not saw-
ing and hammering and planing, he took long walks up
and down Coniston Water, and was surprised deep in
thought at several places.

Nathan Bass's story-and-a-half house, devoid of paint,
faced the road, and behind it was the shed, or barn, that
served as the tannery, and between the tannery and Coniston Water were the vats.   The rain flew in silvery
spray, and the drops shone like jewels on the coat of a

Florence Scovel Shinn

"Mr. Worthington was downright distinguished-looking under his gray beaver."

young man who stood looking in at the tannery door.
Young Jake Wheeler, son of the village spendthrift, was
driving a lean white horse round in a ring: to the horse
was attached a beam, and on the beam a huge round stone
rolled on a circular oak platform. Jethro Bass, who was
engaged in pushing hemlock bark under the stone to be
crushed, straightened. Of the three, the horse had seen
the visitor first, and stopped in his tracks.

"Jethro!" whispered Jake, tingling with an excitement that was but natural. Jethro had begun to sweep
the finer pieces of bark toward the centre. "It's the
city man, walked up here from Brampton."

It was indeed Mr. Worthington, slightly more sunburned and less citified-looking than on his arrival, and
he wore a woollen cap of Brampton make. Even then,
despite his wavy hair and delicate appearance, Isaac
Worthington had the hawklike look which became famous
in later years, and at length he approached Jethro and
fixed his eye upon him.

"Kind of slow work, isn't it?" remarked Mr. Worthington.

The white horse was the only one to break the silence
that followed, by sneezing with all his might.

"How is the tannery business in these parts?" essayed
Mr. Worthington again.

"Thinkin' of it?" said Jethro. "T-thinkin' of it, be
you?"

"No," answered Mr. Worthington, hastily. "If I
were," he added, "I'd put in new machinery. That horse
and stone is primitive."

"What kind of machinery would you put in?" asked
Jethro.

"Ah," answered Worthington, "that will interest you.
All New Englanders are naturally progressive, I take it."

"W-what was it you took?"

"I was merely remarking on the enterprise of New
Englanders," said Worthington, flushing. "On my journey up here, beside the Merrimac, I had the opportunity to
inspect the new steam-boiler, the fulling-mill, the splitting-

machine, and other remarkable improvements. In fact, these suggested one or two little things to me, which might be of interest to you."

"Well," said Jethro, "they might, and then again they mightn't. Guess it depends."

"Depends!" exclaimed the man of leisure, "depends on what?"

"H-how much you know about it."

Young Mr. Worthington, instead of being justly indignant, laughed and settled himself comfortably on a pile of bark. He thought Jethro a character, and he was not mistaken. On the other hand, Mr. Worthington displayed a knowledge of the fulling-mill and splitting-machine and the process of tanneries in general that was surprising. Jethro, had Mr. Worthington but known it, was more interested in *animate* machines : more interested in Mr. Worthington than the fulling-mill or, indeed, the tannery business.

At length the visitor fell silent, his sense of superiority suddenly gone. Others had had this same feeling with Jethro, even the minister; but the man of leisure (who was nothing of the sort) merely felt a kind of bewilderment.

"Callatin' to live in Brampton — be you?" asked Jethro.

"I am living there now."

"C-callatin' to set up a mill some day?"

Mr. Worthington fairly leaped off the bark pile.

"What makes you say that?" he demanded.

"G-guesswork," said Jethro, starting to shovel again, "g-guesswork."

To take a walk in the wild, to come upon a bumpkin in cowhide boots crushing bark, to have him read within twenty minutes a cherished and well-hidden ambition which Brampton had not discovered in a month (and did not discover for many years) was sufficiently startling. Well might Mr. Worthington tremble for his other ambitions, and they were many.

Jethro stepped out, passing Mr. Worthington as though he had already forgotten that gentleman's existence, and seized an armful of bark that lay under cover of a lean-to. Just then, heralded by a brightening of the western sky, a girl appeared down the road, her head bent a little as in thought, and if she saw the group by the tannery house she gave no sign. Two of them stared at her — Jake Wheeler and Mr. Worthington. Suddenly Jake, implike, turned and stared at Worthington.

"Cynthy Ware, the minister's daughter," he said.

"Haven't I seen her in Brampton?" inquired Mr. Worthington, little thinking of the consequences of the question.

"Guess you have," answered Jake. "Cynthy goes to the Social Library, to git books. She knows more'n the minister himself, a sight more."

"Where does the minister live?" asked Mr. Worthington.

Jake pulled him by the sleeve toward the road, and pointed to the low gable of the little parsonage under the elms on the hill beyond the meeting-house. The visitor gave a short glance at it, swung around and gave a longer glance at the figure disappearing in the other direction. He did not suspect that Jake was what is now called a news agency. Then Mr. Worthington turned to Jethro, who was stooping over the bark.

"If you come to Brampton, call and see me," he said. "You'll find me at Silas Wheelock's."

He got no answer, but apparently expected none, and he started off down the Brampton road in the direction Cynthia had taken.

"That makes another," said Jake, significantly, "and Speedy Bates says he never looks at wimmen. Godfrey, I wish I could see Moses now."

Mr. Worthington had not been quite ingenuous with Jake. To tell the truth, he had made the acquaintance of the Social Library and Miss Lucretia, and that lady had sung the praises of her favorite. Once out of sight of Jethro, Mr. Worthington quickened his steps, passed the store, where he was remarked by two of Jonah's customers, and his blood leaped when he saw the girl in front of

him, walking faster now. Yes, it is a fact that Isaac
Worthington's blood once leaped. He kept on, but when
near her had a spasm of fright to make his teeth fairly
chatter, and than another spasm followed, for Cynthia had
turned around.

"How do you do, Mr. Worthington?" she said, dropping him a little courtesy. Mr. Worthington stopped in
his tracks, and it was some time before he remembered to
take off his woollen cap and sweep the mud with it.

"You know my name!" he exclaimed.

"It is known from Tarleton Four Corners to Harwich,"
said Cynthia, "all that distance. To tell the truth," she
added, "those are the boundaries of my world." And
Mr. Worthington being still silent, "How do you like
being a big frog in a little pond?"

"If it were your pond, Miss Cynthia," he responded
gallantly, "I should be content to be a little frog."

"Would you?" she said; "I don't believe you."

This was not subtle flattery, but the truth — Mr. Worth-
ington would never be content to be a little anything.
So he had been judged twice in an afternoon, once by
Jethro and again by Cynthia.

"Why don't you believe me?" he asked ecstatically.

"A woman's instinct, Mr. Worthington, has very little
reason in it."

"I hear, Miss Cynthia," he said gallantly, "that your
instinct is fortified by learning, since Miss Penniman tells
me that you are quite capable of taking a school in
Boston."

"Then I should be doubly sure of your character," she
retorted with a twinkle.

"Will you tell my fortune?" he said gayly.

"Not on such a slight acquaintance," she replied.
"Good-by, Mr. Worthington."

"I shall see you in Brampton," he cried, "I — I have
seen you in Brampton."

She did not answer this confession, but left him, and
presently disappeared beyond the triangle of the green,
while Mr. Worthington pursued his way to Brampton by

"'All that distance.'"

the road,— his thoughts that evening not on waterfalls or machinery. As for Cynthia's conduct, I do not defend or explain it, for I have found out that the best and wisest of women can at times be coquettish.

It was that meeting which shook the serenity of poor Moses, and he learned of it when he went to Jonah Winch's store an hour later. An hour later, indeed, Coniston was discussing the man of leisure in a new light. It was possible that Cynthia might take him, and Deacon Ira Perkins made a note the next time he went to Brampton to question Silas Wheelock on Mr. Worthington's origin, habits, and orthodoxy.

Cynthia troubled herself very little about any of these. Scarcely any purpose in the world is single, but she had had a purpose in talking to Mr. Worthington, besides the pleasure it gave her. And the next Saturday, when she rode off to Brampton, some one looked through the cracks in the tannery shed and saw that she wore her new bonnet.

There is scarcely a pleasanter place in the world than Brampton Street on a summer's day. Down the length of it runs a wide green, shaded by spreading trees, and on either side, tree-shaded, too, and each in its own little plot, gabled houses of that simple, graceful architecture of our forefathers. Some of these had fluted pilasters and cornices, the envy of many a modern architect, and fan-shaped windows in dormer and doorway. And there was the church, then new, that still stands to the glory of its builders; with terraced steeple and pillared porch and the widest of checker-paned sashes to let in the light on high-backed pews and gallery.

The celebrated Social Library, halfway up the street, occupied part of Miss Lucretia's little house; or, it might better be said, Miss Lucretia boarded with the Social Library. There Cynthia hitched her horse, gave greeting to Mr. Ezra Graves and others who paused, and, before she was fairly in the door, was clasped in Miss Lucretia's arms. There were new books to be discussed, arrived by the stage the day before; but scarce half an hour had passed before Cynthia started guiltily at a timid knock, and Miss Lucretia rose briskly.

"It must be Ezra Graves come for the Gibbon," she said. "He's early." And she went to the door. Cynthia thought it was not Ezra. Then came Miss Lucretia's voice from the entry: —

"Why, Mr. Worthington! Have you read the 'Last of the Mohicans' already?"

There he stood, indeed, the man of leisure, and to-day he wore his beaver hat. No, he had not yet read the 'Last of the Mohicans.' There were things in it that Mr. Worthington would like to discuss with Miss Penniman. Was it not a social library? At this juncture there came a giggle from within that made him turn scarlet, and he scarcely heard Miss Lucretia offering to discuss the whole range of letters. Enter Mr. Worthington, bows profoundly to Miss Lucretia's guest, his beaver in his hand, and the discussion begins, Cynthia taking no part in it. Strangely enough, Mr. Worthington's remarks on American Indians are not only intelligent, but interesting. The clock strikes four, Miss Lucretia starts up, suddenly remembering that she has promised to read to an invalid, and with many regrets from Mr. Worthington, she departs. Then he sits down again, twirling his beaver, while Cynthia looks at him in quiet amusement.

"I shall walk to Coniston again, next week," he announced.

"What an energetic man!" said Cynthia.

"I want to have my fortune told."

"I hear that you walk a great deal," she remarked, "up and down Coniston Water. I shall begin to think you romantic, Mr. Worthington — perhaps a poet."

"I don't walk up and down Coniston Water for that reason," he answered earnestly.

"Might I be so bold as to ask the reason?" she ventured.

Great men have their weaknesses. And many, close-mouthed with their own sex, will tell their cherished hopes to a woman, if their interests are engaged. With a bas-relief of Isaac Worthington in the town library to-day (his own library), and a full-length portrait of him in the capitol of the state, who shall deny this title to greatness?

He leaned a little toward her, his face illumined by his subject, which was himself.

"I will confide in you," he said, "that some day I shall build here in Brampton a woollen mill which will be the best of its kind. If I gain money, it will not be to hoard it or to waste it. I shall try to make the town better for it, and the state, and I shall try to elevate my neighbors."

Cynthia could not deny that these were laudable ambitions.

"Something tells me," he continued, "that I shall succeed. And that is why I walk on Coniston Water — to choose the best site for a dam."

"I am honored by your secret, but I feel that the responsibility you repose in me is too great," she said.

"I can think of none in whom I would rather confide," said he.

"And am I the only one in all Brampton, Harwich, and Coniston who knows this?" she asked.

Mr. Worthington laughed.

"The only one of importance," he answered. "This week, when I went to Coniston, I had a strange experience. I left the brook at a tannery, and a most singular fellow was in the shed shovelling bark. I tried to get him to talk, and told him about some new tanning machinery I had seen. Suddenly he turned on me and asked me if I was 'callatin' to set up a mill.' He gave me a queer feeling. Do you have many such odd characters in Coniston, Miss Cynthia? You're not going?"

Cynthia had risen, and all of the laughter was gone from her eyes. What had happened to make her grow suddenly grave, Isaac Worthington never knew.

"I have to get my father's supper," she said.

He, too, rose, puzzled and disconcerted at this change in her.

"And may I not come to Coniston?" he asked.

"My father and I should be glad to see you, Mr. Worthington," she answered.

He untied her horse and essayed one more topic.

"You are taking a very big book," he said. "May I look at the title?"

She showed it to him in silence. It was the "Life of Napoleon Bonaparte."

CHAPTER V

ISAAC WORTHINGTON came to Coniston not once, but many times, before the snow fell; and afterward, too, in Silas Wheelock's yellow sleigh through the great drifts under the pines, the chestnut Morgan trotting to one side in the tracks. On one of these excursions he fell in with that singular character of a bumpkin who had interested him on his first visit, in coonskin cap and overcoat and mittens. Jethro Bass was plodding in the same direction, and Isaac Worthington, out of the goodness of his heart, invited him into the sleigh. He was scarcely prepared for the bumpkin's curt refusal, but put it down to native boorishness, and thought no more about it — then.

What troubled Mr. Worthington infinitely more was the progress of his suit; for it had become a suit, though progress is a wrong word to use in connection with it. So far had he got, — not a great distance, — and then came to what he at length discovered was a wall, and apparently impenetrable. He was not even allowed to look over it. Cynthia was kind, engaging, even mirthful, at times, save when he approached it; and he became convinced that a certain sorrow lay in the forbidden ground. The nearest he had come to it was when he mentioned again, by accident, that life of Napoleon.

That Cynthia would accept him, nobody doubted for an instant. It would be madness not to. He was orthodox, so Deacon Ira had discovered, of good habits, and there was the princely four hundred a year — almost a minister's salary! Little people guessed that there was no love-making — only endless discussions of books beside the great centre chimney, and discussions of Isaac Worthington's career.

It is a fact — for future consideration — that Isaac Worthington proposed to Cynthia Ware, although neither Speedy Bates nor Deacon Ira Perkins heard him do so. It had been very carefully prepared, that speech, and was a model of proposals for the rising young men of all time. Mr. Worthington preferred to offer himself for what he was going to be — not for what he was. He tendered to Cynthia a note for a large amount, payable in some twenty years, with interest. The astonishing thing to record is that in twenty years he could have more than paid the note, although he could not have foreseen at that time the Worthington Free Library and the Truro Railroad, and the stained-glass window in the church and the great marble monument on the hill — to another woman. All of these things, and more, Cynthia might have had if she had only accepted that promise to pay! But she did not accept it. He was a trifle more robust than when he came to Brampton in the summer, but perhaps she doubted his promise to pay.

It may have been guessed, although the language we have used has been purposely delicate, that Cynthia was already in love with — somebody else. Shame of shames and horror of horrors — with Jethro Bass! With Strength, in the crudest form in which it is created, perhaps, but yet with Strength. The strength might gradually and eventually be refined. Such was her hope, when she had any. It is hard, looking back upon that virginal and cultured Cynthia, to be convinced that she could have loved passionately, and such a man! But love she did, and passionately, too, and hated herself for it, and prayed and struggled to cast out what she believed, at times, to be a devil.

The ancient allegory of Cupid and the arrows has never been improved upon: of Cupid, who should never in the world have been trusted with a weapon, who defies all game laws, who shoots people in the bushes and innocent bystanders generally, the weak and the helpless and the strong and self-confident! There is no more reason in it than that. He shot Cynthia Ware, and what she suffered in secret Coniston never guessed. What parallels in history shall I quote to bring home the enormity of such a mésalliance? Orthodox Coniston would have gone into sackcloth and ashes, — was soon to go into these, anyway.

I am not trying to keep the lovers apart for any mere purposes of fiction, — this is a true chronicle, and they stayed apart most of that winter. Jethro went about his daily tasks, which were now become manifold, and he wore the locket on its little chain himself. He did not think that Cynthia loved him — yet, but he had the effrontery to believe that she might, some day; and he was content to wait. He saw that she avoided him, and he was too proud to go to the parsonage and so incur ridicule and contempt.

Jethro was content to wait. That is a clew to his character throughout his life. He would wait for his love, he would wait for his hate: he had waited ten years before putting into practice the first step of a little scheme which he had been gradually developing during that time, for which he had been amassing money, and the life of Napoleon Bonaparte, by the way, had given him some valuable ideas. Jethro, as well as Isaac D. Worthington, had ambitions, although no one in Coniston had hitherto guessed them except Jock Hallowell — and Cynthia Ware, after her curiosity had been aroused.

Even as Isaac D. Worthington did not dream of the Truro Railroad and of an era in the haze of futurity, it did not occur to Jethro Bass that his ambitions tended to the making of another era that was at hand. Makers of eras are too busy thinking about themselves and like immediate matters to worry about history. Jethro never heard the expression about "cracks in the Constitution," and would not have known what it meant, — he merely had the desire to get on top. But with Established Church Coniston tight in the saddle (in the person of Moses Hatch, Senior), how was he to do it?

As the winter wore on, and March town meeting ap-

proached, strange rumors of a Democratic ticket began
to drift into Jonah Winch's store, — a Democratic ticket
headed by Fletcher Bartlett, of all men, as chairman of
the board. Moses laughed when he first heard of
it, for Fletcher was an easy-going farmer of the
Methodist persuasion who was always in debt, and the
other members of the ticket, so far as Moses could learn
of it — were remarkable neither for orthodoxy or solidity.
The rumors persisted, and still Moses laughed, for the
senior selectman was a big man with flesh on him, who
could laugh with dignity.

"Moses," said Deacon Lysander Richardson as they
stood on the platform of the store one sunny Saturday
in February, "somebody's put Fletcher up to this. He
hain't got sense enough to act that independent all by
himself."

"You be always croakin', Lysander," answered Moses.

Cynthia Ware, who had come to the store for buttons
for Speedy Bates, who was making a new coat for the
minister, heard these remarks, and stood thoughtfully
staring at the blue coat-tails of the elders. A brass button was gone from Deacon Lysander's, and she wanted
to sew it on. Suddenly she looked up, and saw Jock
Hallowell standing beside her. Jock winked — and Cynthia blushed and hurried homeward without a word. She
remembered, vividly enough, what Jock had told her the
spring before, and several times during the week that
followed she thought of waylaying him and asking what
he knew. But she could not summon the courage. As a
matter of fact, Jock knew nothing, but he had a theory.
He was a strange man, Jock, who whistled all day on roof
and steeple and meddled with nobody's business, as a rule.
What had impelled him to talk to Cynthia in the way he
had must remain a mystery.

Meanwhile the disquieting rumors continued to come
in. Jabez Miller, on the north slope, had told Samuel
Todd, who told Ephraim Williams, that he was going to
vote for Fletcher. Moses Hatch hitched up his team and
went out to see Jabez, spent an hour in general conversation, and then plumped the question, taking, as he said,

Florence Scovel Shinn

" ' You be always croakin', Lysander.' "

that means of finding out. Jabez hemmed and hawed, said his farm was mortgaged; spoke at some length about the American citizen, however humble, having a right to vote as he chose. A most unusual line for Jabez, and the whole matter very mysterious and not a little ominous. Moses drove homeward that sparkling day, shutting his eyes to the glare of the ice crystals on the pines, and thinking profoundly. He made other excursions, enough to satisfy himself that this disease, so new and unheard of (the right of the unfit to hold office), actually existed. Where the germ began that caused it, Moses knew no better than the deacon, since those who were suspected of leanings toward Fletcher Bartlett were strangely secretive. The practical result of Moses' profound thought was a meeting, in his own house, without respect to party, Democrats and Whigs alike, opened by a prayer from the minister himself. The meeting, after a futile session, broke up dismally. Sedition and conspiracy existed ; a chief offender and master mind there was, somewhere. But who was he?

Good Mr. Ware went home, troubled in spirit, shaking his head. He had a cold, and was not so strong as he used to be, and should not have gone to the meeting at all. At supper, Cynthia listened with her eyes on her plate while he told her of the affair.

"Somebody's behind this, Cynthia," he said. "It's the most astonishing thing in my experience that we cannot discover who has incited them. All the unattached people in the town seem to have been organized." Mr. Ware was wont to speak with moderation even at his own table. He said unattached — not ungodly.

Cynthia kept her eyes on her plate, but she felt as though her body were afire. Little did the minister imagine, as he went off to write his sermon, that his daughter might have given him the clew to the mystery. Yes, Cynthia guessed ; and she could not read that evening because of the tumult of her thoughts. What was her duty in the matter? To tell her father her suspicions? They were only suspicions, after all, and she could make no accusations. And Jethro! Although she condemned him, there was something in the situation that appealed to a most reprehensible sense of humor. Cynthia caught herself smiling once or twice, and knew that it was wicked. She excused Jethro, and told herself that, with his lack of training, he could know no better. Then an idea came to her, and the very boldness of it made her grow hot again. She would appeal to him: tell him that that power he had over other men could be put to better and finer uses. She would appeal to him, and he would abandon the matter. That the man loved her with the whole of his rude strength she was sure, and that knowledge had been the only salve to her shame.

So far we have only suspicions ourselves; and, strange to relate, if we go around Coniston with Jethro behind his little red Morgan, we shall come back with nothing but — suspicions. They will amount to convictions, yet we cannot prove them. The reader very naturally demands some specific information — how did Jethro do it? I confess that I can only indicate in a very general way: I can prove nothing. Nobody ever could prove anything against Jethro Bass. Bring the following evidence before any grand jury in the country, and see if they don't throw it out of court.

Jethro, in the course of his weekly round of strictly business visits throughout the town, drives into Samuel Todd's farmyard, and hitches on the sunny side of the red barns. The *town* of Coniston, it must be explained for the benefit of those who do not understand the word "town" in the New England sense, was a tract of country about ten miles by ten, the most thickly settled portion of which was the *village* of Coniston, consisting of twelve houses. Jethro drives into the barnyard, and Samuel Todd comes out. He is a little man, and has a habit of rubbing the sharp ridge of his nose.

"Haow be you, Jethro?" says Samuel. "Killed the brindle Thursday. Finest hide you ever seed."

"G-goin' to town meetin' Tuesday — g-goin' to town meetin' Tuesday — Sam'l?" says Jethro.

"I was callatin' to, Jethro."

"Democrat — hain't ye — Democrat?"

"Callate to be."

"How much store do ye set by that hide?"

Samuel rubs his nose. Then he names a price that the hide might fetch, under favorable circumstances, in Boston. Jethro does not wince.

"Who d'ye callate to vote for, Sam'l?"

Samuel rubs his nose.

"Heerd they was a-goin' to put up Fletcher and Amos Cuthbert, an' Sam Price for Moderator." (What a convenient word is *they* when used politically!) "Hain't made up my mind, clear," says Samuel.

"C-comin' by the tannery after town meetin'?" inquired Jethro, casually.

"Don't know but what I kin."

"F-fetch the hide — f-fetch the hide."

And Jethro drives off, with Samuel looking after him, rubbing his nose. "No bill," says the jury — if you can get Samuel into court. But you can't. Even Moses Hatch can get nothing out of Samuel, who then talks Jacksonian principles and the rights of an American citizen.

Let us pursue this matter a little farther, and form a committee of investigation. Where did Mr. Todd learn anything about Jacksonian principles? From Mr. Samuel Price, whom *they* have spoken of for Moderator. And where did Mr. Price learn of these principles? Any one in Coniston will tell you that Mr. Price makes a specialty of orators and oratory, and will hold forth at the drop of a hat in Jonah Winch's store or anywhere else. Who is Mr. Price? He is a tall, sallow young man of eight and twenty, with a wedge-shaped face, a bachelor and a Methodist, who farms in a small way on the southern slope, and saves his money. He has become almost insupportable since *they* have named him for Moderator.

Get Mr. Sam Price into court. Here is a man who assuredly knows who *they* are: if we are not much mistaken, he is *their* mouthpiece. Get an eel into court.

There is only one man in town who can hold an eel, and he isn't on the jury. Mr. Price will talk plentifully, in his nasal way; but he won't tell you anything.

Mr. Price has been nominated to fill Deacon Lysander Richardson's shoes in the following manner: One day in the late autumn a man in a coonskin cap stops beside Mr. Price's woodpile, where Mr. Price has been chopping wood, pausing occasionally to stare off through the purple haze at the south shoulder of Coniston Mountain.

" Haow be you, Jethro ? " says Mr. Price, nasally.

" D-Democrats are talkin' some of namin' you Moderator next meetin'," says the man in the coonskin cap.

" Want to know ! " ejaculates Mr. Price, dropping the axe and straightening up in amazement. For Mr. Price's ambition soared no higher, and he had made no secret of it. " Wal ! Whar'd you hear that, Jethro ? "

" H-heerd it round — some. D-Democrat — hain't you — Democrat ? "

" Always callate to be."

" J-Jacksonian Democrat ? "

" Guess I be."

Silence for a while, that Mr. Price may feel the gavel in his hand, which he does.

" Know somewhat about Jacksonian principles, don't ye — know somewhat ? "

" Callate to," says Mr. Price, proudly.

" T-talk 'em up, Sam — t-talk 'em up. C-canvass, Sam."

With these words of brotherly advice Mr. Bass went off down the road, and Mr. Price chopped no more wood that night ; but repeated to himself many times in his nasal voice, " I want to know ! " In the course of the next few weeks various gentlemen mentioned to Mr. Price that he had been spoken of for Moderator, and he became acquainted with the names of the other candidates on the same mysterious ticket who were mentioned. Whereupon he girded up his loins and went forth and preached the word of Jacksonian Democracy in all the farmhouses roundabout, with such effect that Samuel

Todd and others were able to talk with some fluency
about the rights of American citizens.

Question before the Committee, undisposed of : Who
nominated Samuel Price for Moderator? Samuel Price
gives the evidence, tells the court he does not know, and
is duly cautioned and excused.

Let us call, next, Mr. Eben Williams, if we can.
Moses Hatch, Senior, has already interrogated him with
all the authority of the law and the church, for Mr.
Williams is orthodox, though the deacons have to remind
him of his duty once in a while. Eben is timid, and
replies to us, as to Moses, that he has heard of the Democratic ticket, and callates that Fletcher Bartlett, who has
always been the leader of the Democratic party, has
named the ticket. He did not mention Jethro Bass to
Deacon Hatch. Why should he? What has Jethro
Bass got to do with politics?

Eben lives on a southern spur, next to Amos Cuthbert,
where you can look off for forty miles across the billowy
mountains of the west. From no spot in Coniston town
is the sunset so fine on distant Farewell Mountain, and
Eben's sheep feed on pastures where only mountain-bred
sheep can cling and thrive. Coniston, be it known, at
this time is one of the famous wool towns of New England: before the industry went West, with other indus-
tries. But Eben Williams's sheep do not wholly belong
to him — they are mortgaged — and Eben's farm is mortgaged.

Jethro Bass — Eben testifies to us — is in the habit of
visiting him once a month, perhaps, when he goes to
Amos Cuthbert's. Just friendly calls. Is it not a fact
that Jethro Bass holds his mortgage? Yes, for eight
hundred dollars. How long has he held that mortgage?
About a year and a half. Has the interest been paid
promptly? Well, the fact is that Eben hasn't paid any
interest yet.

Now let us take the concrete incident. Before that
hypocritical thaw early in February, Jethro called upon
Amos Cuthbert — not so surly then as he has since be-

For

SENIOR SELECTMAN, FLETCHER BARTLETT.

> (*Farm and buildings on Thousand Acre Hill mortgaged to Jethro Bass.*)

SECOND SELECTMAN, AMOS CUTHBERT.

> (*Farm and buildings on Town's End Ridge mortgaged to Jethro Bass.*)

THIRD SELECTMAN, CHESTER PERKINS.

> (*Sop of some kind to the Established Church party. Horse and cow mortgaged to Jethro Bass, though his father, the tithing-man, doesn't know it.*)

MODERATOR, SAMUEL PRICE.

> (*Natural ambition — love of oratory and Jacksonian principles.*)

> etc., etc.

The notes are mine, not Moses's. Strange that they didn't occur to Moses. What a wealthy man has our hero become at thirty-one! Jethro Bass was rich beyond the dreams of avarice — for Coniston. Truth compels me to admit that the sum total of all his mortgages did not amount to nine thousand dollars; but that was a large sum of money for Coniston in those days, and even now. Nathan Bass had been a saving man, and had left to his son one-half of this fortune. If thrift and the ability to gain wealth be qualities for a hero, Jethro had them — in those days.

The Sunday before March meeting, it blew bitter cold, and Priest Ware, preaching in mittens, denounced sedition in general. Underneath him, on the first landing of the high pulpit, the deacons sat with knitted brows, and the

"Priest Ware, preaching in mittens."

key-note from Isaiah Prescott's pitch pipe sounded like a mournful echo of the mournful wind without.

Monday was ushered in with that sleet storm to which the almanacs still refer, and another scarcely less important event occurred that day which we shall have to pass by for the present; on Tuesday, the sleet still raging, came the historic town meeting. Deacon Moses Hatch, his chores done and his breakfast and prayers completed, fought his way with his head down through a white waste to the meeting-house door, and unlocked it, and shivered as he made the fire. It was certainly not good election weather, thought Moses, and others of the orthodox persuasion, high in office, were of the same opinion as they stood with parted coat tails before the stove. Whoever had stirred up and organized the hordes, whoever was the author of that ticket of the discontented, had not counted upon the sleet. Heaven-sent sleet, said Deacon Ira Perkins, and would not speak to his son Chester, who sat down just then in one of the rear slips. Chester had become an agitator, a Jacksonian Democrat, and an outcast, to be prayed for but not spoken to.

We shall leave them their peace of mind for half an hour more, those stanch old deacons and selectmen, who did their duty by their fellow-citizens as they saw it and took no man's bidding. They could not see the trackless roads over the hills, now becoming tracked, and the bent figures driving doggedly against the storm, each impelled by a motive : each motive strengthened by a master mind until it had become imperative. Some, like Eben Williams behind his rickety horse, came through fear ; others through ambition ; others were actuated by both ; and still others were stung by the pain of the sleet to a still greater jealousy and envy, and the remembrance of those who had been in power. I must not omit the conscientious Jacksonians who were misguided enough to believe in such a ticket.

The sheds were not large enough to hold the teams that day. Jethro's barn and tannery were full, and many other barns in the village. And now the peace of mind

of the orthodox is a thing of the past. Deacon Lysander
Richardson, the moderator, sits aghast in his high place
as they come trooping in, men who have not been to town
meeting for ten years. Deacon Lysander, with his white
band of whiskers that goes around his neck like a six-
teenth-century ruff under his chin, will soon be a memory.
Now enters one, if Deacon Lysander had known it —
symbolic of the new Era. One who, though his large
head is bent, towers over most of the men who make way
for him in the aisle, nodding but not speaking, and takes
his place in the chair under the platform on the right of
the meeting-house under one of the high, three-part windows. That chair was always his in future years, and there
he sat afterward, silent, apparently taking no part. But
not a man dropped a ballot into the box whom Jethro
Bass did not see and mark.

And now, when the meeting-house is crowded as it has
never been before, when Jonah Winch has arranged his
dinner booth in the corner, Deacon Lysander raps for
order and the minister prays. They proceed, first, to
elect a representative to the General Court. The Jacksonians do not contest that seat, — this year, — and Isaiah
Prescott, fourteenth child of Timothy, the Stark hero,
father of a young Ephraim whom we shall hear from
later, is elected. And now ! Now for a sensation, now
for disorder and misrule !

"Gentlemen," says Deacon Lysander, "you will prepare your ballots for the choice of the first Selectman."

The Whigs have theirs written out, — Deacon Moses
Hatch. But who has written out these others that are
being so assiduously passed around ? Sam Price, perhaps,
for he is passing them most assiduously. And what name
is written on them ? Fletcher Bartlett, of course ; that
was on the ticket. Somebody is tricked again. That
is not the name on the ticket. Look over Sam Price's
shoulder and you will see the name — Jethro Bass.

It bursts from the lips of Fletcher Bartlett himself —
of Fletcher, inflammable as gunpowder.

"Gentlemen, I withdraw as your candidate, and nomi-
nate a better and an abler man, — Jethro Bass."

" Jethro Bass for Chairman of the Selectmen ! "

The cry is taken up all over the meeting-house, and rises high above the hiss of the sleet on the great windows. Somebody's got on the stove, to add to the confusion and horror. The only man in the whole place who is not excited is Jethro Bass himself, who sits in his chair regardless of those pressing around him. Many years afterward he confessed to some one that he was surprised — and this is true. Fletcher Bartlett had surprised and tricked him, but was forgiven. Forty men are howling at the moderator, who is pounding on the table with a blacksmith's blows. Squire Asa Northcutt, with his arms fanning like a windmill from the edge of the platform, at length shouts down everybody else — down to a hum. Some listen to him : hear the words " infamous outrage" — " if Jethro Bass is elected Selectman, Coniston will never be able to hold up her head among her sister towns for very shame." (Momentary blank, for somebody has got on the stove again, a scuffle going on there.) " I see it all now," says the Squire — (marvel of perspicacity!) " Jethro Bass has debased and debauched this town — " (blank again, and the squire points a finger of rage and scorn at the unmoved offender in the chair) " he has bought and intimidated men to do his bidding. He has sinned against heaven, and against the spirit of that most immortal of documents — " (Blank again. Most unfortunate blank, for this is becoming oratory, but somebody from below has seized the squire by the leg.) Squire Northcutt is too dignified and elderly a person to descend to rough and tumble, but he did get his leg liberated and kicked Fletcher Bartlett in the face. Oh, Coniston, that such scenes should take place in your town meeting ! By this time another is orating, Mr. Sam Price, Jackson Democrat. There was no shorthand reporter in Coniston in those days, and it is just as well, perhaps, that the accusations and recriminations should sink into oblivion.

At last, by mighty efforts of the peace loving in both parties, something like order is restored, the ballots are in the box, and Deacon Lysander is counting them : not like another moderator I have heard of, who spilled the votes on the floor until his own man was elected. No. Had they registered his own death sentence, the deacon would have counted them straight, and needed no town clerk to verify his figures. But when he came to pronounce the vote, shame and sorrow and mortification overcame him. Coniston, his native town, which he had served and revered, was dishonored, and it was for him, Lysander Richardson, to proclaim her disgrace. The deacon choked, and tears of bitterness stood in his eyes, and there came a silence only broken by the surging of the sleet as he rapped on the table.

"Seventy-five votes have been cast for Jethro Bass — sixty-three for Moses Hatch. Necessary for a choice, seventy — and Jethro Bass is elected senior Selectman."

The deacon sat down, and men say that a great sob shook him, while Jacksonian Democracy went wild — not looking into future years to see what they were going wild about. Jethro Bass Chairman of the Board of Selectmen, in the honored place of Deacon Moses Hatch! Bourbon royalists never looked with greater abhorrence on the Corsican adventurer and usurper of the throne than did the orthodox in Coniston on this tanner, who had earned no right to aspire to any distinction, and who by his wiles had acquired the highest office in the town government. Fletcher Bartlett in, as a leader of the irresponsible opposition, would have been calamity enough. But Jethro Bass!

This man whom they had despised was the master mind who had organized and marshalled the loose vote, was the author of that ticket, who sat in his corner unmoved alike by the congratulations of his friends and the maledictions of his enemies; who rose to take his oath of office as unconcerned as though the house were empty, albeit Deacon Lysander could scarcely get the words out. And then Jethro sat down again in his chair — not to leave it for six and thirty years. From this time forth that chair became a seat of power, and of dominion over a state.

Thus it was that Jock Hallowell's prophecy, so lightly uttered, came to pass.

How the remainder of that Jacksonian ticket was elected, down to the very hog-reeves, and amid what turmoil of the Democracy and bitterness of spirit of the orthodox, I need not recount. There is no moral to the story, alas — it was one of those things which inscrutable heaven permitted to be done. After that dark town-meeting day some of those stern old fathers became broken men, and it is said in Coniston that this calamity to righteous government, and not the storm, gave to Priest Ware his death-stroke.

CHAPTER VI

"DEEP AS FIRST LOVE, AND WILD WITH ALL REGRET"

And now we must go back for a chapter — a very short chapter — to the day before that town meeting which had so momentous an influence upon the history of Coniston and of the state. That Monday, too, it will be remembered, dawned in storm, the sleet hissing in the wide throats of the centre-chimneys, and bearing down great boughs of trees until they broke in agony. Dusk came early, and howling darkness that hid a muffled figure on the ice-bound road staring at the yellow cracks in the tannery door. Presently the figure crossed the yard; the door, flying open, released a shaft of light that shot across the white ground, revealed a face beneath a hood to him who stood within.

"Jethro!"

She darted swiftly past him, seizing the door and drawing it closed after her. A lantern hung on the central post and flung its rays upon his face. Her own, mercifully, was in the shadow, and burning now with a shame that was insupportable. Now that she was there, beside him, her strength failed her, and her courage — courage that she had been storing for this dread undertaking throughout the whole of that dreadful day. Now that she was there, she would have given her life to have been able to retrace her steps, to lose herself in the wild, dark places of the mountain.

"Cynthy!" His voice betrayed the passion which her presence had quickened.

The words she would have spoken would not come. She could think of nothing but that she was alone with him, and in bodily terror of him. She turned to the door again, to grasp the wooden latch; but he barred the way, and she fell back.

"Let me go," she cried. "I did not mean to come. Do you hear? — let me go!"

To her amazement he stepped aside — a most unaccountable action for him. More unaccountable still, she did not move, now that she was free, but stood poised for flight, held by she knew not what.

"G-go if you've a mind to, Cynthy — if you've a mind to."

"I-I've come to say something to you," she faltered. It was not at all the way she had pictured herself as saying it.

"H-haven't took Moses — have you?"

"Oh," she cried, "do you think I came here to speak of such a thing as that?"

"H-haven't took — Moses, have you?"

She was trembling, and yet she could almost have smiled at this well-remembered trick of pertinacity.

"No," she said, and immediately hated herself for answering him.

"H-haven't took that Worthington cuss?"

He was jealous!

"I didn't come to discuss Mr. Worthington," she replied.

"Folks say it's only a matter of time," said he. "Made up your mind to take him, Cynthy? M-made up your mind?"

"You've no right to talk to me in this way," she said, and added, the words seeming to slip of themselves from her lips, "Why do you do it?"

"Because I'm — interested," he said.

"You haven't shown it," she flashed back, forgetting the place, and the storm, and her errand even, forgetting that Jake Wheeler, or any one in Coniston, might come and surprise her there.

He took a step toward her, and she retreated. The light struck her face, and he bent over her as though searching it for a sign. The cape on her shoulders rose and fell as she breathed.

" 'Twahn't charity, Cynthy — was it? 'Twahn't charity?"

"It was you who called it such," she answered, in a low voice.

A sleet-charged gust hurled itself against the door, and the lantern flickered.

"Wahn't it charity?"

"It was friendship, Jethro. You ought to have known that, and you should not have brought back the book."

"Friendship," he repeated, "y-you said *friendship?*"

"Yes."

"M-meant friendship?"

"Yes," said Cynthia, but more faintly, and yet with a certain delicious fright as she glanced at him shyly. Surely there had never been a stranger man! Now he was apparently in a revery.

"G-guess it's because I'm not good enough to be anything more," he remarked suddenly. "Is that it?"

"You have not tried even to be a friend," she said.

"H-how about Worthington?" he persisted. "Just friends with him?"

"I won't talk about Mr. Worthington," cried Cynthia, desperately, and retreated toward the lantern again.

"J-just friends with Worthington?"

"Why?" she asked, her words barely heard above the gust, "why do you want to know?"

He came after her. It was as if she had summoned some unseen, uncontrollable power, only to be appalled by it, and the mountain-storm without seemed the symbol of it. His very voice seemed to partake of its strength.

"Cynthy," he said, "if you'd took *him*, I'd have killed him. Cynthy, I love you — I want you to be my woman—"

"Your woman!"

He caught her, struggling wildly, terror-stricken, in his arms, beat down her hands, flung back her hood, and kissed her forehead — her hair, blown by the wind — her lips. In that moment she felt the mystery of heaven and hell, of all kinds of power. In that moment she was like a seed flying in the storm above the mountain spruces — whither, she knew not, cared not. There was one thought that drifted across the chaos like a blue light of the spirit: Could she control the storm? Could she say whither the winds might blow, where the seed might be planted? Then she found herself listening, struggling no longer, for he held her powerless. Strangest of all, most hopeful of all, his own mind was working, though his soul rocked with passion.

"Cynthy — ever sence we stopped that day on the road in Northcutt's woods, I've thought of nothin' but to marry you — m-marry you. Then you give me that book — I hain't had much education, but it come across me if you was to help me that way — And when I seed you with Worthington, I could have killed him easy as breakin' bark."

"Hush, Jethro."

She struggled free and leaped away from him, panting, while he tore open his coat and drew forth something which gleamed in the lantern's rays — a silver locket. Cynthia scarcely saw it. Her blood was throbbing in her temples, she could not reason, but she knew that the appeal for the sake of which she had stooped must be delivered now.

"Jethro," she said, "do you know why I came here — why I came to *you?*"

"No," he said. "No. W-wanted me, didn't you? Wanted me — I wanted you, Cynthy."

"I would never have come to you for that," she cried, "*never.*"

"L-love me, Cynthy — love me, don't you?"

How could he ask, seeing that she had been in his arms, and had not fled? And yet she must go through with what she had come to do, at any cost.

"Jethro, I have come to speak to you about the town meeting to-morrow."

He halted as though he had been struck, his hand tightening over the locket.

F

" T-town meetin' ? "

" Yes. All this new organization is your doing," she cried. " Do you think that I am foolish enough to believe that Fletcher Bartlett or Sam Price planned this thing? No, Jethro. I know who has done it, and I could have told them if they had asked me."

He looked at her, and the light of a new admiration was in his eye.

" Knowed it — did you? "

" Yes," she answered, a little defiantly, " I did."

" H-how'd you know it — how'd you know it, Cynthy? " How did she know it, indeed?

" I guessed it," said Cynthia, desperately, " knowing you, I guessed it."

" A-always thought you was smart, Cynthy."

" Tell me, did you do this thing ? "

" Th-thought you knowed it — th-thought you knowed it."

" I believe that these men are doing your bidding."

" Hain't you guessin' a little mite too much, Cynthy ? "

" Jethro," she said, " you told me just now that — that you loved me. Don't touch me ! " she cried, when he would have taken her in his arms again. " If you love me, you will tell me why you have done such a thing."

What instinct there was in the man which forbade him speaking out to her, I know not. I do believe that he would have confessed, if he could. Isaac Worthington had been impelled to reveal his plans and aspirations, but Jethro Bass was as powerless in this supreme moment of his life as was Coniston Mountain to move the granite on which it stood. Cynthia's heart sank, and a note of passionate appeal came into her voice.

" Oh, Jethro! " she cried, " this is not the way to use your power, to compel men like Eben Williams and Samuel Todd and — and Lyman Hull, who is a drunkard and a vagabond, to come in and vote for those who are not fit to hold office." She was using the minister's own arguments. " We have always had clean men, and honorable and good men."

He did not speak, but dropped his hands to his sides. His thoughts were not to be fathomed, yet Cynthia took the movement for silent confession, — which it was not, — and stood appalled at the very magnitude of his accomplishment, astonished at the secrecy he had maintained. She had heard that his name had been mentioned in the meeting at the house of Moses Hatch as having taken part in the matter, and she guessed something of certain of his methods. But she had felt his force, and knew that this was not the only secret of his power.

What might he not aspire to, if properly guided? No, she did not believe him to be unscrupulous — but merely ignorant: a man who was capable of such love as she felt was in him, a man whom she could love, could not mean to be unscrupulous. Defence of him leaped to her own lips.

"You did not know what you were doing," she said. "I was sure of it, or I would not have come to you. Oh, Jethro! you must stop it — you must prevent this election."

Her eyes met his, her own pleading, and the very wind without seemed to pause for his answer. But what she asked was impossible. That wind which he himself had loosed, which was to topple over institutions, was rising, and he could no more have stopped it then than he could have hushed the storm.

"You will not do what I ask — now?" she said, very slowly. Then her voice failed her, she drew her hands together, and it was as if her heart had ceased to beat. Sorrow and anger and fierce shame overwhelmed her, and she turned from him in silence and went to the door.

"Cynthy," he cried hoarsely, "Cynthy!"

"You must never speak to me again," she said, and was gone into the storm.

Yes, she had failed. But she did not know that she had left something behind which he treasured as long as he lived.

* * * * * * *

In the spring, when the new leaves were green on the slopes of Coniston, Priest Ware ended a life of faithful service. The high pulpit, taken from the old meeting house, and the cricket on which he used to stand and the Bible from which he used to preach have remained objects of veneration in Coniston to this day. A fortnight later many tearful faces gazed after the Truro coach as it galloped out of Brampton in a cloud of dust, and one there was, watching unseen from the spruces on the hill, who saw within it a girl dressed in black, dry-eyed, staring from the window.

CHAPTER VII

"AND STILL THE AGES ROLL, UNMOVED"

OUT of the stump of a blasted tree in the Coniston woods a flower will sometimes grow, and even so the story which I have now to tell springs from the love of Cynthia Ware and Jethro Bass. The flower, when it came to bloom, was fair in life, and I hope that in these pages it will not lose too much of its beauty and sweetness.

For a little while we are going to gallop through the years as before we have ambled through the days, although the reader's breath may be taken away in the process. How Cynthia Ware went over the Truro Pass to Boston, and how she became a teacher in a high school there, — largely through the kindness of that Miss Lucretia Penniman of whom we have spoken, who wrote in Cynthia's behalf to certain friends she had in that city; how she met one William Wetherell, no longer a clerk in Mr. Judson's jewellery shop, but a newspaper man with I know not what ambitions — and limitations in strength of body and will; how, many, many years afterward, she nursed him tenderly through a sickness and — married him, is all told in a paragraph. Marry him she did, to take care of him, and told him so. She made no secret of the maternal in this love.

One evening, the summer after their marriage, they were walking in the Mall under the great elms that border the Common on the Tremont Street side. They often used to wander there, talking of the books he was to write when strength should come and a little leisure, and sometimes their glances would linger longingly on

Colonnade Row that Bulfinch built across the way, where
dwelt the rich and powerful of the city — and yet he
would not have exchanged their lot for his.   Could he
have earned with his own hands such a house, and set
Cynthia there in glory, what happiness !   But, I stray.

They were walking in the twilight, for the sun had
sunk all red in the marshes of the Charles, when there
chanced along a certain Mr. Judson, a jeweller, taking
the air likewise.   So there came into Wetherell's mind that
amusing adventure with the country lad and the locket.
His name, by reason of some strange quality in it, he had
never forgotten, and suddenly he recalled that the place
the countryman had come from was Coniston.

"Cynthia," said her husband, when Mr. Judson was
gone, "did you know any one in Coniston named Jethro
Bass ? "

She did not answer him.   And, thinking she had not
heard, he spoke again.

"Why do you ask ? " she said, in a low tone, without
looking at him.

He told her the story.   Not until the end of it did the
significance of the name engraved come to him — Cynthy.
"Cynthy, from Jethro."

"Why, it might have been you ! " he said jestingly.
"Was he an admirer of yours, Cynthia, that strange, uncouth countryman?   Did he give you the locket ? "

"No," she answered, "he never did."

Wetherell glanced at her in surprise, and saw that her
lip was quivering, that tears were on her lashes.   She laid
her hand on his arm.

"William," she said, drawing him to a bench, "come,
let us sit down, and I will tell you the story of Jethro
Bass.   We have been happy together, you and I, for I
have found peace with you.   I have tried to be honest
with you, William, and I will always be so.   I told you
before we were married that I loved another man.   I have
tried to forget him, but as God is my judge, I cannot.
I believe I shall love him until I die."

They sat in the summer twilight, until darkness

Forbes Sene Shine ————

"'I will tell you the story of Jethro Bass.'"

fell, and the lights gleamed through the leaves, and
a deep, cool breath coming up from the sea stirred the
leaves above their heads. That she should have loved
Jethro seemed as strange to her as to him, and yet Wetherell was to feel the irresistible force of him. Hers was
not a love that she chose, or would have chosen, but something elemental that cried out from the man to her, and
drew her. Something that had in it now, as of yore,
much of pain and even terror, but drew her. Strangest
of all was that William Wetherell understood and was not
jealous of this thing : which leads us to believe that some
essence of virility was lacking in him, some substance that
makes the fighters and conquerors in this world. In
such mood he listened to the story of Jethro Bass.

" My dear husband," said Cynthia, when she had finished,
her hand tightening over his, " I have never told you this
for fear that it might trouble you as it has troubled me.
I have found in your love sanctuary, and all that remains
of myself I have given to you."

" You have found a weakling to protect, and an invalid
to nurse," he answered. " To have your compassion,
Cynthia, is all I crave."

* * * * * * *

So they lived through the happiest and swiftest years of
his life, working side by side, sharing this strange secret
between them. And after that night Cynthia talked to
him often of Coniston, until he came to know the mountain that lay along the western sky, and the sweet hillsides by Coniston Water under the blue haze of autumn,
aye, and clothed in the colors of spring, the bright blossoms of thorn and apple against the tender green of the
woods and fields. So he grew to love the simple people
there, but little did he foresee that he was to end his life
among them !

But so it came to pass. She was taken from him, who
had been the one joy and inspiration of his weary days,
and he was driven, wandering, into unfrequented streets
that he might not recall the places where she had once

trod, and through the wakeful nights her voice haunted him, — its laughter, its sweet notes of seriousness; little ways and manners of her look came to twist his heart, and he prayed God to take him, too, until it seemed that Cynthia frowned upon him for his weakness. One mild Sunday afternoon, he took little Cynthia by the hand and led her, toddling, out into the sunny Common, where he used to walk with her mother, and the infant prattle seemed to bring at last a strange peace to his storm-tossed soul.

For many years these Sunday walks in the Common were Wetherell's greatest pleasure and solace, and it seemed as though little Cynthia had come into the world with an instinct, as it were, of her mission that lent to her infant words a sweet gravity and weight. Many people used to stop and speak to the child, among them a great physician whom they grew to know. He was there every Sunday, and at length it came to be a habit with him to sit down on the bench and take Cynthia on his knee, and his stern face would soften as he talked to her.

One Sunday when Cynthia was eight years old he missed them, and the next, and at dusk he strode into their little lodging behind the hill and up to the bedside. He glanced at Wetherell, patting Cynthia on the head the while, and bade her cheerily to go out of the room. But she held tight hold of her father's hand and looked up at the doctor bravely.

" I am taking care of my father," she said.

" So you shall, little woman," he answered. " I would that we had such nurses as you at the hospital. Why didn't you send for me at once?"

" I wanted to," said Cynthia.

" Bless her good sense," said the doctor; "she has more than you, Wetherell. Why didn't you take her advice? If your father does not do as I tell him, he will be a very sick man indeed. He must go into the country and stay there."

" But I must live, Doctor," said William Wetherell.

The doctor looked at Cynthia.

Florence Scovel Shinn

"Led her, toddling, out into the sunny Common."

"You will not live if you stay here," he replied.

"Then he will go," said Cynthia, so quietly that he gave her another look, strange and tender and comprehending. He sat and talked of many things : of the great war that was agonizing the nation ; of the strong man who, harassed and suffering himself, was striving to guide it, likening Lincoln unto a physician. So the doctor was wont to take the minds of patients from themselves. And before he left he gave poor Wetherell a fortnight to decide.

As he lay on his back in that room among the chimney tops trying vainly to solve the problem of how he was to earn his salt in the country, a visitor was climbing the last steep flight of stairs. That visitor was none other than Sergeant Ephraim Prescott, son of Isaiah of the pitchpipe, and own cousin of Cynthia Ware's. Sergeant Ephraim was just home from the war and still clad in blue, and he walked with a slight limp by reason of a bullet he had got in the Wilderness, and he had such an honest, genial face that little Cynthia was on his knee in a moment.

"How be you, Will? Kind of poorly, I callate. So Cynthy's b'en took," he said sadly. "Always thought a sight of Cynthy. Little Cynthy favors her some. Yes, thought I'd drop in and see how you be on my way home."

Sergeant Ephraim had much to say about the great war, and about Coniston. True to the instincts of the blood of the Stark hero, he had left the plough and the furrow at the first call, forty years of age though he was. But it had been otherwise with many in Coniston and Brampton and Harwich. Some of these, when the drafting came, had fled in bands to the mountain and defied capture. Mr. Dudley Worthington, now a mill owner, had found a substitute; Heth Sutton of Clovelly had been drafted and had driven over the mountain to implore Jethro Bass abjectly to get him out of it. In short, many funny things had happened — funny things to Sergeant Ephraim, but not at all to William Wetherell, who sympathized with Heth in his panic.

"So Jethro Bass has become a great man," said Wetherell.

"Great!" Ephraim ejaculated. "Guess he's the biggest man in the state to-day. Queer how he got his power — began twenty-four years ago when I wahn't but twenty. I call that town meetin' to mind as if 'twas yesterday — never was such an upset. Jethro's be'n first Selectman ever sence, though he turned Republican in '60. Old folks don't fancy Jethro's kind of politics much, but times change. Jethro saved my life, I guess."

"Saved your life!" exclaimed Wetherell.

"Got me a furlough," said Ephraim. "Guess I would have died in the hospital if he hadn't got it so all-fired quick, and he druv down to Brampton to fetch me back. You'd have thought I was General Grant the way folks treated me."

"You went back to the war after your leg healed?" Wetherell asked, in wondering admiration of the man's courage.

"Well," said Ephraim, simply, "the other boys was gettin' full of bullets and dysentery, and it didn't seem just right. The leg troubles me some on wet days, but not to amount to much. You hain't thinkin' of dyin' yourself, be ye, William?"

William was thinking very seriously of it, but it was Cynthia who spoke, and startled them both.

"The doctor says he will die if he doesn't go to the country."

"Somethin' like consumption, William?" asked Ephraim.

"So the doctor said."

"So I callated," said Ephraim. "Come back to Coniston with me; there hain't a healthier place in New England."

"How could I support myself in Coniston?" Wetherell asked.

Ephraim ruminated. Suddenly he stuck his hand into the bosom of his blue coat, and his face lighted and even flushed as he drew out a crumpled letter.

"It don't take much gumption to run a store, does it, William? Guess you could run a store, couldn't you?"

"I would try anything," said Wetherell.

"Well," said Ephraim, "there's the store at Coniston. With folks goin' West, and all that, nobody seems to want it much." He looked at the letter. "Lem Hallowell says there hain't nobody to take it."

"Jonah Winch's!" exclaimed Wetherell.

"Jonah made it go, but that was before all this hullaba-loo about Temperance Cadets and what not. Jonah sold good rum, but now you can't get nothin' in Coniston but hard cider and potato whiskey. Still, it's the place for somebody without much get-up," and he eyed his cousin by marriage. "Better come and try it, William."

So much for dreams! Instead of a successor to Irving and Emerson, William Wetherell became a successor to Jonah Winch.

That journey to Coniston was full of wonder to Cynthia, and of wonder and sadness to Wetherell, for it was the way his other Cynthia had come to Boston. From the state capital the railroad followed the same deep valley as the old coach road, but ended at Truro, and then they took stage over Truro Pass for Brampton, where honest Ephraim awaited them and their slender luggage with a team. Brampton, with its wide-shadowed green, and terrace-steepled church; home once of the Social Library and Lucretia Penniman, now famous; home now of Isaac Dudley Worthington, whose great mills the stage driver had pointed out to them on Coniston Water as they entered the town.

Then came a drive through the cool evening to Conis-ton, Ephraim showing them landmarks. There was Deacon Lysander's house, where little Rias Richardson lived now; and on that slope and hidden in its forest nook, among the birches and briers, the little schoolhouse where Cynthia had learned to spell; here, where the road made an aisle in the woods, she had met Jethro. The choir of the birds was singing an evening anthem now as then, to the lower notes of Coniston Water, and the moist, hothouse fragrance of the ferns rose from the deep places.

At last they came suddenly upon the little hamlet of

Coniston itself. There was the flagpole and the triangular green, scene of many a muster ; Jonah Winch's store, with its horse block and checker-paned windows, just as Jonah had left it ; Nathan Bass's tannery shed, now weather-stained and neglected, for Jethro lived on Thousand Acre Hill now; the Prescott house, home of the Stark hero, where Ephraim lived, "innocent of paint" (as one of Coniston's sons has put it), "innocent of paint as a Coniston maiden's face"; the white meeting-house, where Priest Ware had preached — and the parsonage. Cynthia and Wetherell loitered in front of it, while the blue shadow of the mountain deepened into night, until Mr. Satterlee, the minister, found them there, and they went in and stood reverently in the little chamber on the right of the door, which had been Cynthia's.

Long Wetherell lay awake that night, in his room at the gable-end over the store, listening to the rustling of the great oak beside the windows, to the whippoorwills calling across Coniston Water. But at last a peace descended upon him, and he slept: yes, and awoke with the same sense of peace at little Cynthia's touch, to go out into the cool morning, when the mountain side was in myriad sheens of green under the rising sun. Behind the store was an old-fashioned garden, set about by a neat stone wall, hidden here and there by the masses of lilac and currant bushes, and at the south of it was a great rose-covered boulder of granite. And beyond, through the foliage of the willows and the low apple trees which Jonah Winch had set out, Coniston Water gleamed and tumbled. Under an arching elm near the house was the well, stone-rimmed, with its long pole and crotch, and bucket all green with the damp moss which clung to it.

Ephraim Prescott had been right when he had declared that it did not take much gumption to keep store in Coniston. William Wetherell merely assumed certain obligations at the Brampton bank, and Lem Hallowell, Jock's son, who now drove the Brampton stage, brought the goods to the door. Little Rias Richardson was willing to come in and help move the barrels, and on such occasions wore carpet slippers to save his shoes. William still had time for his books; in that Coniston air he began to feel stronger, and to wonder whether he might not be a Washington Irving yet. And yet he had one worry and one fear, and both of these concerned one man, — Jethro Bass. Him, by her own confession, Cynthia Ware had loved to her dying day, hating herself for it: and he, William Wetherell, had married this woman whom Jethro had loved so violently, and must always love — so Wetherell thought: that was the worry. How would Jethro treat him? that was the fear. William Wetherell was not the most courageous man in the world.

Jethro Bass had not been in Coniston since William's arrival. No need to ask where he was. Jake Wheeler, Jethro's lieutenant in Coniston, gave William a glowing account of that Throne Room in the Pelican Hotel at the capital, from whence Jethro ruled the state during the sessions of the General Court. This legislature sat to him as a sort of advisory committee of three hundred and fifty : an expensive advisory committee to the people, relic of an obsolete form of government. Many stories of the now all-powerful Jethro William heard from the little coterie which made their headquarters in his store — stories of how those methods of which we have read were gradually spread over other towns and other counties. Not that Jethro held mortgages in these towns and counties, but the local lieutenants did, and bowed to him as an overlord. There were funny stories, and grim stories of vengeance which William Wetherell heard and trembled at. Might not Jethro wish to take vengeance upon him?

One story he did not hear, because no one in Coniston knew it. No one knew that Cynthia Ware and Jethro Bass had ever loved each other.

At last, toward the end of June, it was noised about that the great man was coming home for a few days. One beautiful afternoon William Wetherell stood on the platform of the store, looking off at Coniston, talking to Moses

Hatch — young Moses, who is father of six children now
and has forgotten Cynthia Ware. Old Moses sleeps on
the hillside, let us hope in the peace of the orthodox and
the righteous. A cloud of dust arose above the road to
the southward, and out of it came a country wagon drawn
by a fat horse, and in the wagon the strangest couple
Wetherell had ever seen. The little woman who sat re-
tiringly at one end of the seat was all in brilliant colors
from bonnet to flounce, like a paroquet, red and green
predominating. The man, big in build, large-headed,
wore an old-fashioned blue swallow-tailed coat with brass
buttons, a stock, and coonskin hat, though it was summer,
and the thumping of William Wetherell's heart told him
that this was Jethro Bass. He nodded briefly at Moses
Hatch, who greeted him with genial obsequiousness.

"Legislatur' through?" shouted Moses.

The great man shook his head and drove on.

"Has Jethro Bass ever been a member of the Legislature?" asked the storekeeper, for the sake of something
to say.

"Never would take any office but Chairman of the
Selectmen," answered Moses, who apparently bore no
ill will for his father's sake. "Jethro kind of fathers
the Legislatur', I guess, though I don't take much stock
in politics. Goes down sessions to see that they don't
get too gumptious and kick off the swaddlin' clothes."

"And — was that his wife?" Wetherell asked, hesitatingly.

"Aunt Listy, they call her. Nobody ever knew how he
come to marry her. Jethro went up to Wisdom once, in
the centre of the state, and come back with her. Funny
place to bring a wife from — Wisdom! Funnier place to
bring Listy from. He loads her down with them ribbons
and gewgaws — all the shades of the rainbow! Says he
wants her to be the best-dressed woman in the state.
Callate she is," added Moses, with conviction. "Listy's
a fine woman, but all she knows is enough to say, 'Yes,
Jethro,' and 'No, Jethro.' Guess that's all Jethro wants
in a wife; but he certainly is good to her."

"And why has he come back before the Legislature's over?" said Wetherell.

"Cuttin' of his farms. Always comes back hayin' time. That's the way Jethro spends the money he makes in politics, and he hain't no more of a farmer than —"
Moses looked at Wetherell.

"Than I'm a storekeeper," said the latter, smiling.

"Than I'm a lawyer," said Moses, politely.

They were interrupted at this moment by the appearance of Jake Wheeler and Sam Price, who came gaping out of the darkness of the store.

"Was that Jethro, Mose?" demanded Jake. "Guess we'll go along up and see if there's any orders."

"I suppose the humblest of God's critturs has their uses," Moses remarked contemplatively, as he watched the retreating figures of Sam and Jake. "Leastwise that's Jethro's philosophy. When you come to know him, you'll notice how much those fellers walk like him. Never seed a man who had so many imitators. Some of 'em's took to talkin' like him, even to stutterin'. Bijah Bixby, over to Clovelly, comes pretty nigh it, too."

Moses loaded his sugar and beans into his wagon, and drove off.

An air of suppressed excitement seemed to pervade those who came that afternoon to the store to trade and talk — mostly to talk. After such purchases as they could remember were made, they lingered on the barrels and on the stoop, in the hope of seeing Jethro, whose habit it was, apparently, to come down and dispense such news as he thought fit for circulation. That Wetherell shared this excitement, too, he could not deny, but for a different cause. At last, when the shadows of the big trees had crept across the green, he came, the customers flocking to the porch to greet him, Wetherell standing curiously behind them in the door. Heedless of the dust, he strode down the road with the awkward gait that was all his own, kicking up his heels behind. And behind him, heels kicking up likewise, followed Jake and Sam, Jethro apparently oblivious of their presence. A modest silence was

maintained from the stoop, broken at length by Lem Hallowell, who (men said) was an exact reproduction of Jock,
the meeting-house builder. Lem alone was not abashed
in the presence of greatness.

"How be you, Jethro?" he said heartily. "Air the
Legislatur' behavin' themselves?"

"B-bout as common," said Jethro.

Surely nothing very profound in this remark, but received as though it were Solomon's.

Be prepared for a change in Jethro, after the galloping
years. He is now fifty-seven, but he might be any age.
He is still smooth-shaven, his skin is clear, and his eye is
bright, for he lives largely on bread and milk, and eschews
stimulants. But the lines in his face have deepened and
his big features seem to have grown bigger.

"Who be you thinkin' of for next governor, Jethro?"
queries Rias Richardson, timidly.

"They say Alvy Hopkins of Gosport is willin' to pay
for it," said Chester Perkins, sarcastically. Chester, we
fear, is a born agitator, fated to remain always in opposition. He is still a Democrat, and Jethro, as is well known,
has extended the mortgage so as to include Chester's
farm.

"Wouldn't give a Red Brook Seedling for Alvy,"
ejaculated the nasal Mr. Price.

"D-don't like Red Brook Seedlings, Sam? D-don't
like 'em?" said Jethro. He had parted his blue coat tails
and seated himself on the stoop, his long legs hanging
over it.

"Never seed a man who had a good word to say for
'em," said Mr. Price, with less conviction.

"Done well on mine," said Jethro, "d-done well. I
was satisfied with my Red Brook Seedlings."

Mr. Price's sallow face looked as if he would have con-
tradicted another man.

"Haow was that, Jethro?" piped up Jake Wheeler,
voicing the general desire.

Jethro looked off into the blue space beyond the mountain line.

"G-got mine when they first come round — seed cost me considerable. Raised more than a hundred bushels — L-Listy put some of 'em on the table — t-then gave some to my old hoss Tom. Tom said: 'Hain't I always been a good beast, Jethro? Hain't I carried you faithful, summer and winter, for a good many years? And now you give me Red Brook Seedlings?'"

Here everybody laughed, and stopped abruptly, for Jethro still looked contemplative.

"Give some of 'em to the hogs. W-wouldn't touch 'em. H-had over a hundred bushels on hand — n-new variety. W-what's that feller's name down to Ayer, Massachusetts, deals in all kinds of seeds? Ellett — that's it. Wrote to Ellett, said I had a hundred bushels of Red Brooks to sell, as fine a lookin' potato as I had in my cellar. Made up my mind to take what he offered, if it was only five cents. He wrote back a dollar a bushel. I-I was always satisfied with my Red Brook Seedlings, Sam. But I never raised any more — n-never raised any more."

Uproarious laughter greeted the end of this story, and continued in fits as some humorous point recurred to one or the other of the listeners. William Wetherell perceived that the conversation, for the moment at least, was safely away from politics, and in that dubious state where it was difficult to reopen. This was perhaps what Jethro wanted. Even Jake Wheeler was tongue-tied, and Jethro appeared to be lost in reflection.

At this instant a diversion occurred — a trifling diversion, so it seemed at the time. Around the corner of the store, her cheeks flushed and her dark hair flying, ran little Cynthia, her hands, browned already by the Coniston sun, filled with wild strawberries.

"See what I've found, Daddy!" she cried, "see what I've found!"

Jethro Bass started, and flung back his head like a man who has heard a voice from another world, and then he looked at the child with a kind of stupefaction. The cry died on Cynthia's lips, and she stopped, gazing up at him with wonder in her eyes.

"'M-may I call you Cynthy?'"

" F-found strawberries ? " said Jethro, at last.

" Yes," she answered. She was very grave and serious now, as was her manner in dealing with people.

" S-show 'em to me," said Jethro.

Cynthia went to him, without embarrassment, and put her hand on his knee. Not once had he taken his eyes from her face. He put out his own hand with an awkward, shy movement, picked a strawberry from her fingers, and thrust it in his mouth.

" Mm," said Jethro, gravely. " Er — what's your name, little gal — what's your name ? "

" Cynthia."

There was a long pause.

" Er-er — Cynthia ? " he said at length, " Cynthia ? "

" Cynthia."

" Er-er, Cynthia — not Cynthy ? "

" Cynthia," she said again.

He bent over her and lowered his voice.

" M-may I call you Cynthy — Cynthy ? " he asked.

" Y-yes," answered Cynthia, looking up to her father and then glancing shyly at Jethro.

His eyes were on the mountain, and he seemed to have forgotten her until she reached out to him, timidly, another strawberry. He seized her little hand instead and held it between his own — much to the astonishment of his friends.

" Whose little gal be you ? " he asked.

" Dad's."

" She's Will Wetherell's daughter," said Lem Hallowell. " He's took on the store. Will," he added, turning to Wetherell, " let me make you acquainted with Jethro Bass."

Jethro rose slowly, and towered above Wetherell on the stoop. There was an inscrutable look in his black eyes, as of one who sees without being seen. Did he know who William Wetherell was ? If so, he gave no sign, and took Wetherell's hand limply.

" Will's kinder hipped on book-l'arnin'," Lemuel continued kindly. " Come here to keep store for his health. Guess you may have heerd, Jethro, that Will married Cynthy Ware. You call Cynthy to mind, don't ye?"

Jethro Bass dropped Wetherell's hand, but answered nothing.

CHAPTER VIII

IT IS SOMETHING TO HAVE DREAMED

A WEEK passed, and Jethro did not appear in the village, report having it that he was cutting his farms on Thousand Acre Hill. When Jethro was farming, — so it was said, — he would not stop to talk politics even with the President of the United States were that dignitary to lean over his pasture fence and beckon to him. On a sultry Friday morning, when William Wetherell was seated at Jonah Winch's desk in the cool recesses of the store slowly and painfully going over certain troublesome accounts which seemed hopeless, he was thrown into a panic by the sight of one staring at him from the far side of a counter. History sometimes reverses itself.

" What can I do for you — Mr. Bass ? " asked the store-keeper, rather weakly.

" Just stepped in — stepped in," he answered. " W-where's Cynthy ? "

" She was in the garden — shall I get her ? "

" No," he said, parting his coat tails and seating himself on the counter. " Go on figurin', don't mind me."

The thing was manifestly impossible. Perhaps Wetherell indicated as much by his answer.

" Like storekeepin' ? " Jethro asked presently, perceiving that he did not continue his work.

" A man must live, Mr. Bass," said Wetherell ; " I had to leave the city for my health. I began life keeping store," he added, " but I little thought I should end it so."

" Given to book-l'arnin' then, wahn't you ? " Jethro remarked. He did not smile, but stared at the square of

87

light that was the doorway, "Judson's jewellery store,
wahn't it? Judson's?"

"Yes, Judson's," Wetherell answered, as soon as he
recovered from his amazement. There was no telling
from Jethro's manner whether he were enemy or friend;
whether he bore the storekeeper a grudge for having
attained to a happiness that had not been his.

"Hain't made a great deal out of life, hev you? N-not
a great deal?" Jethro observed at last.

Wetherell flushed, although Jethro had merely stated a
truth which had often occurred to the storekeeper himself.

"It isn't given to all of us to find Rome in brick and
leave it in marble," he replied a little sadly.

Jethro Bass looked at him quickly.

"Er — what's that?" he demanded. "F-found Rome
in brick, left it in marble. Fine thought." He ruminated a little. "Never writ anything — did you — never
writ anything?"

"Nothing worth publishing," answered poor William
Wetherell.

"J-just dreamed — dreamed and kept store. S-something to have dreamed — eh — something to have
dreamed?"

Wetherell forgot his uneasiness in the unexpected turn
the conversation had taken. It seemed very strange to
him that he was at last face to face again with the man
whom Cynthia Ware had never been able to drive from
her heart. Would he mention her? Had he continued
to love her, in spite of the woman he had married and
adorned? Wetherell asked himself these questions before
he spoke.

"It is more to have accomplished," he said.

"S-something to have dreamed," repeated Jethro, rising
slowly from the counter. He went toward the doorway
that led into the garden, and there he halted and stood
listening.

"C-Cynthy!" he said, "C-Cynthy!"

Wetherell dropped his pen at the sound of the name on
Jethro's lips. But it was little Cynthia he was calling —

little Cynthia in the garden. The child came at his voice, and stood looking up at him silently.

"H-how old be you, Cynthy?"

"Nine," answered Cynthia, promptly.

"L-like the country, Cynthy — like the country better than the city?"

"Oh, yes," said Cynthia.

"And country folks? L-like country folks better than city folks?"

"I didn't know many city folks," said Cynthia. "I liked the old doctor who sent Daddy up here ever so much, and I liked Mrs. Darwin."

"Mis' Darwin?"

"She kept the house we lived in. She used to give me cookies," said Cynthia, "and bread to feed the pigeons."

"Pigeons? F-folks keep pigeons in the city?"

"Oh, no," said Cynthia, laughing at such an idea; "the pigeons came on the roof under our window, and they used to fly right up on the window-sill and feed out of my hand. They kept me company while Daddy was away, working. On Sundays we used to go into the Common and feed them, before Daddy got sick. The Common was something like the country, only not half as nice."

"C-couldn't pick flowers in the Common and go bare-foot — c-couldn't go barefoot, Cynthy?"

"Oh, no," said Cynthia, laughing again at his sober face.

"C-couldn't dig up the Common and plant flowers — could you?"

"Of course you couldn't."

"P-plant 'em out there?" asked Jethro.

"Oh, yes," cried Cynthia; "I'll show you." She hesitated a moment, and then thrust her hand into his. "Do you want to see?"

"Guess I do," said he, energetically, and she led him into the garden, pointing out with pride the rows of sweet peas and pansies, which she had made herself. Impelled by a strange curiosity, William Wetherell went to the

door and watched them. There was a look on the face of
Jethro Bass that was new to it as he listened to the child
talk of the wondrous things around them that summer's
day, — the flowers and the bees and the brook (they
must go down and stand on the brink of it), and the songs
of the vireo and the hermit thrush.

"Hain't lonely here, Cynthy — hain't lonely here?" he
said.

"Not in the country," said Cynthia. Suddenly she
lifted her eyes to his with a questioning look. "Are you
lonely, sometimes?"

He did not answer at once.

"Not with you, Cynthy — not with you."

By all of which it will be seen that the acquaintance was
progressing. They sat down for a while on the old millstone that formed the step, and there discussed Cynthia's
tastes. She was too old for dolls, Jethro supposed. Yes,
Cynthia was too old for dolls. She did not say so, but the
only doll she had ever owned had become insipid when the
delight of such a reality as taking care of a helpless father
had been thrust upon her. Books, suggested Jethro. Books
she had known from her earliest infancy: they had been
piled around that bedroom over the roof. Books and book
lore and the command of the English tongue were William
Wetherell's only legacies to his daughter, and many an
evening that spring she had read him to sleep from classic
volumes of prose and poetry I hesitate to name, for fear
you will think her precocious. They went across the
green to Cousin Ephraim Prescott's harness shop, where
Jethro had tied his horse, and it was settled that Cynthia
liked books.

On the morning following this extraordinary conversation, Jethro Bass and his wife departed for the state capital. Listy was bedecked in amazing greens and yellows,
and Jethro drove, looking neither to the right nor left, his
coat tails hanging down behind the seat, the reins lying
slack across the plump quarters of his horse — the same
fat Tom who, by the way, had so indignantly spurned the
Red Brook Seedlings. And Jake Wheeler went along to

bring back the team from Brampton. To such base uses are political lieutenants sometimes put, although Jake would have told you it was an honor, and he came back to the store that evening fairly bristling with political secrets which he could not be induced to impart.

One evening a fortnight later, while the lieutenant was holding forth in commendably general terms on the politics of the state to a speechless if not wholly admiring audience, a bomb burst in their midst. William Wetherell did not know that it was a periodical bomb, like those flung at regular intervals from the Union mortars into Vicksburg. These bombs, at any rate, never failed to cause consternation and fright in Coniston, although they never did any harm. One thing noticeable, they were always fired in Jethro's absence. And the bombardier was always Chester Perkins, son of the most unbending and rigorous of tithing-men, but Chester resembled his father in no particular save that he, too, was a deacon and a pillar of the church. Deacon Ira had been tall and gaunt and sunken and uncommunicative. Chester was stout, and said to perspire even in winter, apoplectic, irascible, talkative, and still, as has been said, a Democrat. He drove up to the store this evening to the not inappropriate rumble of distant thunder, and he stood up in his wagon in front of the gathering and shook his fist in Jake Wheeler's face.

" This town's tired of puttin' up with a King," he cried. " Yes, King — I said it, and I don't care who hears me. It's time to stop this one-man rule. You kin go and tell him I said it, Jake Wheeler, if you've a mind to. I guess there's plenty who'll do that."

An uneasy silence followed — the silence which cries treason louder than any voice. Some shifted uneasily, and spat, and Jake Wheeler thrust his hands in his pockets and walked away, as much as to say that it was treason even to listen to such talk. Lem Hallowell seemed unperturbed.

" On the rampage agin, Chet? " he remarked.

" You'd ought to know better, Lem," cried the enraged

Chester; "hain't the hull road by the Four Corners ready
to drop into the brook? What be you a-goin' to do
about it?"

"I'll show you when I git to it," answered Lem, quietly.
And show them he did.

"Git to it!" shouted Chester, scornfully, "I'll git to
it. I'll tell you right now I'm a candidate for the Chairman of the Selectmen, if town meetin' is eight months
away. An', Sam Price, I'll expect the Democrats to git
into line."

With this ultimatum Chester drove away as rapidly as
he had come.

"I want to know!" said Sam Price, an exclamation
peculiarly suited to his voice. But nevertheless Sam
might be counted on in each of these little rebellions.
He, too, had remained steadfast to Jacksonian principles,
and he had never forgiven Jethro about a little matter
of a state office which he (Sam) had failed to obtain.

Before he went to bed Jake Wheeler had written a letter which he sent off to the state capital by the stage the
next morning. In it he indicted no less than twenty of
his fellow-townsmen for treason; and he also thought it
wise to send over to Clovelly for Bijah Bixby, a lieutenant
in that section, to come and look over the ground and
ascertain by his well-known methods how far the treason
had eaten into the body politic. Such was Jake's ordinary
procedure when the bombs were fired, for Mr. Wheeler
was nothing if not cautious.

Three mornings later, a little after seven o'clock, when
the storekeeper and his small daughter were preparing to
go to Brampton upon a very troublesome errand, Chester
Perkins appeared again. It is always easy to stir up dis-
satisfaction among the ne'er-do-wells (Jethro had once
done it himself), and during the three days which had
elapsed since Chester had flung down the gauntlet there
had been more or less of downright treason heard in the
store. William Wetherell, who had perplexities of his
own, had done his best to keep out of the discussions that
had raged on his cracker boxes and barrels, for his head

"He indicted no less than twenty of his fellow-townsmen."

was a jumble of figures which would not come right. And
now as he stood there in the freshness of the early summer morning, waiting for Lem Hallowell's stage, poor
Wetherell's heart was very heavy.

"Will Wetherell," said Chester, "you be a gentleman
and a student, hain't you? Read history, hain't you?"

"I have read some," said William Wetherell.

"I callate that a man of parts," said Chester, "such as
you be, will help us agin corruption and a dic'tator. I'm
a-countin' on you, Will Wetherell. You've got the store,
and you kin tell the boys the difference between right and
wrong. They'll listen to you, because you're eddicated."

"I don't know anything about politics," answered Wetherell, with an appealing glance at the silent group, — group
that was always there. Rias Richardson, who had donned
the carpet slippers preparatory to tending store for the
day, shuffled inside. Deacon Lysander, his father, would
not have done so.

"You know somethin' about history and the Constitoo-
tion, don't ye?" demanded Chester, truculently. "Jethro
Bass don't hold your mortgage, does he? Bank in Brampton holds it — hain't that so? You hain't afeard of Jethro
like the rest on 'em, be you?"

"I don't know what right you have to talk to me that
way, Mr. Perkins," said Wetherell.

"What right? Jethro holds my mortgage — the hull
town knows it — and he kin close me out to-morrow if he's
a mind to — "

"See here, Chester Perkins," Lem Hallowell interposed,
as he drove up with the stage, "what kind of free principles be you preachin'? You'd ought to know better'n
coerce."

"What be you a-goin' to do about that Four Corners
road?" Chester cried to the stage driver.

"I give 'em till to-morrow night to fix it," said Lem.
"Git in, Will. Cynthy's over to the harness shop with
Eph. We'll stop as we go 'long."

"Give 'em till to-morrow night!" Chester shouted
after them. "What you goin' to do then?"

But Lem did not answer this inquiry. He stopped at the harness shop, where Ephraim came limping out and lifted Cynthia to the seat beside her father, and they joggled off to Brampton. The dew still lay in myriad drops on the red herd's-grass, turning it to lavender in the morning sun, and the heavy scent of the wet ferns hung in the forest. Lem whistled, and joked with little Cynthia, and gave her the reins to drive, and at last they came in sight of Brampton Street, with its terrace-steepled church and line of wagons hitched to the common rail, for it was market day. Father and daughter walked up and down, hand in hand, under the great trees, and then they went to the bank.

It was a brick building on a corner opposite the common, imposing for Brampton, and very imposing to Wetherell. It seemed like a tomb as he entered its door, Cynthia clutching his fingers, and never but once in his life had he been so near to leaving all hope behind. He waited patiently by the barred windows until the clerk, who was counting bills, chose to look up at him.

"Want to draw money?" he demanded.

The words seemed charged with irony. William Wetherell told him, falteringly, his name and business, and he thought the man looked at him compassionately.

"You'll have to see Mr. Worthington," he said; "he hasn't gone to the mills yet."

"Dudley Worthington?" exclaimed Wetherell.

The teller smiled.

"Yes. He's the president of this bank."

He opened a door in the partition, and leaving Cynthia dangling her feet from a chair, Wetherell was ushered, not without trepidation, into the great man's office, and found himself at last in the presence of Mr. Isaac D. Worthington, who used to wander up and down Coniston Water searching for a mill site.

He sat behind a table covered with green leather, on which papers were laid with elaborate neatness, and he wore a double-breasted skirted coat of black, with braided lapels, a dark purple blanket-cravat with a large red

cameo pin. And Mr. Worthington's features harmonized
perfectly with this costume — those of a successful, am-
bitious man who followed custom and convention blindly;
clean-shaven, save for reddish chops, blue eyes of extreme
keenness, and thin-lipped mouth which had been tightening year by year as the output of the Worthington Mills
increased.

"Well, sir," he said sharply, "what can I do for you?"

"I am William Wetherell, the storekeeper at Coniston."

"Not the Wetherell who married Cynthia Ware!"

No, Mr. Worthington did not say that. He did not
know that Cynthia Ware was married, or alive or dead,
and — let it be confessed at once — he did not care.

This is what he did say : —

"Wetherell — Wetherell. Oh, yes, you've come about
that note — the mortgage on the store at Coniston." He
stared at William Wetherell, drummed with his fingers on
the table, and smiled slightly. "I am happy to say that
the Brampton Bank does not own this note any longer.
If we did, — merely as a matter of business, you understand" (he coughed), — "we should have had to foreclose."

"Don't own the note!" exclaimed Wetherell. "Who
does own it?"

"We sold it a little while ago — since you asked for
the extension — to Jethro Bass."

"Jethro Bass!" Wetherell's feet seemed to give way
under him, and he sat down.

"Mr. Bass is a little quixotic — that is a charitable
way to put it — quixotic. He does — strange things like
this once in a while."

The storekeeper found no words to answer, but sat
mutely staring at him. Mr. Worthington coughed again.

"You appear to be an educated man. Haven't I heard
some story of your giving up other pursuits in Boston
to come up here for your health? Certainly I place you
now. I confess to a little interest in literature myself —
in libraries."

In spite of his stupefaction at the news he had just

received, Wetherell thought of Mr. Worthington's beaver hat, and of that gentleman's first interest in libraries, for Cynthia had told the story to her husband.

"It is perhaps an open secret," continued Mr. Worthington, "that in the near future I intend to establish a free library in Brampton. I feel it my duty to do all I can for the town where I have made my success, and there is nothing which induces more to the popular welfare than a good library." Whereupon he shot at Wetherell another of his keen looks. "I do not talk this way ordinarily to my customers, Mr. Wetherell," he began; "but you interest me, and I am going to tell you something in confidence. I am sure it will not be betrayed."

"Oh, no," said the bewildered storekeeper, who was in no condition to listen to confidences.

He went quietly to the door, opened it, looked out, and closed it softly. Then he looked out of the window.

"Have a care of this man Bass," he said, in a lower voice. "He began many years ago by debauching the liberties of that little town of Coniston, and since then he has gradually debauched the whole state, judges and all. If I have a case to try" (he spoke now with more intensity and bitterness), "concerning my mills, or my bank, before I get through I find that rascal mixed up in it somewhere, and unless I arrange matters with him, I—"

He paused abruptly, his eyes going out of the window, pointing with a long finger at a grizzled man crossing the street with a yellow and red horse blanket thrown over his shoulders.

"That man, Judge Baker, holding court in this town now, Bass owns body and soul."

"And the horse blanket?" Wetherell queried, irresistibly.

Dudley Worthington did not smile.

"Take my advice, Mr. Wetherell, and pay off that note somehow." An odor of the stable pervaded the room, and a great unkempt grizzled head and shoulders, horse blanket and all, were stuck into it.

H

" Mornin', Dudley," said the head, " busy ? "

" Come right in, Judge," answered Mr. Worthington. " Never too busy to see you." The head disappeared. " Take my advice, Mr. Wetherell."

And then the storekeeper went into the bank.

For some moments he stood dazed by what he had heard, the query ringing in his head : Why had Jethro Bass bought that note ? Did he think that the storekeeper at Coniston would be of use to him, politically ? The words Chester Perkins had spoken that morning came back to Wetherell as he stood in the door. And how was he to meet Jethro Bass again with no money to pay even the interest on the note ? Then suddenly he missed Cynthia, hurried out, and spied her under the trees on the common so deep in conversation with a boy that she did not perceive him until he spoke to her. The boy looked up, smiling frankly at something Cynthia had said to him. He had honest, humorous eyes, and a browned, freckled face, and was, perhaps, two years older than Cynthia.

" What's the matter ? " said Wetherell.

Cynthia's face was flushed, and she was plainly vexed about something.

" I gave her a whistle," said the boy, with a little laugh of vexation, " and now she says she won't take it because I owned up I made it for another girl."

Cynthia held it out to him, not deigning to appeal her case.

" You must take it back," she said.

" But I want you to have it," said the boy.

" It wouldn't be right for me to take it when you made it for somebody else."

After all, people with consciences are born, not made. But this was a finer distinction than the boy had ever met with in his experience.

" I didn't know you when I made the whistle," he objected, puzzled and downcast.

" That doesn't make any difference."

" I like you better than the other girl."

Florence Scovel Shinn

"'Mornin', Dudley.'"

99

"You have no right to," retorted the casuist; "you've known her longer."

"That doesn't make any difference," said the boy; "there are lots of people I don't like I have always known. This girl doesn't live in Brampton, anyway."

"Where does she live?" demanded Cynthia, — which was a step backward.

"At the state capital. Her name's Janet Duncan. There, do you believe me now?"

William Wetherell had heard of Janet Duncan's father, Alexander Duncan, who had the reputation of being the richest man in the state. And he began to wonder who the boy could be.

"I believe you," said Cynthia; "but as long as you made it for her, it's hers. Will you take it?"

"No," said he, determinedly.

"Very well," answered Cynthia. She laid down the whistle beside him on the rail, and went off a little distance and seated herself on a bench. The boy laughed.

"I like that girl," he remarked; "the rest of 'em take everything I give 'em, and ask for more. She's prettier'n any of 'em, too."

"What is your name?" Wetherell asked him, curiously, forgetting his own troubles.

"Bob Worthington."

"Are you the son of Dudley Worthington?"

"Everybody asks me that," he said; "I'm tired of it. When I grow up, they'll have to stop it."

"But you should be proud of your father."

"I am proud of him, everybody's proud of him, Brampton's proud of him — he's proud of himself. That's enough, ain't it?" He eyed Wetherell somewhat defiantly, then his glance wandered to Cynthia, and he walked over to her. He threw himself down on the grass in front of her, and lay looking up at her solemnly. For a while she continued to stare inflexibly at the line of market wagons, and then she burst into a laugh.

"Thought you wouldn't hold out forever," he remarked.

"It's because you're so foolish," said Cynthia, "that's

Florence Scovel Shinn

"Deep in conversation with a boy."

why I laughed." Then she grew sober again and held out her hand to him. "Good-by."

"Where are you going?"

"I must go back to my father. I — I think he doesn't feel very well."

"Next time I'll make a whistle for you," he called after her.

"And give it to somebody else," said Cynthia.

She had hold of her father's hand by that, but he caught up with her, very red in the face.

"You know that isn't true," he cried angrily, and taking his way across Brampton Street, turned, and stood staring after them until they were out of sight.

"Do you like him, Daddy?" asked Cynthia.

William Wetherell did not answer. He had other things to think about.

"Daddy?"

"Yes."

"Does your trouble feel any better?"

"Some, Cynthia. But you mustn't think about it."

"Daddy, why don't you ask Uncle Jethro to help you?"

At the name Wetherell started as if he had had a shock.

"What put him into your head, Cynthia?" he asked sharply. "Why do you call him 'Uncle Jethro'?"

"Because he asked me to. Because he likes me, and I like him."

The whole thing was a riddle he could not solve — one that was best left alone. They had agreed to walk back the ten miles to Coniston, to save the money that dinner at the hotel would cost. And so they started, Cynthia flitting hither and thither along the roadside, picking the stately purple iris flowers in the marshy places, while Wetherell pondered.

CHAPTER IX

SHAKE HANDS WITH MR. BIJAH BIXBY

WHEN William Wetherell and Cynthia had reached the last turn in the road in Northcutt's woods, quarter of a mile from Coniston, they met the nasal Mr. Samuel Price driving silently in the other direction. The word "silently" is used deliberately, because to Mr. Price appertained a certain ghostlike quality of flitting, and to Mr. Price's horse and wagon likewise. He drew up for a brief moment when he saw Wetherell.

"Wouldn't hurry back if I was you, Will."

"Why not?"

Mr. Price leaned out of the wagon.

"Bije has come over from Clovelly to spy araound a little mite."

It was evident from Mr. Price's manner that he regarded the storekeeper as a member of the reform party.

"What did he say, Daddy?" asked Cynthia, as Wetherell stood staring after the flitting buggy in bewilderment.

"I haven't the faintest idea, Cynthia," answered her father, and they walked on.

"Don't you know who 'Bije' is?"

"No," said her father, "and I don't care."

It was almost criminal ignorance for a man who lived in that part of the country not to know Bijah Bixby of Clovelly, who was paying a little social visit to Coniston that day on his way home from the state capital, — tending, as it were, Jethro's flock. Still, Wetherell must be excused because he was an impractical literary man with troubles of his own. But how shall we chronicle Bijah's rank and precedence in the Jethro army, in which there are neither shoulder-straps nor annual registers? To designate him as the Chamberlain of that hill Rajah, the Honorable Heth Sutton, would not be far out of the way. The Honorable Heth, whom we all know and whom we shall see presently, is the man of substance and of broad acres in Clovelly: Bijah merely owns certain mortgages in that town, but he had created the Honorable Heth (politically) as surely as certain prime ministers we could name have created their sovereigns. The Honorable Heth was Bijah's creation, and a grand creation he was, as no one will doubt when they see him.

Bijah — as he will not hesitate to tell you — took Heth down in his pocket to the Legislature, and has more than once delivered him, in certain *blocks* of five and ten, and four and twenty, for certain considerations. The ancient Song of Sixpence applies to Bijah, but his pocket was generally full of proxies instead of rye, and the Honorable Heth was frequently one of the four and twenty blackbirds. In short, Bijah was the working bee, and the Honorable Heth the ornamental drone.

I do not know why I have dwelt so long on such a minor character as Bijah, except that the man fascinates me. Of all the lieutenants in the state, his manners bore the closest resemblance to those of Jethro Bass. When he walked behind Jethro in the corridors of the Pelican, kicking up his heels behind, he might have been taken for Jethro's shadow. He was of a good height and size, smooth-shaven, with little eyes that kindled, and his mouth moved not at all when he spoke: unlike Jethro, he "used" tobacco.

When Bijah had driven into Coniston village and hitched his wagon to the rail, he went direct to the store. Chester Perkins and others were watching him with various emotions from the stoop, and Bijah took a seat in the midst of them, characteristically engaging in conversation without the usual conventional forms of greeting, as if he had been there all day.

"H-how much did you git for your wool, Chester — h-how much?"

"Guess you hain't here to talk about wool, Bije," said Chester, red with anger.

"Kind of neglectin' the farm lately, I hear," observed Bijah.

"Jethro Bass sent you up to find out how much I was neglectin' it," retorted Chester, throwing all caution to the winds.

"Thinkin' of upsettin' Jethro, be you? Thinkin' of upsettin' Jethro?" remarked Bije, in a genial tone.

"Folks in Clovelly hain't got nothin' to do with it, if I am," said Chester.

"Leetle early for campaignin', Chester, leetle early."

"We do our campaignin' when we're a mind to."

Bijah looked around.

"Well, that's funny. I could have took oath I seed Rias Richardson here."

There was a deep silence.

"And Sam Price," continued Bijah, in pretended astonishment, "wahn't he settin' on the edge of the stoop when I drove up?"

Another silence, broken only by the enraged breathing of Chester, who was unable to retort. Moses Hatch laughed. The discreet departure of these gentlemen certainly had its comical side.

"Rias as indoostrious as ever, Mose?" inquired Bijah.

"He has his busy times," said Mose, grinning broadly.

"See you've got the boys with their backs up, Chester," said Bijah.

"Some of us are sick of tyranny," cried Chester; "you kin tell that to Jethro Bass when you go back, if he's got time to listen to you buyin' and sellin' out of railroads."

"Hear Jethro's got the Grand Gulf Road in his pocket to do as he's a mind to with," said Moses, with a view to drawing Bijah out. But the remark had exactly the opposite effect, Bijah screwing up his face into an expression of extraordinary secrecy and cunning.

"How much did you git out of it, Bije?" demanded Chester.

"Hain't looked through my clothes yet," said Bijah, his face screwed up tighter than ever. "N-never look through my clothes till I git home, Chester, it hain't safe."

It has become painfully evident that Mr. Bixby is that rare type of man who can sit down under the enemy's ramparts and smoke him out. It was a rule of Jethro's code either to make an effective departure or else to remain and compel the other man to make an ineffective departure. Lem Hallowell might have coped with him; but the stage was late, and after some scratching of heads and delving for effectual banter (through which Mr. Bixby sat genial and unconcerned), Chester's followers took their leave, each choosing his own pretext.

In the meantime William Wetherell had entered the store by the back door — unperceived, as he hoped. He had a vehement desire to be left in peace, and to avoid politics and political discussions forever — vain desire for the storekeeper of Coniston. Mr. Wetherell entered the store, and to take his mind from his troubles, he picked up a copy of Byron: gradually the conversation on the stoop died away, and just as he was beginning to congratulate himself and enjoy the book, he had an unpleasant sensation of some one approaching him measuredly. Wetherell did not move; indeed, he felt that he could not — he was as though charmed to the spot. He could have cried aloud, but the store was empty, and there was no one to hear him. Mr. Bixby did not speak until he was within a foot of his victim's ear. His voice was very nasal, too.

"Wetherell, hain't it?"

The victim nodded helplessly.

"Want to see you a minute."

"What is it?"

"Where can we talk private?" asked Mr. Bixby, looking around.

"There's no one here," Wetherell answered. "What do you wish to say?"

"If the boys was to see me speakin' to you, they might git suspicious — you understand," he confided, his manner conveying a hint that they shared some common policy.

" I don't meddle with politics," said Wetherell, desperately.

" Ex'actly! " answered Bijah, coming even closer. " I knowed you was a level-headed man, moment I set eyes on you. Made up my mind I'd have a little talk in private with you — you understand. The boys hain't got no reason to suspicion you care anything about politics, have they ? "

" None whatever."

" You don't pay no attention to what they say ? "

" None."

" You *hear* it ? "

" Sometimes I can't help it."

" Ex'actly ! You *hear* it."

" I told you I couldn't help it."

" Want you should vote right when the time comes," said Bijah. " D-don't want to see such an intelligent man go wrong an' be sorry for it — you understand. Chester Perkins is hare-brained. Jethro Bass runs things in this state."

" Mr. Bixby — "

" You understand," said Bijah, screwing up his face. " Guess your watch is a-comin' out." He tucked it back caressingly, and started for the door — the back door. Involuntarily Wetherell put his hand to his pocket, felt something crackle under it, and drew the something out. To his amazement it was a ten-dollar bill.

" Here ! " he cried so sharply in his fright that Mr. Bixby turned around. Wetherell ran after him. " Take this back ! "

" Guess you got me," said Bijah. " W-what is it ? "

" This money is yours," cried Wetherell, so loudly that Bijah started and glanced at the front of the store.

" Guess you made some mistake," he said, staring at the storekeeper with such amazing innocence that he began to doubt his senses, and clutched the bill to see if it was real.

" But I had no money in my pocket," said Wetherell, perplexedly. And then, gaining indignation, " Take this to the man who sent you, and give it back to him."

But Bijah merely whispered caressingly in his ear, " Nobody sent me, — you understand, — nobody sent me," and was gone. Wetherell stood for a moment, dazed by the man's audacity, and then, hurrying to the front stoop, the money still in his hand, he perceived Mr. Bixby in the sunlit road walking, Jethro-fashion, toward Ephraim Prescott's harness shop.

" Why, Daddy," said Cynthia, coming in from the garden, " where did you get all that money? Your troubles must feel better."

" It is not mine," said Wetherell, starting. And then, quivering with anger and mortification, he sank down on the stoop to debate what he should do.

" Is it somebody else's?" asked the child, presently.

" Yes."

" Then why don't you give it back to them, Daddy?"

How was Wetherell to know, in his fright, that Mr. Bixby had for once indulged in an overabundance of zeal in Jethro's behalf? He went to the door, laughter came to him across the green from the harness shop, and his eye following the sound, fastened on Bijah seated comfortably in the midst of the group there. Bitterly the storekeeper comprehended that, had he possessed courage, he would have marched straight after Mr. Bixby and confronted him before them all with the charge of bribery. The blood throbbed in his temples, and yet he sat there, trembling, despising himself, repeating that he might have had the courage if Jethro Bass had not bought the mortgage. The fear of the man had entered the storekeeper's soul.

" Does it belong to that man over there?" asked Cynthia.

" Yes."

" I'll take it to him, Daddy," and she held out her hand.

" Not now," Wetherell answered nervously, glancing at the group. He went into the store, addressed an envelope to " Mr. Bijah Bixby of Clovelly," and gave it to

Cynthia.   " When he comes back for his wagon, hand it
to him," he said, feeling that he would rather, at that
moment, face the devil himself than Mr. Bixby.

Half an hour later, Cynthia gave Mr. Bixby the envelope as he unhitched his horse; and so deftly did Bijah slip
it into his pocket, that he must certainly have misjudged
its contents.   None of the loungers at Ephraim's remarked
the transaction.

If Jethro had indeed instructed Bijah to look after his
flock at Coniston, it was an ill-conditioned move, and some
of the flock resented it when they were quite sure that
Bijah was climbing the notch road toward Clovelly.
The discussion (from which the storekeeper was provi-
dentially omitted) was in full swing when the stage
arrived, and Lem Hallowell's voice silenced the uproar.
It was Lem's boast that he never had been and never
would be a politician.

" Why don't you folks quit railin' against Jethro and
do somethin'?" he said.   " Bije turns up here, and you all
scatter like a flock of crows.   I'm tired of makin' com-
plaints about that Brampton road, and to-day the hull
side of it give way, and put me in the ditch.   Sure as the
sun rises to-morrow, I'm goin' to make trouble for Jethro."

" What be you a-goin' to do, Lem?"

" Indict the town," replied Lem, vigorously.   " Who is
the town?   Jethro, hain't he?   Who has charge of the
highways?   Jethro Bass, Chairman of the Selectmen.
I've spoke to him, time and agin, about that piece, and he
hain't done nothin'.   To-night I go to Harwich and git
the court to app'int an agent to repair that road, and
the town'll hev to pay the bill."

The boldness of Lem's intention for the moment took
away their breaths, and then the awe-stricken hush which
followed his declaration was broken by the sound of Chester's fist hammering on the counter.

" That's the sperrit," he cried; " I'll go along with you,
Lem."

" No, you won't," said Lem, " you'll stay right whar
you be."

" Chester wants to git credit for the move," suggested Sam Price, slyly.

" It's a lie, Sam Price," shouted Chester.   " What made you sneak off when Bije Bixby come ? "

" Didn't sneak off," retorted Sam, indignantly, through his nose ; " forgot them eggs I left to home."

" Sam," said Lem, with a wink at Moses Hatch, " you hitch up your hoss and fetch me over to Harwich to git that indictment.   Might git a chance to see that lady."

" Wal, now, I wish I could, Lem, but my hoss is stun lame."

There was a roar of laughter, during which Sam tried to look unconcerned.

" Mebbe Rias'll take me over," said Lem, soberly. " You hitch up, Rias ? "

" He's gone," said Joe Northcutt, " slid out the door when you was speakin' to Sam."

" Hain't none of you folks got spunk enough to carry me over to see the jedge ? " demanded Lem ; " my hosses ain't fit to travel to-night."   Another silence followed, and Lem laughed contemptuously but good-naturedly, and turned on his heel.   " Guess I'll walk, then," he said.

" You kin have my white hoss, Lem," said Moses Hatch.

" All right," said Lem; " I'll come round and hitch up soon's I git my supper."

An hour later, when Cynthia and her father and Milli-cent Skinner — who condescended to assist in the work and cooking of Mr. Wetherell's household — were seated at supper in the little kitchen behind the store, the head and shoulders of the stage-driver were thrust in at the window, his face shining from its evening application of soap and water.   He was making eyes at Cynthia.

" Want to go to Harwich, Will ? " he asked.

William set his cup down quickly.

" You hain't afeard, be you ? " he continued.   " Most folks that hasn't went West or died is afeard of Jethro Bass."

" Daddy isn't afraid of him, and I'm not," said Cynthia.

" That's right, Cynthy," said Lem, leaning over and giving a tug to the pigtail that hung down her back; "there hain't nothin' to be afeard of."

"I like him," said Cynthia; "he's very good to me."

"You stick to him, Cynthy," said the stage driver. "Ready, Will?"

It may readily be surmised that Mr. Wetherell did not particularly wish to make this excursion, the avowed object of which was to get Mr. Bass into trouble. But he went, and presently he found himself jogging along on the mountain road to Harwich. From the crest of Town's End ridge they looked upon the western peaks tossing beneath a golden sky. The spell of the evening's beauty seemed to have fallen on them both, and for a long time Lem spoke not a word, and nodded smilingly but absently to the greetings that came from the farm doorways.

"Will," he said at last, "you acted sensible. There's no mite of use of your gettin' mixed up in politics. You're too good for 'em."

"Too good!" exclaimed the storekeeper.

"You're eddicated," Lem replied, with a tactful attempt to cover up a deficiency; "you're a gentleman, ef you do keep store."

Lemuel apparently thought that gentlemen and politics were contradictions. He began to whistle, while Wetherell sat and wondered that any one could be so care-free on such a mission. The day faded, and went out, and the lights of Harwich twinkled in the valley. Wetherell was almost tempted to mention his trouble to this man, as he had been to Ephraim: the fear that each might think he wished to borrow money held him back.

"Jethro's all right," Lem remarked, "but if he neglects the road, he's got to stand for it, same's any other. I writ him twice to the capital, and give him fair warning afore he went. He knows I hain't doin' of it for politics. I've often thought," Lem continued, "that ef some smart, good woman could have got hold of him when he was young, it would have made a big difference. What's the matter?"

"Have you room enough?"

"I guess I've got the hull seat," said Lem. "As I was

sayin', if some able woman had married Jethro and made him look at things a little mite different, he would have b'en a big man. He has all the earmarks. Why, when he comes back to Coniston, them fellers'll hunt their holes like rabbits, mark my words."

" You don't think — "

" Don't think what ? "

" I understand he holds the mortgages of some of them," said Wetherell.

" Shouldn't blame him a great deal ef he did git tired and sell Chester out soon. This thing happens regular as leap year."

" Jethro Bass doesn't seem to frighten you," said the storekeeper.

" Well," said Lem, " I hain't afeard of him, that's so. For the life of me, I can't help likin' him, though he does things that I wouldn't do for all the power in Christendom. Here's Jedge Parkinson's house."

Wetherell remained in the wagon while Lemuel went in to transact his business. The judge's house, outlined in the starlight, was a modest dwelling with a little porch and clambering vines, set back in its own garden behind a picket fence. Presently, from the direction of the lines of light in the shutters, came the sound of voices, Lem's deep and insistent, and another, pitched in a high nasal key, deprecatory and protesting. There was still another, a harsh one that growled something unintelligible, and Wetherell guessed, from the fragments which he heard, that the judge before sitting down to his duty was trying to dissuade the stage driver from a step that was foolhardy. He guessed likewise that Lem was not to be dissuaded. At length a silence followed, then the door swung open, and three figures came down the illuminated path.

" Like to make you acquainted with Jedge Abner Parkinson, Mr. Wetherell, and Jim Irving. Jim's the sheriff of Truro County, and I guess the jedge don't need any recommendation as a lawyer from me. You won't mind stayin' awhile with the jedge while Jim and I go down town with the team ? You're both literary folks."

Wetherell followed the judge into the house. He was sallow, tall and spare and stooping, clean-shaven, with a hooked nose and bright eyes — the face of an able and adroit man, and he wore the long black coat of the politician-lawyer. The room was filled with books, and from these Judge Parkinson immediately took his cue, probably through a fear that Wetherell might begin on the subject of Lemuel's errand. However, it instantly became plain that the judge was a true book lover, and despite the fact that Lem's visit had disturbed him not a little, he soon grew animated in a discussion on the merits of Sir Walter Scott, paced the room, pitched his nasal voice higher and higher, covered his table with volumes of that author to illustrate his meaning. Neither of them heard a knock, and they both stared dumfounded at the man who filled the doorway.

It was Jethro Bass !

He entered the room with characteristic unconcern, as if he had just left it on a trivial errand, and without a " How do you do ?" or a " Good evening," parted his coat tails, and sat down in the judge's armchair. The judge dropped the volume of Scott on the desk, and as for Wetherell, he realized for once the full meaning of the biblical expression of a man's tongue cleaving to the roof of his mouth ; the gleam of one of Jethro's brass buttons caught his eye and held it fascinated.

" Literary talk, Judge ? " said Jethro.   " D-don't mind me — go on."

" Thought you were at the capital," said the judge, reclaiming some of his self-possession.

" Good many folks thought so," answered Jethro, " g-good many folks."

There was no conceivable answer to this, so the judge sat down with an affectation of ease. He was a man on whom dignity lay heavily, and was not a little ruffled because Wetherell had been a witness of his discomfiture. He leaned back in his chair, then leaned forward, stretching his neck and clearing his throat, a position in which he bore a ludicrous resemblance to a turkey gobbler.

I

"Most through the Legislature?" inquired the judge.

" 'Bout as common," said Jethro.

There was a long silence, and, forgetful for the moment of his own predicament, Wetherell found a fearful fascination in watching the contortions of the victim whose punishment was to precede his. It had been one of the delights of Louis XI to contemplate the movements of a certain churchman whom he had had put in a cage, and some inkling of the pleasure to be derived from this pastime of tyrants dawned on Wetherell. Perhaps the judge, too, thought of this as he looked at "Quentin Durward" on the table.

"I was just sayin' to Lem Hallowell," began the judge, at last, "that I thought he was a little mite hasty —"

"Er — indicted us, Judge?" said Jethro.

The judge and Wetherell heard the question with different emotions. Mr. Parkinson did not seem astonished at the miracle which had put Jethro in possession of this information, but heaved a long sigh of relief, as a man will when the worst has at length arrived.

"I had to, Jethro — couldn't help it. I tried to get Hallowell to wait till you come back and talk it over friendly, but he wouldn't listen ; said the road was dangerous, and that he'd spoken about it too often. He said he hadn't anything against you."

"Didn't come in to complain," said Jethro, "didn't come in to complain. Road is out of repair. W-what's the next move?"

"I'm sorry, Jethro — I swan I'm sorry." He cleared his throat. "Well," he continued in his judicial manner, "the court has got to appoint an agent to repair that road, the agent will present the bill, and the town will have to pay the bill — whatever it is. It's too bad, Jethro, that you have allowed this to be done."

"You say you've got to app'int an agent?"

"Yes — I'm sorry —"

"Have you app'inted one ?"

"No."

"G-got any candidates ?"

The judge scratched his head.

" Well, I don't know as I have."

" Well, *have* you ? "

" No," said the judge.

" A-any legal objection to my bein' app'inted ? " asked Jethro.

The judge looked at him and gasped.   But the look was an involuntary tribute of admiration.

" Well," he said hesitatingly, " I don't know as there is, Jethro.   No, there's no legal objection to it."

" A-any other kind of objection ? " said Jethro.

The judge appeared to reflect.

" Well, no," he said at last, " I don't know as there is."

" Well, *is* there ? " said Jethro, again.

" No," said the judge, with the finality of a decision. A smile seemed to be pulling at the corners of his mouth.

" Well, I'm a candidate," said Jethro.

" Do you tell me, Jethro, that you want me to appoint you agent to fix that road ? "

" I — I'm a candidate."

" Well," said the judge, rising, " I'll do it."

" When ? " said Jethro, sitting still.

" I'll send the papers over to you within two or three days."

" O-ought to be done right away, Judge.   Road's in bad shape."

" Well, I'll send the papers over to you to-morrow."

" How long would it take to make out that app'intment — how long ? "

" It wouldn't take but a little while."

" I'll wait," said Jethro.

" Do you want to take the appointment along with you to-night ? " asked the judge, in surprise.

" G-guess that's about it."

Without a word the judge went over to his table, and for a while the silence was broken only by the scratching of his pen.

" Er — interested in roads, — Will, — interested in roads ? "

The judge stopped writing to listen, since it was now the turn of the other victim.

"Not particularly," answered Mr. Wetherell, whose throat was dry.

"C-come over for the drive — c-come over for the drive ? "

"Yes," replied the storekeeper, rather faintly.

"H-how's Cynthy ? " said Jethro.

The storekeeper was too astonished to answer. At that moment there was a heavy step in the doorway, and Lem Hallowell entered the room. He took one long look at Jethro and bent over and slapped his hand on his knee, and burst out laughing.

"So here you be ! " he cried. "By Godfrey! ef you don't beat all outdoors, Jethro. Wal, I got ahead of ye for once, but you can't say I didn't warn ye. Come purty nigh bustin' the stage on that road to-day, and now I'm a-goin' to hev an agent app'inted."

"W-who's the agent ? " said Jethro.

"We'll git one. Might app'int Will, there, only he don't seem to want to get mixed up in it."

"There's the agent," cried the judge, holding out the appointment to Jethro.

"Wh-what ! " ejaculated Lem.

Jethro took the appointment, and put it in his cowhide wallet.

"Be you the agent?" demanded the amazed stage driver.

"C-callate to be," said Jethro, and without a smile or another word to any one he walked out into the night, and after various exclamations of astonishment and admiration, the stage driver followed.

No one, indeed, could have enjoyed this unexpected coup of Jethro's more than Lem himself, and many times on their drive homeward he burst into loud and unexpected fits of laughter at the sublime conception of the Chairman of the Selectmen being himself appointed road agent.

"Will," said he, "don't you tell this to a soul. We'll have some fun out of some of the boys to-morrow."

The storekeeper promised, but he had an unpleasant presentiment that he himself might be one of the boys in question.

"How do you suppose Jethro Bass knew you were going to indict the town?" he asked of the stage driver.

Lem burst into fresh peals of laughter, but this was something which he did not attempt to answer.

CHAPTER X

HOW THE REBELLION WAS QUENCHED

It so happened that there was a certain spinster whom Sam Price had been trying to make up his mind to marry for ten years or more, and it was that gentleman's habit to spend at least one day in the month in Harwich for the purpose of paying his respects. In spite of the fact that his horse had been "stun lame" the night before, Mr. Price was able to start for Harwich, via Brampton, very early the next morning. He was driving along through Northcutt's woods with one leg hanging over the wheel, humming through his nose what we may suppose to have been a love-ditty, and letting his imagination run riot about the lady in question, when he nearly fell out of his wagon. The cause of this was the sight of fat Tom coming around a corner, with Jethro Bass behind him. Lem Hallowell and the storekeeper had kept their secret so well that Sam, if he was thinking about Jethro at all, believed him at that moment to be seated in the Throne Room at the Pelican House, in the capital.

Mr. Price, however, was one of an adaptable nature, and by the time he had pulled up beside Jethro he had recovered sufficiently to make a few remarks on farming subjects, and finally to express a polite surprise at Jethro's return.

"But you come a little mite late, hain't you, Jethro?" he asked finally, with all of the indifference he could assume.

"H-how's that, Sam — how's that?"

"It's too bad, — I swan it is, — but Lem Hallowell rode over to Harwich last night and indicted the town for

118

that piece of road by the Four Corners. Took Will
Wetherell along with him."

"D-don't say so !" said Jethro.

"I callate he done it," responded Sam, pulling a long
face.   "The court'll hev to send an agent to do the job,
and I guess you'll hev to foot the bill, Jethro."

"C-court'll hev to app'int an agent ?"

"I callate."

"Er — you a candidate — Sam — you a candidate ? "

"Don't know but what I be," answered the usually wary
Mr. Price.

"G-goin' to Harwich — hain't you ?"

"Mebbe I be, and mebbe I hain't," said Sam, not able to
repress a self-conscious snicker.

"M-might as well be you as anybody, Sam," said Jethro,
as he drove on.

It was not strange that the idea, thus planted, should grow
in Mr. Price's favor as he proceeded.   He had been surprised at Jethro's complaisance, and he wondered whether,
after all, he had done well to help Chester stir people up
at this time.   When he reached Harwich, instead of presenting himself promptly at the spinster's house, he went
first to the office of Judge Parkinson, as became a prudent
man of affairs.

Perhaps there is no need to go into the details of Mr.
Price's discomfiture on the occasion of this interview.
The judge was by nature of a sour disposition, but he
haw-hawed so loudly as he explained to Mr. Price the
identity of the road agent that the judge of probate in the
next office thought his colleague had gone mad.   Afterward Mr. Price stood for some time in the entry, where
no one could see him, scratching his head and repeating
his favorite exclamation, "I want to know !"   It has been
ascertained that he omitted to pay his respects to the
spinster on that day.

Cyamon Johnson carried the story back to Coniston,
where it had the effect of eliminating Mr. Price from local
politics for some time to come.

That same morning Chester Perkins was seen by many

driving wildly about from farm to farm, supposedly haranguing his supporters to make a final stand against the tyrant, but by noon it was observed by those naturalists who were watching him that his activity had ceased. Chester arrived at dinner time at Joe Northcutt's, whose land bordered on the piece of road which had caused so much trouble, and Joe and half a dozen others had been at work there all morning under the road agent whom Judge Parkinson had appointed. Now Mrs. Northcutt was Chester's sister, a woman who in addition to other qualities possessed the only sense of humor in the family. She ushered the unsuspecting Chester into the kitchen, and there, seated beside Joe and sipping a saucer of very hot coffee, was Jethro Bass himself. Chester halted in the doorway, his face brick-red, words utterly failing him, while Joe sat horror-stricken, holding aloft on his fork a smoking potato. Jethro continued to sip his coffee.

"B-busy times, Chester," he said, "b-busy times."

Chester choked. Where were the burning words of denunciation which came so easily to his tongue on other occasions? It is difficult to denounce a man who insists upon drinking coffee.

"Set right down, Chester," said Mrs. Northcutt, behind him.

Chester sat down, and to this day he cannot account for that action. Once seated, habit asserted itself, and he attacked the boiled dinner with a ferocity which should have been exercised against Jethro.

"I suppose the stores down to the capital is finer than ever, Mr. Bass," remarked Mrs. Northcutt.

"So-so, Mis' Northcutt, so-so."

"I was there ten years ago," remarked Mrs. Northcutt, with a sigh of reminiscence, "and I never see such fine silks and bonnets in my life. Now I've often wanted to ask you, did you buy that bonnet with the trembly jet things for Mis' Bass?"

"That bonnet come out full better'n I expected," answered Jethro, modestly.

"You have got taste in wimmin's fixin's, Mr. Bass.

Strange ! Now I wouldn't let Joe choose my things for worlds."

So the dinner progressed, Joe with his eyes on his plate, Chester silent, but bursting with anger and resentment, until at last Jethro pushed back his chair, and said good day to Mrs. Northcutt and walked out.   Chester got up instantly and went after him, and Joe, full of forebodings, followed his brother-in-law ! Jethro was standing calmly on the grass plot, whittling a toothpick.   Chester stared at him a moment, and then strode off toward the barn, unhitched his horse and jumped in his wagon.   Something prompted him to take another look at Jethro, who was still whittling.

"C-carry me down to the road, Chester — c-carry me down to the road ? " said Jethro.

Joe Northcutt's knees gave way under him, and he sat down on a sugar kettle.   Chester tightened up his reins so suddenly that his horse reared, while Jethro calmly climbed into the seat beside him and they drove off. It was some time before Joe had recovered sufficiently to arise and repair to the scene of operations on the road.

It was Joe who brought the astounding news to the store that evening.   Chester was Jethro's own candidate for senior Selectman! Jethro himself had said so, that he would be happy to abdicate in Chester's favor, and make it unanimous — Chester having been a candidate so many times, and disappointed.

"Whar's Chester ? " said Lem Hallowell.

Joe pulled a long face.

"Just come from his house, and he hain't done a lick of work sence noon time.   Jest sets in a corner — won't talk, won't eat — jest sets thar."

Lem sat down on the counter and laughed until he was forced to brush the tears from his cheeks at the idea of Chester Perkins being Jethro's candidate.   Where was reform now ? If Chester were elected, it would be in the eyes of the world as Jethro's man. No wonder he sat in a corner and refused to eat.

" Guess you'll ketch it next, Will, for goin' over to
Harwich with Lem," Joe remarked playfully to the storekeeper, as he departed.

These various occurrences certainly did not tend to
allay the uneasiness of Mr. Wetherell. The next afternoon, at a time when a slack trade was slackest, he had
taken his chair out under the apple tree and was sitting
with that same volume of Byron in his lap — but he was
not reading. The humorous aspects of the doings of
Mr. Bass did not particularly appeal to him now ; and he
was, in truth, beginning to hate this man whom the fates
had so persistently intruded into his life. William Wetherell was not, it may have been gathered, what may be
called vindictive. He was a sensitive, conscientious person whose life should have been in the vale ; and yet at
that moment he had a fierce desire to confront Jethro Bass
and — and destroy him. Yes, he felt equal to that.

Shocks are not very beneficial to sensitive natures.
William Wetherell looked up, and there was Jethro Bass
on the doorstep.

" G-great resource — readin' — great resource," he remarked.

In this manner Jethro snuffed out utterly that passion to destroy, and another sensation took its place —
a sensation which made it very difficult for William Wetherell to speak, but he managed to reply that reading had
been a great resource to him. Jethro had a parcel in his
hand, and he laid it down on the step beside him; and
he seemed, for once in his life, to be in a mood for conversation.

" It's hard for me to read a book," he observed. " I own
to it — it's a little mite hard. H-hev to kind of spell it
out in places. Hain't had much time for readin'. But it's
kind of pleasant to l'arn what other folks has done in the
world by pickin' up a book. T-takes your mind off
things — don't it ? "

Wetherell felt like saying that his reading had not been
able to do that lately. Then he made the plunge, and
shuddered as he made it.

"Mr. Bass — I — I have been waiting to speak to you about that mortgage."

"Er — yes," he answered, without moving his head, "er — about the mortgage."

"Mr. Worthington told me that you had bought it."

"Yes, I did — yes, I did."

"I'm afraid you will have to foreclose," said Wetherell; "I cannot reasonably ask you to defer the payments any longer."

"If I foreclose it, what will you do?" he demanded abruptly.

There was but one answer — Wetherell would have to go back to the city and face the consequences. He had not the strength to earn his bread on a farm.

"If I'd a b'en in any hurry for the money — g-guess I'd a notified you," said Jethro.

"I think you had better foreclose, Mr. Bass," Wetherell answered; "I can't hold out any hopes to you that it will ever be possible for me to pay it off. It's only fair to tell you that."

"Well," he said, with what seemed a suspicion of a smile, "I don't know but what that's about as honest an answer as I ever got."

"Why did you do it?" Wetherell cried, suddenly goaded by another fear; "why did you buy that mortgage?"

But this did not shake his composure.

"H-have a little habit of collectin' 'em," he answered, "same as you do books. G-guess some of 'em hain't as valuable."

William Wetherell was beginning to think that Jethro knew something also of such refinements of cruelty as were practised by Caligula. He drew forth his cowhide wallet and produced from it a folded piece of newspaper which must, Wetherell felt sure, contain the mortgage in question.

"There's one power I always wished I had," he observed, "the power to make folks see some things as I see 'em. I was acrost the Water to-night, on my hill farm, when the sun set, and the sky up thar above the mountain was all golden bars, and the river all a-flamin' purple, just as if it had been dyed by some of them Greek gods you're readin' about. Now if I could put them things on paper, I wouldn't care a haycock to be President. No, sir."

The storekeeper's amazement as he listened to this speech may be imagined. Was this Jethro Bass? If so, here was a side of him the existence of which no one suspected. Wetherell forgot the matter in hand.

"Why don't you put that on paper?" he exclaimed.

Jethro smiled, and made a deprecating motion with his thumb.

"Sometimes when I hain't busy, I drop into the state library at the capital and enjoy myself. It's like goin' to another world without any folks to bother you. Er — er — there's books I'd like to talk to you about — sometime."

"But I thought you told me you didn't read much, Mr. Bass?"

He made no direct reply, but unfolded the newspaper in his hand, and then Wetherell saw that it was only a clipping.

"H-happened to run across this in a newspaper — if this hain't this county, I wahn't born and raised here. If it hain't Coniston Mountain about seven o'clock of a June evening, I never saw Coniston Mountain. Er — listen to this."

Whereupon he read, with a feeling which Wetherell had not supposed he possessed, an extract : and as the storekeeper listened his blood began to run wildly. At length Jethro put down the paper without glancing at his companion.

"There's somethin' about that that fetches you spinnin' through the air," he said slowly. "Sh-showed it to Jim Willard, editor of the *Newcastle Guardian*. Er — what do you think he said?"

"I don't know," said Wetherell, in a low voice.

"Willard said, 'Bass, w-wish you'd find me that man. I'll give him five dollars every week for a letter like that — er — five dollars a week.'"

He paused, folded up the paper again and put it in his pocket, took out a card and handed it to Wetherell.

James G. Willard, Editor.

Newcastle Guardian.

" That's his address," said Jethro.   " Er — guess you'll know what to do with it.   Er — five dollars a week — five dollars a week."

" How did you know I wrote this article ? " said Wetherell, as the card trembled between his fingers.

" K-knowed the place was Coniston seen from the east, knowed there wahn't any one in Brampton or Harwich could have done it — g-guessed the rest — guessed the rest."

Wetherell could only stare at him like a man who, with the halter about his neck, has been suddenly reprieved. But Jethro Bass did not appear to be waiting for thanks. He cleared his throat, and had Wetherell not been in such a condition himself, he would actually have suspected him of embarrassment.

" Er — Wetherell ? "

" Yes ? "

" W-won't say nothin' about the mortgage — p-pay it when you can."

This roused the storekeeper to a burst of protest, but he stemmed it.

" Hain't got the money, have you ? "

" No — but — "

" If I needed money, d'ye suppose I'd bought the mortgage ? "

" No," answered the still bewildered Wetherell, " of course not."   There he stuck, that other suspicion of political coercion suddenly rising uppermost.   Could this be what the man meant ?   Wetherell put his hand to his head, but he did not dare to ask the question.   Then Jethro Bass fixed his eyes upon him.

" Hain't never mixed any in politics — hev you — n-never mixed any ? "

Wetherell's heart sank.

" No," he answered.

" D-don't — take my advice — d-don't."

" What ! " cried the storekeeper, so loudly that he frightened himself.

" D-don't," repeated Jethro, imperturbably.

There was a short silence, the storekeeper being unable to speak. Coniston Water, at the foot of the garden, sang the same song, but it seemed to Wetherell to have changed its note from sorrow to joy.

" H-hear things, don't you — hear things in the store ? "

" Yes."

" Don't hear 'em. Keep out of politics, Will, s-stick to storekeepin' and — and literature."

Jethro got to his feet and turned his back on the storekeeper and picked up the parcel he had brought.

" C-Cynthy well ? " he inquired.

" I — I'll call her," said Wetherell, huskily. " She — she was down by the brook when you came."

But Jethro Bass did not wait. He took his parcel and strode down to Coniston Water, and there he found Cynthia seated on a rock with her toes in a pool.

" How be you, Cynthy ? " said he, looking down at her.

" I'm well, Uncle Jethro," said Cynthia.

" R-remembered what I told you to call me, hev you," said Jethro, plainly pleased. " Th-that's right. Cynthy ? "

Cynthia looked up at him inquiringly.

" S-said you liked books — didn't you? S-said you liked books?"

" Yes, I do," she replied simply, " very much."

He undid the wrapping of the parcel, and there lay disclosed a book with a very gorgeous cover. He thrust it into the child's lap.

" It's ' Robinson Crusoe ' ! " she exclaimed, and gave a little shiver of delight that made ripples in the pool. Then she opened it — not without awe, for William Wetherell's books were not clothed in this magnificent manner. "It's full of pictures," cried Cynthia. "See, there he is making a ship!"

"Y-you read it, Cynthy?" asked Jethro, a little anxiously.

No, Cynthia hadn't.

"L-like it, Cynthy — l-like it?" said he, not quite so anxiously.

Cynthia looked up at him with a puzzled expression.

"F-fetched it up from the capital for you, Cynthy — for you."

"For me!"

A strange thrill ran through Jethro Bass as he gazed upon the wonder and delight in the face of the child.

"F-fetched it for you, Cynthy."

For a moment Cynthia sat very still, and then she slowly closed the book and stared at the cover again, Jethro looking down at her the while. To tell the truth, she found it difficult to express the emotions which the event had summoned up.

"Thank you — Uncle Jethro," she said.

Jethro, however, understood. He had, indeed, never failed to understand her from the beginning. He parted his coat tails and sat down on the rock beside her, and very gently opened the book again, to the first chapter.

"G-goin' to read it, Cynthy?"

"Oh, yes," she said, and trembled again.

"Er — read it to me?"

So Cynthia read "Robinson Crusoe" to him while the summer afternoon wore away, and the shadows across the pool grew longer and longer.

CHAPTER XI

MR. WORTHINGTON BECOMES A REFORMER

THUS William Wetherell became established in Coniston, and was started at last — poor man — upon a life that was fairly tranquil. Lem Hallowell had once covered him with blushes by unfolding a newspaper in the store and reading an editorial beginning : "We publish to-day a new and attractive feature of the *Guardian*, a weekly contribution from a correspondent whose modesty is to be compared only with his genius as a writer. We are confident that the readers of our paper will appreciate the letter in another column signed 'W.W.'" And from that day William was accorded much of the deference due to a litterateur which the fates had hitherto denied him. Indeed, during the six years which we are about to skip over so lightly, he became a marked man in Coniston, and it was voted in town meeting that he be intrusted with that most important of literary labors, the Town History of Coniston.

During this period, too, there sprang up the strangest of intimacies between him and Jethro Bass. Surely no more dissimilar men than these have ever been friends, and that the friendship was sometimes misjudged was one of the clouds on William Wetherell's horizon. As the years went on he was still unable to pay off the mortgage ; and sometimes, indeed, he could not even meet the interest, in spite of the princely sum he received from Mr. Willard of the *Guardian*. This was one of the clouds on Jethro's horizon, too, if men had but known it, and he took such moneys as Wetherell insisted upon giving him grudgingly enough. It is needless to say that he refrained from making use of Mr. Wetherell politically, although no poorer vessel for political purposes was ever constructed. It is quite as needless to say, perhaps, that Chester Perkins never got to be Chairman of the Board of Selectmen.

After Aunt Listy died, Jethro was more than ever to be found, when in Coniston, in the garden or the kitchen behind the store. Yes, Aunt Listy is dead. She has flitted through these pages as she flitted through life itself, arrayed by Jethro like the rainbow, and quite as shadowy and unreal. There is no politician of a certain age in the state who does not remember her walking, clad in dragon-fly colors, through the streets of the capital on Jethro's arm, or descending the stairs of the Pelican House to supper. None of Jethro's detractors may say that he ever failed in kindness to her, and he loved her as much as was in his heart to love any woman after Cynthia Ware. As for Aunt Listy, she never seemed to feel any resentment against the child Jethro brought so frequently to Thousand Acre Hill. Poor Aunt Listy ! some people used to wonder whether she ever felt any emotion at all. But I believe that she did, in her own way.

It is a well-known fact that Mr. Bijah Bixby came over from Clovelly, to request the place of superintendent of the funeral, a position which had already been filled. A special office, too, was created on this occasion for an old supporter of Jethro's, Senator Peleg Hartington of Brampton. He was made chairman of the bearers, of whom Ephraim Prescott was one.

After this, as we have said, Jethro was more than ever at the store — or rather in that domestic domain behind it which Wetherell and Cynthia shared with Miss Millicent Skinner. Moses Hatch was wont to ask Cynthia how her daddies were. It was he who used to clear out the road to the little schoolhouse among the birches when the snow almost buried the little village, and on sparkling mornings after the storms his oxen would stop to breathe in front of the store, a cluster of laughing children clinging to the snow-plough and tumbling over good-natured Moses in

K

"Through the streets of the capital on Jethro's arm."

their frolics.   Cynthia became a country girl, and grew
long and lithe of limb, and weather-burnt, and acquired
an endurance that spoke wonders for the life-giving air of
Coniston.   But she was a serious child, and Wetherell and
Jethro sometimes wondered whether she was ever a child
at all.   When Eben Hatch fell from the lumber pile on
the ice, it was she who bound the cut in his head; and
when Tom Richardson unexpectedly embraced the schoolhouse stove, Cynthia, not Miss Rebecca Northcutt, took
charge of the situation.

It was perhaps inevitable, with such a helpless father,
that the girl should grow up with a sense of responsibility,
being what she was.   Did William Wetherell go to Brampton, Cynthia examined his apparel, and he was marched
shamefacedly back to his room to change; did he read too
late at night, some unseen messenger summoned her out
of her sleep, and he was packed off to bed.   Miss Millicent
Skinner, too, was in a like mysterious way compelled to
abdicate her high place in favor of Cynthia, and Wetherell
was utterly unable to explain how this miracle was accomplished.   Not only did Millicent learn to cook, but Cynthia, at the age of fourteen, had taught her.   Some wit
once suggested that the national arms of the United States
should contain the emblem of crossed frying-pans, and
Millicent was in this respect a true American.   When
Wetherell began to suffer from her pies and doughnuts,
the revolution took place — without stampeding, or recriminations, or trouble of any kind.   One evening he
discovered Cynthia, decked in an apron, bending over the
stove, and Millicent looking on with an expression that
was (for Millicent) benign.

This was to some extent explained, a few days later,
when Wetherell found himself gazing across the counter
at the motherly figure of Mrs. Moses Hatch, who held the
well-deserved honor of being the best cook in Coniston.

"Hain't had so much stomach trouble lately, Will?" she
remarked.

"No," he answered, surprised; "Cynthia is learning to
cook."

"Cynthia became a country girl."

"Guess she is," said Mrs. Moses. "That gal is worth any seven grown-up women in town. And she was four nights settin' in my kitchen before I knowed what she was up to."

"So you taught her, Amanda?"

"I taught her some. She callated that Milly was killin' you, and I guess she was."

During her school days, Jethro used frequently to find himself in front of the schoolhouse when the children came trooping out — quite by accident, of course. Winter or summer, when he went away on his periodical trips, he never came back without a little remembrance in his carpet bag, usually a book, on the subject of which he had spent hours in conference with the librarian at the state library at the capital. But in June of the year when Cynthia was fifteen, Jethro yielded to that passion which was one of the man's strangest characteristics, and appeared one evening in the garden behind the store with a bundle which certainly did not contain a book. With all the gravity of a ceremony he took off the paper, and held up in relief against the astonished Cynthia a length of cardinal cloth. William Wetherell, who was looking out of the window, drew his breath, and even Jethro drew back with an exclamation at the change wrought in her. But Cynthia snatched the roll from his hand and wound it up with a feminine deftness.

"Wh-what's the matter, Cynthy?"

"Oh, I can't wear that, Uncle Jethro," she said.

"C-can't wear it! Why not?"

Cynthia sat down on the grassy mound under the apple tree and clasped her hands across her knees. She looked up at him and shook her head.

"Don't you see that I couldn't wear it, Uncle Jethro?"

"Why not?" he demanded. "Ch-change it if you've a mind to hev green."

She shook her head, and smiled at him a little sadly.

"T-took me a full hour to choose that, Cynthy," said he. "H-had to go to Boston, so I got it there."

He was, indeed, grievously disappointed at this reception of his gift, and he stood eying the cardinal cloth very mournfully as it lay on the paper. Cynthia, remorseful, reached up and seized his hand.

"Sit down here, Uncle Jethro." He sat down on the mound beside her, very much perplexed. She still held his hand in hers. "Uncle Jethro," she said slowly, "you mustn't think I'm not grateful."

"N-no," he answered; "I don't think that, Cynthy. I know you be."

"I am grateful — I'm very grateful for everything you give me, although I should love you just as much if you didn't give me anything."

She was striving very hard not to offend him, for in some ways he was as sensitive as Wetherell himself. Even Coniston folk had laughed at the idiosyncrasy which Jethro had of dressing his wife in brilliant colors, and the girl knew this.

"G-got it for you to wear to Brampton on the Fourth of July, Cynthy," he said.

"Uncle Jethro, I couldn't wear that to Brampton!"

"You'd look like a queen," said he.

"But I'm not a queen," objected Cynthia.

"Rather hev somethin' else?"

"Yes," she said, looking at him suddenly with the gleam of laughter in her eyes, although she was on the verge of tears.

"Wh-what?" Jethro demanded.

"Well," said Cynthia, demurely gazing down at her ankles, "shoes and stockings." The barefooted days had long gone by.

Jethro laughed. Perhaps some inkling of her reasons came to him, for he had a strange and intuitive understanding of her. At any rate, he accepted her decision with a meekness which would have astonished many people who knew only that side of him which he showed to the world. Gently she released her hand, and folded up the bundle again and gave it to him.

"B-better keep it — hadn't you?"

"No, you keep it. And I will wear it for you when I am rich, Uncle Jethro."

Florence Scovel Shinn

"Tom Richardson unexpectedly embraced the schoolhouse stove."

Jethro did keep it, and in due time the cardinal cloth had its uses. But Cynthia did not wear it on the Fourth of July.

That was a great day for Brampton, being not only the nation's birthday, but the hundredth year since the adventurous little band of settlers from Connecticut had first gazed upon Coniston Water at that place. Early in the morning wagon loads began to pour into Brampton Street from Harwich, from Coniston, from Tarleton Four Corners, and even from distant Clovelly, and Brampton was banner-hung for the occasion — flags across the stores, across the dwellings, and draped along the whole breadth of the meeting-house; but for sheer splendor the newly built mansion of Isaac D. Worthington outshone them all. Although its owner was a professed believer in republican simplicity, no such edifice ornamented any town to the west of the state capital. Small wonder that the way in front of it was blocked by a crowd lost in admiration of its Gothic proportions! It stands to-day one of many monuments to its builder, with its windows of one pane (unheard-of magnificence), its tower of stone, its porch with pointed arches and scroll-work. No fence divides its grounds from the public walk, and on the smooth-shaven lawn between the ornamental flower beds and the walk stand two stern mastiffs of iron, emblematic of the solidity and power of their owner. It was as much to see this house as to hear the oratory that the countryside flocked to Brampton that day.

All the day before Cynthia and Milly, and many another housewife, had been making wonderful things for the dinners they were to bring, and stowing them in the great basket ready for the early morning start. At six o'clock Jethro's three-seated farm wagon was in front of the store. Cousin Ephraim Prescott, in a blue suit and an army felt hat with a cord, got up behind, a little stiffly by reason of that Wilderness bullet; and there were also William Wetherell and Lem Hallowell, his honest face shining, and Sue, his wife, and young Sue and Jock and Lilian, all a-quiver with excitement in their Sunday best.

And as they drove away there trotted up behind them Moses and Amandy Hatch, with their farm team, and all the little Hatches, — Eben and George and Judy and Liza. As they jogged along they drank in the fragrance of the dew-washed meadows and the pines, and a great blue heron stood knee-deep on the far side of Deacon Lysander's old mill-pond, watching them philosophically as they passed.

It was eight o'clock when they got into the press of Brampton Street, and there was a hush as they made their way slowly through the throng, and many a stare at the curious figure in the old-fashioned blue swallowtail and brass buttons and tall hat, driving the farm wagon. Husbands pointed him out to their wives, young men to sisters and sweethearts, some openly, some discreetly. "There goes Jethro Bass," and some were bold enough to say, "Howdy, Jethro?" Jake Wheeler was to be observed in the crowd ahead of them, hurried for once out of his Jethro step, actually running toward the tavern, lest such a one arrive unheralded. Commotion is perceived on the tavern porch, — Mr. Sherman, the proprietor, bustling out, Jake Wheeler beside him; a chorus of " How be you, Jethros?" from the more courageous there, — but the farm team jogs on, leaving a discomfited gathering, into the side street, up an alley, and into the cool, ammonia-reeking sheds of lank Jim Sanborn's livery stable. No obsequiousness from lank Jim, who has the traces slipped and the reins festooned from the bits almost before Jethro has lifted Cynthia to the floor. Jethro, walking between Cynthia and her father, led the way, Ephraim, Lem, and Sue Hallowell following, the children, in unwonted shoes and stockings, bringing up the rear. The people parted, and presently they found themselves opposite the new-scrolled band stand among the trees, where the Harwich band in glittering gold and red had just been installed. The leader, catching sight of Jethro's party, and of Ephraim's corded army hat, made a bow, waved his baton, and they struck up "Marching through Georgia." It was, of course, not dignified to cheer, but I think that the

blood of every man and woman and child ran faster with
the music, and so many of them looked at Cousin Ephraim
that he slipped away behind the line of wagons.   So the
day began.

"Jest to think of bein' that rich, Will!" exclaimed
Amanda Hatch to the storekeeper, as they stood in the
little group which had gathered in front of the first citizen's new mansion.   "I own it scares me.   Think how
much that house must hev cost, and even them dogs,"
said Amanda, staring at the mastiffs with awe.   "They
tell me he has a grand piano from New York, and
guests from Boston — railroad presidents.   I call Isaac
Worthington to mind when he wahn't but a slip of a boy
with a cough, runnin' after Cynthy Ware."   She glanced
down at Cynthia with something of compassion.   "Just
to think, child, he might have be'n your father!"

"I'm glad he isn't," said Cynthia, hotly.

"Of course, of course," replied the good-natured and
well-intentioned Amanda, "I'd sooner have your father
than Isaac Worthington.   But I was only thinkin' how nice
it would be to be rich."

Just then one of the glass-panelled doors of this house
opened, and a good-looking lad of seventeen came out.

"That's Bob Worthington," said Amanda, determined
that they should miss nothing.   "My! it wahn't but the
other day when he put on long pants.   It won't be a
great while before he'll go into the mills and git all that
money.   Guess he'll marry some city person.   He'd ought
to take you, Cynthy."

"I don't want him," said Cynthia, the color flaming
into her cheeks.   And she went off across the green in
search of Jethro.

There was a laugh from the honest country folk who
had listened.   Bob Worthington came to the edge of the
porch and stood there, frankly scanning the crowd, with
an entire lack of self-consciousness.   Some of them shifted
nervously, with the New Englander's dislike of being
caught in the act of sight-seeing.

"What in the world is he starin' at me for?" said

Amanda, backing behind the bulkier form of her husband.
" As I live, I believe he's comin' here."

Young Mr. Worthington was, indeed, descending the
steps and walking across the lawn toward them, nodding
and smiling to acquaintances as he passed. To Wetherell's astonishment he made directly for the place where he
was standing and held out his hand.

" How do you do, Mr. Wetherell ? " he said.   " Perhaps
you don't remember me, — Bob Worthington."

" I can't say that I should have known you," answered
the storekeeper.   They were all absurdly silent, thinking
of nothing to say and admiring the boy because he was at
ease.

" I hope you have a good seat at the exercises," he said,
pressing Wetherell's hand again, and before he could
thank him, Bob was off in the direction of the band stand.

" One thing," remarked Amanda, " he ain't much like
his dad.   You'd never catch Isaac Worthington bein'
that common."

Just then there came another interruption for William
Wetherell, who was startled by the sound of a voice in his
ear — a nasal voice that awoke unpleasant recollections.
He turned to confront, within the distance of eight inches,
the face of Mr. Bijah Bixby of Clovelly screwed up into
a greeting.   The storekeeper had met Mr. Bixby several
times since that first memorable meeting, and on each
occasion, as now, his hand had made an involuntary
movement to his watch pocket.

" Hain't seed you for some time, Will," remarked Mr.
Bixby; "goin' over to the exercises ?   We'll move along
that way," and he thrust his hand under Mr. Wetherell's
elbow.   " Whar's Jethro ? "

"He's here somewhere," answered the storekeeper,
helplessly, moving along in spite of himself.

" Keepin' out of sight, you understand," said Bijah, with
a knowing wink, as much as to say that Mr. Wetherell
was by this time a past master in Jethro tactics.   Mr.
Bixby could never disabuse his mind of a certain inter-
pretation which he put on the storekeeper's intimacy with

Jethro.   "You done well to git in with him, Will.
Didn't think you had it in you when I first looked you
over."

Mr. Wetherell wished to make an indignant denial, but
he didn't know exactly how to begin.

"Smartest man in the United States of America — guess
you know that," Mr. Bixby continued amiably.   "*They*
can't git at him unless he wants 'em to.   There's a railroad president at Isaac Worthington's who'd like to git at
him to-day, — guess you know that, — Steve Merrill."

Mr. Wetherell didn't know, but he was given no time
to say so.

"Steve Merrill, of the Grand Gulf and Northern.   *He*
hain't here to see Worthington ; he's here to see Jethro,
when Jethro's a mind to.   Guess you understand."

"I know nothing about it," answered Wetherell, shortly.
Mr. Bixby gave him a look of infinite admiration, as
though he could not have pursued any more admirable line.

"I know Steve Merrill better'n I know you," said Mr.
Bixby, "and he knows me.   Whenever he sees me at the
state capital he says, 'How be you, Bije?' just as natural
as if *I* was a railroad president, and slaps me on the back.
When be you goin' to the capital, Will?   You'd ought
to come down and be thar with the boys on this Truro
Bill.   You could reach some on 'em the rest of us couldn't
git at."

William Wetherell avoided a reply to this very pointed
inquiry by escaping into the meeting-house, where he
found Jethro and Cynthia and Ephraim already seated
halfway up the aisle.

On the platform, behind a bank of flowers, are the velvet-
covered chairs which contain the dignitaries of the
occasion.   The chief of these is, of course, Mr. Isaac Worthington, the one with the hawklike look, sitting next to
the Rev. Mr. Sweet, who is rather pudgy by contrast.
On the other side of Mr. Sweet, next to the parlor organ
and the quartette, is the genial little railroad president
Mr. Merrill, batting the flies which assail the unprotected
crown of his head, and smiling benignly on the audience.

Suddenly his eye becomes fixed, and he waves a fat hand vigorously at Jethro, who answers the salute with a nod of unwonted cordiality for him. Then comes a hush, and the exercises begin.

There is a prayer, of course, by the Rev. Mr. Sweet, and a rendering of "My Country" and "I would not Change my Lot," and other choice selections by the quartette; and an original poem recited with much feeling by a lady admirer of Miss Lucretia Penniman, and the "Hymn to Coniston" declaimed by Mr. Gamaliel Ives, president of the Brampton Literary Club. But the crowning event is, of course, the oration by Mr. Isaac D. Worthington, the first citizen, who is introduced under that title by the chairman of the day; and as the benefactor of Brampton, who has bestowed upon the town the magnificent gift which was dedicated such a short time ago, the Worthington Free Library.

Mr. Isaac D. Worthington stood erect beside the table, his hand thrust into the opening of his coat, and spoke at the rate of one hundred and eight words a minute, for exactly one hour. He sketched with much skill the creed of the men who had fought their way through the forests to build their homes by Coniston Water, who had left their clearings to risk their lives behind Stark and Ethan Allen for that creed; he paid a graceful tribute to the veterans of the Civil War, scattered among his hearers — a tribute, by the way, which for some reason made Ephraim very indignant. Mr. Worthington went on to outline the duty of citizens of the present day, as he conceived it, and in this connection referred, with becoming modesty, to the Worthington Free Library. He had made his money in Brampton, and it was but right that he should spend it for the benefit of the people of Brampton. The library, continued Mr. Worthington when the applause was over, had been the dream of a certain delicate youth who had come, many years ago, to Brampton for his health. (It is a curious fact, by the way, that Mr. Worthington seldom recalled the delicate youth now, except upon public occasions.)

"At the rate of one hundred and eight words a minute."

Yes, the dream of that youth had been to benefit in some way that community in which circumstances had decreed that he should live, and in this connection it might not be out of place to mention a bill then before the Legislature of the state, now in session. If the bill became a law, the greatest modern factor of prosperity, the railroad, would come to Brampton. The speaker was interrupted here by more applause. Mr. Worthington did not deem it dignified or necessary to state that the railroad to which he referred was the Truro Railroad; and that he, as the largest stockholder, might indirectly share that prosperity with Brampton. That would be wandering too far from his subject, which, it will be recalled, was civic duties. He took a glass of water, and went on to declare that he feared — sadly feared — that the ballot was not held as sacred as it had once been. He asked the people of Brampton, and of the state, to stop and consider who in these days made the laws and granted the franchises. Whereupon he shook his head very slowly and sadly, as much as to imply that, if the Truro Bill did not pass, the corruption of the ballot was to blame. No, Mr. Worthington could think of no better subject on this Birthday of Independence than a recapitulation of the creed of our forefathers, from which we had so far wandered.

In short, the first citizen, as became him, had delivered the first reform speech ever heard in Brampton, and the sensation which it created was quite commensurate to the occasion. The presence in the audience of Jethro Bass, at whom many believed the remarks to have been aimed, added no little poignancy to that sensation, although Jethro gave no outward signs of the terror and remorse by which he must have been struck while listening to Mr. Worthington's ruminations of the corruption of the ballot. Apparently unconscious of the eyes upon him, he walked out of the meeting-house with Cynthia by his side, and they stood waiting for Wetherell and Ephraim under the maple tree there.

The beribboned members of the Independence Day committee were now on the steps, and behind them came Isaac

Worthington and Mr. Merrill. The people, scenting a dramatic situation, lingered. Would the mill owner speak to the boss? The mill owner, with a glance at the boss, did nothing of the kind, but immediately began to talk rapidly to Mr. Merrill. That gentleman, however, would not be talked to, but came running over to Jethro and seized his hand, leaving Mr. Worthington to walk on by himself.

"Jethro," cried the little railroad president, " upon my word. Well, well. And Miss Jethro," he took off his hat to Cynthia, "well, well. Didn't know you had a girl, Jethro."

"W-wish she was mine, Steve," said Jethro. "She's a good deal to me as it is. Hain't you, Cynthy?"

"Yes," said Cynthia.

"Well, well," said Mr. Merrill, staring at her, " you'll have to look out for her some day — keep the boys away from her — eh? Upon my word! Well, Jethro," said he, with a twinkle in his eye, "are you goin' to reform? I'll bet you've got an annual over my road in your pocket right now."

"Enjoy the speech-makin', Steve?" inquired Mr. Bass, solemnly.

Mr. Merrill winked at Jethro, and laughed heartily.

"Keep the boys away from her, Jethro," he repeated, laying his hand on the shoulder of the lad who stood beside him. "It's a good thing Bob's going off to Harvard this fall. Seems to me I heard about some cutting up at Andover — eh, Bob?"

Bob grinned, showing a line of very white teeth.

Mr. Merrill took Jethro by the arm and led him off a little distance, having a message of some importance to give him, the purport of which will appear later. And Cynthia and Bob were left face to face. Of course Bob could have gone on, if he had wished it.

"Don't remember me, do you?" he said.

"I do now," said Cynthia, looking at him rather timidly through her lashes. Her face was hot, and she had been very uncomfortable during Mr. Merrill's remarks. Furthermore, Bob had not taken his eyes off her.

"I remembered you right away," he said reproachfully ; "I saw you in front of the house this morning, and you ran away."

"I didn't run away," replied Cynthia, indignantly.

"It looked like it to me," said Bob. "I suppose you were afraid I was going to give you another whistle."

Cynthia bit her lip, and then she laughed. Then she looked around to see where Jethro was, and discovered that they were alone in front of the meeting-house. Ephraim and her father had passed on while Mr. Merrill was talking.

"What's the matter?" asked Bob.

"I'm afraid they've gone," said Cynthia. "I ought to be going after them. They'll miss me."

"Oh, no, they won't," said Bob, easily, "let's sit down under the tree. They'll come back."

Whereupon he sat down under the maple. But Cynthia remained standing, ready to fly. She had an idea that it was wrong to stay — which made it all the more delightful.

"Sit down — Cynthia," said he.

She glanced down at him, startled. He was sitting, with his legs crossed, looking up at her intently.

"I like that name," he observed. "I like it better than any girl's name I know. Do be good-natured and sit down." And he patted the ground close beside him.

She laughed again. The laugh had in it an exquisite note of shyness, which he liked.

"Why do you want me to sit down?" she asked suddenly.

"Because I want to talk to you."

"Can't you talk to me standing up?"

"I suppose I could," said Bob, "but I shouldn't be able to say such nice things to you."

The corners of her mouth trembled a little.

"And whose loss would that be?" she asked.

Bob Worthington was surprised at this retort, and correspondingly delighted. He had not expected it in a country storekeeper's daughter, and he stared at Cynthia so frankly that she blushed again, and turned away. He

L

was a young man who, it may be surmised, had had some experience with the other sex at Andover and elsewhere. He had not spent all of his life in Brampton.

"I've often thought of you since that day when you wouldn't take the whistle," he declared. "What are you laughing at?"

"I'm laughing at you," said Cynthia, leaning against the tree, with her hands behind her.

"You've been laughing at me ever since you've stood there," he said, aggrieved that his declarations should not be taken more seriously.

"What have you thought about me?" she demanded. She was really beginning to enjoy this episode.

"Well —" he began, and hesitated — and broke down and laughed — Cynthia laughed with him.

"I can tell you what I didn't think," said Bob.

"What?" asked Cynthia, falling into the trap.

"I didn't think you'd be so — so good-looking," said he, quite boldly.

"And I didn't think you'd be so rude," responded Cynthia. But though she blushed again, she was not exactly displeased.

"What are you going to do this afternoon?" he asked. "Let's go for a walk."

"I'm going back to Coniston."

"Let's go for a walk now," said he, springing to his feet. "Come on."

Cynthia looked at him and shook her head smilingly.

"Here's Uncle Jethro —"

"Uncle Jethro!" exclaimed Bob, "is he your uncle?"

"Oh, no, not really. But he's just the same. He's very good to me."

"I wonder whether he'd mind if I called him Uncle Jethro, too," said Bob, and Cynthia laughed at the notion. This young man was certainly very comical, and very frank. "Good-by," he said; "I'll come to see you some day in Coniston."

CHAPTER XII

" A TIME TO WEEP, AND A TIME TO LAUGH "

THAT evening, after Cynthia had gone to bed, William Wetherell sat down at Jonah Winch's desk in the rear of the store to gaze at a blank sheet of paper until the Muses chose to send him subject-matter for his weekly letter to the *Guardian*. The window was open, and the cool airs from the mountain spruces mingled with the odors of corn meal and kerosene and calico print. Jethro Bass, who had supped with the storekeeper, sat in the wooden armchair silent, with his head bent. Sometimes he would sit there by the hour while Wetherell wrote or read, and take his departure when he was so moved without saying good night. Presently Jethro lifted his chin, and dropped it again ; there was a sound of wheels without, and, after an interval, a knock at the door.

William Wetherell dropped his pen with a start of surprise, as it was late for a visitor in Coniston. He glanced at Jethro, who did not move, and then he went to the door and shot back the great forged bolt of it, and stared out. On the edge of the porch stood a tallish man in a double-breasted frock coat.

" Mr. Worthington ! " exclaimed the storekeeper.

Mr. Worthington coughed and pulled at one of his mutton-chop whiskers, and seemed about to step off the porch again. It was, indeed, the first citizen and reformer of Brampton. No wonder William Wetherell was mystified.

" Can I do anything for you ? " he asked. " Have you missed your way ? "

Wetherell thought he heard him muttering, " No, no,"

and then he was startled by another voice in his ear.   It was Jethro who was standing beside him.

"G-guess he hain't missed his way a great deal.   Er — come in — come in."

Mr. Worthington took a couple of steps forward.

"I understood that you were to be alone," he remarked, addressing Jethro with an attempted severity of manner.

"Didn't say so — d-didn't say so, did I?" answered Jethro.

"Very well," said Mr. Worthington, "any other time will do for this little matter."

"Er — good night," said Jethro, shortly, and there was the suspicion of a gleam in his eye as Mr. Worthington turned away.   The mill-owner, in fact, did not get any farther than the edge of the porch before he wheeled again.

"The affair which I have to discuss with you is of a private nature, Mr. Bass," he said.

"So I callated," said Jethro.

"You may have the place to yourselves, gentlemen," Wetherell put in uneasily, and then Mr. Worthington came as far as the door, where he stood looking at the storekeeper with scant friendliness.   Jethro turned to Wetherell.

"You a politician, Will?" he demanded.

"No," said Wetherell.

"You a business man?"

"No," he said again.

"You ever tell folks what you hear other people say?"

"Certainly not," the storekeeper answered; "I'm not interested in other people's business."

"Ex'actly," said Jethro.   "Guess you'd better stay."

"But I don't care to stay," Wetherell objected.

"S-stay to oblige me — stay to oblige me?" he asked.

"Well, yes, if you put it that way," Wetherell said, beginning to get some amusement out of the situation.

He did not know what Jethro's object was in this matter; perhaps others may guess.

Mr. Worthington, who had stood by with ill-disguised impatience during this colloquy, now broke in.

"It is most unusual, Mr. Bass, to have a third person present at a conference in which he has no manner of concern. I think on the whole, since you have insisted upon my coming to you —"

"H-hain't insisted that I know of," said Jethro.

"Well," said Mr. Worthington, "never mind that. Perhaps it would be better for me to come to you some other time, when you are alone."

In the meantime Wetherell had shut the door, and they had gradually walked to the rear of the store. Jethro parted his coat tails, and sat down again in the armchair. Wetherell, not wishing to be intrusive, went to his desk again, leaving the first citizen standing among the barrels.

"W-what other time?" Jethro asked.

"Any other time," said Mr. Worthington.

"What other time?"

"To-morrow night?" suggested Mr. Worthington, striving to hide his annoyance.

"B-busy to-morrow night," said Jethro.

"You know that what I have to talk to you about is of the utmost importance," said Worthington. "Let us say Saturday night."

"B-busy Saturday night," said Jethro. "Meet you to-morrow."

"What time?"

"Noon," said Jethro, "noon."

"Where?" asked Mr. Worthington, dubiously.

"Band stand in Brampton Street," said Jethro, and the storekeeper was fain to bend over his desk to conceal his laughter, busying himself with his books. Mr. Worthington sat down with as much dignity as he could muster on one of Jonah's old chairs, and Jonah Winch's clock ticked and ticked, and Wetherell's pen scratched and scratched on his weekly letter to Mr. Willard, although he knew that he was writing the sheerest nonsense. As a matter of fact, he tore up the sheets the next morning without reading them. Mr. Worthington unbuttoned his coat, fumbled in his pocket, and pulled out two cigars, one of which he pushed toward Jethro, who shook his head. Mr. Worthington lighted his cigar and cleared his throat.

"Perhaps you have observed, Mr. Bass," he said, "that this is a rapidly growing section of the state — that the people hereabouts are every day demanding modern and efficient means of communication with the outside world."

"Struck you as a mill owner, has it?" said Jethro.

"I do not care to emphasize my private interests," answered Mr. Worthington, at last appearing to get into his stride again. "I wish to put the matter on broader grounds. Men like you and me ought not to be so much concerned with our own affairs as with those of the population amongst whom we live. And I think I am justified in putting it to you on these grounds."

"H-have to be justified, do you — have to be justified?" Jethro inquired. "Er — why?"

This was a poser, and for a moment he stared at Jethro, blankly, until he decided how to take it. Then he crossed his legs and blew smoke toward the ceiling.

"It is certainly fairer to everybody to take the broadest view of a situation," he remarked; "I am trying to regard this from the aspect of a citizen, and I am quite sure that it will appeal to you in the same light. If the spirit which imbued the founders of this nation means anything, Mr. Bass, it means that the able men who are given a chance to rise by their own efforts must still retain the duties and responsibilities of the humblest citizens. That, I take it, is our position, Mr. Bass, — yours and mine."

Mr. Worthington had uncrossed his legs, and was now by the inspiration of his words impelled to an upright position. Suddenly he glanced at Jethro, and started — for Jethro had sunk down on the small of his back, his chin on his chest, in an attitude of lassitude if not of oblivion. There was a silence perhaps a little disconcerting for Mr. Worthington, who chose the opportunity to relight his cigar.

"G-got through?" said Jethro, without moving, "g-got through?"

"Through?" echoed Mr. Worthington, "through what?"

" T-through Sunday-school," said Jethro.

Worthington dropped his match and stamped on it, and Wetherell began to wonder how much the man would stand. It suddenly came over the storekeeper that the predicament in which Mr. Worthington found himself — whatever it was — must be a very desperate one. He half rose in his chair, sat down again, and lighted another match.

" Er — director in the Truro Road, hain't you, Mr. Worthington ? " asked Jethro, without looking at him.

" Yes."

" Er — principal stockholder — ain't you ? "

" Yes — but that is neither here nor there, sir."

" Road don't pay — r-road don't pay, does it ? "

" It certainly does not."

" W-would pay if it went to Brampton and Harwich ? "

" Mr. Bass, the company consider that they are pledged to the people of this section to get the road through. I am not prepared to say whether the road would pay, but it is quite likely that it would not."

" Ch-charitable organization ? " said Jethro, from the depths of his chair.

" The pioneers in such matters take enormous risks for the benefit of the community, sir. We believe that we are entitled to a franchise, and in my opinion the General Court are behaving disgracefully in refusing us one. I will not say all I think about that affair, Mr. Bass. I am convinced that influences are at work — " He broke off with a catch in his throat.

" T-tried to get a franchise, did you ? "

" I am not here to quibble with you, Mr. Bass. We tried to get it by every legitimate means, and failed, and you know it as well as I do."

" Er — Heth Sutton didn't sign his receipt — er — did he ? "

The storekeeper, not being a politician, was not aware that the somewhat obscure reference of Jethro's to the Speaker of the House concerned an application which Mr. Worthington was supposed to have made to that gentleman, who had at length acknowledged his inability to oblige, and had advised Mr. Worthington to go to head-quarters. And Mr. Stephen Merrill, who had come to Brampton out of the kindness of his heart, had only arranged this meeting in a conversation with Jethro that day, after the reform speech.

Mr. Worthington sprang to his feet, and flung out a hand toward Jethro.

"Prove your insinuations, sir," he cried; "I defy you to prove your insinuations."

But Jethro still sat unmoved.

"H-Heth in the charitable organization, too?" he asked.

"People told me I was a fool to believe in honesty, but I thought better of the lawmakers of my state. I'll tell you plainly what they said to me, sir. They said, 'Go to Jethro Bass.'"

"Well, so you have, hain't you? So you have."

"Yes, I have. I've come to appeal to you in behalf of the people of your section to allow that franchise to go through the present Legislature."

"Er — come to appeal, have you — come to appeal?"

"Yes," said Mr. Worthington, sitting down again; "I have come to-night to appeal to you in the name of the farmers and merchants of this region — your neighbors, — to use your influence to get that franchise. I have come to you with the conviction that I shall not have appealed in vain."

"Er — appealed to Heth in the name of the farmers and merchants?"

"Mr. Sutton is Speaker of the House."

"F-farmers and merchants elected him," remarked Jethro, as though stating a fact.

Worthington coughed.

"It is probable that I made a mistake in going to Sutton," he admitted.

"If I w-wanted to catch a pike, w-wouldn't use a pin-hook."

"I might have known," remarked Worthington, after a pause, "that Sutton could not have been elected Speaker without your influence."

Jethro did not answer that, but still remained sunk in his chair. To all appearances he might have been asleep.

"W-worth somethin' to the farmers and merchants to get that road through — w-worth somethin', ain't it?"

Wetherell held his breath. For a moment Mr. Worthington sat very still, his face drawn, and then he wet his lips and rose slowly.

"We may as well end this conversation, Mr. Bass," he said, and though he tried to speak firmly his voice shook; "it seems to be useless. Good night."

He picked up his hat and walked slowly toward the door, but Jethro did not move or speak. Mr. Worthington reached the door, opened it, and the night breeze started the lamp to smoking. Wetherell got up and turned it down, and the first citizen was still standing in the doorway. His back was toward them, but the fingers of his left hand working convulsively caught Wetherell's eye and held it; save for the ticking of the clock and the chirping of the crickets in the grass, there was silence. Then Mr. Worthington closed the door softly, hesitated, turned, and came back and stood before Jethro.

"Mr. Bass," he said, "we've got to have that franchise."

William Wetherell glanced at the countryman who, without moving in his chair, without raising his voice, had brought the first citizen of Brampton to his knees. The thing frightened the storekeeper, revolted him, and yet its drama held him fascinated. By some subtle process which he had actually beheld, but could not fathom, this cold Mr. Worthington, this bank president who had given him sage advice, this preacher of political purity, had been reduced to a frenzied supplicant. He stood bending over Jethro.

"What's your price? Name it, for God's sake."

"B-better wait till you get the bill — hadn't you?— b-better wait till you get the bill."

"Will you put the franchise through?"

"Goin' down to the capital soon?" Jethro inquired.

"I'm going down on Thursday."

"B-better come in and see me," said Jethro.

"Very well," answered Mr. Worthington ; "I'll be in at two o'clock on Thursday." And then, without another word to either of them, he swung on his heel and strode quickly out of the store. Jethro did not move.

William Wetherell's hand was trembling so that he could not write, and he could not trust his voice to speak. Although Jethro had never mentioned Isaac Worthington's name to him, Wetherell knew that Jethro hated the first citizen of Brampton.

At length, when the sound of the wheels had died away, Jethro broke the silence.

"Er — didn't laugh — did he, Will ? Didn't laugh once — did he?"

"Laugh !" echoed the storekeeper, who himself had never been further from laughter in his life.

"M-might have let him off easier if he'd laughed," said Jethro, "if he'd laughed just once, m-might have let him off easier."

And with this remark he went out of the store and left Wetherell alone.

CHAPTER XIII

MR. WETHERELL DESCENDS INTO THE ARENA

THE weekly letter to the *Newcastle Guardian* was not finished that night, but Coniston slept, peacefully, unaware of Mr. Worthington's visit; and never, indeed, discovered it, since the historian for various reasons of his own did not see fit to insert the event in his plan of the Town History. Before another sun had set Jethro Bass had departed for the state capital, not choosing to remain to superintend the haying of the many farms which had fallen into his hand, — a most unusual omission for him.

Presently rumors of a mighty issue about the Truro Railroad began to be discussed by the politicians at the Coniston store, and Jake Wheeler held himself in instant readiness to answer a summons to the capital — which never came.

Delegations from Brampton and Harwich went to petition the Legislature for the franchise, and the *Brampton Clarion* and *Harwich Sentinel* declared that the people of Truro County recognized in Isaac Worthington a great and public-spirited man, who ought by all means to be the next governor — if the franchise went through.

One evening Lem Hallowell, after depositing a box of trimmings at Ephraim Prescott's harness shop, drove up to the platform of the store with the remark that "things were gittin' pretty hot down to the capital in that franchise fight."

"Hain't you b'en sent for yet, Jake?" he cried, throwing his reins over the backs of his sweating Morgans; "well, that's strange. Guess the fight hain't as hot as we hear about. Jethro hain't had to call out his best men."

155

"I'm a-goin' down if there's trouble," declared Jake, who consistently ignored banter.

"Better git up and git," said Lem; "there's three out of the five railroads against Truro, and Steve Merrill layin' low. Bije Bixby's down there, and Heth Sutton, and Abner Parkinson, and all the big bugs. Better git aboard, Jake."

At this moment the discussion was interrupted by the sight of Cynthia Wetherell coming across the green with an open letter in her hand.

"It's a message from Uncle Jethro," she said.

The announcement was sufficient to warrant the sensation it produced on all sides.

"'Tain't a *letter* from Jethro, is it?" exclaimed Sam Price, overcome by a pardonable curiosity. For it was well known that one of Jethro's fixed principles in life was embodied in his own motto, "Don't write — send."

"It's very funny," answered Cynthia, looking down at the paper with a puzzled expression. "'Dear Cynthia: Judge Bass wished me to say to you that he would be pleased if you and Will would come to the capital and spend a week with him at the Pelican House, and see the sights. The judge says Rias Richardson will tend store. Yours truly, P. Hartington.' That's all," said Cynthia, looking up.

For a moment you could have heard a pine needle drop on the stoop. Then Rias thrust his hands in his pockets and voiced the general sentiment.

"Well, I'll be — goldurned!" said he.

"Didn't say nothin' about Jake?" queried Lem.

"No," answered Cynthia, "that's all — except two pieces of cardboard with something about the Truro Railroad and our names. I don't know what they are." And she took them from the envelope.

"Guess I could tell you if I was pressed," said Lem, amid a shout of merriment from the group.

"Air you goin', Will?" said Sam Price, pausing with his foot on the step of his buggy, that he might have the complete news before he left.

"Godfrey, Will," exclaimed Rias, breathlessly, "you hain't a-goin' to throw up a chance to stay a hull week at the Pelican, be you?" The mere possibility of refusal overpowered Rias.

* * * * * * *

Those who are familiar with that delightful French song which treats of the leave-taking of one Monsieur Dumollet will appreciate, perhaps, the attentions which were showered upon William Wetherell and Cynthia upon their departure for the capital next morning. Although Mr. Wetherell had at one time been actually a resident of Boston, he received quite as many cautions from his neighbors as Monsieur Dumollet. *Billets doux* and pistols were, of course, not mentioned, but it certainly behooved him, when he should have arrived at that place of intrigues, to be on the lookout for cabals.

They took the stage-coach from Brampton over the pass: picturesque stage-coach with its apple-green body and leather springs, soon to be laid away forever if the coveted Truro Franchise Bill becomes a law; stage-coach which pulls up defiantly beside its own rival at Truro station, where our passengers take the train down the pleasant waterways and past the little white villages among the fruit trees to the capital. The thrill of anticipation was in Cynthia's blood, and the flush of pleasure on her cheeks, when they stopped at last under the sheds. The conductor snapped his fingers and cried, "This way, Judge," and there was Jethro in his swallow-tailed coat and stove-pipe hat awaiting them. He seized Wetherell's carpet-bag with one hand and Cynthia's arm with the other, and shouldered his way through the people, who parted when they saw who it was.

"Uncle Jethro," cried Cynthia, breathlessly, "I didn't know you were a judge. What are you judge of?"

"J-judge of clothes, Cynthy. D-don't you wish you had the red cloth to wear here?"

"No, I don't," said Cynthia. "I'm glad enough to be here without it."

"G-glad to hev you in any fixin's, Cynthy," he said, giving her arm a little squeeze, and by that time they were up the hill and William Wetherell quite winded. For Jethro was strong as an ox, and Cynthia's muscles were like an Indian's.

They were among the glories of Main Street now. The capital was then, and still remains, a typically beautiful New England city, with wide streets shaded by shapely maples and elms, with substantial homes set back amidst lawns and gardens. Here on Main Street were neat brick business buildings and banks and shops, with the parklike grounds of the Capitol farther on, and everywhere, from curb to doorway, were knots of men talking politics; broad-faced, sunburned farmers in store clothes, with beards that hid their shirt fronts; keen-featured, sallow, country lawyers in long black coats crumpled from much sitting on the small of the back; country storekeepers with shrewd eyes, and local proprietors and manufacturers.

"Uncle Jethro, I didn't know you were such a great man," she said.

"H-how did ye find out, Cynthy?"

"The way people treat you here. I knew you were great, of course," she hastened to add.

"H-how do they treat me?" he asked, looking down at her.

"You know," she answered. "They all stop talking when you come along and stare at you. But why don't you speak to them?"

Jethro smiled and squeezed her arm again, and then they were in the corridor of the famous Pelican Hotel, hazy with cigar smoke and filled with politicians. Some were standing, hanging on to pillars, gesticulating, some were ranged in benches along the wall, and a chosen few were in chairs grouped around the spittoons. Upon the appearance of Jethro's party, the talk was hushed, the groups gave way, and they accomplished a kind of triumphal march to the desk. The clerk, descrying them, desisted abruptly from a conversation across the cigar counter, and with all the form of a ceremony dipped the pen with a flourish into the ink and handed it to Jethro.

"Your rooms are ready, Judge," he said.

As they started for the stairs, Jethro and Cynthia leading the way, Wetherell felt a touch on his elbow and turned to confront Mr. Bijah Bixby — at very close range, as usual.

"C-come down at last, Will?" he said. "Thought ye would. Need everybody this time — you understand."

"I came on pleasure," retorted Mr. Wetherell, somewhat angrily.

Mr. Bixby appeared hugely to enjoy the joke.

"So I callated," he cried, still holding Wetherell's hand in a mild, but persuasive grip. "So I callated. Guess I done you an injustice, Will."

"How's that?"

"You're a leetle mite smarter than I thought you was. So long. Got a leetle business now — you understand — a leetle business."

Was it possible, indeed, for the simple-minded to come to the capital and not become involved in cabals? With some misgivings William Wetherell watched Mr. Bixby disappear among the throng, kicking up his heels behind, and then went upstairs. On the first floor Cynthia was standing by an open door.

"Dad," she cried, "come and see the rooms Uncle Jethro's got for us!" She took Wetherell's hand and led him in. "See the lace curtains, and the chandelier, and the big bureau with the marble top."

Jethro had parted his coat tails and seated himself enjoyably on the bed.

"D-don't come often," he said, "m-might as well have the best."

"Jethro," said Wetherell, coughing nervously and fumbling in the pocket of his coat, "you've been very kind to us, and we hardly know how to thank you. I-I didn't have any use for these."

He held out the pieces of cardboard which had come in Cynthia's letter. He dared not look at Jethro, and his eye was fixed instead upon the somewhat grandiose signature of Isaac D. Worthington, which they bore. Jethro took them and tore them up, and slowly tossed the pieces into a cuspidor conveniently situated near the foot of the bed. He rose and thrust his hands into his pockets.

" Er — when you get freshened up, come into Number 7," he said.

Number 7 ! But we shall come to that later. Supper first, in a great pillared dining room filled with notables, if we only had the key. Jethro sits silent at the head of the table eating his crackers and milk, with Cynthia on his left and William Wetherell on his right. Poor William, greatly embarrassed by his sudden projection into the lime-light, is helpless in the clutches of a lady-waitress who is demanding somewhat fiercely that he make an immediate choice from a list of dishes which she is shooting at him with astonishing rapidity. But who is this, sitting beside him, who comes to William's rescue, and demands that the lady repeat the bill of fare ? Surely a notable, for he has a generous presence, and jet-black whiskers which catch the light, which give the gentleman, as Mr. Bixby remarked, " quite a settin'." Yes, we have met him at last. It is none other than the Honorable Heth Sutton, Rajah of Clovelly, Speaker of the House, who has condescended to help Mr. Wetherell.

His chamberlain, Mr. Bijah Bixby, sits on the other side of the Honorable Heth, and performs the presentation of Mr. Wetherell. But Mr. Sutton, as becomes a man of high position, says little after he has rebuked the waitress, and presently departs with a carefully chosen toothpick ; whereupon Mr. Bixby moves into the vacant seat — not to Mr. Wetherell's unqualified delight.

" I've knowed him ever sence we was boys," said Mr. Bixby ; " you saw how intimate we was. When he wants a thing done, he says, ' Bije, you go out and git 'em.' Never counts the cost. He was nice to you — wahn't he, Will ? " And then Mr. Bixby leaned over and whispered in Mr. Wetherell's ear, " He knows — you understand — he knows."

" Knows what ? " demanded Mr. Wetherell.

Mr. Bixby gave him another admiring look.

"Knows you didn't come down here with Jethro jest to see the sights."

At this instant the talk in the dining room fell flat, and looking up William Wetherell perceived a portly, rubicund man of middle age being shown to his seat by the head waiter. The gentleman wore a great, glittering diamond in his shirt, and a watch chain that contained much fine gold. But the real cause of the silence was plainly in the young woman who walked beside him, and whose effective entrance argued no little practice and experience. She was of a type that catches the eye involuntarily and holds it, — tall, well-rounded, fresh-complexioned, with heavy coils of shimmering gold hair. Her gown, which was far from unbecoming, was in keeping with those gifts with which nature had endowed her. She carried her head high, and bestowed swift and evidently fatal glances to right and left during her progress through the room. Mr. Bixby's voice roused the storekeeper from this contemplation of the beauty.

"That's Alvy Hopkins of Gosport and his daughter. Fine gal, hain't she? Ever sence she come down here t'other day she's stirred up more turmoil than any railroad bill I ever seed. She was most suffocated at the governor's ball with fellers tryin' to git dances — some of 'em old fellers, too. And you understand about Alvy ? "

" What about him ? "

"Alvy says he's a-goin' to be the next governor, or fail up." Mr. Bixby's voice sank to a whisper, and he spoke into Mr. Wetherell's ear. "Alvy says he has twenty-five thousand dollars to put in if necessary. I'll introduce you to him, Will," he added meaningly. "Guess you can help him some — you understand ? "

"Mr. Bixby ! " cried Mr. Wetherell, putting down his knife and fork.

"There ! " said Mr. Bixby, reassuringly, " 'twon't be no bother. I know him as well as I do you — call each other by our given names. Guess I was the first man he sent for last

M

spring. He knows I go through all them river towns.
He says, ' Bije, you git 'em.' I understood."

William Wetherell began to realize the futility of trying
to convince Mr. Bixby of his innocence in political matters, and glanced at Jethro.

"You wouldn't think he was listenin', would you, Will ? "
Mr. Bixby remarked.

" Listening ? "

" Ears are sharp as a dog's. Callate he kin hear as
far as the governor's table, and he don't look as if he knows
anything. One way he built up his power — listenin'
when they're talkin' sly out there in the rotunda. They're
almighty surprised when they l'arn he knows what they're
up to. Guess you understand how to go along by quiet
and listen when they're talkin' sly."

" I never did such a thing in my life," cried William
Wetherell, indignantly aghast.

But Mr. Bixby winked.

" So long, Will," he said, " see you in Number 7."

Never, since the days of Pompadour and Du Barry, until
modern American politics were invented, has a state been
ruled from such a place as Number 7 in the Pelican House
— familiarly known as the Throne Room. In this historic
cabinet there were five chairs, a marble-topped table, a
pitcher of iced water, a bureau, a box of cigars and a Bible,
a chandelier with all the gas jets burning, and a bed,
whereon sat such dignitaries as obtained an audience, —
railroad presidents, governors and ex-governors and prospective governors, the Speaker, the President of the Senate,
Bijah Bixby, Peleg Hartington, mighty chiefs from the
North Country, and lieutenants from other parts of the
state. These sat on the bed by preference. Jethro sat in
a chair by the window, and never took any part in the discussions that raged, but listened. Generally there was
some one seated beside him who talked persistently in his
ear ; as at present, for instance, Mr. Chauncey Weed,
Chairman of the Committee on Corporations of the House,
who took the additional precaution of putting his hand to
his mouth when he spoke.

Mr. Stephen Merrill was in the Throne Room that evening, and confidentially explained to the bewildered William Wetherell the exact situation in the Truro Franchise fight. Inasmuch as it has become our duty to describe this celebrated conflict, — in a popular and engaging manner, if possible, — we shall have to do so through Mr. Wetherell's eyes, and on his responsibility. The biographies of some of the gentlemen concerned have since been published, and for some unaccountable reason contain no mention of the Truro franchise.

"All Gaul," said Mr. Merrill — he was speaking to a literary man — "all Gaul is divided into five railroads. I am one, the Grand Gulf and Northern, the impecunious one. That is the reason I'm so nice to everybody, Mr. Wetherell. The other day a conductor on my road had a shock of paralysis when a man paid his fare. Then there's Balch, president of the 'Down East' road, as we call it. Balch and I are out of this fight, — we don't care whether Isaac D. Worthington gets his franchise or not, or I wouldn't be telling you this. The two railroads which don't want him to get it, because the Truro would eventually become a competitor with them, are the Central and the Northwestern. Alexander Duncan is president of the Central."

"Alexander Duncan!" exclaimed Wetherell. "He's the richest man in the state, isn't he?"

"Yes," said Mr. Merrill, "and he lives in a big square house right here in the capital. He ain't a bad fellow, Duncan. You'd like him. He loves books. I wish you could see his library."

"I'm afraid there's not much chance of that," answered Wetherell.

"Well, as I say, there's Duncan, of the Central, and the other is Lovejoy, of the Northwestern. Lovejoy's a bachelor and a skinflint. Those two, Duncan and Lovejoy, are using every means in their power to prevent Worthington from getting that franchise. Have I made myself clear?"

"Do you think Mr. Worthington will get it?" asked

Wetherell, who had in mind a certain nocturnal visit at his store.

Mr. Merrill almost leaped out of his chair at the question. Then he mopped his face, and winked very deliberately at the storekeeper. Then Mr. Merrill laughed.

"Well, well," he said, "for a man who comes down here to stay with Jethro Bass to ask me that!" Whereupon Mr. Wetherell flushed, and began to perspire himself. "Didn't you hear Isaac D. Worthington's virtuous appeal to the people at Brampton?" said Mr. Merrill.

"Yes," replied Wetherell, getting redder.

"I like you, Will," said Mr. Merrill, unexpectedly, "darned if I don't. I'll tell you what I know about it, and you can have a little fun while you're here, lookin' on, only it won't do to write about it to the *Newcastle Guardian*. Guess Willard wouldn't publish it, anyhow. I suppose you know that Jethro pulls the strings, and we little railroad presidents dance. We're the puppets now, but after a while, when I'm crowded out, all these little railroads will get together and there'll be a row worth looking at, or I'm mistaken. But to go back to Worthington," continued Mr. Merrill, "he made a little mistake with his bill in the beginning. Instead of going to Jethro, he went to Heth Sutton, and Heth got the bill as far as the Committee on Corporations, and there she's been ever since, with our friend Chauncey Weed, who's whispering over there."

"Mr. Sutton couldn't even get it out of the Committee!" exclaimed Wetherell.

"Not an inch. Jethro saw this thing coming about a year ago, and he took the precaution to have Chauncey Weed and the rest of the Committee in his pocket — and of course Heth Sutton's always been there."

William Wetherell thought of that imposing and manly personage, the Honorable Heth Sutton, being in Jethro's pocket, and marvelled. Mr. Chauncey Weed seemed of a species better able to thrive in the atmosphere of pockets.

"Well, as I say, there was the Truro Franchise Bill

sound asleep in the Committee, and when Isaac D. Worthington saw that his little arrangement with Heth Sutton wasn't any good, and that the people of the state didn't have anything more to say about it than the Crow Indians, and that the end of the session was getting nearer and nearer, he got desperate and went to Jethro, I suppose. You know as well as I do that Jethro has agreed to put the bill through."

"Then why doesn't he get the Committee to report it and put it through?" asked Wetherell.

"Bless your simple literary nature," exclaimed Mr. Merrill, "Jethro's got more power than any man in the state, but that isn't saying that he doesn't have to fight occasionally. He has to fight now. He has seven of the twelve senators hitched, and the governor. But Duncan and Lovejoy have bought up all the loose blocks of representatives, and it is supposed that the franchise forces only control a quorum. The end of the session is a week off, and never in all my experience have I seen a more praiseworthy attendance on the part of members."

"Do you mean that they are being paid to remain in their seats?" cried the amazed Mr. Wetherell.

"Well," answered Mr. Merrill, with a twinkle in his eye, "that is a little bald and — and unparliamentary, perhaps, but fairly accurate. Our friend Jethro is confronted with a problem to tax even his faculties, and to look at him, a man wouldn't suspect he had a care in the world."

Jethro was apparently quite as free from anxiety the next morning when he offered, after breakfast, to show Wetherell and Cynthia the sights of the town, though Wetherell could not but think that the Throne Room and the Truro Franchise Bill were left at a very crucial moment to take care of themselves. Jethro talked to Cynthia — or rather, Cynthia talked to Jethro upon innumerable subjects ; they looked upon the statue of a great statesman in the park, and Cynthia read aloud the quotation graven on the rock of the pedestal, "The People's Government, made for the People, made by the

People, and answerable to the People." After that they went into the state library, where Wetherell was introduced to the librarian, Mr. Storrow. They did not go into the State House because, as everybody knows, Jethro Bass never went there. Mr. Bijah Bixby and other lieutenants might be seen in the lobbies, and the governor might sign bills in his own apartment there, but the real seat of government was that Throne Room into which we have been permitted to enter.

They walked out beyond the outskirts of the town, where there was a grove or picnic ground which was also used as a park by some of the inhabitants. Jethro liked the spot, and was in the habit sometimes of taking refuge there when the atmosphere of the Pelican House became too thick. The three of them had sat down on one of the board benches to rest, when presently two people were seen at a little distance walking among the trees, and the sight of them, for some reason, seemed to give Jethro infinite pleasure.

"Why," exclaimed Cynthia, "one of them is that horrid girl everybody was looking at in the dining room last night."

"D-don't like her, Cynthy?" said Jethro.

"No," said Cynthia, "I don't."

"Pretty — hain't she — pretty?"

"She's brazen," declared Cynthia.

It was, indeed, Miss Cassandra Hopkins, daughter of that Honorable Alva who — according to Mr. Bixby — was all ready with a certain sum of money to be the next governor. Miss Cassandra was arrayed fluffily in cool, pink lawn, and she carried a fringed parasol, and she was gazing upward with telling effect into the face of the gentleman by her side. This would have all been very romantic if the gentleman had been young and handsome, but he was certainly not a man to sweep a young girl off her feet. He was tall, angular, though broad-shouldered, with a long, scrawny neck that rose out of a very low collar, and a large head, scantily covered with hair — a head that gave a physical as well as a mental effect of hardness. His smooth-shaven face seemed to bear witness that

"It was, indeed, Miss Cassandra Hopkins."

its owner was one who had pushed frugality to the borders
of a vice. It was not a pleasant face, but now it wore an
almost benign expression under the influence of Miss Cassandra's eyes. So intent, apparently, were both of them
upon each other that they did not notice the group on the
bench at the other side of the grove. William Wetherell
ventured to ask Jethro who the man was.

"N-name's Lovejoy," said Jethro.

"Lovejoy!" ejaculated the storekeeper, thinking of
what Mr. Merrill had told him of the opponents of the
Truro Franchise Bill. "President of the 'Northwestern'
Railroad?"

Jethro gave his friend a shrewd look.

"G-gettin' posted — hain't you, Will?" he said.

"Is she going to marry that old man?" asked Cynthia.

Jethro smiled a little. "G-guess not," said he, "guess
not, if the old man can help it. Nobody's married him yet,
and hain't likely to."

Jethro was unusually silent on the way back to the hotel,
but he did not seem to be worried or displeased. He only
broke his silence once, in fact, when Cynthia called his
attention to a large poster of some bloodhounds on a fence,
announcing the fact in red letters that "Uncle Tom's
Cabin" would be given by a certain travelling company
at the Opera House the next evening.

"L-like to go, Cynthy?"

"Oh, Uncle Jethro, do you think we can go?"

"Never b'en to a show — hev you — never b'en to a
show?"

"Never in my life," said Cynthia.

"We'll all go," said Jethro, and he repeated it once or
twice as they came to Main Street, seemingly greatly
tickled at the prospect. And there was the Truro Franchise Bill hanging over him, with only a week left of
the session, and Lovejoy's and Duncan's men sitting so
tight in their seats! William Wetherell could not understand it.

CHAPTER XIV

IN WHICH THE BACK SEATS ARE HEARD FROM

HALF an hour later, when Mr. Wetherell knocked timidly at Number 7, — drawn thither by an irresistible curiosity, — the door was opened by a portly person who wore a shining silk hat and ample gold watch chain. The gentleman had, in fact, just arrived; but he seemed perfectly at home as he laid down his hat on the marble-topped bureau, mopped his face, took a glass of iced water at a gulp, chose a cigar, and sank down gradually on the bed. Mr. Wetherell recognized him instantly as the father of the celebrated Cassandra.

"Well, Jethro," said the gentleman, "I've got to come into the Throne Room once a day anyhow, just to make sure you don't forget me — eh?"

"A-Alvy," said Jethro, "I want you to shake hands with a particular friend of mine, Mr. Will Wetherell of Coniston. Er — Will, the Honorable Alvy Hopkins of Gosport."

Mr. Hopkins rose from the bed as gradually as he had sunk down upon it, and seized Mr. Wetherell's hand impressively. His own was very moist.

"Heard you was in town, Mr. Wetherell," he said heartily. "If Jethro calls you a particular friend, it means something, I guess. It means something to me, anyhow."

"Will hain't a politician," said Jethro. "Er — Alvy?"

"Hello!" said Mr. Hopkins.

"Er — Will don't talk."

"If Jethro had been real tactful," said the Honorable Alvy, sinking down again, "he'd have introduced me as the next governor of the state. Everybody knows I want to be governor, everybody knows I've got twenty thousand dollars in the bank to pay for that privilege. Everybody knows I'm going to be governor if Jethro says so."

William Wetherell was a little taken aback at this ingenuous statement of the gentleman from Gosport. He looked out of the window through the foliage of the park, and his eye was caught by the monument there in front of the State House, and he thought of the inscription on the base of it, "The People's Government." The Honorable Alva had not mentioned the people — undoubtedly.

"Yes, Mr. Wetherell, twenty thousand dollars." He sighed. "Time was when a man could be governor for ten. Those were the good old days — eh, Jethro?"

"A-Alvy, 'Uncle Tom's Cabin's' comin' to town to-morrow — to-morrow."

"You don't tell me," said the Honorable Alva, acquiescing cheerfully in the change of subject. "We'll go. Pleased to have you, too, Mr. Wetherell."

"Alvy," said Jethro, again, "'Uncle Tom's Cabin' comes to town to-morrow."

Mr. Hopkins stopped fanning himself, and glanced at Jethro questioningly.

"A-Alvy, that give you an idea?" said Jethro, mildly.

Mr. Wetherell looked blank: it gave him no idea whatsoever, except of little Eva and the bloodhounds. For a few moments the Honorable Alva appeared to be groping, too, and then his face began to crease into a smile of comprehension.

"By Godfrey, Jethro, but you are smart!" he exclaimed, with involuntary tribute; "you mean buy up the theatre?"

"C-callate you'll find it's bought up."

"You mean *pay* for it?" said Mr. Hopkins.

"You've guessed it, Alvy, you've guessed it."

Mr. Hopkins gazed at him in admiration, leaned out of the perpendicular, and promptly drew from his trousers' pocket a roll of stupendous proportions. Wetting his thumb, he began to push aside the top bills.

" How much is it ? " he demanded.

But Jethro put up his hand.

" No hurry, Alvy — n-no hurry. H-Honorable Alvy Hopkins of Gosport — p-patron of the theatre. Hain't the first time you've b'en a patron, Alvy."

" Jethro," said Mr. Hopkins, solemnly, putting up his money, " I'm much obliged to you. I'm free to say I'd never have thought of it. If you ain't the all-firedest smartest man in America to-day, — I don't except any, even General Grant, — then I ain't the next governor of this state."

Whereupon he lapsed into an even more expressive silence, his face still glowing.

" Er — Alvy," said Jethro. presently, " what's the name of your gal ? "

" Well," said Mr. Hopkins, " I guess you've got me. We did christen her Lily, but she didn't turn out exactly Lily. She ain't the type," said Mr. Hopkins, slowly, not without a note of regret, and lapsed into silence.

" W-what did you say her name was, Alvy ? "

" I guess her name's Cassandra," said the Honorable Alva.

" C-Cassandry ? "

" Well, you see," he explained a trifle apologetically, " she's kind of taken some matters in her own hands, my gal. Didn't like Lily, and it didn't seem to fit her anyway, so she called herself Cassandra. Read it in a book. It means, ' inspirer of love,' or some such poetry ; but I don't deny that it goes with her better than Lily would."

" Sh-she's a good deal of a gal, Alvy — fine-appearin' gal, Alvy."

" Upon my word, Jethro, I didn't know you ever looked at a woman. But I suppose you couldn't help lookin' at my gal — she does seem to draw men's eyes as if she was magnetized some way." Mr. Hopkins did not speak as though this quality of his daughter gave him unmixed delight. " But she's a good-hearted gal, Cassy is, high-spirited, and I won't deny she's handsome and smart.

She'll kind of grace my position when I'm governor. But to tell you the truth, Jethro, one old friend to another, durned if I don't wish she was married. It's a terrible thing for a father to say, I know, but I'd feel easier about her if she was married to some good man who could hold her. There's young Joe Turner in Gosport, he'd give his soul to have her, and he'd do. Cassy says she's after bigger game than Joe. She's young — that's her only excuse. Funny thing happened night before last," continued Mr. Hopkins, laughing. " Lovejoy saw her, and he's b'en out of his head ever since. Al must be pretty near my age, ain't he ? Well, there's no fool like an old fool."

" A-Alvy — introduce me to Cassandry sometime — will you ? "

" Why, certainly," answered Mr. Hopkins, heartily, " I'll bring her in here. And now how about gettin' an adjournment to-morrow night for 'Uncle Tom's Cabin' ? These night sessions kind of interfere."

Half an hour later, when the representatives were pouring into the rotunda for dinner, a crowd was pressing thickly around the desk to read a placard pinned on the wall above it. The placard announced the coming of Mr. Glover's Company for the following night, and that the Honorable Alva Hopkins of Gosport, ex-Speaker of the House, had bought three hundred and twelve seats for the benefit of the members. And the Honorable Alva himself, very red in the face and almost smothered, could be dimly discerned at the foot of the stairs trying to fight his way out of a group of over-enthusiastic friends and admirers. Alva — so it was said on all sides — was doing the right thing.

So it was that one sensation followed another at the capital, and the politicans for the moment stopped buzzing over the Truro Franchise Bill to discuss Mr. Hopkins and his master-stroke. The afternoon *Chronicle* waxed enthusiastic on the subject of Mr. Hopkins's generosity, and predicted that, when Senator Hartington made the motion in the upper house and Mr. Jameson in the lower, the General Court would unanimously agree that there would be no evening session on the following day.   The Honorable Alva was the hero of the hour.

That afternoon Cynthia and her father walked through the green park to make their first visit to the State House. They stood hand in hand on the cool, marble-paved floor of the corridor, gazing silently at the stained and battered battle-flags behind the glass, and Wetherell seemed to be listening again to the appeal of a great President to a great Country in the time of her dire need — the soul calling on the body to fight for itself.   Wetherell seemed to feel again the thrill he felt when he saw the blue-clad men of this state crowded in the train at Boston : and to hear again the cheers, and the sobs, and the prayers as he looked upon the blood that stained stars and stripes alike with a holy stain.   With that blood the country had been consecrated, and the state — yes, and the building where they stood.   So they went on up the stairs, reverently, nor heeded the noise of those in groups about them, and through a door into the great hall of the representatives of the state.

Life is a mixture of emotions, a jumble of joy and sorrow and reverence and mirth and flippancy, of right feeling and heresy.   In the morning William Wetherell had laughed at Mr. Hopkins and the twenty thousand dollars he had put in the bank to defraud the people ; but now he could have wept over it, and as he looked down upon the three hundred members of that House, he wondered how many of them represented their neighbors who supposedly had sent them here — and how many Mr. Lovejoy's railroad, Mr. Worthington's railroad, or another man's railroad.

But gradually he forgot the battle-flags, and his mood changed.   Perhaps the sight of Mr. Speaker Sutton towering above the House, the very essence and bulk of authority, brought this about.   He aroused in Wetherell unwilling admiration and envy when he arose to put a question in his deep voice, or rapped sternly with his gavel to silence the tumult of voices that arose from time to time ; or while some member was speaking, or the clerk was reading a bill at breathless speed, he turned with wonderful nonchalance to listen to the conversation of the gentlemen on the bench beside him, smiled, nodded, pulled his whiskers, at once conscious and unconscious of his high position. And, most remarkable of all to the storekeeper, not a man of the three hundred, however obscure, could rise that the Speaker did not instantly call him by name.

William Wetherell was occupied by such reflections as these when suddenly there fell a hush through the House. The clerk had stopped reading, the Speaker had stopped conversing, and, seizing his gavel, looked expectantly over the heads of the members and nodded. A sleek, comfortably dressed man arose smilingly in the middle of the House, and subdued laughter rippled from seat to seat as he addressed the chair.

"Mr. Jameson of Wantage."

Mr. Jameson cleared his throat impressively and looked smilingly about him.

"Mr. Speaker and gentlemen of the House," he said, "if I desired to arouse the enthusiasm — the just enthusiasm — of any gathering in this House, or in this city, or in this state, I should mention the name of the Honorable Alva Hopkins of Gosport. I think I am right."

Mr. Jameson was interrupted, as he no doubt expected, by applause from floor and gallery. He stood rubbing his hands together, and it seemed to William Wetherell that the Speaker did not rap as sharply with his gavel as he had upon other occasions.

"Gentlemen of the House," continued Mr. Jameson, presently, "the Honorable Alva Hopkins, whom we all know and love, has with unparalleled generosity — unparalleled, I say — bought up three hundred and twelve seats in Foster's Opera House for to-morrow night" (renewed applause), "in order that every member of this august body may have the opportunity to witness that most classic of histrionic productions, 'Uncle Tom's Cabin.'" (Loud applause, causing the Speaker to rap sharply.) "That we may show a proper appreciation of this compliment, I move you, Mr. Speaker, that the House adjourn not later than six o'clock to-morrow, Wednesday evening, not to meet again until Thursday morning."

Mr. Jameson of Wantage handed the resolution to a page and sat down amidst renewed applause. Mr. Wetherell noticed that many members turned in their seats as they clapped, and glancing along the gallery he caught a flash of red and perceived the radiant Miss Cassandra herself leaning over the rail, her hands clasped in ecstasy. Mr. Lovejoy was not with her — he evidently preferred to pay his attentions in private.

"There she is again," whispered Cynthia, who had taken an instinctive and extraordinary dislike to Miss Cassandra. Then Mr. Sutton rose majestically to put the question.

"Gentlemen, are you ready for the question?" he cried. "All those in favor of the resolution of the gentleman from Wantage, Mr. Jameson — " the Speaker stopped abruptly. The legislators in the front seats swung around, and people in the gallery craned forward to see a member standing at his seat in the extreme rear of the hall. He was a little man in an ill-fitting coat, his wizened face clean-shaven save for the broom-shaped beard under his chin, which he now held in his hand. His thin, nasal voice was somehow absurdly penetrating as he addressed the chair. Mr. Sutton was apparently, for once, taken by surprise, and stared a moment, as though racking his brain for the name.

"The gentleman from Suffolk, Mr. Heath," he said, and smiling a little, sat down.

The gentleman from Suffolk, still holding on to his beard, pitched in without preamble.

"We farmers on the back seats don't often git a chance to be heard, Mr. Speaker," said he, amidst a general tittering from the front seats. "We come down here without any l'arnin' of parli'ment'ry law, and before we know what's happened the session's over, and we hain't said nothin'." (More laughter.) "There's b'en a good many times when I wanted to say somethin', and this time I made up my mind I was a-goin' to — law or no law."

(Applause, and a general show of interest in the gentleman from Suffolk.) "Naow, Mr. Speaker, I hain't ag'in' 'Uncle Tom's Cabin.' It's a good play, and it's done an almighty lot of good. And I hain't sayin' nothin' ag'in' Alvy Hopkins nor his munificence. But I do know there's a sight of little bills on that desk that won't be passed if we don't set to-morrow night — little bills that are big bills for us farmers. That thar woodchuck bill, for one." (Laughter.) "My constituents want I should have that bill passed. We don't need a quorum for them bills, but we need *time*. Naow, Mr. Speaker, I say let all them that wants to go and see 'Uncle Tom's Cabin' go and see it, but let a few of us fellers that has woodchuck bills and other things that we've got to git through come down here and pass 'em. You kin put 'em on the docket, and I guess if anything comes along that hain't jest right for everybody, somebody can challenge a quorum and bust up the session. That's all."

The gentleman from Suffolk sat down amidst thunderous applause, and before it died away Mr. Jameson was on his feet, smiling and rubbing his hands together, and was recognized.

"Mr. Speaker," he said, as soon as he could be heard, "if the gentleman from Suffolk desires to pass woodchuck bills" (renewed laughter), "he can do so as far as I'm concerned. I guess I know where most of the members of this House will be to-morrow night —" (Cries of 'You're right,' and sharp rapping of the gavel.) "Mr. Speaker, I withdraw my resolution."

"The gentleman from Wantage," said the Speaker, smiling broadly now, "withdraws his resolution."

As William Wetherell was returning to the Pelican House, pondering over this incident, he almost ran into a distinguished-looking man walking briskly across Main Street.

"It was Mr. Worthington !" said Cynthia, looking after him.

But Mr. Worthington had a worried look on his face, and was probably too much engrossed in his own thoughts

to notice his acquaintances.   He had, in fact, just come
from the Throne Room, where he had been to remind Jethro
that the session was almost over, and to ask him what he
meant to do about the Truro Bill.   Jethro had given
him no satisfaction.

"Duncan and Lovejoy have their people paid to sit
there night and day," Mr. Worthington had said.   "We've
got a bare majority on a full House; but you don't seem to
dare to risk it.   What are you going to do about it, Mr.
Bass?"

"W-want the bill to pass — don't you?"

"Certainly," Mr. Worthington had cried, on the edge of
losing his temper.

"L-left it to me — didn't you?"

"Yes, but I'm entitled to know what's being done.   I'm
paying for it."

"H-hain't paid for it yet — hev you?"

"No, I most assuredly haven't."

"B-better wait till you do."

There was very little satisfaction in this, and Mr.
Worthington had at length been compelled to depart,
fuming, to the house of his friend the enemy, Mr. Duncan,
there to attempt for the twentieth time to persuade Mr.
Duncan to call off his dogs who were sitting with such
praiseworthy pertinacity in their seats.   As the two
friends walked on the lawn, Mr. Worthington tried to
explain, likewise for the twentieth time, that the extension of the Truro Railroad could in no way lessen the
Canadian traffic of the Central, Mr. Duncan's road.   But
Mr. Duncan could not see it that way, and stuck to his
present ally, Mr. Lovejoy, and refused point blank to call
off his dogs.   Business was business.

It is an apparently inexplicable fact, however, that Mr.
Worthington and his son Bob were guests at the Duncan
mansion at the capital.   Two countries may not be allies,
but their sovereigns may be friends.   In the present instance, Mr. Duncan and Mr. Worthington's railroads were
opposed, diplomatically, but another year might see the
Truro Railroad and the Central acting as one.   And Mr.

N

Worthington had no intention whatever of sacrificing Mr.
Duncan's friendship. The first citizen of Brampton possessed one quality so essential to greatness — that of looking into the future, and he believed that the time would
come when an event of some importance might create a
perpetual alliance between himself and Mr. Duncan. In
short, Mr. Duncan had a daughter, Janet, and Mr. Worthington, as we know, had a son. And Mr. Duncan, in
addition to his own fortune, had married one of the richest
heiresses in New England. *Prudens futuri*, that was Mr.
Worthington's motto.

The next morning Cynthia, who was walking about the
town alone, found herself gazing over a picket fence at a
great square house with a very wide cornice that stood by
itself in the centre of a shade-flecked lawn. There were
masses of shrubbery here and there, and a greenhouse, and a
latticed summer-house: and Cynthia was wondering what
it would be like to live in a great place like that, when a
barouche with two shining horses in silver harness drove
past her and stopped before the gate. Four or five girls
and boys came laughing out on the porch, and one of them,
who held a fishing-rod in his hand, Cynthia recognized.
Startled and ashamed, she began to walk on as fast as she
could in the opposite direction, when she heard the sound
of footsteps on the lawn behind her, and her own name
called in a familiar voice. At that she hurried the faster;
but she could not run, and the picket fence was half
a block long, and Bob Worthington had an advantage over
her. Of course it was Bob, and he did not scruple to run,
and in a few seconds he was leaning over the fence in front
of her. Now Cynthia was as red as a peony by this time,
and she almost hated him.

"Well, of all people, Cynthia Wetherell!" he cried;
"didn't you hear me calling after you?"

"Yes," said Cynthia.

"Why didn't you stop?"

"I didn't want to," said Cynthia, glancing at the distant
group on the porch, who were watching them. Suddenly
she turned to him defiantly. "I didn't know you were in
that house, or in the capital," she said.

"And I didn't know you were," said Bob, upon whose masculine intelligence the meaning of her words was entirely lost. "If I had known it, you can bet I would have looked you up. Where are you staying?"

"At the Pelican House."

"What!" said Bob, "with all the politicians? How did you happen to go there?"

"Mr. Bass asked my father and me to come down for a few days," answered Cynthia, her color heightening again. Life is full of contrasts, and Cynthia was becoming aware of some of them.

"Uncle Jethro?" said Bob.

"Yes, Uncle Jethro," said Cynthia, smiling in spite of herself. He always made her smile.

"Uncle Jethro owns the Pelican House," said Bob.

"Does he? I knew he was a great man, but I didn't know how great he was until I came down here."

Cynthia said this so innocently that Bob repented his flippancy on the spot. He had heard occasional remarks of his elders about Jethro.

"I didn't mean quite that," he said, growing red in his turn. "Uncle Jethro — Mr. Bass — is a great man — of course. That's what I meant."

"And he's a very good man," said Cynthia, who understood now that he had spoken a little lightly of Jethro, and resented it.

"I'm sure of it," said Bob, eagerly. Then Cynthia began to walk on, slowly, and he followed her on the other side of the fence. "Hold on," he cried, "I haven't said half the things I want to say — yet."

"What do you want to say?" asked Cynthia, still walking. "I have to go."

"Oh, no, you don't! Wait just a minute — won't you?"

Cynthia halted, with apparent unwillingness, and put out her toe between the pickets. Then she saw that there was a little patch on that toe, and drew it in again.

"What do you want to say?" she repeated. "I don't believe you have anything to say at all." And suddenly she flashed a look at him that made his heart thump.

"I do — I swear I do," he protested. "I'm coming down to the Pelican to-morrow morning to get you to go for a walk."

Cynthia could not but think that the remoteness of the time he set was scarce in keeping with his ardent tone.

"I have something else to do to-morrow morning," she answered.

"Then I'll come to-morrow afternoon," said Bob, instantly.

"Who lives here?" she asked irrelevantly.

"Mr. Duncan. I'm visiting the Duncans."

At this moment a carryall joined the carriage at the gate. Cynthia glanced at the porch again. The group there had grown larger, and they were still staring. She began to feel uncomfortable again, and moved on slowly.

"Mayn't I come?" asked Bob, going after her, and scraping the butt of the rod along the palings.

"Aren't there enough girls here to satisfy you?" asked Cynthia.

"They're enough — yes," he said, "but none of 'em could hold a candle to you."

Cynthia laughed outright.

"I believe you tell them all something like that," she said.

"I don't do any such thing," he retorted, and then he laughed himself, and Cynthia laughed again.

"I like you because you don't swallow everything whole," said Bob, "and — well, for a good many other reasons." And he looked into her face with such frank admiration that Cynthia blushed and turned away.

"I don't believe a word you say," she answered, and started to walk off, this time in earnest.

"Hold on," cried Bob. They were almost at the end of the fence by this, and the pickets were sharp and rather high, or he would have climbed them.

Cynthia paused hesitatingly.

"I'll come at two o'clock to-morrow," said he; "we're

going on a picnic to-day, to Dalton's Bend, on the river. I wish I could get out of it."

Just then there came a voice from the gateway.

"Bob! Bob Worthington!"

They both turned involuntarily. A slender girl with light brown hair was standing there, waving at him.

"Who's that?" asked Cynthia.

"That?" said Bob, in some confusion, "oh, that's Janet Duncan."

"Good-by," said Cynthia.

"I'm coming to-morrow," he called after her, but she did not turn. In a little while she heard the carryall behind her clattering down the street, its passengers laughing and joking merrily. Her face burned, for she thought that they were laughing at her; she wished with all her heart that she had not stopped to talk with him at the palings. The girls, indeed, were giggling as the carryall passed, and she heard somebody call out his name, but nevertheless he leaned out of the seat and waved his hat at her, amid a shout of laughter. Poor Cynthia! She did not look at him. Tears of vexation were in her eyes, and the light of her joy at this visit to the capital flickered, and she wished she were back in Coniston. She thought it would be very nice to be rich, and to live in a great house in a city, and to go on picnics.

The light flickered, but it did not wholly go out. If it has not been shown that Cynthia was endowed with a fair amount of sense, many of these pages have been written in vain. She sat down for a while in the park and thought of the many things she had to be thankful for — not the least of which was Jethro's kindness. And she remembered that she was to see "Uncle Tom's Cabin" that evening.

Such are the joys and sorrows of fifteen!

CHAPTER XV

THE WOODCHUCK SESSION

Mr. Amos Cuthbert named it so — our old friend Amos who lives high up in the ether of Town's End ridge, and who now represents Coniston in the Legislature. He is the same silent, sallow person as when Jethro first took a mortgage on his farm, only his skin is beginning to resemble dried parchment, and he is a trifle more cantankerous. On the morning of that memorable day when "Uncle Tom's Cabin" came to the capital, Amos had entered the Throne Room and given vent to his feelings in regard to the gentleman in the back seat who had demanded an evening sitting on behalf of the farmers.

"Don't that beat all!" cried Amos. "Let them have their darned woodchuck session; there won't nobody go to it. For cussed, crisscross contrariness, give me a moss-back Democrat from a one-hoss, one-man town like Suffolk. I'm a-goin' to see the show."

"G-goin' to the show, be you, Amos?" said Jethro.

"Yes, I be," answered Amos, bitterly. "I hain't a-goin' nigh the house to-night." And with this declaration he departed.

"I wonder if he really is going?" queried Mr. Merrill, looking at the ceiling. And then he laughed.

"Why shouldn't he go?" asked William Wetherell.

Mr. Merrill's answer to this question was a wink, whereupon he, too, departed. And while Wetherell was pondering over the possible meaning of these words the Honorable Alva Hopkins entered, wreathed in smiles, and closed the door behind him.

"It's all fixed," he said, taking a seat near Jethro in the window.

"S-seen your gal — Alvy — seen your gal?"

Mr. Hopkins gave a glance at Wetherell.

"Will don't talk," said Jethro, and resumed his inspection through the lace curtains of what was going on in the street.

"Cassandry's got him to go," said Mr. Hopkins. "It's all fixed, as sure as Sunday. If it misses fire, then I'll never mention the governorship again. But if it don't miss fire," and the Honorable Alva leaned over and put his hand on Jethro's knee, "if it don't miss fire, I get the nomination. Is that right?"

"Y-you've guessed it, Alvy."

"That's all I want to know," declared the Honorable Alva; "when you say that much, you never go back on it. And you can go ahead and give the orders, Jethro. I have to see that the boys get the tickets. Cassandry's got a head on her shoulders, and she kind of wants to be governor, too." He got as far as the door, when he turned and bestowed upon Jethro a glance of undoubted tribute. "You've done a good many smart things," said he, "but I guess you never beat this, and never will."

"H-hain't done it yet, Alvy," answered Jethro, still looking out through the window curtains at the ever changing groups of gentlemen in the street. These groups had a never ceasing interest for Jethro Bass.

Mr. Wetherell didn't talk, but had he been the most incurable of gossips he felt that he could have done no damage to this mysterious affair, whatever it was. In a certain event, Mr. Hopkins was promised the governorship: so much was plain. And it was also evident that Miss Cassandra Hopkins was in some way to be instrumental. William Wetherell did not like to ask Jethro, but he thought a little of sounding Mr. Merrill, and then he came to the conclusion that it would be wiser for him not to know.

"Er — Will," said Jethro, presently, "you know Heth Sutton — Speaker Heth Sutton?"

"Yes."

"Er — wouldn't mind askin' him to step in and see me before the session — if he was comin' by — would you?"

"Certainly not."

"Er — if he was comin' by," said Jethro.

Mr. Wetherell found Mr. Speaker Sutton glued to a pillar in the rotunda below. He had some difficulty in breaking through the throng that pressed around him, and still more in attracting his attention, as Mr. Sutton took no manner of notice of the customary form of placing one's hand under his elbow and pressing gently up. Summoning up his courage, Mr. Wetherell tried the second method of seizing him by the buttonhole. He paused in his harangue, one hand uplifted, and turned and glanced at the storekeeper abstractedly.

"Mr. Bass asked me to tell you to drop into Number 7," said Wetherell, and added, remembering express instructions, "if you were going by."

Wetherell had not anticipated the magical effect this casual message would have on Mr. Sutton, nor had he thought that so large and dignified a body would move so rapidly. Before the astonished gentlemen who had penned him in could draw a breath, Mr. Sutton had reached the stairway and was mounting it with an agility that did him credit. Five minutes later Wetherell saw the Speaker descending again, the usually impressive quality of his face slightly modified by the twitching of a smile.

Thus the day passed, and the gentlemen of the Lovejoy and Duncan factions sat as tight as ever in their seats, and the Truro Franchise bill still slumbered undisturbed in Mr. Chauncey Weed's committee.

At supper there was a decided festal air about the dining room of the Pelican House, the little band of agricultural gentlemen who wished to have a session not being patrons of that exclusive hotel. Many of the Solons had sent home for their wives, that they might do the utmost justice to the Honorable Alva's hospitality. Even Jethro, as he ate his crackers and milk, had a new coat with bright brass buttons, and Cynthia, who wore a fresh gingham which Miss Sukey Kittredge of Coniston had helped to design, so far relented in deference to Jethro's taste as to tie a red bow at her throat.

The middle table under the chandelier was the immediate firmament of Miss Cassandra Hopkins. And there, beside the future governor, sat the president of the "Northwestern" Railroad, Mr. Lovejoy, as the chief of the revolving satellites. People began to say that Mr. Lovejoy was hooked at last, now that he had lost his head in such an unaccountable fashion as to pay his court in public; and it was very generally known that he was to make one of the Honorable Alva's immediate party at the performance of "Uncle Tom's Cabin."

Mr. Speaker Sutton, of course, would have to forego the pleasure of the theatre as a penalty of his high position. Mr. Merrill, who sat at Jethro's table next to Cynthia that evening, did a great deal of joking with the Honorable Heth about having to preside over a woodchuck session, which the Speaker, so Mr. Wetherell thought, took in astonishingly good part, and seemed very willing to make the great sacrifice which his duty required of him.

After supper Mr. Wetherell took a seat in the rotunda. As an observer of human nature, he had begun to find a fascination in watching the group of politicians there. First of all he encountered Mr. Amos Cuthbert, his little coal-black eyes burning brightly, and he was looking very irritable indeed.

"So you're going to the show, Amos?" remarked the storekeeper, with an attempt at cordiality.

To his bewilderment, Amos turned upon him fiercely.

"Who said I was going to the show?" he snapped.

"You yourself told me."

"You'd ought to know whether I'm a-goin' or not," said Amos, and walked away.

While Mr. Wetherell sat meditating upon this inexplicable retort, a retired, scholarly looking gentleman with a white beard, who wore spectacles, came out of the door leading from the barber shop and quietly took a seat beside him. The storekeeper's attention was next distracted by the sight of one who wandered slowly but ceaselessly from group to group, kicking up his heels behind, and halting always in the rear of the speakers. Needless to say that this was our friend Mr. Bijah Bixby, who was following out his celebrated tactics of "going along by when they were talkin' sly." Suddenly Mr. Bixby's eye alighted on Mr. Wetherell, who by a stretch of imagination conceived that it expressed both astonishment and approval, although he was wholly at a loss to understand these sentiments. Mr. Bixby winked — Mr. Wetherell was sure of that. But to his surprise, Bijah did not pause in his rounds to greet him.

Mr. Wetherell was beginning to be decidedly uneasy, and was about to go upstairs, when Mr. Merrill came down the rotunda whistling, with his hands in his pockets. He stopped whistling when he spied the storekeeper, and approached him in his usual hearty manner.

"Well, well, this is fortunate," said Mr. Merrill; "how are you, Duncan? I want you to know Mr. Wetherell. Wetherell writes that weekly letter for the *Guardian* you were speaking to me about last year. Will, this is Mr. Alexander Duncan, president of the 'Central.'"

"How do you do, Mr. Wetherell?" said the scholarly gentleman with the spectacles, putting out his hand. "I'm glad to meet you, very glad, indeed. I read your letters with the greatest pleasure."

Mr. Wetherell, as he took Mr. Duncan's hand, had a variety of emotions which may be imagined, and need not be set down in particular.

"Funny thing," Mr. Merrill continued, "I was looking for you, Duncan. It occurred to me that you would like to meet Mr. Wetherell. I was afraid you were in Boston."

"I have just got back," said Mr. Duncan.

"I wanted Wetherell to see your library. I was telling him about it."

"I should be delighted to show it to him," answered Mr. Duncan. That library, as is well known, was a special weakness of Mr. Duncan's.

Poor William Wetherell, who was quite overwhelmed by the fact that the great Mr. Duncan had actually read his letters and liked them, could scarcely utter a sensible word. Almost before he realized what had happened he was following Mr. Duncan out of the Pelican House, when the storekeeper was mystified once more by a nudge and another wink from Mr. Bixby, conveying unbounded admiration.

"Why don't you write a book, Mr. Wetherell?" inquired the railroad president, when they were crossing the park.

"I don't think I could do it," said Mr. Wetherell, modestly. Such incense was overpowering, and he immediately forgot Mr. Bixby.

"Yes, you can," said Mr. Duncan, "only you don't know it. Take your letters for a beginning. You can draw people well enough, when you try. There was your description of the lonely hill-farm on the spur — I shall always remember that: the gaunt farmer, toiling every minute between sun and sun; the thin, patient woman bending to a task that never changed or lightened; the children growing up and leaving one by one, some to the cities, some to the West, until the old people are left alone in the evening of life — to the sunsets and the storms. Of course you must write a book."

Mr. Duncan quoted other letters, and William Wetherell thrilled. Poor man! he had had little enough incense in his time, and none at all from the great. They came to the big square house with the cornice which Cynthia had seen the day before, and walked across the lawn through the open door. William Wetherell had a glimpse of a great drawing-room with high windows, out of which was wafted the sound of a piano and of youthful voices and laughter, and then he was in the library. The thought of one man owning all those books overpowered him. There they were, in stately rows, from the floor to the high ceiling, and a portable ladder with which to reach them.

Mr. Duncan, understanding perhaps something of the storekeeper's embarrassment, proceeded to take down his treasures: first editions from the shelves, and folios and missals from drawers in a great iron safe in one corner and laid them on the mahogany desk. It was the railroad president's hobby, and could he find an appreciative guest, he was happy. It need scarcely be said that he found William Wetherell appreciative, and possessed of a knowledge of Shaksperiana and other matters that astonished his host as well as pleased him. For Wetherell had found his tongue at last.

After a while Mr. Duncan drew out his watch and gave a start.

"By George!" he exclaimed, "it's after eight o'clock. I'll have to ask you to excuse me to-night, Mr. Wetherell. I'd like to show you the rest of them — can't you come around to-morrow afternoon?"

Mr. Wetherell, who had forgotten his own engagement and "Uncle Tom's Cabin," said he would be happy to come. And they went out together and began to walk toward the State House.

"It isn't often I find a man who knows anything at all about these things," continued Mr. Duncan, whose heart was quite won. "Why do you bury yourself in Coniston?"

"I went there from Boston for my health," said the storekeeper.

"Jethro Bass lives there, doesn't he?" said Mr. Duncan, with a laugh. "But I suppose you don't know anything about politics."

"I know nothing at all," said Mr. Wetherell, which was quite true. He had been in dreamland, but now the fact struck him again, with something of a shock, that this mild-mannered gentleman was one of those who had been paying certain legislators to remain in their seats. Wetherell thought of speaking to Mr. Duncan of his friendship with Jethro Bass, but the occasion passed.

"I wish to heaven I didn't have to know anything about politics," Mr. Duncan was saying; "they disgust me. There's a little matter on now, about an extension of the Truro Railroad to Harwich, which wouldn't interest you, but you can't conceive what a nuisance it has been to watch that House day and night, as I've had to. It's no joke to have that townsman of yours, Jethro Bass, opposed to you. I won't say anything against him, for he may be a friend of yours, and I have to use him sometimes myself." Mr. Duncan sighed. "It's all very sordid and annoying. Now this evening, for instance, when we might have enjoyed ourselves with those books, I've got to go to the House, just because some backwoods farmers want to talk about woodchucks. I suppose it's foolish," said Mr. Duncan; "but Bass has tricked us so often that I've got into the habit of being watchful. I should have been here twenty minutes ago."

By this time they had come to the entrance of the State House, and Wetherell followed Mr. Duncan in, to have a look at the woodchuck session himself. Several members hurried by and up the stairs, some of them in their Sunday black ; and the lobby above seemed, even to the storekeeper's unpractised eye, a trifle active for a woodchuck session. Mr. Duncan muttered something, and quickened his gait a little on the steps that led to the gallery. This place was almost empty. They went down to the rail, and the railroad president cast his eye over the House.

"Good God!" he said sharply, "there's almost a quorum here." He ran his eye over the members. "There *is* a quorum here."

Mr. Duncan stood drumming nervously with his fingers on the rail, scanning the heads below. The members were scattered far and wide through the seats, like an army in open order, listening in silence to the droning voice of the clerk. Moths burned in the gas flames, and June-bugs hummed in at the high windows and tilted against the walls. Then Mr. Duncan's finger nails whitened as his thin hands clutched the rail, and a sense of a pending event was upon Wetherell. Slowly he realized that he was listening to the Speaker's deep voice.

" ' The Committee on Corporations, to whom was referred House Bill Number 109, entitled, *An Act to extend the Truro Railroad to Harwich*, having considered the same, report the same with the following resolution: Resolved, that the bill ought to pass. Chauncey Weed, for the Committee.'"

The Truro Franchise! The lights danced, and even a sudden weakness came upon the storekeeper. Jethro's trick! The Duncan and Lovejoy representatives in the theatre, the adherents of the bill here! Wetherell saw Mr. Duncan beside him, a tense figure leaning on the rail, calling to some one below. A man darted up the centre, another up the side aisle. Then Mr. Duncan flashed at William Wetherell from his blue eye such a look of anger as the storekeeper never forgot, and he, too, was gone. Tingling and perspiring, Wetherell leaned out over the railing as the Speaker rapped calmly for order. Hysteric laughter, mingled with hoarse cries, ran over the House, but the Honorable Heth Sutton did not even smile.

A dozen members were on their feet shouting to the chair. One was recognized, and that man Wetherell perceived with amazement to be Mr. Jameson of Wantage, adherent of Jethro's — he who had moved to adjourn for "Uncle Tom's Cabin"! A score of members crowded into the aisles, but the Speaker's voice again rose above the tumult.

"The doorkeepers will close the doors! Mr. Jameson of Wantage moves that the report of the Committee be accepted, and on this motion a roll-call is ordered."

The doorkeepers, who must have been inspired, had already slammed the doors in the faces of those seeking wildly to escape. The clerk already had the little, short-legged desk before him and was calling the roll with incredible rapidity. Bewildered and excited as Wetherell was, and knowing as little of parliamentary law as the gentleman who had proposed the woodchuck session, he began to form some sort of a notion of Jethro's generalship, and he saw that the innocent rural members who belonged to Duncan and Lovejoy's faction had tried to get away before the roll-call, destroy the quorum, and so adjourn the House. These, needless to say, were not par-

liamentarians, either.   They had lacked a leader, they
were stunned by the suddenness of the onslaught, and
had not moved quickly enough.   Like trapped animals,
they wandered blindly about for a few moments, and then
sank down anywhere.   Each answered the roll-call sul-
lenly, out of necessity, for every one of them was a marked
man.   Then Wetherell remembered the two members who
had escaped, and Mr. Duncan, and fell to calculating how
long it would take these to reach Foster's Opera House,
break into the middle of an act, and get out enough partisans to come back and kill the bill.   Mr. Wetherell
began to wish he could witness the scene there, too, but
something held him here, shaking with excitement, listening to each name that the clerk called.

Would the people at the theatre get back in time?

Despite William Wetherell's principles, whatever these
may have been, he was so carried away that he found himself with his watch in his hand, counting off the minutes
as the roll-call went on.   Foster's Opera House was some
six squares distant, and by a liberal estimate Mr. Duncan
and his advance guard ought to get back within twenty
minutes of the time he left.   Wetherell was not aware
that people were coming into the gallery behind him; he
was not aware that one sat at his elbow until a familiar
voice spoke directly into his ear.

" Er — Will — held Duncan pretty tight — didn't you?
He's a hard one to fool, too.   Never suspected a mite, did
he?   Look out for your watch!"

Mr. Bixby seized it or it would have fallen.   If his life
had depended on it, William Wetherell could not have
spoken a word to Mr. Bixby then.

" You done well, Will, sure enough," that gentleman
continued to whisper.   " And Alvy's gal done well, too
— you understand.   I guess she's the only one that
ever snarled up Al Lovejoy so that he didn't know
where he was at.   But it took a fine, delicate touch for
her job and yours, Will.   Godfrey, this is the quickest
roll-call I ever seed!   They've got halfway through Truro
County.   That fellow can talk faster than a side-show
ticket-seller at a circus."

The clerk was, indeed, performing prodigies of pronuncia-
tion. When he reached Wells County, the last, Mr. Bixby
so far lost his habitual *sang froid* as to hammer on the rail
with his fist.

"If there hain't a quorum, we're done for," he said.
"How much time has gone away? Twenty minutes!
Godfrey, some of 'em may break loose and git here in
five minutes!"

"Break loose?" Wetherell exclaimed involuntarily.

Mr. Bixby screwed up his face.

"You understand. Accidents is liable to happen."

Mr. Wetherell didn't understand in the least, but just
then the clerk reached the last name on the roll; an instant of absolute silence, save for the June-bugs, followed,
while the assistant clerk ran over his figures deftly and
handed them to Mr. Sutton, who leaned forward to receive
them.

"One hundred and twelve gentlemen have voted in the
affirmative and forty-eight in the negative, and the report
of the Committee is accepted."

"Ten more'n a quorum!" ejaculated Mr. Bixby, in a
voice of thanksgiving, as the turmoil below began again.
It seemed as though every man in the opposition was on his
feet and yelling at the chair: some to adjourn; some to
indefinitely postpone; some demanding roll-calls; others
swearing at these — for a division vote would have opened
the doors. Others tried to get out, and then ran down
the aisles and called fiercely on the Speaker to open the
doors, and threatened him. But the Honorable Heth
Sutton did not lose his head, and it may be doubted
whether he ever appeared to better advantage than at that
moment. He had a voice like one of the Clovelly bulls
that. fed in his own pastures in the valley, and by sheer
bellowing he got silence, or something approaching it, —
the protests dying down to a hum; had recognized another
friend of the bill, and was putting another question.

"Mr. Gibbs of Wareham moves that the rules of the
House be so far suspended that this bill be read a second
and third time by its title, and be put upon its final pas-

sage at this time.   And on this motion," thundered Mr. Sutton, above the tide of rising voices, "the yeas and nays are called for. *The doorkeepers will keep the doors shut.*"

"Abbey of Ashburton."

The nimble clerk had begun on the roll almost before the Speaker was through, and checked off the name. Bijah Bixby mopped his brow with a blue pocket-handkerchief.

"My God," he said, "what a risk Jethro's took ! they can't git through another roll-call. Jest look at Heth ! Ain't he carryin' it magnificent? Hain't as ruffled as I be. I've knowed him ever sence he wahn't no higher'n that desk. Never would have b'en in politics if it hadn't b'en for me.   Funny thing, Will — you and I was so excited we never thought to look at the clock. Put up your watch.   Godfrey, what's this ? "

The noise of many feet was heard behind them. Men and women were crowding breathlessly into the gallery.

"Didn't take it long to git noised araound," said Mr. Bixby.   "Say, Will, they're bound to have got at 'em in the thea'tre. Don't see how they held 'em off, c-cussed if I do."

The seconds ticked into minutes, the air became stifling, for now the front of the gallery was packed.   Now, if ever, the fate of the Truro Franchise hung in the balance, and, perhaps, the rule of Jethro Bass.   And now, as in the distance, came a faint, indefinable stir, not yet to be identified by Wetherell's ears as a sound, but registered somewhere in his brain as a warning note.   Bijah Bixby, as sensitive as he, straightened up to listen, and then the whispering was hushed.   The members below raised their heads, and some clutched the seats in front of them and looked up at the high windows.   Only the Speaker sat like a wax statue of himself, and glanced neither to the right nor to the left.

"Harkness of Truro," said the clerk.

"He's almost to Wells County again," whispered Bijah, excitedly.   "I didn't callate he could do it.   Will ? "

o

" Yes ? "

" Will — you hear somethin' ? "

A distant shout floated with the night breeze in at the windows ; a man on the floor got to his feet and stood straining : a commotion was going on at the back of the gallery, and a voice was heard crying out : —

" For the love of God, let me through ! "

Then Wetherell turned to see the crowd at the back parting a little, to see a desperate man in a gorgeous white necktie fighting his way toward the rail. He wore no hat, his collar was wilted, and his normally ashen face had turned white. And, strangest of all, clutched tightly in his hand was a pink ribbon.

" It's Al Lovejoy," said Bijah, laconically.

Unmindful of the awe-stricken stares he got from those about him when his identity became known, Mr. Lovejoy gained the rail and shoved aside a man who was actually making way for him. Leaning far out, he scanned the house with inarticulate rage while the roll-call went monotonously on. Some of the members looked up at him and laughed ; others began to make frantic signs, indicative of helplessness ; still others telegraphed him obvious advice about reënforcements which, if anything, increased his fury. Mr. Bixby was now fanning himself with the blue handkerchief.

" I hear 'em ! " he said, " I hear 'em, Will ! "

And he did. The unmistakable hum of the voices of many men and the sound of feet on stone flagging shook the silent night without. The clerk read off the last name on the roll.

" Tompkins of Ulster."

His assistant lost no time now. A mistake would have been fatal, but he was an old hand. Unmindful of the rumble on the wooden stairs below, Mr. Sutton took the list with an admirable deliberation.

" One hundred and twelve gentlemen have voted in the affirmative, forty-eight in the negative, the rules of the House are suspended, and " (the clerk having twice mumbled the title of the bill) " the question is : Shall the bill pass? As many as are of opinion that the bill pass will say *Aye*, contrary minded *No*."

Feet were in the House corridor now, and voices rising there, and noises that must have been scuffling — yes, and beating of door panels. Almost every member was standing, and it seemed as if they were all shouting, — " personal privilege," "fraud," "trickery," "open the doors." Bijah was slowly squeezing the blood out of William Wetherell's arm.

" The doorkeepers has the keys in their pockets !" Mr. Bixby had to shout, for once.

Even then the Speaker did not flinch. By a seeming miracle he got a semblance of order, recognized his man, and his great voice rang through the hall and drowned all other sounds.

" And on this question a roll-call is ordered. *The door-keepers will close the doors!*"

Then, as in reaction, the gallery trembled with a roar of laughter. But Mr. Sutton did not smile. The clerk scratched off the names with lightning rapidity, scarce waiting for the answers. Every man's color was known, and it was against the rules to be present and fail to vote. The noise in the corridors grew louder, some one dealt a smashing kick on a panel, and Wetherell ventured to ask Mr. Bixby if he thought the doors would hold.

"They can break in all they've a mind to now," he chuckled ; " the Truro Franchise is safe."

" What do you mean ?" Wetherell demanded excitedly.

" If a member hain't present when a question is put, he can't git into a roll-call," said Bijah.

The fact that the day was lost was evidently brought home to those below, for the strife subsided gradually, and finally ceased altogether. The whispers in the gallery died down, the spectators relaxed a little. Lovejoy alone remained tense, though he had seated himself on a bench, and the hot anger in which he had come was now cooled into a vindictiveness that set the hard lines of his face even harder. He still clutched the ribbon. The last part of that famous roll-call was conducted so quietly that

a stranger entering the House would have suspected nothing unusual.   It was finished in absolute silence.

"One hundred and twelve gentlemen have voted in
the affirmative, forty-eight in the negative, and the bill
passes.   The House will attend to the title of the bill."

"An act to extend the Truro Railroad to Harwich,"
said the clerk, glibly.

"Such will be the title of the bill unless otherwise
ordered by the House," said Mr. Speaker Sutton.   "The
doorkeepers will open the doors."

Somebody moved to adjourn, the motion was carried,
and thus ended what has gone down to history as the
Woodchuck Session.   Pandemonium reigned.   One hundred and forty belated members fought their way in at the
four entrances, and mingled with them were lobbyists of
all sorts and conditions, residents and visitors to the
capital, men and women to whom the drama of "Uncle
Tom's Cabin" was as nothing to that of the Truro Franchise Bill.   It was a sight to look down upon.   Fierce
wrangles began in a score of places, isolated personal remarks rose above the din, but your New Englander rarely
comes to blows ; in other spots men with broad smiles
seized others by the hands and shook them violently,
while Mr. Speaker Sutton seemed in danger of suffoca-
tion by his friends.   His enemies, for the moment, could
get nowhere near him.   On this scene Mr. Bijah Bixby
gazed with pardonable pleasure.

"Guess there wahn't a mite of trouble about the river
towns," he said, "I had 'em in my pocket.   Will, let's
amble round to the thea'tre.   We ought to git in two
acts."

William Wetherell went.   There is no need to go into
the psychology of the matter.   It may have been numb-
ness ; it may have been temporary insanity caused by the
excitement of the battle he had witnessed, for his brain
was in a whirl ; or Mr. Bixby may have hypnotized him.
As they walked through the silent streets toward the
Opera House, he listened perforce to Mr. Bixby's comments upon some of the innumerable details which Jethro

had planned and quietly carried out while sitting in the window of the Throne Room. A great light dawned on William Wetherell, but too late.

Jethro's trusted lieutenants (of whom, needless to say, Mr. Bixby was one) had been commanded to notify such of their supporters whose fidelity and secrecy could be absolutely depended upon to attend the Woodchuck Session; and, further to guard against surprise, this order had not gone out until the last minute (hence Mr. Amos Cuthbert's conduct). The seats of these members at the theatre had been filled by accommodating townspeople and visitors. Forestalling a possible vote on the morrow to recall and reconsider, there remained some sixty members whose loyalty was unquestioned, but whose reputation for discretion was not of the best. So much for the parliamentary side of the affair, which was a revelation of generalship and organization to William Wetherell. By the time he had grasped it they were come in view of the lights of Foster's Opera House, and they perceived, among a sprinkling of idlers, a conspicuous and meditative gentleman leaning against a pillar. He was ludicrously tall and ludicrously thin, his hands were in his trousers pockets, and the skirts of his Sunday broadcloth coat hung down behind him awry. One long foot was crossed over the other and rested on the point of the toe, and his head was tilted to one side. He had, on the whole, the appearance of a rather mournful stork. Mr. Bixby approached him gravely, seized him by the lower shoulder, and tilted him down until it was possible to speak into his ear. The gentleman apparently did not resent this, although he seemed in imminent danger of being upset.

"How be you, Peleg? Er — you know Will?"

"No," said the gentleman.

Mr. Bixby seized Mr. Wetherell under the elbow, and addressed himself to the storekeeper's ear.

"Will, I want you to shake hands with Senator Peleg Hartington, of Brampton. This is Will Wetherell, Peleg, — from Coniston — you understand."

The senator took one hand from his pocket.

"How be *you?*" he said. Mr. Bixby was once more pulling down on his shoulder.

"H-haow was it here?" he demanded.

"Almighty funny," answered Senator Hartington, sadly, and waved at the lobby. "There wahn't standin' room in the place."

"Jethro Bass Republican Club come and packed the entrance," explained Mr. Bixby with a wink. "You understand, Will? Go on, Peleg."

"Sidewalk *and* street, too," continued Mr. Hartington, slowly. "First come along Ball of Towles, hollerin' like blazes. They crumpled him all up and lost him. Next come old man Duncan himself."

"Will kep' Duncan," Mr. Bixby interjected.

"That was wholly an accident," exclaimed Mr. Wetherell, angrily.

"Will wahn't born in the country," said Mr. Bixby.

Mr. Hartington bestowed on the storekeeper a mournful look, and continued: —

"Never seed Duncan sweatin' before. He didn't seem to grasp why the boys was there."

"Didn't seem to understand," put in Mr. Bixby, sympathetically.

"'For God's sake, gentlemen,' says he, 'let me in! The Truro Bill!' 'The Truro Bill hain't in the thea'tre, Mr. Duncan,' says Dan Everett. Cussed if I didn't come near laughin'. 'That's "Uncle Tom's Cabin," Mr. Duncan,' says Dan. 'You're a dam fool,' says Duncan. I didn't know he was profane. 'Make room for Mr. Duncan,' says Dan, 'he wants to see the show.' 'I'm a-goin' to see you in jail for this, Everett,' says Duncan. They let him push in about half a rod, and they swallowed *him*. He was makin' such a noise that they had to close the doors of the thea'tre — so's not to disturb the play-actors."

"You understand," said Mr. Bixby to Wetherell. Whereupon he gave another shake to Mr. Hartington, who had relapsed into a sort of funereal meditation.

"Well," resumed that personage, "there was some more come, hollerin' about the Truro Bill. Not many. Guess they'll all have to git their wimmen-folks to press their clothes to-morrow.   Then Duncan wanted to git out again, but 'twan't ex'actly convenient.   Callated he was suffo-catin' — seemed to need air.   Little mite limp when he broke loose, Duncan was."

The Honorable Peleg stopped again, as if he were over-come by the recollection of Mr. Duncan's plight.

"Er — er — Peleg ! "

Mr. Hartington started.

"What'd they do? — what'd they do ? "

"Do ? "

"How'd they git notice to 'em ? "

"Oh," said Mr. Hartington, "cussed if that *wahn't* funny.   Let's see, where was I ?   After a while they went over t'other side of the street, talkin' sly, waitin' for the act to end.   But goldarned if it ever did end."

For once Mr. Bixby didn't seem to understand.

"D-didn't end ? "

"No," explained Mr. Hartington ; "seems they hitched a kind of nigger minstrel show right on to it — banjos and thingumajigs in front of the curtain while they was chang-in' scenes, *and* they hitched the second act right on to that.   Nobody come out of the thea'tre at all.   Funny notion, wahn't it ? "

Mr. Bixby's face took on a look of extreme cunning. He smiled broadly and poked Mr. Wetherell in an ex-tremely sensitive portion of his ribs.   On such occasions the nasal quality of Bijah's voice seemed to grow.

"You see ? " he said.

"Know that little man, Gibbs, don't ye ? " inquired Mr. Hartington.

"Airley Gibbs, hain't it ?   Runs a livery business daown to Rutgers, on Lovejoy's railroad," replied Mr. Bixby, promptly.   "I know him.   Knew old man Gibbs well's I do you.   Mean cuss."

"This Airley's smart — wahn't quite smart enough, though.   His bright idea come a little mite late.   Hunted up old Christy, got the key to his law office right here in the Duncan Block, went up through the skylight, clumb down to the roof of Randall's store next door, shinned up the lightnin' rod on t'other side, and stuck his head plump into the Opery House window."

" I want to know ! " ejaculated Mr. Bixby.

" Somethin' terrible pathetic was goin' on on the stage," resumed Mr. Hartington, "the folks didn't see him at first, — they was all cryin' and everythin' was still, but Airley wahn't affected. As quick as he got his breath he hollered right out loud's he could : ' The Truro Bill's up in the House, boys. We're skun if you don't git thar quick.' Then they tell me the lightnin' rod give way ; anyhow, he came down on Randall's gravel roof considerable hard, I take it."

Mr. Hartington, apparently, had an aggravating way of falling into mournful revery and of forgetting his subject. Mr. Bixby was forced to jog him again.

" Yes, they did," he said, " they did. They come out like the thea'tre was afire. There was some delay in gettin' to the street, but not much — not much. All the Republican Clubs in the state couldn't have held 'em then, and the profanity they used wahn't especially edifyin'."

" Peleg's a deacon — you understand," said Mr. Bixby. " Say, Peleg, where was Al Lovejoy ? "

" Lovejoy come along with the first of 'em. Must have hurried some — they tell me he was settin' way down in front alongside of Alvy Hopkins's gal, and when Airley hollered out she screeched *and* clutched on to Al, and Al said somethin' he hadn't ought to and tore off one of them pink gew-gaws she was covered with. He was the *maddest* man I ever see. Some of the club was crowded inside, behind the seats, standin' up to see the show. Al was so anxious to git through he hit Si Dudley in the mouth — injured him some, I guess. Pity, wahn't it ? "

" Si hain't in politics, you understand," said Mr. Bixby. " Callate Si paid to git in there, didn't he, Peleg? "

" Callate he did," assented Senator Hartington.

A long and painful pause followed. There seemed, indeed, nothing more to be said. The sound of applause floated out of the Opera House doors, around which the remaining loiterers were clustered.

" Goin' in, be you, Peleg ? " inquired Mr. Bixby.

Mr. Hartington shook his head.

" Will and me had a notion to see somethin' of the show," said Mr. Bixby, almost apologetically. "I kep' my ticket."

"Well," said Mr. Hartington, reflectively, "I guess you'll find some of the show left. That hain't b'en hurt much, so far as I can ascertain."

*   *   *   *   *   *   *

The next afternoon, when Mr. Isaac D. Worthington happened to be sitting alone in the office of the Truro Railroad at the capital, there came a knock at the door, and Mr. Bijah Bixby entered. Now, incredible as it may seem, Mr. Worthington did not know Mr. Bixby — or rather, did not remember him. Mr. Worthington had not had at that time much of an experience in politics, and he did not possess a very good memory for faces.

Mr. Bixby, who had, as we know, a confidential and winning manner, seated himself in a chair very close to Mr. Worthington — somewhat to that gentleman's alarm.

"How be you?" said Bijah, "I-I've got a little bill here — you understand."

Mr. Worthington didn't understand, and he drew his chair away from Mr. Bixby's.

"I don't know anything about it, sir," answered the president of the Truro Railroad, indignantly; "this is neither the manner nor the place to present a bill. I don't want to see it."

Mr. Bixby moved his chair up again. "Callate you will want to see this bill, Mr. Worthington," he insisted, not at all abashed. "Jethro Bass sent it — you understand — it's *engrossed*."

Whereupon Mr. Bixby drew from his capacious pocket a roll, tied with white ribbon, and pressed it into Mr. Worthington's hands. It was the Truro Franchise Bill.

It is safe to say that Mr. Worthington understood.

CHAPTER XVI

"CYNTHIA LOVED YOU"

THERE are certain instruments used by scientists so delicate that they have to be wrapped in cotton wool and kept in dustless places, and so sensitive that the slightest shock will derange them. And there are certain souls which cannot stand the jars of life — souls created to register thoughts and sentiments too fine for those of coarser construction. Such was the soul of the storekeeper of Coniston. Whether or not he was one of those immortalized in the famous Elegy, it is not for us to say. A celebrated poet who read the letters to the *Guardian* — at Miss Lucretia Penniman's request — has declared Mr. Wetherell to have been a genius. He wrote those letters, as we know, after he had piled his boxes and rolled his barrels into place; after he had added up the columns in his ledger and recorded, each week, the small but ever increasing deficit which he owed to Jethro Bass. Could he have been removed from the barrels and the ledgers, and the debts and the cares and the implications, what might we have had from his pen? That will never be known.

We left him in the lobby of the Opera House, but he did not go in to see the final act of "Uncle Tom's Cabin." He made his way, alone, back to the hotel, slipped in by a side entrance, and went directly to his room, where Cynthia found him, half an hour later, seated by the open window in the dark.

"Aren't you well, Dad?" she asked anxiously. "Why didn't you come to see the play?"

"I — I was detained Cynthia," he said. "Yes — I am well."

202

She sat down beside him and felt his forehead and his hands, and the events of the evening which were on her lips to tell him remained unspoken.

"You ought not to have left Coniston," she said; "the excitement is too much for you. We will go back to-morrow."

"Yes, Cynthia, we will go back to-morrow."

"In the morning?"

"On the early train," said Wetherell, "and now you must go to sleep."

"I am glad," said Cynthia, as she kissed him good night. "I have enjoyed it here, and I am grateful to Uncle Jethro for bringing us, but — but I like Coniston best."

William Wetherell could have slept but a few hours. When he awoke the sparrows were twittering outside, the fresh cool smells of the morning were coming in at his windows, and the sunlight was just striking across the roofs through the green trees of the Capitol Park. The remembrance of a certain incident of the night before crept into his mind, and he got up and drew on his clothes and thrust his few belongings into the carpet-bag, and knocked on Cynthia's door. She was already dressed, and her eyes rested searchingly on his face.

"Dad, you aren't well. I know it," she said.

But he denied that he was not.

Her belongings were in a neat little bundle under her arm. But when she went to put them in the bag she gave an exclamation, knelt down, took everything out that he had packed, and folded each article over again with amazing quickness. Then she made a rapid survey of the room lest she had forgotten anything, closed the bag, and they went out and along the corridor. But when Wetherell turned to go down the stairs, she stopped him.

"Aren't you going to say goodby to Uncle Jethro?"

"I—I would rather go on and get in the train, Cynthia," he said. "Jethro will understand."

Cynthia was worried, but she did not care to leave him; and she led him, protesting, into the dining room. He had a sinking fear that they might meet Jethro there, but only a few big-boned countrymen were scattered about, attended by sleepy waitresses. Lest Cynthia might suspect how his head was throbbing, Wetherell tried bravely to eat his breakfast. He did not know that she had gone out, while they were waiting, and written a note to Jethro, explaining that her father was ill, and that they were going back to Coniston. After breakfast, when they went to the desk, the clerk stared at them in astonishment.

"Going, Mr. Wetherell?" he exclaimed.

"I find that I have to get back," stammered the storekeeper. "Will you tell me the amount of my bill?"

"Judge Bass gave me instructions that he would settle that."

"It is very kind of Mr. Bass," said Wetherell, "but I prefer to pay it myself."

The man hesitated.

"The judge will be very angry, Mr. Wetherell."

"Kindly give me the bill."

The clerk made it out and handed it over in silence. Wetherell had in his pocket the money from several contributions to the *Guardian*, and he paid him. Then they set out for the station, bought their tickets and hurried past the sprinkling of people there. The little train for Truro was standing under the sheds, the hissing steam from the locomotive rising perpendicular in the still air of the morning, and soon they were settled in one of the straight-backed seats. The car was almost empty, for few people were going up that day, and at length, after what seemed an eternity of waiting, they started, and soon were in the country once more — in that wonderful Truro valley with its fruit trees and its clover scents; with its sparkling stream that tumbled through the passes and mirrored between green meadow-banks the blue and white of the sky. How hungrily they drank in the freshness of it.

They reached Truro village at eleven. Outside the little tavern there, after dinner, the green stage was drawn up; and Tom the driver cracked his long whip over the Morgan leaders and they started, swaying in the sand ruts and jolting over the great stones that cropped out of the road. Up they climbed, through narrow ways in the forest — ways hedged with alder and fern and sumach and wild grape, adorned with oxeye daisies and tiger lilies, and the big purple flowers which they knew and loved so well. They passed, too, wild lakes overhung with primeval trees, where the iris and the water-lily grew among the fallen trunks and the water-fowl called to each other across the blue stretches. And at length, when the sun was beginning visibly to fall, they came out into an open cut on the western side and saw again the long line of Coniston once more against the sky.

"Dad," said Cynthia, as she gazed, "don't you love it better than any other place in the world?"

He did. But he could not answer her.

An hour later, from the hilltops above Isaac Worthington's mills, they saw the terraced steeple of Brampton church, and soon the horses were standing with drooping heads and wet sides in front of Mr. Sherman's tavern in Brampton Street; and Lem Hallowell, his honest face aglow with joy, was lifting Cynthia out of the coach as if she were a bundle of feathers.

"Upon my word," he cried, "this is a little might sudden! What's the matter with the capital, Will? Too wicked and sophisticated down thar to suit ye?" By this time, Wetherell, too, had reached the ground, and as Lem Hallowell gazed into his face the laughter in his own died away and gave place to a look of concern. "Don't wonder ye come back," he said, "you're as white as Moses's hoss."

"He isn't feeling very well, Lem;" said Cynthia.

"Jest tuckered, that's all," answered Lem; "you git him right into the stage, Cynthy, I won't be long. Hurry them things off, Tom," he called, and himself seized a huge crate from the back of the coach and flung it on his shoulder. He had his cargo on in a jiffy, clucked to his horses, and they turned into the familiar road to Coniston just as the sun was dipping behind the south end of the mountain.

"They'll be surprised some, and disappointed some," said Lem, cheerily; "they was kind of plannin' a little celebration when you come back, Will — you and Cynthy. Amandy Hatch was a-goin' to bake a cake, and the minister was callatin' to say some word of welcome. Wahn't goin' to be anything grand — jest homelike. But you was right to come if you was tuckered. I guess Cynthy fetched you. Rias he kep' store and done it well, — brisker'n I ever see him, Rias was. Wait till I put some of them things back, and make you more comfortable, Will."

He moved a few parcels and packages from Wetherell's feet and glanced at Cynthia as he did so. The mountain cast its vast blue shadow over forest and pasture, and above the pines the white mist was rising from Coniston Water — rising in strange shapes. Lem's voice seemed to William Wetherell to have given way to a world-wide silence, in the midst of which he sought vainly for Cynthia and the stage driver. Most extraordinary of all, out of the silence and the void came the checker-paned windows of the store at Coniston, then the store itself, with the great oaks bending over it, then the dear familiar faces, — Moses and Amandy, Eph Prescott limping toward them, and little Rias Richardson in an apron with a scoop shovel in his hand, and many others. They were not smiling at the storekeeper's return — they looked very grave. Then somebody lifted him tenderly from the stage and said: —

"Don't you worry a mite, Cynthy. Jest tuckered, that's all."

William Wetherell was "just tuckered." The great Dr. Coles, authority on pulmonary troubles, who came all the way from Boston, could give no better verdict than that. It was Jethro Bass who had induced Dr. Coles to come to Coniston — much against the great man's inclination, and to the detriment of his patients: Jethro who, on receiving Cynthia's note, had left the capital on the next train and had come to Coniston, and had at once gone to Boston for the specialist.

"I do not know why I came," said the famous physician to Dr. Abraham Rowell of Tarleton, "I never shall know. There is something about that man Jethro Bass which compels you to do his will. He has a most extraordinary personality. Is this storekeeper a great friend of his?"

"The only intimate friend he had in the world," answered Dr. Rowell; "none of us could ever understand it. And as for the girl, Jethro Bass worships her."

"If nursing could cure him, I'd trust her to do it. She's a natural-born nurse."

The two physicians were talking in low tones in the little garden behind the store when Jethro came out of the doorway.

"He looks as if he were suffering, too," said the Boston physician, and he walked toward Jethro and laid a hand upon his shoulders. "I give him until winter, my friend," said Dr. Coles.

Jethro Bass sat down on the doorstep — on that same millstone where he had talked with Cynthia many years before — and was silent for a long while. The doctor was used to scenes of sorrow, but the sight of this man's suffering unnerved him, and he turned from it.

"D-doctor?" said Jethro, at last.

The doctor turned again. "Yes?" he said.

"D-doctor — if Wetherell hadn't b'en to the capital — would he have lived — if he hadn't been to the capital?"

"My friend," said Dr. Coles, "if Mr. Wetherell had always lived in a warm house, and had always been well fed, and helped over the rough places and shielded from the storms, he might have lived — longer. It is a marvel to me that he has lived so long."

And then the doctor went way, back to Boston. Many times in his long professional life had the veil been lifted for him — a little. But as he sat in the train he said to himself that in this visit to the hamlet of Coniston he had had the strangest glimpse of all.

William Wetherell rallied, as Dr. Coles had predicted,

from that first sharp attack, and one morning they brought
up a reclining chair which belonged to Mr. Satterlee,
the minister, and set it in the window.   There, in the still
days of the early autumn, Wetherell looked down upon the
garden he had grown to love, and listened to the song
of Coniston Water.   There Cynthia, who had scarcely
left his side, read to him from Keats and Shelley and
Tennyson — yet the thought grew on her that he did not
seem to hear.   Even that wonderful passage of Milton's,
beginning " So sinks the day-star in the ocean bed, " which
he always used to beg her to repeat, did not seem to move
him now.

The neighbors came and sat with him, but he would
not often speak.   Cheery Lem Hallowell and his wife,
and Cousin Ephraim, to talk about the war, hobbling
slowly up the stairs — for rheumatism had been added
to that trouble of the Wilderness bullet now, and Ephraim
was getting along in years ; and Rias Richardson stole up
in his carpet slippers ; and Moses, after his chores were
done, and Amandy with her cakes and delicacies, which
he left untouched — though Amandy never knew it.   Yes,
and Jethro came.   Day by day he would come silently
into the room, and sit silently for a space, and go as
silently out of it.   The farms were neglected now on
Thousand Acre Hill.   William Wetherell would take his
hand, and speak to him, but do no more than that.

There were times when Cynthia leaned over him, listening as he breathed to know whether he slept or were
awake.   If he were not sleeping, he would speak her name:
he repeated it often in those days, as though the sound
of it gave him comfort ; and he would fall asleep with
it on his lips, holding her hand, and thinking, perhaps,
of that other Cynthia who had tended and nursed and
shielded him in other days.   Then she would steal
down the stairs to Jethro on the doorstep : to Jethro
who would sit there for hours at a time, to the wonder
and awe of his neighbors.   Although they knew that he
loved the storekeeper as he loved no other man, his was
a grief that they could not understand.

Cynthia used to go to Jethro in the garden. Sorrow had brought them very near together ; and though she had loved him before, now he had become her reliance and her refuge. The first time Cynthia saw him, when the worst of the illness had passed and the strange and terrifying apathy had come, she had hidden her head on his shoulder and wept there. Jethro kept that coat, with the tear stains on it, to his dying day, and never wore it again.

"Sometimes — sometimes I think if he hadn't gone to the capital, Cynthy, this mightn't hev come," he said to her once.

"But the doctor said that didn't matter, Uncle Jethro," she answered, trying to comfort him. She, too, believed that something had happened at the capital.

"N-never spoke to you about anything there — n-never spoke to you, Cynthia ?"

"No, never," she said. "He — he hardly speaks at all, Uncle Jethro."

One bright morning after the sun had driven away the frost, when the sumachs and maples beside Coniston Water were aflame with red, Rias Richardson came stealing up the stairs and whispered something to Cynthia.

"Dad," she said, laying down her book, "it's Mr. Merrill. Will you see him ?"

William Wetherell gave her a great fright. He started up from his pillows, and seized her wrist with a strength which she had not thought remained in his fingers.

"Mr. Merrill !" he cried — "Mr. Merrill here !"

"Yes," answered Cynthia, agitatedly, "he's downstairs — in the store."

"Ask him to come up," said Wetherell, sinking back again, "ask him to come up."

Cynthia, as she stood in the passage, was of two minds about it. She was thoroughly frightened, and went first to the garden to ask Jethro's advice. But Jethro, so Milly Skinner said, had gone off half an hour before, and did not know that Mr. Merrill had arrived. Cynthia went back again to her father.

P

"Where's Mr. Merrill?" asked Wetherell.

"Dad, do you think you ought to see him? He — he might excite you."

"I insist upon seeing him, Cynthia."

William Wetherell had never said anything like that before. But Cynthia obeyed him, and presently led Mr. Merrill into the room. The kindly little railroad president was very serious now. The wasted face of the store-keeper, enhanced as it was by the beard, gave Mr. Merrill such a shock that he could not speak for a few moments — he who rarely lacked for cheering words on any occasion. A lump rose in his throat as he went over and stood by the chair and took the sick man's hand.

"I am glad you came, Mr. Merrill," said Wetherell, simply, "I wanted to speak to you. Cynthia, will you leave us alone for a few minutes?"

Cynthia went, troubled and perplexed, wondering at the change in him. He had had something on his mind — now she was sure of it — something which Mr. Merrill might be able to relieve.

It was Mr. Merrill who spoke first when she was gone.

"I was coming up to Brampton," he said, "and Tom Collins, who drives the Truro coach, told me you were sick. I had not heard of it."

Mr. Merrill, too, had something on his mind, and did not quite know how to go on. There was in William Wetherell, as he sat in the chair with his eyes fixed on his visitor's face, a dignity which Mr. Merrill had not seen before — had not thought the man might possess.

"I was coming to see you, anyway," Mr. Merrill said. "I did you a wrong — though as God judges me, I did not think of it at the time. It was not until Alexander Duncan spoke to me last week that I thought of it at all."

"Yes," said Wetherell.

"You see," continued Mr. Merrill, wiping his brow, for he found the matter even more difficult than he had imagined, — "it was not until Duncan told me how you had acted in his library that I guessed the truth — that I remembered myself how you had acted. I knew that you were not mixed up in politics, but I also knew that you were an intimate friend of Jethro's, and I thought that you had been let into the secret of the woodchuck session. I don't defend the game of politics as it is played, Mr. Wetherell, but all of us who are friends of Jethro's are generally willing to lend a hand in any little manœuvre that is going on, and have a practical joke when we can. It was not until I saw you sitting there beside Duncan that the idea occurred to me. It didn't make a great deal of difference whether Duncan or Lovejoy got to the House or not, provided they didn't learn of the matter too early, because some of their men had been bought off that day. It suited Jethro's sense of humor to play the game that way — and it was very effective. When I saw you there beside Duncan I remembered that he had spoken about the *Guardian* letters, and the notion occurred to me to get him to show you his library. I have explained to him that you were innocent. I — I hope you haven't been worrying."

William Wetherell sat very still for a while, gazing out of the window, but a new look had come into his eyes.

" Jethro Bass did not know that you — that you had — used me ? " he asked at length.

" No," replied Mr. Merrill, thickly, "no. He didn't know a thing about it — he doesn't know it now, I believe."

A smile came upon Wetherell's face, but Mr. Merrill could not look at it.

" You have made me very happy," said the storekeeper, tremulously. " I — I have no right to be proud — I have taken his money — he has supported my daughter and myself all these years. But he had never asked me to — to do anything, and I liked to think that he never would."

Mr. Merrill could not speak. The tears were streaming down his cheeks.

" I want you to promise me, Mr. Merrill," he went on presently, " I want you to promise me that you will never speak to Jethro of this, or to my daughter, Cynthia."

Mr. Merrill merely nodded his head in assent. Still he could not speak.

"They might think it was this that caused my death. It was not. I know very well that I am worn out, and that I should have gone soon in any case. And I must leave Cynthia to him. He loves her as his own child."

William Wetherell, his faith in Jethro restored, was facing death as he had never faced life. Mr. Merrill was greatly affected.

"You must not speak of dying, Wetherell," said he, brokenly. "Will you forgive me?"

"There is nothing to forgive, now that you have explained matters, Mr. Merrill," said the storekeeper, and he smiled again. "If my fibre had been a little tougher, this thing would never have happened. There is only one more request I have to make. And that is, to assure Mr. Duncan, from me, that I did not detain him purposely."

"I will see him on my way to Boston," answered Mr. Merrill.

Then Cynthia was called. She was waiting anxiously in the passage for the interview to be ended, and when she came in one glance at her father's face told her that he was happier. She, too, was happier.

"I wish you would come every day, Mr. Merrill," she said, when they descended into the garden after the three had talked awhile. "It is the first time since he fell ill that he seems himself."

Mr. Merrill's answer was to take her hand and pat it. He sat down on the millstone and drew a deep breath of that sparkling air and sighed, for his memory ran back to his own innocent boyhood in the New England country. He talked to Cynthia until Jethro came.

"I have taken a fancy to this girl, Jethro," said the little railroad president, "I believe I'll steal her; a fellow can't have too many of 'em, you know. I'll tell you one thing, — you won't keep her always shut up here in Coniston. She's much too good to waste on the desert air." Perhaps Mr. Merrill, too, had been thinking of the Elegy that morning. "I don't mean to run down Coniston — it's one of the most beautiful places I ever saw. But seriously, Jethro, you and Wetherell ought to send her to

school in Boston after a while. She's about the age of
my girls, and she can live in my house. Ain't I right?"

" D-don't know but what you be, Steve," Jethro answered
slowly.

" I am right," declared Mr. Merrill, " you'll back me
in this, I know it. Why, she's like your own daughter.
You remember what I say. I *mean* it. — "What are you
thinking about, Cynthia?"

" I couldn't leave Dad and Uncle Jethro," she said.

" Why, bless your soul," said Mr. Merrill, " bring Dad
along. We'll find room for him. And I guess Uncle
Jethro will get to Boston twice a month if you're there."

And Mr. Merrill got into the buggy with Mr. Sherman
and drove away to Brampton, thinking of many things.

" S-Steve's a good man," said Jethro. " C-come up
here from Brampton to see your father — did he?"

" Yes," answered Cynthia, " he is very kind." She
was about to tell Jethro what a strange difference this
visit had made in her father's spirits, but some instinct
kept her silent. She knew that Jethro had never ceased
to reproach himself for inviting Wetherell to the capital,
and she was sure that something had happened there
which had disturbed her father and brought on that fearful apathy. But the apathy was dispelled now, and she
shrank from giving Jethro pain by mentioning the fact.

He never knew, indeed, until many years afterward,
what had brought Stephen Merrill to Coniston. When
Jethro went up the stairs that afternoon, he found William
Wetherell alone, looking out over the garden with a new
peace and contentment in his eyes. Jethro drew breath
when he saw that look, as if a great load had been lifted
from his heart.

" F-feelin' some better to-day, Will?" he said.

" I am well again, Jethro," replied the storekeeper,
pressing Jethro's hand for the first time in months.

" S-soon be, Will," said Jethro, " s-soon be."

Wetherell, who was not speaking of the welfare of the
body, did not answer.

" Jethro," he said presently, " there is a little box lying

in the top of my trunk over there in the corner.   Will you
get it for me ? ''

Jethro rose and opened the rawhide trunk and handed
the little rosewood box to his friend.   Wetherell took it
and lifted the lid reverently, with that same smile on his
face and far-off look in his eyes, and drew out a small
daguerreotype in a faded velvet frame.   He gazed at the
picture a long time, and then he held it out to Jethro ;
and Jethro looked at it, and his hand trembled.

It was a picture of Cynthia Ware.   And who can say
what emotions it awoke in Jethro's heart ?   She was older
than the Cynthia he had known, and yet she did not seem
so.   There was the same sweet, virginal look in the gray
eyes, and the same exquisite purity in the features.   He
saw her again — as if it were yesterday — walking in the
golden green light under the village maples, and himself
standing in the tannery door ; he saw the face under the
poke bonnet on the road to Brampton, and heard the
thrush singing in the woods.   And — if he could only
blot out that scene from his life ! — remembered her, a
transformed Cynthia, — remembered that face in the lan-
tern-light when he had flung back the hood that shaded
it ; and that hair which he had kissed, wet, then, from the
sleet.   Ah, God, for that briefest of moments she had
been his !

So he stared at the picture as it lay in the palm of his
hand, and forgot him who had been her husband.   But at
length he started, as from a dream, and gave it back to
Wetherell, who was watching him.   Her name had never
been mentioned between the two men, and yet she had
been the one woman in the world to both.

" It is strange," said William Wetherell, " it is strange
that I should have had but two friends in my life, and that
she should have been one and you the other.   She found
me destitute and brought me back to life and married me,
and cared for me until she died.   And after that — you
cared for me."

" You — you mustn't think of that, Will, 'twahn't much
what I did — no more than any one else would hev done."

"It was everything," answered the storekeeper, simply ; "each of you came between me and destruction. There is something that I have always meant to tell you, Jethro, — something that it may be a comfort for you to know. Cynthia loved you."

Jethro Bass did not answer. He got up and stood in the window, looking out.

"When she married me," Wetherell continued steadily, "she told me that there was one whom she had never been able to drive from her heart. And one summer evening, — how well I recall it! — we were walking under the trees on the Mall and we met my old employer, Mr. Judson, the jeweller. He put me in mind of the young country-man who had come in to buy a locket, and I asked her if she knew you. Strange that I should have remembered your name, wasn't it? It was then that she led me to a bench and confessed that you were the man whom she could not forget. I used to hate you then — as much as was in me to hate. I hated and feared you when I first came to Coniston. But now I can tell you — I can even be happy in telling you."

Jethro Bass groaned. He put his hand to his throat as though he were stifling. Many, many years ago he had worn the locket there. And now? Now an impulse seized him, and he yielded to it. He thrust his hand in his coat and drew out a cowhide wallet, and from the wallet the oval locket itself. There it was, tarnished with age, but with that memorable inscription still legible, — "Cynthy, from Jethro"; not Cynthia, but Cynthy. How the years fell away as he read it! He handed it in silence to the storekeeper, and in silence went to the window again. Jethro Bass was a man who could find no outlet for his agony in speech or tears.

"Yes," said Wetherell, "I thought you would have kept it. Dear, dear, how well I remember it! And I remember how I patronized you when you came into the shop. I believed I should live to be something in the world, then. Yes, she loved you, Jethro. I can die more easily now that I have told you — it has been on my mind all these years."

The locket fell open in William Wetherell's hand, for the clasp had become worn with time, and there was a picture of little Cynthia within: of little Cynthia,—not so little now, — a photograph taken in Brampton the year before. Wetherell laid it beside the daguerreotype.

"She looks like her, he said aloud; "but the child is more vigorous, more human — less like a spirit. I have always thought of Cynthia Ware as a spirit."

Jethro turned at the words, and came and stood looking over Wetherell's shoulder at the pictures of mother and daughter. In the rosewood box was a brooch and a gold ring — Cynthia Ware's wedding ring — and two small slips of yellow paper. William Wetherell opened one of these, disclosing a little braid of brown hair. He folded the paper again and laid it in the locket, and handed that to Jethro.

"It is all I have to give you," he said, "but I know that you will cherish it, and cherish her, when I am gone. She — she has been a daughter to both of us."

"Yes," said Jethro, "I will."

William Wetherell lived but a few days longer. They laid him to rest at last in the little ground which Captain Timothy Prescott had hewn out of the forest with his axe, where Captain Timothy himself lies under his slate head-stone with the quaint lettering of bygone days. That same autumn Jethro Bass made a pilgrimage to Boston, and now Cynthia Ware sleeps there, too, beside her husband, amid the scenes she loved so well.

BOOK II

CHAPTER I

IN THE TANNERY HOUSE

ONE day, in the November following William Wetherell's death, Jethro Bass astonished Coniston by moving to the little cottage in the village which stood beside the disused tannery, and which had been his father's. It was known as the tannery house. His reasons for this step, when at length discovered, were generally commended: they were, in fact, a disinclination to leave a girl of Cynthia's tender age alone on Thousand Acre Hill while he journeyed on his affairs about the country. The Rev. Mr. Satterlee, gaunt, red-faced, but the six feet of him a man and a Christian, from his square-toed boots to the bleaching yellow hair around his temples, offered to become her teacher. For by this time Cynthia had exhausted the resources of the little school among the birches.

The four years of her life in the tannery house which are now briefly to be chronicled were, for her, full of happiness and peace. Though the young may sorrow, they do not often mourn. Cynthia missed her father; at times, when the winds kept her wakeful at night, she wept for him. But she loved Jethro Bass and served him with a devotion that filled his heart with strange ecstasies — yes, and forebodings. In all his existence he had never known a love like this. He may have imagined it once, back in the bright days of his youth; but the dreams of its fulfilment had fallen far short of the exquisite touch of the reality in which he now spent his days at home. In summer, when she sat, in the face of all the conventions of the village, reading under the but-

217

ternut tree before the house, she would feel his eyes upon her, and the mysterious yearning in them would startle her. Often during her lessons with Mr. Satterlee in the parlor of the parsonage she would hear a noise outside and perceive Jethro leaning against the pillar. Both Cynthia and Mr. Satterlee knew that he was there, and both, by a kind of tacit agreement, ignored the circumstance.

Cynthia, in this period, undertook Jethro's education, too. She could have induced him to study the making of Latin verse by the mere asking. During those days which he spent at home, and which he had grown to value beyond price, he might have been seen seated on the ground with his back to the butternut tree while Cynthia read aloud from the well-worn books which had been her father's treasures, — books that took on marvels of meaning from her lips. Cynthia's powers of selection were not remarkable at this period, and perhaps it was as well that she never knew the effect of the various works upon the hitherto untamed soul of her listener. Milton and Tennyson and Longfellow awoke in him by their very music troubled and half-formed regrets ; Carlyle's " Frederick the Great" set up tumultuous imaginings ; but the " Life of Jackson" (as did the story of Napoleon long ago) stirred all that was masterful in his blood. Unlettered as he was, Jethro had a power which often marks the American of action — a singular grasp of the application of any sentence or paragraph to his own life ; and often, about this time, he took away the breath of a judge or a senator by flinging at them a chunk of Carlyle or Parton.

It was perhaps as well that Cynthia was not a woman at this time, and that she had grown up with him, as it were. His love, indeed, was that of a father for a daughter ; but it held within it as a core the revived love of his youth for Cynthia, her mother. Tender as were the manifestations of this love, Cynthia never guessed the fires within, for there was in truth something primeval in the fierceness of his passion. She was his now — his alone, to cherish and sweeten the declining years of his life, and when by a chance Jethro looked upon her and thought of the suitor who was to come in the fulness of her years, he burned with a hatred which it is given few men to feel. It was well for Jethro that these thoughts came not often.

Sometimes, in the summer afternoons, they took long drives through the town behind Jethro's white horse on business. "Jethro's gal," as Cynthia came to be affectionately called, held the reins while Jethro went in to talk to the men folk. One August evening found Cynthia thus beside a poplar in front of Amos Cuthbert's farmhouse, a poplar that shimmered green-gold in the late afternoon, and from the buggy-seat Cynthia looked down upon a thousand purple hilltops and mountain peaks of another state. The view aroused in the girl visions of the many wonders which life was to hold, and she did not hear the sharp voice beside her until the woman had spoken twice. Jethro came out in the middle of the conversation, nodded to Mrs. Cuthbert, and drove off.

"Uncle Jethro," asked Cynthia, presently, "what is a mortgage?"

Jethro struck the horse with the whip, an uncommon action with him, and the buggy was jerked forward sharply over the boulders.

"Er — who's b'en talkin' about mortgages, Cynthy?" he demanded.

"Mrs. Cuthbert said that when folks had mortgages held over them they had to take orders whether they liked them or not. She said that Amos had to do what you told him because there was a mortgage. That isn't so, is it?"

Jethro did not speak. Presently Cynthia laid her hand over his.

"Mrs. Cuthbert is a spiteful woman," she said. "I know the reason why people obey you — it's because you're so great. And Daddy used to tell me so."

A tremor shook Jethro's frame and the hand on which hers rested, and all the way down the mountain valleys to Coniston village he did not speak again. But Cynthia was used to his silences, and respected them.

To Ephraim Prescott, who, as the days went on, found it more and more difficult to sew harness on account of his rheumatism, Jethro was not only a great man but a hero. For Cynthia was vaguely troubled at having found one discontent. She was wont to entertain Ephraim on the days when his hands failed him, when he sat sunning himself before his door; and she knew that he was honest. "Who's b'en talkin' to you, Cynthia?" he cried. "Why, Jethro's the biggest man I know, and the best. I don't like to think where some of us would have b'en if he hadn't given us a lift."

"But he has enemies, Cousin Eph," said Cynthia, still troubled.

"What great man hain't?" exclaimed the soldier. "Jethro's enemies hain't worth thinkin' about."

The thought that Jethro had enemies was very painful to Cynthia, and she wanted to know who they were that she might show them a proper contempt if she met them. Lem Hallowell brushed aside the subject with his usual bluff humor, and pinched her cheek and told her not to trouble her head; Amanda Hatch dwelt upon the inherent weakness in the human race, and the Rev. Mr. Satterlee faced the question once, during a history lesson. The nation's heroes came into inevitable comparison with Jethro Bass. Was Washington so good a man? and would not Jethro have been as great as the Father of his Country if he had had the opportunities?

The answers sorely tried Mr. Satterlee's conscience, albeit he was not a man of the world. It set him thinking. He liked Jethro, this man of rugged power whose word had become law in the state. He knew best that side of him which Cynthia saw; and — if the truth be told — as a native of Coniston Mr. Satterlee felt in the bottom of his heart a certain pride in Jethro. The minister's opinions well represented the attitude of his time. He had not given thought to the subject — for such matters had come to be taken for granted. A politician now was a politician, his ways and standards set apart from those of other citizens, and not to be judged by men without the pale of public life. Mr. Satterlee in his limited vision did not then trace the matter to its source, did not reflect that Jethro Bass himself was almost wholly responsible in that state for the condition of politics and politicians. Coniston was proud of Jethro, prouder of him than ever since his last great victory in the Legislature, which brought the Truro Railroad through to Harwich and settled their towns-man more firmly than ever before in the seat of power. Every statesman who drove into their little mountain village and stopped at the tannery house made their blood beat faster. Senators came, and representatives, and judges, and governors, " to git their orders," as Rias Richardson briefly put it, and Jethro could make or un-make them at a word. Each was scanned from the store where Rias now reigned supreme, and from the harness shop across the road. Some drove away striving to bite from their lips the tell-tale smile which arose in spite of them; others tried to look happy, despite the sentence of doom to which they had listened.

Jethro Bass was indeed a great man to make such as these tremble or rejoice. When he went abroad with Cynthia awheel or afoot, some took off their hats — an unheard-of thing in Coniston. If he stopped at the store, they scanned his face for the mood he was in before venturing their remarks ; if he lingered for a moment in front of the house of Amanda Hatch, the whole village was advised of the circumstance before nightfall.

Two personages worthy of mention here visited the tannery house during the years that Cynthia lived with Jethro. The Honorable Heth Sutton drove over from Clovelly attended by his prime minister, Mr. Bijah Bixby. The Honorable Heth did not attempt to conceal the smile with which he went away, and he stopped at the store long enough to enable Rias to produce certain refreshments from depths unknown to the United States Internal Revenue authorities. Mr. Sutton shook hands with every-body, including Jake Wheeler. Well he might. He came

to Coniston a private citizen, and drove away to all intents
and purposes a congressman: the darling wish of his life
realized after heaven knows how many caucuses and conventions of disappointment, when Jethro had judged it
expedient for one reason or another that a north countryman should go. By the time the pair reached Brampton,
Chamberlain Bixby was introducing his chief as Congressman Sutton, and by this title he was known for many
years to come.

Another day, when the snow lay in great billows on the
ground and filled the mountain valleys, when the pines
were rusty from the long winter, two other visitors drove
to Coniston in a two-horse sleigh. The sun was shining
brightly, the wind held its breath, and the noon-day warmth
was almost like that of spring. Those who know the mountain country will remember the joy of many such days. Cynthia, standing in the sun on the porch, breathing deep of
the pure air, recognized, as the sleigh drew near, the somewhat portly gentleman driving, and the young woman
beside him regally clad in furs who looked patronizingly
at the tannery house as she took the reins. The young
woman was Miss Cassandra Hopkins, and the portly
gentleman, the Honorable Alva himself, patron of the
drama, who had entered upon his governorship and now
wished to be senator.

"Jethro Bass home?" he called out.

"Mr. Bass is home," answered Cynthia. The girl in
the sleigh murmured something, laughing a little, and
Cynthia flushed. Mr. Hopkins gave a somewhat peremp-
tory knock at the door and was admitted by Millicent
Skinner, but Cynthia stood staring at Cassandra in the
sleigh, some instinct warning her of a coming skirmish.

"Do you live here all the year round?"

"Of course," said Cynthia.

Miss Cassandra shrugged as though that were beyond
her comprehension.

"I'd die in a place like this," she said. "No balls, or
theatres. Doesn't your father take you around the
state?"

"My father's dead," said Cynthia.

"Oh ! Your name's Cynthia Wetherell, isn't it ? You know Bob Worthington, don't you ? He's gone to Harvard now, but he was a great friend of mine at Andover."

Cynthia didn't answer. It would not be fair to say that she felt a pang, though it might add to the romance of this narrative. But her dislike for the girl in the sleigh decidedly increased. How was she, in her inexperience, to know that the radiant beauty in furs was what the boys at Phillips Andover called an "old stager."

"So you live with Jethro Bass," was Miss Cassandra's next remark. "He's rich enough to take you round the state and give you everything you want."

"I have everything I want," replied Cynthia.

"I shouldn't call living here having everything I wanted," declared Miss Hopkins, with a contemptuous glance at the tannery house.

"I suppose you wouldn't," said Cynthia.

Miss Hopkins was nettled. She was out of humor that day, besides she shared some of her father's political ambition. If he went to Washington, she went too.

"Didn't you know Jethro Bass was rich ? " she demanded, imprudently. "Why, my father gave twenty thousand dollars to be governor, and Jethro Bass must have got half of it."

Cynthia's eyes were of that peculiar gray which, lighted by love or anger, once seen, are never forgotten. One hand was on the dashboard of the cutter, the other had seized the seat. Her voice was steady, and the three words she spoke struck Miss Hopkins with startling effect.

Miss Hopkins's breath was literally taken away, and for once she found no retort. Let it be said for her that this was a new experience with a new creature. A demure country girl turn into a wildcat before her very eyes ! Perhaps it was as well for both that the door of the house opened and the Honorable Alva interrupted their talk, and without so much as a glance at Cynthia he got hurriedly into the sleigh and drove off. When Cynthia turned, the points of color still high in her cheeks and the light still ablaze in her eyes, she surprised Jethro gazing at her from the porch, and some sorrow she felt rather than beheld stopped the confession on her lips. It would be unworthy of her even to repeat such slander, and the color surged again into her face for very shame of her anger. Cassandra Hopkins had not been worthy of it.

Jethro did not speak, but slipped his hand into hers, and thus they stood for a long time gazing at the snow fields between the pines on the heights of Coniston.

The next summer was the first which the painter — pioneer of summer visitors there — spent at Coniston. He was an unsuccessful painter, who became, by a process which he himself does not to-day completely understand, a successful writer of novels. As a character, however, he himself confesses his inadequacy, and the chief interest in him for the readers of this narrative is that he fell deeply in love with Cynthia Wetherell at nineteen. It is fair to mention in passing that other young men were in love with Cynthia at this time, notably Eben Hatch — history repeating itself. Once, in a moment of madness, Eben confessed his love, the painter never did : and he has to this day a delicious memory which has made Cynthia the heroine of many of his stories. He boarded with Chester Perkins, and he was humored by the village as a harmless but amiable lunatic.

The painter had never conceived that a New England conscience and a temper of no mean proportions could dwell together in the body of a wood nymph. When he had first seen Cynthia among the willows by Coniston Water, he had thought her a wood nymph. But she scolded him for his impropriety with so unerring a choice of words that he fell in love with her intellect, too. He spent much of his time to the neglect of his canvases under the butternut tree in front of Jethro's house trying to persuade Cynthia to sit for her portrait ; and if Jethro himself had not overheard one of these arguments, the portrait never would have been painted. Jethro focussed a look upon the painter.

" Er — painter-man, be you ?   Paint Cynthy's picture ? "

"But I don't want to be painted, Uncle Jethro. I won't be painted!"

"H-how much for a good picture? Er — only want the best — only want the best."

The painter said a few things, with pardonable heat, to the effect — well, never mind the effect. His remarks made no impression whatever upon Jethro.

"Er — paint the picture — paint the picture, and then we'll talk about the price. Er — wait a minute."

He went into the house, and they heard him lumbering up the stairs. Cynthia sat with her back to the artist, pretending to read, but presently she turned to him.

"I'll never forgive you — never, as long as I live," she cried, "and I won't be painted!"

"N-not to please me, Cynthy?" It was Jethro's voice.

Her look softened. She laid down the book and went up to him on the porch and put her hand on his shoulder.

"Do you really want it so much as all that, Uncle Jethro?" she said.

"Callate I do, Cynthy," he answered. He held a bundle covered with newspaper in his hand, he looked down at Cynthia.

He seated himself on the edge of the porch and for the moment seemed lost in revery. Then he began slowly to unwrap the newspaper from the bundle: there were five layers of it, but at length he disclosed a bolt of cardinal cloth.

"Call this to mind, Cynthy?"

"Yes," she answered with a smile.

"H-how's this for the dress, Mr. Painter-man?" said Jethro, with a pride that was ill-concealed.

The painter started up from his seat and took the material in his hands and looked at Cynthia. He belonged to a city club where he was popular for his knack of devising costumes, and a vision of Cynthia as the daughter of a Doge of Venice arose before his eyes. Wonder of wonders, the daughter of a Doge discovered in a New England hill village! The painter seized his pad and pencil and with a few strokes, guided by inspiration,

Q

sketched the costume then and there and held it up to
Jethro, who blinked at it in astonishment. But Jethro
was suspicious of his own sensations.

"Er — well — Godfrey — g-guess that'll do." Then
came the involuntary: "W-wouldn't a-thought you had
it in you. How about it, Cynthy?" and he held it up
for her inspection.

"If you are pleased, it's all I care about, Uncle Jethro,"
she answered, and then, her face suddenly flushing, "You
must promise me on your honor that nobody in Coniston
shall know about it, 'Mr. Painter-man.'"

After this she always called him "Mr. Painter-man,"
— when she was pleased with him.

So the cardinal cloth was come to its usefulness at last.
It was inevitable that Sukey Kittredge, the village seam-
stress, should be taken into confidence. It was no small
thing to take Sukey into confidence, for she was the legitimate successor in more ways than one of Speedy Bates,
and much of Cynthia and the artist's ingenuity was spent
upon devising a form of oath which would hold Sukey
silent. Sukey, however, got no small consolation from
the sense of the greatness of the trust confided in her, and
of the uproar she could make in Coniston if she chose.
The painter, to do him justice, was the real dressmaker,
and did everything except cut the cloth and sew it together.
He sent to friends of his in the city for certain paste
jewels and ornaments, and one day Cynthia stood in the
old tannery shed — hastily transformed into a studio —
before a variously moved audience. Sukey, having ad-
justed the last pin, became hysterical over her handiwork,
Millicent Skinner stared open-mouthed, words having
failed her for once, and Jethro thrust his hands in his
pockets in a quiet ecstasy of approbation.

"A-always had a notion that cloth'd set you off,
Cynthy," said he, "er — next time I go to the state capital you come along — g-guess it'll surprise 'em some."

"I guess it would, Uncle Jethro," said Cynthia, laughing.

Jethro postponed two political trips of no small importance to be present at the painting of that picture, and he would sit silently by the hour in a corner of the shed watching every stroke of the brush.   Never stood Doge's daughter in her jewels and seed pearls amidst stranger surroundings, — the beam, and the centre post around which the old white horse had toiled in times gone by, and all the piled-up, disused machinery of forgotten days. And never was Venetian lady more unconscious of her environment than Cynthia.

The portrait was of the head and shoulders alone, and when he had given it the last touch, the painter knew that, for once in his life, he had done a good thing.   Never before, perhaps, had the fire of such inspiration been given him.   Jethro, who expressed himself in terms (for him) of great enthusiasm, was for going to Boston immediately to purchase a frame commensurate with the importance of such a work of art, but the artist had his own views on that subject and sent to New York for this also.

The day after the completion of the picture a rugged figure in rawhide boots and coonskin cap approached Chester Perkins's house, knocked at the door, and inquired for the "Painter-man."   It was Jethro.   The "Painter-man" forthwith went out into the rain behind the shed, where a somewhat curious colloquy took place.

"G-guess I'm willin' to pay you full as much as it's worth," said Jethro, producing a cowhide wallet.   "Er — what figure do you allow it comes to with the frame?"

The artist was past taking offence, since Jethro had long ago become for him an engrossing study.

"I will send you the bill for the frame, Mr. Bass," he said, "the picture belongs to Cynthia."

"Earn your livin' by paintin', don't you — earn your livin'?"

The painter smiled a little bitterly.

"No," he said, "if I did, I shouldn't be — alive.   Mr. Bass, have you ever done anything the pleasure of doing which was pay enough, and to spare?"

Jethro looked at him, and something very like admiration came into the face that was normally expressionless.

He put up his wallet a little awkwardly, and held out his hand more awkwardly.

" You be more of a feller than I thought for," he said, and strode off through the drizzle toward Coniston. The painter walked slowly to the kitchen, where Chester Perkins and his wife were sitting down to supper.

" Jethro got a mortgage on you, too ? " asked Chester.

The artist had his reward, for when the picture was hung at length in the little parlor of the tannery house it became a source of pride to Coniston second only to Jethro himself.

CHAPTER II

TIME passes, and the engines of the Truro Railroad are now puffing in and out of the yards of Worthington's mills in Brampton, and a fine layer of dust covers the old green stage which has worn the road for so many years over Truro Gap. If you are ever in Brampton, you can still see the stage, if you care to go into the back of what was once Jim Sanborn's livery stable, now owned by Mr. Sherman of the Brampton House.

Conventions and elections had come and gone, and the Honorable Heth Sutton had departed triumphantly to Washington, cheered by his neighbors in Clovelly. Chamberlain Bixby was left in charge there, supreme. Who could be more desirable as a member of Congress than Mr. Sutton, who had so ably served his party (and Jethro) by holding the House against the insurgents in the matter of the Truro Bill? Mr. Sutton was, moreover, a gentleman, an owner of cattle and land, a man of substance whom lesser men were proud to mention as a friend — a very hill-Rajah with stock in railroads and other enterprises, who owed allegiance and paid tribute alone to the Great Man of Coniston.

Mr. Sutton was one who would make himself felt even in the capital of the United States — felt and heard. And he had not been long in the Halls of Congress before he made a speech which rang under the very dome of the Capitol. So said the Brampton and Harwich papers, at least, though rivals and detractors of Mr. Sutton declared that they could find no matter in it which related to the subject of a bill, but that is neither here nor there. The

oration began with a lengthy tribute to the resources and
history of his state, and ended by a declaration that the
speaker was in Congress at no man's bidding, but as the
servant of the common people of his district.

Under the lamp of the little parlor in the tannery
house, Cynthia (who has now arrived at the very serious
age of nineteen) was reading the papers to Jethro and
came upon Mr. Sutton's speech. There were four columns
of it, but Jethro seemed to take delight in every word;
and portions of the noblest parts of it, indeed, he had Cynthia read over again. Sometimes, in the privacy of his
home, Jethro was known to chuckle, and to Cynthia's
surprise he chuckled more than usual that evening.

"Uncle Jethro," she said at length, when she had laid
the paper down, "I thought that you sent Mr. Sutton to
Congress."

Jethro leaned forward.

"What put that into your head, Cynthy?" he asked.

"Oh," answered the girl, "everybody says so, — Moses
Hatch, Rias, and Cousin Eph. Didn't you?"

Jethro looked at her, as she thought, strangely.

"You're too young to know anything about such
things, Cynthy," he said, "too young."

"But you make all the judges and senators and congressmen in the state, I know you do. Why," exclaimed
Cynthia, indignantly, "why does Mr. Sutton say the
people elected him when he owes everything to you?"

Jethro arose abruptly and flung a piece of wood into the
stove, and then he stood with his back to her. Her instinct told her that he was suffering, though she could not
fathom the cause, and she rose swiftly and drew him
down into the chair beside her.

"What is it?" she said anxiously. "Have you got
rheumatism, too, like Cousin Eph? All old men seem to
have rheumatism."

"No, Cynthy, it hain't rheumatism," he managed to answer; "wimmen folks hadn't ought to mix up in politics.
They — they don't understand 'em, Cynthy."

"But I shall understand them some day, because I am

your daughter — now that — now that I have only you, I am your daughter, am I not?"

"Yes, yes," he answered huskily, with his hand on her hair.

"And I know more than most women now," continued Cynthia, triumphantly. "I'm going to be such a help to you soon — very soon. I've read a lot of history, and I know some of the Constitution by heart. I know why old Timothy Prescott fought in the Revolution — it was to get rid of kings, wasn't it, and to let the people have a chance? The people can always be trusted to do what is right, can't they, Uncle Jethro?"

Jethro was silent, but Cynthia did not seem to notice that. After a space she spoke again: —

"I've been thinking it all out about you, Uncle Jethro."

"A-about me?"

"Yes, I know why you are able to send men to Congress and make judges of them. It's because the people have chosen you to do all that for them — you are so great and good."

Jethro did not answer.

Although the month was March, it was one of those wonderful still nights that sometimes come in the mountain-country when the wind is silent in the notches and the stars seem to burn nearer to the earth. Cynthia awoke and lay staring for an instant at the red planet which hung over the black and ragged ridge, and then she arose quickly and knocked at the door across the passage.

"Are you ill, Uncle Jethro?"

"No," he answered, "no, Cynthy. Go to bed. Er — I was just thinkin' — thinkin', that's all, Cynthy."

Though all his life he had eaten sparingly, Cynthia noticed that he scarcely touched his breakfast the next morning, and two hours later he went unexpectedly to the state capital. That day, too, Coniston was clothed in clouds, and by afternoon a wild March snowstorm was sweeping down the face of the mountain, piling against doorways and blocking the roads. Through the storm Cynthia fought her way to the harness shop, for Ephraim

Prescott had taken to his bed, bound hand and foot by rheumatism.

Much of that spring Ephraim was all but helpless, and Cynthia spent many days nursing him and reading to him. Meanwhile the harness industry languished. Cynthia and Ephraim knew, and Coniston guessed, that Jethro was taking care of Ephraim, and strong as was his affection for Jethro the old soldier found dependence hard to bear. He never spoke of it to Cynthia, but he used to lie and dream through the spring days of what he might have done if the war had not crippled him. For Ephraim Prescott, like his grandfather, was a man of action — a keen, intelligent American whose energy, under other circumstances, might have gone toward the making of the West. Ephraim, furthermore, had certain principles which some in Coniston called cranks ; for instance, he would never apply for a pension, though he could easily have obtained one. Through all his troubles, he held grimly to the ideal which meant more to him than ease and comfort, — that he had served his country for the love of it.

With the warm weather he was able to be about again, and occasionally to mend a harness, but Doctor Rowell shook his head when Jethro stopped his buggy in the road one day to inquire about Ephraim. Whereupon Jethro went on to the harness shop. The inspiration, by the way, had come from Cynthia.

"Er — Ephraim, how'd you like to be postmaster? H-haven't any objections to that kind of a job, hev you ? "

"Why no," said Ephraim. "We hain't agoin' to hev a post-office at Coniston — air we ? "

"H-how'd you like to be postmaster at Brampton ? " demanded Jethro, abruptly.

Ephraim dropped the trace he was shaving.

"Postmaster at Brampton!" he exclaimed.

"H-how'd you like it ? " said Jethro again.

"Well," said Ephraim, " *I* hain't got any objections."

Jethro started out of the shop, but paused again at the door.

"W-won't say nothin' about it, will you, Eph?" he inquired.

"Not till I *git* it," answered Ephraim. The sorrows of three years were suddenly lifted from his shoulders, and for an instant Ephraim wanted to dance until he remembered the rheumatism and the Wilderness leg. Suddenly a thought struck him, and he hobbled to the door and called out after Jethro's retreating figure. Jethro returned.

"Well?" he said, "well?"

"What's the pay?" said Ephraim, in a whisper.

Jethro named the sum instantly, also in a whisper.

"You don't tell me!" said Ephraim, and sank stupefied into the chair in front of the shop, where lately he had spent so much of his time.

Jethro chuckled twice on his way home : he chuckled twice again to Cynthia's delight at supper, and after supper he sent Millicent Skinner to find Jake Wheeler. Jake, as usual, was kicking his heels in front of the store, talking to Rias and others about the coming Fourth of July celebration at Brampton. Brampton, as we know, was famous for its Fourth of July celebrations. Not neglecting to let it be known that Jethro had sent for him, Jake hurried off through the summer twilight to the tannery house, bowed ceremoniously to Cynthia under the butternut tree, and discovered Jethro behind the shed. It was usually Jethro's custom to allow the other man to begin the conversation, no matter how trivial the subject — a method which had commended itself to Mr. Bixby and other minor politicians who copied him. And usually the other man played directly into Jethro's hands. Jake Wheeler always did, and now, to cover the awkwardness of the silence, he began on the Brampton celebration.

"They tell me Heth Sutton's a-goin' to make the address — seems prouder than ever since he went to Congress. I guess you'll tell him what to say when the time comes, Jethro."

"Er — goin' to Clovelly after wool this week, Jake?"

"I *kin* go to-morrow," said Jake, scenting an affair.

"Er — goin' to Clovelly after wool this week, Jake?"

Jake reflected. He saw it was expedient that this errand should not smell of haste.

" I was goin' to see Cutter on Friday," he answered.

" Er — if you should happen to meet Heth — "

" Yes," interrupted Jake.

" If *by chance* you should happen to meet Heth, or Bije " (Jethro knew that Jake never went to Clovelly without a conference with one or the other of these personages, if only to be able to talk about it afterward at the store), ' er — what would you say to 'em ? "

" Why," said Jake, scratching his head for the answer, " I'd tell him you was at Coniston."

" Think we'll have rain, Jake ? " inquired Jethro, blandly.

Jake wended his way back to the store, filled with renewed admiration for the great man. Jethro had given him no instructions whatever, could deny before a jury if need be that he had sent him (Jake) to Clovelly to tell Heth Sutton to come to Coniston for instructions on the occasion of his Brampton speech. And Jake was filled with a mysterious importance when he took his seat once more in the conclave.

Jake Wheeler, although in many respects a fool, was one of the most efficient pack of political hounds that the state has ever known. By six o'clock on Friday morning he was descending a brook valley on the Clovelly side of the mountain, and by seven was driving between the forest and river meadows of the Rajah's domain, and had come in sight of the big white house with its somewhat pretentious bay-windows and Gothic doorway; it might be dubbed the palace of these parts. The wide river flowed below it, and the pastures so wondrously green in the morning sun were dotted with fat cattle and sheep. Jake was content to borrow a cut of tobacco from the superintendent and wander aimlessly around the farm until Mr. Sutton's family prayers and breakfast were accomplished. We shall not concern ourselves with the message or the somewhat lengthy manner in which it was delivered. Jake had merely dropped in by accident, but the Rajah listened coldly while he picked his teeth, said he didn't know whether he was going to Brampton or not — hadn't decided; didn't know whether he could get to Coniston or not — his affairs were multitudinous now. In short, he set Jake to thinking deeply as his horse walked up the western heights of Coniston on the return journey. He had, let it be repeated, a sure instinct once his nose was fairly on the scent, and he was convinced that a war of great magnitude was in the air, and he, Jake Wheeler, was probably the first in all the state to discover it ! His blood leaped at the thought.

The hill-Rajah's defiance, boiled down, could only mean one thing, — that somebody with sufficient power and money was about to lock horns with Jethro Bass. Not for a moment did Jake believe that, for all his pomp and circumstance, the Honorable Heth Sutton was a big enough man to do this. Jake paid to the Honorable Heth all the outward respect that his high position demanded, but he knew the man through and through. He thought of the Honorable Heth's reform speech in Congress, and laughed loudly in the echoing woods. No, Mr. Sutton was not the man to lead a fight. But to whom had he promised his allegiance ? This question puzzled Mr. Wheeler all the way home, and may it be said finally for many days thereafter. He slid into Coniston in the dusk, big with impending events, which he could not fathom. As to giving Jethro the careless answer of the hill-Rajah, that was another matter.

The Fourth of July came at last, nor was any contradiction made in the Brampton papers that the speech of the Honorable Heth Sutton had been cancelled. Instead, advertisements appeared in the *Brampton Clarion* announcing the fact in large letters. When Cynthia read this advertisement to Jethro, he chuckled again. They were under the butternut tree, for the evenings were long now.

"Will you take me to Brampton, Uncle Jethro ? " said she, letting fall the paper on her lap.

" W-who's to get in the hay ? " said Jethro.

"Hay on the Fourth of July!" exclaimed Cynthia, "why, that's — sacrilege! You'd much better come and hear Mr. Sutton's speech — it will do you good."

Cynthia could see that Jethro was intensely amused, for his eyes had a way of snapping on such occasions when he was alone with her. She was puzzled and slightly offended, because, to tell the truth, Jethro had spoiled her.

"Very well, then," she said, "I'll go with the Painter-man."

Jethro came and stood over her, his expression the least bit wistful.

"Er — Cynthy," he said presently, "hain't fond of that Painter-man, be you?"

"Why, yes," said Cynthia, "aren't you?"

"He's fond of you," said Jethro, "sh-shouldn't be surprised if he was in love with you."

Cynthia looked up at him, the corners of her mouth twitching, and then she laughed. The Rev. Mr. Satterlee, writing his Sunday sermon in his study, heard her and laid down his pen to listen.

"Uncle Jethro," said Cynthia, "sometimes I forget that you're a great, wise man, and I think that you are just a silly old goose."

Jethro wiped his face with his blue cotton handkerchief.

"Then you hain't a-goin' to marry the Painter-man?" he said.

"I'm not going to marry anybody," cried Cynthia, contritely; "I'm going to live with you and take care of you all my life."

On the morning of the Fourth, Cynthia drove to Brampton with the Painter-man, and when he perceived that she was dreaming, he ceased to worry her with his talk. He liked her dreaming, and stole many glances at her face of which she knew nothing at all. Through the cool and fragrant woods, past the mill-pond stained blue and white by the sky, and scented clover fields and wayside flowers nodding in the morning air — Cynthia saw these things in the memory of another journey to Brampton.

On that Fourth her father had been with her, and Jethro and Ephraim and Moses and Amanda Hatch and the children. And how well she recalled, too, standing amidst the curious crowd before the great house which Mr. Worthington had just built.

There are weeks and months, perhaps, when we do not think of people, when our lives are full and vigorous, and then perchance a memory will bring them vividly before us — so vividly that we yearn for them. There rose before Cynthia now the vision of a boy as he stood on the Gothic porch of the house, and how he had come down to the wondering country people with his smile and his merry greeting, and how he had cajoled her into lingering in front of the meeting-house. Had he forgotten her? With just a suspicion of a twinge, Cynthia remembered that Janet Duncan she had seen at the capital, whom she had been told was the heiress of the state. When he had graduated from Harvard, Bob would, of course, marry her. That was in the nature of things.

To some the great event of that day in Brampton was to be the speech of the Honorable Heth Sutton in the meeting-house at eleven; others (and this party was quite as numerous) had looked forward to the base-ball game between Brampton and Harwich in the afternoon. The painter would have preferred to walk up meeting-house hill with Cynthia, and from the cool heights look down upon the amphitheatre in which the town was built. But Cynthia was interested in history, and they went to the meeting-house accordingly, where she listened for an hour and a half to the patriotic eloquence of the representative. The painter was glad to see and hear so great a man in the hour of his glory, though so much as a fragment of the oration does not now remain in his memory. In size, in figure, in expression, in the sonorous tones of his voice, Mr. Sutton was everything that a congressman should be. "The people," said Isaac D. Worthington in presenting him, "should indeed be proud of such an able and high-minded representative." We shall have cause to recall that word high-minded.

Many persons greeted Cynthia outside the meeting-house, for the girl seemed genuinely loved by all who knew her — too much loved, her companion thought, by certain spick-and-span young men of Brampton. But they ate the lunch Cynthia had brought, far from the crowd, under the trees by Coniston Water. It was she who proposed going to the base-ball game, and the painter stifled a sigh and acquiesced. Their way brought them down Brampton Street, past a house with great, iron dogs on the lawn, so imposing and cityfied that he hung back and asked who lived there.

" Mr. Worthington," answered Cynthia, making to move on impatiently.

Her escort did not think much of the house, but it interested him as the type which Mr. Worthington had built. On that same Gothic porch, sublimely unconscious of the covert stares and subdued comments of the pas-sers-by, the first citizen himself and the Honorable Heth Sutton might be seen. Mr. Worthington, whose hawklike look had become more pronounced, sat upright, while the Honorable Heth, his legs crossed, filled every nook and cranny of an arm-chair, and an occasional fra-grant whiff from his cigar floated out to those on the tar sidewalk. Although the pedestrians were but twenty feet away, what Mr. Worthington said never reached them ; but the Honorable Heth on public days carried his voice of the Forum around with him.

" Come on," said Cynthia, in one of those startling little tempers she was subject to ; " don't stand there like an idiot."

Then the voice of Mr. Sutton boomed toward them.

" As I understand, Worthington," they heard him say, " you want me to appoint young Wheelock for the Bramp-ton post-office." He stuck his thumb into his vest pocket and recrossed his legs. " I guess it can be arranged."

When the painter at last overtook Cynthia the jewel points he had so often longed to catch upon a canvas were in her eyes. He fell back, wondering how he could so greatly have offended, when she put her hand on his sleeve.

"Did you hear what he said about the Brampton post-office?" she cried.

"The Brampton post-office?" he repeated, dazed.

"Yes," said Cynthia; "Uncle Jethro has promised it to Cousin Ephraim, who will starve without it. Did you hear this man say he would give it to Mr. Wheelock?"

Here was a new Cynthia, aflame with emotions on a question of politics of which he knew nothing. He did understand, however, her concern for Ephraim Prescott, for he knew that she loved the soldier. She turned from the painter now with a gesture which he took to mean that his profession debarred him from such vital subjects, and she led the way to the fair-grounds. There he meekly bought tickets, and they found themselves hurried along in the eager crowd toward the stand.

The girl was still unaccountably angry over that mysterious affair of the post-office, and sat with flushed cheeks staring out on the green field, past the line of buggies and carryalls on the farther side to the southern shoulder of Coniston towering above them all. The painter, already beginning to love his New England folk, listened to the homely chatter about him, until suddenly a cheer starting in one corner ran like a flash of gunpowder around the field, and eighteen young men trotted across the turf. Although he was not a devotee of sport, he noticed that nine of these, as they took their places on the bench, wore blue, — the Harwich Champions. Seven only of those scattering over the field wore white; two young gentlemen, one at second base and the other behind the batter, wore gray uniforms with crimson stockings, and crimson piping on the caps, and a crimson H embroidered on the breast — a sight that made the painter's heart beat a little faster, the honored livery of his own college.

"What are those two Harvard men doing here?" he asked.

Cynthia, who was leaning forward, started, and turned to him a face which showed him that his question had been meaningless. He repeated it.

"Oh," said she, "the tall one, burned brick-red like an Indian, is Bob Worthington."

"He's a good type," the artist remarked.

"You're right, Mister, there hain't a finer young feller anywhere," chimed in Mr. Dodd, a portly person with a tuft of yellow beard on his chin. Mr. Dodd kept the hardware store in Brampton.

"And who," asked the painter, "is the bullet-headed little fellow, with freckles and short red hair, behind the bat?"

"I don't know," said Cynthia, indifferently.

"Why," exclaimed Mr. Dodd, with just a trace of awe in his voice, "that's Somers Duncan, son of Millionnaire Duncan down to the capital. I guess," he added, "I guess them two will be the richest men in the state some day. Duncan come up from Harvard with Bob."

In a few minutes the game was in full swing, Brampton against Harwich, the old rivalry in another form. Every advantage on either side awoke thundering cheers from the partisans; beribboned young women sprang to their feet and waved the Harwich blue at a home run, and were on the verge of tears when the Brampton pitcher struck out their best batsman. But beyond the facts that the tide was turning in Brampton's favor; that young Mr. Worthington stopped a ball flying at a phenomenal speed and batted another at a still more phenomenal speed which was not stopped; that his name and Duncan's were mingled generously in the cheering, the painter remembered little of the game. The exhibition of human passions which the sight of it drew from an undemonstrative race : the shouting, the comments wrung from hardy spirits off their guard, the joy and the sorrow, — such things interested him more. High above the turmoil Coniston, as through the ages, looked down upon the scene impassive.

He was aroused from these reflections by an incident. Some one had leaped over the railing which separated the stand from the field and stood before Cynthia, — a tanned and smiling young man in gray and crimson. His honest eyes were alight with an admiration that was unmistakable to the painter — perhaps to Cynthia also, for a glow that might have been of annoyance or anger, and yet was like the color of the mountain sunrise, answered in her cheek. Mr. Worthington reached out a large brown hand and seized the girl's as it lay on her lap.

"Hello, Cynthia," he cried, "I've been looking for you all day. I thought you might be here. Where were you?"

"Where did you look?" answered Cynthia, composedly, withdrawing her hand.

"Everywhere," said Bob, "up and down the street, all through the hotel. I asked Lem Hallowell, and he didn't know where you were. I only got here last night myself."

"I was in the meeting-house," said Cynthia.

"The meeting-house!" he echoed. "You don't mean to tell me that you listened to that silly speech of Sutton's?"

This remark, delivered in all earnestness, was the signal for uproarious laughter from Mr. Dodd and others sitting near by, attending earnestly to the conversation.

Cynthia bit her lip.

"Yes, I did," she said; "but I'm sorry now."

"I should think you would be," said Bob; "Sutton's a silly, pompous old fool. I had to sit through dinner with him. I believe I could represent the district better myself."

"By gosh!" exploded Mr. Dodd, "I believe you could!"

But Bob paid no attention to him. He was looking at Cynthia.

"Cynthia, you've grown up since I saw you," he said. "How's Uncle Jethro?"

"He's well — thanks," said Cynthia, and now she was striving to put down a smile.

"Still running the state?" said Bob. "You tell him I think he ought to muzzle Sutton. What did he send him down to Washington for?"

"I don't know," said Cynthia.

"What are you going to do after the game?" Bob demanded.

R

"I'm going home, of course," said Cynthia.

His face fell.

"Can't you come to the house for supper and stay for the fireworks?" he begged pleadingly. "We'd be mighty glad to have your friend, too."

Cynthia introduced her escort.

"It's very good of you, Bob," she said, with that New England demureness which at times became her so well, "but we couldn't possibly do it. And then I don't like Mr. Sutton."

"Oh, hang him!" exclaimed Bob. He took a step nearer to her. "Won't you stay this once? I have to go West in the morning."

"I think you are very lucky," said Cynthia.

Bob scanned her face searchingly, and his own fell.

"Lucky!" he cried, "I think it's the worst thing that ever happened to me. My father's so hard-headed when he gets his mind set — he's making me do it. He wants me to see the railroads and the country, so I've got to go with the Duncans. I wanted to stay —" He checked himself, "I think it's a blamed nuisance."

"So do I," said a voice behind him.

It was not the first time that Mr. Somers Duncan had spoken, but Bob either had not heard him or pretended not to. Mr. Duncan's freckled face smiled at them from the top of the railing, his eyes were on Cynthia's face, and he had been listening eagerly. Mr. Duncan's chief characteristic, beyond his freckles, was his eagerness — a quality probably amounting to keenness.

"Hello," said Bob, turning impatiently, "I might have known you couldn't keep away. You're the cause of all my troubles — you and your father's private car."

Somers became apologetic.

"It isn't my fault," he said; "I'm sure I hate going as much as you do. It's spoiled my summer, too."

Then he coughed and looked at Cynthia.

"Well," said Bob, "I suppose I'll have to introduce you. This," he added, dragging his friend over the railing, "is Mr. Somers Duncan."

"I'm awfully glad to meet you, Miss Wetherell," said Somers, fervently; "to tell you the truth, I thought he was just making up yarns."

"Yarns?" repeated Cynthia, with a look that set Mr. Duncan floundering.

"Why, yes," he stammered. "Worthy said that you were up here, but I thought he was crazy the way he talked — I didn't think — "

"Think what?" inquired Cynthia, but she flushed a little.

"Oh, rot, Somers!" said Bob, blushing furiously under his tan; "you ought never to go near a woman — you're the darndest fool with 'em I ever saw."

This time even the painter laughed outright, and yet he was a little sorrowful, too, because he could not be even as these youths. But Cynthia sat serene, the eternal feminine of all the ages, and it is no wonder that Bob Worthington was baffled as he looked at her. He lapsed into an awkwardness quite as bad as that of his friend.

"I hope you enjoyed the game," he said at last, with a formality that was not at all characteristic.

Cynthia did not seem to think it worth while to answer this, so the painter tried to help him out.

"That was a fine stop you made, Mr. Worthington," he said; "wasn't it, Cynthia?"

"Everybody seemed to think so," answered Cynthia, cruelly; "but if I were a man and had hands like that" (Bob thrust them in his pockets), "I believe I could stop a ball, too."

Somers laughed uproariously.

"Good-by," said Bob, with uneasy abruptness, "I've got to go into the field now. When can I see you?"

"When you get back from the West — perhaps," said Cynthia.

"Oh," cried Bob (they were calling him), "I must see you to-night!" He vaulted over the railing and turned. "I'll come back here right after the game," he said; "there's only one more inning."

"We'll come back right after the game," repeated Mr. Duncan.

Bob shot one look at him, — of which Mr. Duncan seemed blissfully unconscious, — and stalked off abruptly to second base.

The artist sat pensive for a few moments, wondering at the ways of women, his sympathies unaccountably enlisted in behalf of Mr. Worthington.

"Weren't you a little hard on him?" he said.

For answer Cynthia got to her feet.

"I think we ought to be going home," she said.

"Going home!" he ejaculated in amazement.

"I promised Uncle Jethro I'd be there for supper," and she led the way out of the grand stand.

So they drove back to Coniston through the level evening light, and when they came to Ephraim Prescott's harness shop the old soldier waved at them cheerily from under the big flag which he had hung out in honor of the day. The flag was silk, and incidentally Ephraim's most valued possession. Then they drew up before the tannery house, and Cynthia leaped out of the buggy and held out her hand to the painter with a smile.

"It was very good of you to take me," she said.

Jethro Bass, rugged, uncouth, in rawhide boots and swallowtail and coonskin cap, came down from the porch to welcome her, and she ran toward him with an eagerness that started the painter to wondering afresh over the contrasts of life. What, he asked himself, had Fate in store for Cynthia Wetherell?

CHAPTER III

JOURNEYS TO GO

"H-HAVE a good time, Cynthy?" said Jethro, looking down into her face. Love had wrought changes in Jethro, mightier changes than he suspected, and the girl did not know how zealous were the sentries of that love, how watchful they were, and how they told him often and again whether her heart, too, was smiling.

"It was very gay," said Cynthia.

"P-painter-man gay?" inquired Jethro.

Cynthia's eyes were on the orange line of the sunset over Coniston, but she laughed a little, indulgently.

"Cynthy?"

"Yes."

"Er—that Painter-man hain't such a bad fellow—w-why didn't you ask him in to supper?"

"I'll give you three guesses," said Cynthia, but she did not wait for them. "It was because I wanted to be alone with you. Milly's gone out, hasn't she?"

"G-gone a-courtin'," said Jethro.

She smiled, and went into the house to see whether Milly had done her duty before she left. It was characteristic of Cynthia not to have mentioned the subject which was agitating her mind until they were seated on opposite sides of the basswood table.

"Uncle Jethro," she said, "I thought you told Mr. Sutton to give Cousin Eph the Brampton post-office? Do you trust Mr. Sutton?" she demanded abruptly.

"Er—why?" said Jethro. "Why?"

"Because I don't," she answered with conviction; "I think he's a big fraud. He must have deceived you,

Uncle Jethro. I can't see why you ever sent him to Congress."

Although Jethro was in no mood for mirth, he laughed in spite of himself, for he was an American. His life-long habit would have made him defend Heth to any one but Cynthia.

"'D you see Heth, Cynthy?" he asked.

"Yes," replied the girl, disgustedly, "I should say I did, but not to speak to him. He was sitting on Mr. Worthington's porch, and I heard him tell Mr. Worthington he would give the Brampton post-office to Dave Wheelock. I don't want you to think that I was eavesdropping," she added quickly; "I couldn't help hearing it."

Jethro did not answer.

"You'll make him give the post-office to Cousin Eph, won't you, Uncle Jethro?"

"Yes," said Jethro, very simply, "I will." He meditated awhile, and then said suddenly, "W-won't speak about it — will you, Cynthy?"

"You know I won't," she answered.

Let it not be thought by any chance that Coniston was given over to revelry and late hours, even on the Fourth of July. By ten o'clock the lights were out in the tannery house, but Cynthia was not asleep. She sat at her window watching the shy moon peeping over Coniston ridge, and she was thinking, to be exact, of how much could happen in one short day and how little in a long month. She was aroused by the sound of wheels and the soft beat of a horse's hoofs on the dirt road: then came stifled laughter, and suddenly she sprang up alert and tingling. Her own name came floating to her through the darkness.

The next thing that happened will be long remembered in Coniston. A tentative chord or two from a guitar, and then the startled village was listening with all its might to the voices of two young men singing "When I first went up to Harvard" — probably meant to disclose the identity of the serenaders, as if that were necessary! Coniston, never having listened to grand opera, was entertained and thrilled, and thought the rendering of the song better on the whole than the church choir could have done it, or even the quartette that sung at the Brampton celebrations behind the flowers. Cynthia had her own views on the subject.

There were five other songs — Cynthia remembers all of them, although she would not confess such a thing. " Naughty, naughty Clara," was another one; the other three were almost wholly about love, some treating it flippantly, others seriously — this applied to the last one, which had many farewells in it. Then they went away, and the crickets and frogs on Coniston Water took up the refrain.

Although the occurrence was unusual, — it might almost be said epoch-making, — Jethro did not speak of it until they had reached the sparkling heights of Thousand Acre Hill the next morning. Even then he did not look at Cynthia.

" Know who that was last night, Cynthy ? " he inquired, as though the matter were a casual one.

" I believe," said Cynthia, heroically, " I believe it was a boy named Somers Duncan — and Bob Worthington."

" Er — Bob Worthington," repeated Jethro, but said nothing more.

Of course Coniston, and presently Brampton, knew that Bob Worthington had serenaded Cynthia — and Coniston and Brampton talked. It is noteworthy that (with the jocular exceptions of Ephraim and Lem Hallowell) they did not talk to the girl herself. The painter had long ago discovered that Cynthia was an individual. She had good blood in her : as a mere child she had shouldered the responsibility of her father; she had a natural aptitude for books — a quality reverenced in the community; she visited, as a matter of habit, the sick and the unfortunate; and lastly (perhaps the crowning achievement) she had bound Jethro Bass, of all men, with the fetters of love. Of course I have ended up by making her a paragon, although I am merely stating what people thought of her. Coniston decided at once that she was to marry the heir to the Brampton Mills.

But the heir had gone West, and as the summer wore on, the gossip died down. Other and more absorbing gossip took its place : never distinctly formulated, but whispered ; always wishing for more definite news that never came. The statesmen drove out from Brampton to the door of the tannery house, as usual, only it was remarked by astute observers and Jake Wheeler that certain statesmen did not come who had been in the habit of coming formerly. In short, those who made it a custom to observe such matters felt vaguely a disturbance of some kind. The organs of the people felt it, and became more guarded in their statements. What no one knew, except Jake and a few in high places, was that a war of no mean magnitude was impending.

There were three men in the State — and perhaps only three — who realized from the first that all former political combats would pale in comparison to this one to come. Similar wars had already started in other states, and when at length they were fought out another twist had been given to the tail of a long-suffering Constitution ; political history in the United States had to be written from an entirely new and unforeseen standpoint, and the unsuspecting people had changed masters.

This was to be a war of extermination of one side or the other. No quarter would be given or asked, and every weapon hitherto known to politics would be used. Of the three men who realized this, and all that would happen if one side or the other were victorious, one was Alexander Duncan, another Isaac D. Worthington, and the third was Jethro Bass.

Jethro would never have been capable of being master of the state had he not foreseen the time when the railroads, tired of paying tribute, would turn and try to exterminate the boss. The really astonishing thing about Jethro's foresight (known to few only) was that he perceived clearly that the time would come when the railroads and other aggregations of capital *would* exterminate the boss, or at least subserviate him. This alone, the writer thinks, gives him some right to greatness. And Jethro

Bass made up his mind that the victory of the railroads, in his state at least, should not come in his day. He would hold and keep what he had fought all his life to gain.

Jethro knew, when Jake Wheeler failed to bring him a message back from Clovelly, that the war had begun, and that Isaac D. Worthington, commander of the railroad forces in the field, had captured his pawn, the hill-Rajah. By getting through to Harwich, the Truro had made a sad muddle in railroad affairs. It was now a connecting link ; and its president, the first citizen of Brampton, a man of no small importance in the state. This fact was not lost upon Jethro, who perceived clearly enough the fight for consolidation that was coming in the next Legislature.

Seated on an old haystack on Thousand Acre Hill, that sits in turn on the lap of Coniston, Jethro smiled as he reflected that the first trial of strength in this mighty struggle was to be over (what the unsuspecting world would deem a trivial matter) the postmastership of Brampton. And Worthington's first move in the game would be to attempt to capture for his faction the support of the Administration itself.

Jethro thought the view from Thousand Acre Hill, especially in September, to be one of the sublimest efforts of the Creator. It was September, first of the purple months in Coniston, not the red-purple of the Maine coast, but the blue-purple of the mountains, the color of the bloom on the Concord grape. His eyes, sweeping the mountain from the notch to the granite ramp of the northern buttress, fell on the weather-beaten little farmhouse in which he had lived for many years, and rested lovingly on the orchard, where the golden early apples shone among the leaves. But Jethro was not looking at the apples.

"Cynthy," he called out abruptly, "h-how'd you like to go to Washington ? "

"Washington ! " exclaimed Cynthia. "When ? "

"N-now — to-morrow." Then he added uneasily, "C-can't you get ready ? "

Cynthia laughed.

"Why, I'll go to-night, Uncle Jethro," she answered.

"Well," he said admiringly, "you hain't one of them clutterin' females. We can get some finery for you in New York, Cynthy. D-don't want any of them town ladies to put you to shame. Er — not that they would," he added hastily — "not that they would."

Cynthia climbed up beside him on the haystack.

"Uncle Jethro," she said solemnly, "when you make a senator or a judge, I don't interfere, do I ?"

He looked at her uneasily, for there were moments when he could not for the life of him make out her drift.

"N-no," he assented, "of course not, Cynthy."

"Why is it that I don't interfere ?"

"I callate," answered Jethro, still more uneasily, "I callate it's because you're a woman."

"And don't you think," asked Cynthia, "that a woman ought to know what becomes her best ?"

Jethro reflected, and then his glance fell on her approvingly.

"G-guess you're right, Cynthy," he said. "I always had some success in dressin' up Listy, and that kind of set me up."

On such occasions he spoke of his wife quite simply. He had been genuinely fond of her, although she was no more than an episode in his life. Cynthia smiled to herself as they walked through the orchard to the place where the horse was tied, but she was a little remorseful. This feeling, on the drive homeward, was swept away by sheer elation at the prospect of the trip before her. She had often dreamed of the great world beyond Coniston, and no one, not even Jethro, had guessed the longings to see it which had at times beset her. Often she had dropped her book to summon up a picture of what a great city was like, to reconstruct the Boston of her early childhood. She remembered the Mall, where she used to walk with her father, and the row of houses where the rich dwelt, which had seemed like palaces. Indeed, when she read of palaces, these houses always came to her mind. And now she was to behold a palace even greater than these, — and the house where the President himself dwelt. But why was Jethro going to Washington?

As if in answer to the question, he drove directly to the harness shop instead of to the tannery house. Ephraim greeted them from within with a cheery hail, and hobbled out and stood between the wheels of the buggy.

"That bridle bust again?" he inquired.

"Er—Ephraim," said Jethro, "how long since you b'en away from Coniston — how long?"

Ephraim reflected.

"I went to Harwich with Moses before that bad spell I had in March," he answered.

Cynthia smiled from pure happiness, for she began to see the drift of things now.

"H-how long since you've b'en in foreign parts?" said Jethro.

"'Sixty-five," answered Ephraim, with astonishing promptness.

"Er — like to go to Washington with us to-morrow — like to go to Washington?"

Ephraim gasped, even as Cynthia had.

"Washin'ton!" he ejaculated.

"Cynthy and I was thinkin' of takin' a little trip," said Jethro, almost apologetically, "and we kind of thought we'd like to have you with us. Didn't we, Cynthy? Er— we might see General Grant," he added meaningly.

Ephraim was a New Englander, and not an adept in expressing his emotions. Both Cynthia and Jethro felt that he would have liked to have said something appropriate if he had known how. What he actually said was: —

"What time to-morrow?"

"C-callate to take the nine o'clock from Brampton," said Jethro.

"I'll report for duty at seven," said Ephraim, and it was then he squeezed the hand that he found in his. He watched them calmly enough until they had disappeared in the barn behind the tannery house, and then his thoughts became riotous. Rumors had been rife that

summer, prophecies of changes to come, and the resigna-
tion of the old man who had so long been postmaster at
Brampton was freely discussed — or rather the matter of
his successor. As the months passed, Ephraim had heard
David Wheelock mentioned with more and more assurance
for the place. He had had many nights when sleep failed
him, but it was characteristic of the old soldier that he
had never once broached the subject since Jethro had
spoken to him two months before. Ephraim had even
looked up the law to see if he was eligible, and found that
he was, since Coniston had no post-office, and was within
the limits of delivery of the Brampton office.

The next morning Coniston was treated to a genuine
surprise. After loading up at the store, Lem Hallowell,
instead of heading for Brampton, drove to the tannery
house, left his horses standing as he ran in, and presently
emerged with a little cowhide trunk that bore the letter
W. Following the trunk came a radiant Cynthia, following Cynthia, Jethro Bass in a stove-pipe hat, with a carpet-bag, and hobbling after Jethro, Ephraim Prescott,
with another carpet-bag. It was remarked in the buzz of
query that followed the stage's departure that Ephraim
wore the blue suit and the army hat with a cord around it
which he kept for occasions. Coniston longed to follow
them, in spirit at least, but even Milly Skinner did not
know their destination.

Fortunately we can follow them. At Brampton station
they got into the little train that had just come over Truro
Pass, and steamed, with many stops, down the valley of
Coniston Water until it stretched out into a wide range
of shimmering green meadows guarded by blue hills veiled
in the morning haze. Then, bustling Harwich, and a wait
of half an hour until the express from the north country
came thundering through the Gap ; then a five-hours' journey down the broad river that runs southward between
the hills, dinner in a huge station amidst a pleasant buzz
of excitement and the ringing of many bells. Then into
another train, through valleys and factory towns and cities
until they came, at nightfall, to the metropolis itself.

Cynthia will always remember the awe with which that first view of New York inspired her, and Ephraim confessed that he, too, had felt it, when he had first seen the myriad lights of the city after the long, dusty ride from the hills with his regiment. For all the flags and bunting it had held in '61, Ephraim thought that city crueller than war itself. And Cynthia thought so, too, as she clung to Jethro's arm between the carriages and the clanging street-cars, and looked upon the riches and poverty around her. There entered her soul that night a sense of that which is the worst cruelty of all — the cruelty of selfishness. Every man going his own pace, seeking to gratify his own aims and desires, unconscious and heedless of the want with which he rubs elbows. Her natural imagination enhanced by her life among the hills, the girl peopled the place in the street lights with all kinds of strange evil-doers of whose sins she knew nothing, — adventurers, charlatans, alert cormorants, who preyed upon the unwary. She shrank closer to Ephraim from a perfumed lady who sat next to her in the car, and was thankful when at last they found themselves in the corridor of the Astor House standing before the desk.

Hotel clerks, especially city ones, are supernatural persons. This one knew Jethro, greeted him deferentially as Judge Bass, and dipped the pen in the ink and handed it to him that he might register. By half-past nine Cynthia was dreaming of Lem Hallowell and Coniston, and Lem was driving a yellow street-car full of queer people down the road to Brampton.

There were few guests in the great dining room when they breakfasted at seven the next morning. New York, in the sunlight, had taken on a more kindly expression, and those who were near by smiled at them and seemed full of good-will. Persons smiled at them that day as they walked the streets or stood spellbound before the shop windows, and some who saw them felt a lump rise in their throats at the memories they aroused of forgotten days: the three seemed to bring the very air of the hills with them into that teeming place, and many who had

"Of their progress along Broadway."

come to the city with high hopes, now in the shackles of drudgery, looked after them. They were a curious party, indeed : the straight, dark girl with the light in her eyes and the color in her cheeks ; the quaint, rugged figure of the elderly man in his swallow-tail and brass buttons and square-toed, country boots ; and the old soldier hobbling along with the aid of his green umbrella, clad in the blue he had loved and suffered for. Had they remained until Sunday, they might have read an amusing account of their visit, — of Jethro's suppers of crackers and milk at the Astor House, of their progress along Broadway. The story was not lacking in pathos, either, and in real human feeling, for the young reporter who wrote it had come, not many years before, from the hills himself. But by that time they had accomplished another marvellous span in their journey, and were come to Washington itself.

CHAPTER IV

"JUDGE BASS AND PARTY"

CYNTHIA was deprived, too, of that thrilling first view of the capital from the train which she had pictured, for night had fallen when they reached Washington likewise. As the train slowed down, she leaned a little out of the window and looked at the shabby houses and shabby streets revealed by the flickering lights in the lamp-posts. Finally they came to a shabby station, were seized upon by a grinning darky hackman, who would not take no for an answer, and were rattled away to the hotel. Although he had been to Washington but once in his life before, as a Lincoln elector, Jethro was greeted as an old acquaintance by this clerk also.

"Glad to see you, Judge," said he, genially. "Train late? You've come purty nigh missin' supper."

A familiar of great men, the clerk was not offended when he got no response to his welcome. Cynthia and Ephraim, intent on getting rid of some of the dust of their journey, followed the colored hall-boy up the stairs. Jethro stood poring over the register, when a distinguished-looking elderly gentleman with a heavy gray beard and eyes full of shrewdness and humor paused at the desk to ask a question.

"Er — Senator?"

The senator (for such he was, although he did not represent Jethro's state) turned and stared, and then held out his hand with unmistakable warmth.

"Jethro Bass," he exclaimed, "upon my word! What are you doing in Washington?"

Jethro took the hand, but he did not answer the question.

" Er — Senator — when can I see the President ? "

" Why," answered the senator, somewhat taken aback, — " why, to-night, if you like. I'm going to the White House in a few minutes and I think I can arrange it."

"T-to-morrow afternoon — t-to-morrow afternoon ? "

The senator cast his eye over the swallow-tail coat and stove-pipe hat tilted back, and laughed.

" Thunder ! " he exclaimed, " you haven't changed a bit. I'm beginning to look like an old man ; but that milk-and-crackers diet seems to keep you young, Jethro. I'll fix it for to-morrow afternoon."

" W-what time — two ? "

" Well, I'll fix it for two to-morrow afternoon. I never could understand you, Jethro ; you don't do things like other men. Do I smell gunpowder ? What's up now — what do you want to see Grant about ? "

Jethro cast his eye around the corridor, where a few men were taking their ease after supper, and looked at the senator mysteriously.

" Any place where we can talk ? " he demanded.

" We can go into the writing room and shut the door," answered the senator, more amused than ever.

When Cynthia came downstairs, Jethro was standing with the gentleman in the corridor leading to the dining room, and she heard the gentleman say as he took his departure : —

" I haven't forgotten what you did for us in '70, Jethro. I'll go right along and see to it now."

Cynthia liked the gentleman's looks, and rightly surmised that he was one of the big men of the nation. She was about to ask Jethro his name when Ephraim came limping along and put the matter out of her mind, and the three went into the almost empty dining room. There they were served with elaborate attention by a darky waiter who had, in some mysterious way, learned Jethro's name and title. Cynthia reflected with pride that Jethro, too, was one of the nation's great men, who could get anything he wanted simply by coming to the capital and asking for it.

s

Ephraim was very much excited on finding himself in Washington, the sight of the place reviving in his mind a score of forgotten incidents of the war. After supper they found seats in a corner of the corridor, where a number of people were scattered about, smoking and talking. It did not occur to Jethro or Cynthia, or even to Ephraim, that these people were all of the male sex, and on the other hand the guests of the hotel were apparently used once in a while to see a lady from the country seated there. At any rate, Cynthia was but a young girl, and her two companions, however unusual their appearance, were clearly most respectable. Jethro, his hands in his pockets and his hat tilted, sat on the small of his back rapt in meditation; Cynthia, her head awhirl, looked around her with sparkling eyes; while Ephraim was smoking a cigar he had saved for just such a festal occasion. He did not see the stout man with the button and corded hat until he was almost on top of him.

"Eph Prescott, I believe!" exclaimed the stout one. "How be you, Comrade?"

Heedless of his rheumatism, Ephraim sprang to his feet and dropped the cigar, which the stout one picked up with much difficulty.

"Well," said Ephraim, in a voice that shook with unwonted emotion, "you kin skin me if it ain't Amasy Beard!" His eye travelled around Amasa's figure. "Wouldn't a-knowed you, I swan, I wouldn't. Why, when I seen you last, Amasy, your stomach was havin' all it could do to git hold of your backbone."

Cynthia laughed outright, and even Jethro sat up and smiled.

"When was it?" said Amasa, still clinging on to Ephraim's hand and incidentally to the cigar, which Ephraim had forgotten; "Beaver Creek, wahn't it?"

"July 10, 1863," said Ephraim, instantly.

Gradually they reached a sitting position, the cigar was restored to its rightful owner, and Mr. Beard was introduced, with some ceremony, to Cynthia and Jethro. From Beaver Creek they began to fight the war over again, backward and forward, much to Cynthia's edification, when her attention was distracted by the entrance of a street band of wind instruments. As the musicians made their way to another corner and began tuning up, she glanced mischievously at Jethro, for she knew his peculiarities by heart. One of these was a most violent detestation of any but the best music. He had often given her this excuse, laughingly, for not going to meeting in Coniston. How he had come by his love for good music, Cynthia never knew — he certainly had not heard much of it.

Suddenly a great volume of sound filled the corridor, and the band burst forth into what many supposed to be "The Watch on the Rhine." Some people were plainly delighted ; the veterans, once recovered from their surprise, shouted their reminiscences above the music, undismayed; Jethro held on to himself until the refrain, when he began to squirm, and as soon as the tune was done and the scattering applause had died down, he reached over and grabbed Mr. Amasa Beard by the knee. Mr. Beard did not immediately respond, being at that moment behind logworks facing a rebel charge ; he felt vaguely that some one was trying to distract his attention, and in some lobe of his brain was registered the fact that that particular knee had gout in it. Jethro increased the pressure, and then Mr. Beard abandoned his logworks and swung around with a snort of pain.

"H-how much do they git for that noise — h-how much do they git ? "

Mr. Beard tenderly lifted the hand from his knee and stared at Jethro with his mouth open, like a man aroused from a bad dream.

"Who ? What noise ? " he demanded.

"The Dutchmen," said Jethro. " H-how much do they git for that noise ? "

"Oh! " Mr. Beard glanced at the band and began to laugh. He thought Jethro a queer customer, no doubt, but he was a friend of Comrade Prescott's. " By gum ! " said Mr. Beard, " I thought for a minute a rebel chainshot had took my leg off. Well, sir, I guess that band gets about two dollars. They've come in here every evening since I've been at the hotel."

" T-two dollars? Is that the price? Er — you say two dollars is their price? "

" Thereabouts," answered Mr. Beard, uneasily. Veteran as he was, Jethro's appearance and earnestness were a little alarming.

" You say two dollars is their price? "

" Thereabouts," shouted Mr. Beard, seating himself on the edge of his chair.

But Jethro paid no attention to him. He rose, unfolding by degrees his six feet two, and strode diagonally across the corridor toward the band leader. Conversation was hushed at the sight of his figure, a titter ran around the walls, but Jethro was oblivious to these things. He drew a great calfskin wallet from an inside pocket of his coat, and the band leader, a florid German, laid down his instrument and made an elaborate bow. Jethro waited until the man had become upright and then held out a two-dollar bill.

" Is that about right for the performance? " he said — " is that about right? "

" Ja, mein Herr," said the man, nodding vociferously.

" I want to pay what's right — I want to pay what's right," said Jethro.

" I thank you very much, sir," said the leader, finding his English, " you haf pay for all."

" P-paid for everything — everything to-night? " demanded Jethro.

The leader spread out his hands.

" You haf pay for one whole evening," said he, and bowed again.

" Then take it, take it," said Jethro, pushing the bill into the man's palm; " but don't you come back to-night — don't you come back to-night."

The amazed leader stared at Jethro — and words failed him. There was something about this man that compelled him to obey, and he gathered up his followers and led the way silently out of the hotel. Roars of laughter and applause arose on all sides ; but Jethro was as one who heard them not as he made his way back to his seat again.

"You did a good job, my friend," said Mr. Beard, approvingly. "I'm going to take Eph Prescott down the street to see some of the boys. Won't you come, too ?"

Mr. Beard doubtless accepted it as one of the man's eccentricities that Jethro did not respond to him, for without more ado he departed arm in arm with Ephraim. Jethro was looking at Cynthia, who was staring toward the desk at the other end of the corridor, her face flushed, and her fingers closed over the arms of her chair. It never occurred to Jethro that she might have been embarrassed.

"W-what's the matter, Cynthy ? " he asked, sinking into the chair beside her.

Her breath caught sharply, but she tried to smile at him. He did not discover what was the matter until long afterward, when he recalled that evening to mind. Jethro was a man used to hotel corridors, used to sitting in an attitude that led the unsuspecting to believe he was half asleep; but no person of note could come or go whom he did not remember. He had seen the distinguished party arrive at the desk, preceded by a host of bell-boys with shawls and luggage. On the other hand, some of the distinguished party had watched the proceeding of paying off the band with no little amusement. Miss Janet Duncan had giggled audibly, her mother had smiled, while her father and Mr. Worthington had pretended to be deeply occupied with the hotel register. Somers was not there. Bob Worthington laughed heartily with the rest until his eye, travelling down the line of Jethro's progress, fell on Cynthia, and now he was striding across the floor toward them. And even in the horrible confusion of that moment Cynthia had a vagrant thought that his clothes had an enviable cut and became him remarkably.

"Well, of all things, to find you here ! " he cried; "this is the best luck that ever happened. I am glad to see you. I was going to steal away to Brampton for a couple of days before the term opened, and I meant to look you up there.

And Mr. Bass," said Bob, turning to Jethro, "I'm glad
to see you too."

Jethro looked at the young man and smiled and held
out his hand. It was evident that Bob was blissfully unaware that hostilities between powers of no mean magnitude
were about to begin; that the generals themselves were on
the ground, and that he was holding treasonable parley
with the enemy. The situation appealed to Jethro, especially as he glanced at the backs of the two gentlemen facing
the desk. These backs seemed to him full of expression.

" Th-thank you, Bob, th-thank you," he answered.

" I like the way you fixed that band," said Bob; " I
haven't laughed as much for a year. You hate music,
don't you? I hope you'll forgive that awful noise we
made outside of your house last July, Mr. Bass."

" You — you make that noise, Bob, you — you make
that?"

" Well," said Bob, " I'm afraid I did most of it. There
was another fellow that helped some and played the guitar.
It was pretty bad," he added, with a side glance at Cynthia, " but it was meant for a compliment."

" Oh," said she, " it was meant for a compliment, was
it?"

" Of course," he answered, glad of the opportunity to turn
his attention entirely to her. " I was for slipping away
right after supper, but my father headed us off."

" Slipping away?" repeated Cynthia.

" You see, he had a kind of a reception and fireworks
afterward. We didn't get away till after nine, and then
I thought I'd have a lecture when I got home."

" Did you?" asked Cynthia.

" No," said Bob, " he didn't know where I'd been."

Cynthia felt the blood rush to her temples, but by habit
and instinct she knew when to restrain herself.

" Would it have made any difference to him where you
had been?" she asked calmly enough.

Bob had a presentiment that he was on dangerous ground.
This new and self-possessed Cynthia was an enigma to
him — certainly a fascinating enigma.

"My father would have thought I was a fool to go off serenading," he answered, flushing. Bob did not like a lie; he knew that his father would have been angry if he had heard he had gone to Coniston; he felt, in the small of his back, that his father was angry now, and guessed the reason.

She regarded him gravely as he spoke, and then her eyes left his face and became fixed upon an object at the far end of the corridor. Bob turned in time to see Janet Duncan swing on her heel and follow her mother up the stairs. He struggled to find words to tide over what he felt was an awkward moment.

"We've had a fine trip," he said, "though I should much rather have stayed at home. The West is a wonderful country, with its cañons and mountains and great stretches of plain. My father met us in Chicago, and we came here. I don't know why, because Washington's dead at this time of the year. I suppose it must be on account of politics." Looking at Jethro with a sudden inspiration, "I hadn't thought of that."

Jethro had betrayed no interest in the conversation. He was seated, as usual, on the small of his back. But he saw a young man of short stature, with a freckled face and close-cropped, curly red hair, come into the corridor by another entrance ; he saw Isaac D. Worthington draw him aside and speak to him, and he saw the young man coming towards them.

"How do you do, Miss Wetherell?" cried the young man joyously, while still ten feet away, "I'm awfully glad to see you, upon my word, I am. How long are you going to be in Washington?"

"I don't know, Mr. Duncan," answered Cynthia.

"Did Worthy know you were here?" demanded Mr. Duncan, suspiciously.

"He did when he saw me," said Cynthia, smiling.

"Not till then?" asked Mr. Duncan. "Say, Worthy, your father wants to see you right away. I'm going to be in Washington a day or two — will you go walking with me to-morrow morning, Miss Wetherell?"

"She's going walking with me," said Bob, not in the best of tempers.

"Then I'll go along," said Mr. Duncan, promptly.

By this time Cynthia got up and was holding out her hand to Bob Worthington. "I'm not going walking with either of you," she said; "I have another engagement. And I think I'll have to say good night, because I'm very tired."

"When can I see you?" Both the young men asked the question at once.

"Oh, you'll have plenty of chances," she answered, and was gone.

The young men looked at each other somewhat blankly, and then down at Jethro, who did not seem to know that they were there, and then they made their way toward the desk. But Isaac D. Worthington and his friends had disappeared.

A few minutes later the distinguished-looking senator with whom Jethro had been in conversation before supper entered the hotel. He seemed preoccupied, and heedless of the salutations he received; but when he caught sight of Jethro he crossed the corridor rapidly and sat down beside him. Jethro did not move. The corridor was deserted now, save for the two.

"Bass," began the senator, "what's the row up in your state?"

"H-haven't heard of any row," said Jethro.

"What did you come to Washington for?" demanded the senator, somewhat sharply.

"Er — vacation," said Jethro, "vacation — to show my gal, Cynthy, the capital."

"Now see here, Bass," said the senator, "I don't forget what happened in '70. I don't object to wading through a swarm of bees to get a little honey for a friend, but I think I'm entitled to know why he wants it."

"G-got the honey?" asked Jethro.

The senator took off his hat and wiped his brow, and then he stole a look at Jethro, with apparently barren results.

"Jethro," he said, "people say you run that state of yours right up to the handle. What's all this trouble about a two-for-a-cent postmastership?"

"H-haven't heard of any trouble," said Jethro.

"Well, there is trouble," said the senator, losing patience at last. "When I told Grant you were here and mentioned that little Brampton matter to him, — it didn't seem much to me, — the bees began to fly pretty thick, I can tell you. I saw right away that somebody had been stirring 'em up. It looks to me, Jethro," said the senator gravely, "it looks to me as if you had something of a rebellion on your hands."

"W-what'd Grant say?" Jethro inquired.

"Well, he didn't say a great deal — he isn't much of a talker, you know, but what he did say was to the point. It seems that your man, Prescott, doesn't come from Brampton, in the first place, and Grant says that while he likes soldiers, he hasn't any use for the kind that want to lie down and make the government support 'em. I'll tell you what I found out. Worthington and Duncan wired the President this morning, and they've gone up to the White House now. They've got a lot of railroad interests back of them, and they've taken your friend Sutton into camp; but I managed to get the President to promise not to do anything until he saw you to-morrow afternoon at two."

Jethro sat silent so long that the senator began to think he wasn't going to answer him at all. In his opinion, he had told Jethro some very grave facts.

"W-when are you going to see the President again?" said Jethro, at last.

"To-morrow morning," answered the senator; "he wants me to walk over with him to see the postmaster-general, who is sick in bed."

"What time do you leave the White House?"

"At eleven," said the senator, very much puzzled.

"Er — Grant ever pay any attention to an old soldier on the street?"

The senator glanced at Jethro, and a twinkle came into his eye.

"Sometimes he has been known to," he answered.

"You — you ever pay any attention to an old soldier on the street?"

Then the senator's eyes began to snap.

"Sometimes I have been known to."

"Er — suppose an old soldier was in front of the White House at eleven o'clock — an old soldier with a gal — suppose?"

The senator saw the point, and took no pains to restrain his admiration.

"Jethro," he said, slapping him on the shoulder, "I'm willing to bet a few thousand dollars you'll run your state for a while yet."

CHAPTER V

COUSIN EPHRAIM'S COMRADE

"Heard you say you was goin' for a walk this morning, Cynthy," Jethro remarked, as they sat at breakfast the next morning.

"Why, of course," answered Cynthia, "Cousin Eph and I are going out to see Washington, and he is to show me the places that he remembers." She looked at Jethro appealingly. "Aren't you coming with us?" she asked.

"M-meet you at eleven, Cynthy," he said.

"Eleven!" exclaimed Cynthia in dismay, "that's almost dinner-time."

"M-meet you in front of the White House at eleven," said Jethro, "plumb in front of it, under a tree."

By half-past seven, Cynthia and Ephraim with his green umbrella were in the street, but it would be useless to burden these pages with a description of all the sights they saw, and with the things that Ephraim said about them, and incidentally about the war. After New York, much of Washington would then have seemed small and ragged to any one who lacked ideals and a national sense, but Washington was to Cynthia as Athens to a Greek. To her the marble Capitol shining on its hill was a sacred temple, and the great shaft that struck upward through the sunlight, though yet unfinished, a fitting memorial to him who had led the barefoot soldiers of the colonies through ridicule to victory. They looked up many institutions and monuments, they even had time to go to the Navy Yard, and they saved the contemplation of the White House till the last. The White House, which

267

Cynthia thought the finest and most graceful mansion in all the world, in its simplicity and dignity, a fitting dwelling for the chosen of the nation. Under the little tree which Jethro had mentioned, Ephraim stood bareheaded before the walls which had sheltered Lincoln, which were now the home of the greatest of his captains, Grant: and wondrous emotions played upon the girl's spirit, too, as she gazed. They forgot the present in the past and the future, and they did not see the two gentlemen who had left the portico some minutes before and were now coming toward them along the sidewalk.

The two gentlemen, however, slowed their steps involuntarily at a sight which was uncommon, even in Washington. The girl's arm was in the soldier's, and her face, which even in repose had a true nobility, now was alight with an inspiration that is seen but seldom in a lifetime. In marble, could it have been wrought by a great sculptor, men would have dreamed before it of high things.

The two, indeed, might have stood for a group, the girl as the spirit, the man as the body which had risked and suffered all for it, and still held it fast. For the honest face of the soldier reflected that spirit as truly as a mirror.

Ephraim was aroused from his thoughts by Cynthia nudging his arm. He started, put on his hat, and stared very hard at a man smoking a cigar who was standing before him. Then he stiffened and raised his hand in an involuntary salute. The man smiled. He was not very tall, he had a closely trimmed light beard that was growing a little gray, he wore a soft hat something like Ephraim's, a black tie on a white pleated shirt, and his eyeglasses were pinned to his vest. His eyes were all kindness.

" How do you do, Comrade ? " he said, holding out his hand.

" General," said Ephraim, " Mr. President," he added, correcting himself, " how be you ? "   He shifted the green umbrella, and shook the hand timidly but warmly.

" *General* will do," said the President, with a smiling

Florence Scovel Shinn

"A man smoking a cigar."

glance at the tall senator beside him, " I like to be called *General*."

" You've growed some older, General," said Ephraim, scanning his face with a simple reverence and affection, " but you hain't changed so much as I'd a thought since I saw you whittlin' under a tree beside the Lacy house in the Wilderness."

" My duty has changed some," answered the President, quite as simply. He added with a touch of sadness, " I liked those days best, Comrade."

" Well, I guess ! " exclaimed Ephraim, " you're general over everything now, but you're not a mite bigger man to me than you was."

The President took the compliment as it was meant.

" I found it easier to run an army than I do to run a country," he said.

Ephraim's blue eyes flamed with indignation.

" I don't take no stock in the bull-dogs and the gold harness at Long Branch and — and all them lies the dratted newspapers print about you,"— Ephraim hammered his umbrella on the pavement as an expression of his feelings, — " and what's more, the people don't."

The President glanced at the senator again, and laughed a little, quietly.

" Thank you, Comrade," he said.

" You're a plain, *common* man," continued Ephraim, paying the highest compliment known to rural New England; " the people think a sight of you, or they wouldn't hev chose you twice, General."

" So you were in the Wilderness ? " said the President, adroitly changing the subject.

" Yes, General. I was pressed into orderly duty the first day — that's when I saw you whittlin' under the tree, and you didn't seem to have no more consarn than if it had been a company drill. Had a cigar then, too. But the second day, May the 6th, I was with the regiment. I'll never forget that day," said Ephraim, warming to the subject, " when we was fightin' Ewell up and down the Orange Turnpike Road, playin' hide-and-seek with the

Johnnies in the woods.   You remember them woods, General ? "

The President nodded, his cigar between his teeth.   He looked as though the scene were coming back to him.

" Never seen such woods," said Ephraim, " scrub oak and pine and cedars and young stuff springin' up until you couldn't see the length of a company, and the Rebs jumpin' and hollerin' around and shoutin' every which way. After a while a lot of them saplings was mowed off clean by the bullets, and then the woods caught afire, and that was hell."

" Were you wounded ? " asked the President, quickly.

" I was hurt some, in the hip," answered Ephraim.

" Some ! " exclaimed Cynthia, " why, you have walked lame ever since."   She knew the story by heart, but the recital of it never failed to stir her blood.   " They carried him out just as he was going to be burned up, in a blanket hung from rifles, and he was in the hospital nine months, and had to come home for a while."

" Cynthy," said Ephraim in gentle reproof, " I callate the General don't want to hear that."

Cynthia flushed, but the President looked at her with an added interest.

" My dear young lady," he said, " that seems to me the vital part of the story.   If I remember rightly," he added, turning again to Ephraim, " the Fifth Corps was on the Orange turnpike.   What brigade were you in ? "

" The third brigade of the First Division," answered Ephraim.

" Griffin's," said the President.   " There were several splendid New England regiments in that brigade.   I sent them with Griffin to help Sheridan at Five Forks."

" I was thar, too," cried Ephraim.

" What ! " said the President, " with the lame hip ? "

" Well, General, I went back, I couldn't help it. I couldn't stay away from the boys — just couldn't. I didn't limp as bad then as I do now.   I wahn't much use anywhere else, and I *had* l'arned to fight.   Five Forks ! " exclaimed Ephraim.   " I call that day to mind as if it was yesterday. I remember how the boys yelled when they told us we was goin' to Sheridan. We got started about daylight, and it took us till four o'clock in the afternoon to git into position. The woods was just comin' a little green, and the white dogwoods was bloomin' around. Sheridan, he galloped up to the line with that black horse of his'n and hollered out, 'Come on, boys, go in at a clean jump or you won't ketch one of 'em.' *You* know how men, even veterans like that Fifth Corps, sometimes hev to be *pushed* into a fight. There was a man from a Maine regiment got shot in the head fust thing. 'I'm killed,' said he. ' Oh, no, you're not,' says Sheridan, 'pick up your gun and go for 'em.' But he was killed. Well, we went for 'em through all the swamps and briers and everything, and Sheridan, thar in front, had got the battle-flag and was rushin' round with it swearin' and prayin' and shoutin', and the first thing we knowed he'd jumped his horse clean over their logworks and landed right on top of the John-nies."

" Yes," said the President, "that was Sheridan, sure enough."

" Mr. President," said the senator, who stood by won-deringly while General Grant had lost himself in this con-versation, " do you realize what time it is ? "

" Yes, yes," said the President, " we must go on. What was your rank, Comrade ? "

" Sergeant, General."

" I hope you have got a good pension for that hip," said the President, kindly. It may be well to add that he was not always so incautious, but this soldier bore the unmistakable stamp of simplicity and sincerity on his face.

Ephraim hesitated.

" He never would ask for a pension, General," said Cynthia.

" What ! " exclaimed the President in real astonish-ment, " are you so rich as all that ? " and he glanced at the green umbrella.

" Well, General," said Ephraim, uncomfortably, " I

never liked the notion of gittin' paid for it. You see, I was what they call a war-Democrat."

" Good Lord ! " said the President, but more to himself. " What do you do now ? "

" I callate to make harness," answered Ephraim.

" Only he can't make it any more on account of his rheumatism, Mr. President," Cynthia put in.

" I think you might call me General, too," he said, with the grace that many simple people found inherent in him. " And may I ask your name, young lady ? "

" Cynthia Wetherell — General," she said smiling.

" That sounds more natural," said the President, and then to Ephraim, " Your daughter ? "

" I couldn't think more of her if she was," answered Ephraim; " Cynthy's pulled me through some tight spells. Her mother was my cousin, General. My name's Prescott — Ephraim Prescott."

" Ephraim Prescott ! " ejaculated the President, sharply, taking his cigar from his mouth, " Ephraim Prescott ! "

" Prescott — that's right — Prescott, General," repeated Ephraim, sorely puzzled by these manifestations of amazement.

" What did you come to Washington for ? " asked the President.

" Well, General, I kind of hate to tell you — I didn't intend to mention that. I guess I won't say nothin' about it," he added, " we've had such a sociable time. I've always b'en a little mite ashamed of it, General, ever since 'twas first mentioned."

" Good Lord!" said the President again, and then he looked at Cynthia. " What is it, Miss Cynthia?" he asked.

It was now Cynthia's turn to be a little confused.

" Uncle Jethro — that is, Mr. Bass " (the President nodded), " went to Cousin Eph when he couldn't make harness any more and said he'd give him the Brampton post-office."

The President's eyes met the senator's, and both gentlemen laughed. Cynthia bit her lip, not seeing any cause

T

for mirth in her remark, while Ephraim looked uncomfortable and mopped the perspiration from his brow.

" He said he'd give it to him, did he?" said the President. " Is Mr. Bass your uncle?"

" Oh, no, General," replied Cynthia, " he's really no relation. He's done everything for me, and I live with him since my father died. He was going to meet us here," she continued, looking around hurriedly, " I'm sure I can't think what's kept him."

" Mr. President, we are half an hour late already," said the senator, hurriedly.

" Well, well," said the President, " I suppose I must go. Good-by, Miss Cynthia," said he, taking the girl's hand warmly. " Good-by, Comrade. If ever you want to see General Grant, just send in your name. Good-by."

The President lifted his hat politely to Cynthia and passed. He said something to the senator which they did not hear, and the senator laughed heartily. Ephraim and Cynthia watched them until they were out of sight.

" Godfrey!" exclaimed Ephraim, " they told me he was hard to talk to. Why, Cynthy, he's as simple as a child."

" I've always thought that all great men must be simple," said Cynthia; " Uncle Jethro is."

" To think that the President of the United States stood talkin' to us on the sidewalk for half an hour," said Ephraim, clutching Cynthia's arm. " Cynthy, I'm glad we didn't press that post-office matter — it was worth more to me than all the post-offices in the Union to have that talk with General Grant."

They waited some time longer under the tree, happy in the afterglow of this wonderful experience. Presently a clock struck twelve.

" Why, it's dinner-time, Cynthy," said Ephraim. " I guess Jethro haint' a-comin' — must hev b'en delayed by some of them politicians."

" It's the first time I ever knew him to miss an appointment," said Cynthia, as they walked back to the hotel.

Jethro was not in the corridor, so they passed on to the dining room and looked eagerly from group to group. Jethro was not there, either, but Cynthia heard some one laughing above the chatter of the guests, and drew back into the corridor. She had spied the Duncans and the Worthingtons making merry by themselves at a corner table, and it was Somers's laugh that she heard. Bob, too, sitting next to Miss Duncan, was much amused about something. Suddenly Cynthia's exaltation over the incident of the morning seemed to leave her, and Bob Worthington's words which she had pondered over in the night came back to her with renewed force. He did not find it necessary to steal away to see Miss Duncan. Why should he have "stolen away" to see her? Was it because she was a country girl, and poor? That was true; but on the other hand, did she not live in the sunlight, as it were, of Uncle Jethro's greatness, and was it not an honor to come to his house and see any one? And why had Mr. Worthington turned his back on Jethro, and sent for Bob when he was talking to them? Cynthia could not understand these things, and her pride was sorely wounded by them.

"Perhaps Jethro's in his room," suggested Ephraim.

And indeed they found him there seated on the bed, poring over some newspapers, and both in a breath demanded where he had been. Ephraim did not wait for an answer.

"We seen General Grant, Jethro," he cried; "while we was waitin' for you under the tree he come up and stood talkin' to us half an hour. Full half an hour, wahn't it, Cynthy?"

"Oh, yes," answered Cynthia, forgetting her own grievance at the recollection; "only it didn't seem nearly that long."

"W-want to know!" exclaimed Jethro, in astonishment, putting down his paper. "H-how did it happen?"

"Come right up and spoke to us," said Ephraim, in a tone he might have used to describe a miracle, "jest as if he was common folk. Never had a more sociable talk with anybody. Why, there was times when I clean forgot he was President of the United States. The boys won't believe it when we git back at Coniston."

And Ephraim, full of his subject, began to recount from the beginning the marvellous affair, occasionally appealing to Cynthia for confirmation. How he had lived over again the Wilderness and Five Forks; how the General had changed since he had seen him whittling under a tree; how the General had asked about his pension.

" D-didn't mention the post-office, did you, Ephraim?"

" Why, no," replied Ephraim, " I didn't like to exactly. You see, we was havin' such a good time I didn't want to spoil it, but Cynthy — "

" I told the President about it, Uncle Jethro; I told him how sick Cousin Eph had been, and that you were going to give him the postmastership because he couldn't work any more with his hands."

The training of a lifetime had schooled Jethro not to betray surprise.

" K-kind of mixin' up in politics, hain't you, Cynthy? P-President say he'd give you the postmastership, Eph?" he asked.

" He didn't say nothin' about it, Jethro," answered Ephraim slowly; " I callate he has other views for the place, and he was too kind to come right out with 'em and spoil our mornin'. You see, Jethro, I wahn't only a sergeant, and Brampton's gittin' to be a big town."

" But, surely," cried Cynthia, who could scarcely wait for him to finish, "surely you're going to give Cousin Eph the post-office, aren't you, Uncle Jethro? All you have to do is to tell the President that you want it for him. Why, I had an idea that we came down for that."

" Now, Cynthy," Ephraim put in, deprecatingly.

" Who else would get the post-office?" asked Cynthia. " Surely you're not going to let Mr. Sutton have it for Dave Wheelock!"

" Er — Cynthy," said Jethro, slyly, " w-what'd you say to me once about interferin' with women's fixin's?"

Cynthia saw the point. She perceived also that the mazes of politics were not to be understood by a young woman, or even by an old soldier. She laughed and seized Jethro's hands and pulled him from the bed.

" We won't get any dinner unless we hurry," she said.

When they reached the dining room she was relieved to discover that the party in the corner had gone.

In the afternoon there were many more sights to be viewed, but they were back in the hotel again by half-past four, because Ephraim's Wilderness leg had its limits of endurance. Jethro (though he had not mentioned the fact to them) had gone to the White House.

It was during the slack hours that our friend the senator, whose interest in the matter of the Brampton post-office outweighed for the present certain grave problems of the Administration in which he was involved, hurried into the Willard Hotel, looking for Jethro Bass. He found him without much trouble in his usual attitude, occupying one of the chairs in the corridor.

" Well," exclaimed the senator, with a touch of eagerness he did not often betray, " did you see Grant ? How about your old soldier ? He's one of the most delightful characters I ever met — simple as a child," and he laughed at the recollection. " That was a masterstroke of yours, Bass, putting him under that tree with that pretty girl. I doubt if you ever did anything better in your life. Did they tell you about it ? "

" Yes," said Jethro, " they told me about it."

" And how about Grant ? What did he say to you ? "

" W-well, I went up there and sent in my card. D-didn't have to wait a great while, as I was pretty early, and soon he came in, smokin' a black cigar, head bent forward a little. D-didn't ask me to sit down, and what talkin' we did we did standin'. D-didn't ask me what he could do for me, what I wanted, or anything else, but just stood there, and I stood there. F-fust time in my life I didn't know how to commence or what to say; looked — looked at me — didn't take his eye off me. After a while I got started, somehow; told him I was there to ask him to appoint Ephraim Prescott to the Brampton post-office — t-told him all about Ephraim from the time he was

rocked in the cradle — never was so hard put that I could
remember.   T-told him how Ephraim shook butternuts
off my father's tree — for all I know.   T-told him all about
Ephraim's war record — leastways all I could call to mind
— and, by Godfrey! before I got through, I wished I'd
listened to more of it.   T-told him about Ephraim's Wilderness bullets — t-told him about Ephraim's rheumatism,
— how it bothered him when he went to bed and when he
got up again."

If Jethro had glanced at his companion, he would have
seen the senator was shaking with silent and convulsive
laughter.

"All the time I talked to him I didn't see a muscle
move in his face," Jethro continued, "so I started in
again, and he looked — looked — looked right at me.
W-wouldn't wink — don't think he winked once while I
was in that room.   I watched him as close as I could, and
I watched to see if a muscle moved or if I was makin' any
impression.   All he would do was to stand there and look
— look — look.   K-kept me there ten minutes and never
opened his mouth at all.   Hardest man to talk to I ever
met — never see a man before but what I could get him
to say somethin', if it was only a cuss word.   I got tired
of it after a while, made up my mind that I had found one
man I couldn't move.   Then what bothered me was to
get out of that room.   If I'd a had a Bible I believe
I'd a read it to him.   I didn't know what to say, but I
did say this after a while : —

" ' W-well, Mr. President, I guess I've kept you long
enough — g-guess you're a pretty busy man.   H-hope
you'll give Mr. Prescott that postmastership.   Er — er —
good-by.'

" ' Wait, sir,' he said.

" ' Yes,' I said, ' I'll wait.'

" ' Thought *you* was goin' to give him that postmastership, Mr. Bass,' he said."

At this point the senator could not control his mirth,
and the empty corridor echoed his laughter.

"By thunder! what did you say to that?"

" Er — I said, 'Mr. President, I thought I was until a while ago.'

" ' And when did you change your mind ? ' says he.

" Then he laughed a little — not much — but he laughed a little.

" ' I understand that your old soldier lives within the limits of the delivery of the Brampton office,' said he.

" ' That's correct, Mr. President,' said I.

" ' Well,' said he, ' I will app'int him postmaster at Brampton, Mr. Bass.'

" ' When ? ' said I.

" Then he laughed a little more.

" ' I'll have the app'intment sent to your hotel this afternoon,' said he.

" ' Then I said to him: ' This has come out full better than I expected, Mr. President. I'm much obliged to you.' He didn't say nothin' more, so I come out."

" Grant didn't say anything about Worthington or Duncan, did he ? " asked the senator, curiously, as he rose to go.

" G-guess I've told you all he said," answered Jethro ; " 'twahn't a great deal."

The senator held out his hand.

" Bass," he said, laughing, " I believe you came pretty near meeting your match. But if Grant's the hardest man in the Union to get anything out of, I've a notion who's the second." And with this parting shot the senator took his departure, chuckling to himself as he went.

As has been said, there were but few visitors in Washington at this time, and the hotel corridor was all but empty. Presently a substantial-looking gentleman came briskly in from the street, nodding affably to the colored porters and bell-boys, who greeted him by name. He wore a flowing Prince Albert coat, which served to dignify a growing portliness, and his coal-black whiskers glistened in the light. A voice, which appeared to come from nowhere in particular, brought the gentleman up standing.

" How be you, Heth ? "

It may not be that Mr. Sutton's hand trembled, but the

ashes of his cigar fell to the floor. He was not used to visitations, and for the instant, if the truth be told, he was not equal to looking around.

"Like Washington, Heth — like Washington?"

Then Mr. Sutton turned. His presence of mind, and that other presence of which he was so proud, seemed for the moment to have deserted him.

"S-stick pretty close to business, Heth, comin' down here out of session time. S-stick pretty close to business, don't you, since the *people* sent you to Congress?"

Mr. Sutton might have offered another man a cigar or a drink, but (as is well known) Jethro was proof against tobacco or stimulants.

"Well," said the Honorable Heth, catching his breath and making a dive, "I am surprised to see you, Jethro," which was probably true.

"Th-thought you might be," said Jethro. "Er — *glad* to see me, Heth — *glad* to see me?"

As has been recorded, it is peculiarly difficult to lie to people who are not to be deceived.

"Why, certainly I am," answered the Honorable Heth, swallowing hard, "certainly I am, Jethro. I meant to have got to Coniston this summer, but I was so busy —"

"Peoples' business, I understand. Er — hear you've gone in for high-minded politics, Heth — r-read a high-minded speech of yours — two high-minded speeches. Always thought you was a high-minded man, Heth."

"How did you like those speeches, Jethro?" asked Mr. Sutton, striving as best he might to make some show of dignity.

"Th-thought they was high-minded," said Jethro.

Then there was a silence, for Mr. Sutton could think of nothing more to say. And he yearned to depart with a great yearning, but something held him there.

"Heth," said Jethro, after a while, "you was always very friendly and obliging. You've done a great many favors for me in your life."

"I've always tried to be neighborly, Jethro," said Mr. Sutton, but his voice sounded a little husky even to himself.

" And I may have done one or two little things for you,
Heth," Jethro continued, "but I can't remember exactly.
Er — can you remember, Heth."

Mr. Sutton was trying with becoming nonchalance to
light the stump of his cigar. He did not succeed this
time. He pulled himself together with a supreme effort.

"I think we've both been mutually helpful, Jethro," he
said, "mutually helpful."

" Well," said Jethro, reflectively, "I don't know as I
could have put it as well as that — there's somethin' in
being an orator."

There was another silence, a much longer one. The
Honorable Heth threw his butt away, and lighted another
cigar. Suddenly, as if by magic, his aplomb returned,
and in a flash of understanding he perceived the situation.
He saw himself once more as the successful congressman,
the trusted friend of the railroad interests, and he saw
Jethro as a discredited boss. He did not stop to reflect
that Jethro did not act like a discredited boss, as a keener
man might have done. But if the Honorable Heth had
been a keener man, he would not have been at that time
a congressman. Mr. Sutton accused himself of having
been stupid in not grasping at once that the tables were
turned, and that now he was the one to dispense the gifts.

" K-kind of fortunate you stopped to speak to me,
Heth. N-now I come to think of it, I *hev* a little favor to
ask of you."

" Ah ! " exclaimed Mr. Sutton, blowing out the smoke ;
"of course anything I can do, Jethro — anything in
reason."

" W-wouldn't ask a high-minded man to do anything
he hadn't ought to," said Jethro ; "the fact is, I'd like to
git Eph Prescott appointed at the Brampton post-office.
You can fix that, Heth — can't you — you can fix that ? "

Mr. Sutton stuck his thumb into his vest pocket and
cleared his throat.

"I can't tell you how sorry I am not to oblige you,
Jethro, but I've arranged to give that post-office to Dave
Wheelock."

"A-arranged it, hev you — a-arranged it?"

"Why, yes," said Mr. Sutton, scarcely believing his own ears. Could it be possible that he was using this patronizingly kind tone to Jethro Bass?

"Well, that's too bad," said Jethro; "g-got it all fixed, hev you?"

"Practically," answered Mr. Sutton, grandly; "indeed, I may go as far as to say that it is as certain as if I had the appointment here in my pocket. I'm sorry not to oblige you, Jethro; but these are matters which a member of Congress must look after pretty closely." He held out his hand, but Jethro did not appear to see it, — he had his in his pockets. "I've an important engagement," said the Honorable Heth, consulting a large gold watch. "Are you going to be in Washington long?"

"G-guess I've about got through, Heth — g-guess I've about got through," said Jethro.

"Well, if you have time, and there's any other little thing, I'm in Room 29," said Mr. Sutton, as he put his foot on the stairway.

"T-told Worthington you got that app'intment for Wheelock — t-told Worthington?" Jethro called out after him.

Mr. Sutton turned and waved his cigar and smiled in acknowledgment of this parting bit of satire. He felt that he could afford to smile. A few minutes later he was ensconced on the sofa of a private sitting room reviewing the incident, with much gusto, for the benefit of Mr. Isaac D. Worthington and Mr. Alexander Duncan. Both of these gentlemen laughed heartily, for the Honorable Heth Sutton knew the art of telling a story well, at least, and was often to be seen with a group around him in the lobbies of Congress.

CHAPTER VI

MR. SUTTON TALKS TO A CONSTITUENT

ABOUT five o'clock that afternoon Ephraim was sitting in his shirt-sleeves by the window of his room, and Cynthia was reading aloud to him an article (about the war, of course) from a Washington paper, which his friend, Mr. Beard, had sent him. There was a knock at the door, and Cynthia opened it to discover a colored hall-boy with a roll in his hand.

"Mistah Ephum Prescott?" he said.

"Yes," answered Ephraim, "that's me."

Cynthia shut the door and gave him the roll, but Ephraim took it as though he were afraid of its contents.

"Guess it's some of them war records from Amasy," he said.

"Oh, Cousin Eph," exclaimed Cynthia, excitedly, "why don't you open it? If you don't, I will."

"Guess you'd better, Cynthy," and he held it out to her with a trembling hand.

Cynthia did open it, and drew out a large document with seals and printing and signatures.

"Cousin Eph," she cried, holding it under his nose, "Cousin Eph, you're postmaster of Brampton!"

Ephraim looked at the paper, but his eyes swam, and he could only make out a dancing, bronze seal.

"I want to know!" he exclaimed. "Fetch Jethro."

But Cynthia had already flown on that errand. Curiously enough, she ran into Jethro in the hall immediately outside of Ephraim's door. Ephraim got to his feet; it was very difficult for him to realize that his troubles were ended, that he was to earn his living at last. He looked at Jethro, and his eyes filled with tears.

"I guess I can't thank you as I'd ought to, Jethro," he said, "leastways, not now."

"I'll thank him for you, Cousin Eph," said Cynthia. And she did.

"D-don't thank me," said Jethro, "I didn't have much to do with it, Eph. Thank the President."

Ephraim did thank the President, in one of the most remarkable letters, from a literary point of view, ever received at the White House. For the art of literature largely consists in belief in what one is writing, and Ephraim's letter had this quality of sincerity, and no lack of vividness as well. He spent most of the evening in composing it.

Cynthia, too, had received a letter that day — a letter which she had read several times, now with a smile, and again with a pucker of the forehead which was meant for a frown. "Dear Cynthia," it said. "Where do you keep yourself? I am sure you would not be so cruel if you knew that I was aching to see you." Aching! Cynthia repeated the word, and remembered the glimpse she had had of him in the dining room with Miss Janet Duncan. "Whenever I have been free" (Cynthia repeated this also, somewhat ironically, although she conceded it the merit of frankness), "Whenever I have been free, I have haunted the corridors for a sight of you. Think of me as haunting the hotel desk for an answer to this, telling me when I can see you — and where. P.S. I shall be around all evening." And it was signed, "Your friend and playmate, R. Worthington."

It is a fact — not generally known — that Cynthia did answer the letter — twice. But she sent neither answer. Even at that age she was given to reflection, and much as she may have approved of the spirit of the letter, she liked the tone of it less. Cynthia did not know a great deal of the world, it is true, but she felt instinctively that something was wrong when Bob resorted to such means of communication. And she was positively relieved, or thought that she was, when she went down to supper and discovered that the table in the corner was empty.

After supper Ephraim had his letter to write, and
Jethro wished to sit in the corridor. But Cynthia had
learned that the corridor was not the place for a girl, so
she explained to Jethro that he would find her in the
parlor if he wanted her, and that she was going there to
read. That parlor Cynthia thought a handsome room,
with its high windows and lace curtains, its long mirrors
and marble-topped tables. She established herself under
a light, on a sofa in one corner, and sat, with the book on
her lap, watching the people who came and went. She
had that delicious sensation which comes to the young when
they first travel — the sensation of being a part of the
great world; and she wished that she knew these people,
and which were the great, and which the little ones.
Some of them looked at her intently, she thought too
intently, and at such times she pretended to read. She
was aroused by hearing some one saying: —

"Isn't this Miss Wetherell?"

Cynthia looked up and caught her breath, for the
young lady who had spoken was none other than Miss
Janet Duncan herself. Seen thus startlingly at close
range, Miss Duncan was not at all like what Cynthia had
expected — but then most people are not. Janet Duncan
was, in fact, one of those strange persons who do not
realize the picture which their names summon up. She
was undoubtedly good-looking; her hair, of a more
golden red than her brother's, was really wonderful; her
neck was slender; and she had a strange, dreamy face that
fascinated Cynthia, who had never seen anything like it.

She put down her book on the sofa and got up, not
without a little tremor at this unexpected encounter.

"Yes, I'm Cynthia Wetherell," she replied.

To add to her embarrassment, Miss Duncan seized both
her hands impulsively and gazed into her face.

"You're really very beautiful," she said. "Do you know
it?"

Cynthia's only answer to this was a blush. She wondered if all city girls were like Miss Duncan.

"I was determined to come up and speak to you the

Florence Scovel Shinn

"'I've been making up stories about you.'"

first chance I had," Janet continued. " I've been making up stories about you."

"Stories!" exclaimed Cynthia, drawing away her hands.

" Romances," said Miss Duncan — "real romances. Sometimes I think I'm going to be a novelist, because I'm always weaving stories about people that I see — people who interest me, I mean. And you look as if you might be the heroine of a wonderful romance."

Cynthia's breath was now quite taken away.

" Oh," she said, " I had never thought that I looked like that."

" But you do," said Miss Duncan ; " you've got all sorts of possibilities in your face — you look as if you might have lived for ages."

" As old as that ? " exclaimed Cynthia, really startled.

" Perhaps I don't express myself very well," said the other, hastily ; " I wish you could see what I've written about you already. I can do it so much better with pen and ink. I've started quite a romance already."

" What is it ? " asked Cynthia, not without interest.

"Sit down on the sofa and I'll tell you," said Miss Duncan; " I've done it all from your face, too. I've made you a very poor girl brought up by peasants, only you are really of a great family, although nobody knows it. A rich duke sees you one day when he is hunting and falls in love with you, and you have to stand a lot of suffering and persecution because of it, and say nothing. I believe you could do that," added Janet, looking critically at Cynthia's face.

" I suppose I could if I had to," said Cynthia, "but I shouldn't like it."

" Oh, it would do you good," said Janet ; " it would ennoble your character. Not that it needs it," she added hastily. " And I could write another story about that quaint old man who paid the musicians to go away, and who made us all laugh so much."

Cynthia's eye kindled.

" Mr. Bass isn't a quaint old man," she said ; "he's the greatest man in the state."

Miss Duncan's patronage had been of an unconscious kind. She knew that she had offended, but did not quite realize how.

"I'm so sorry," she cried, "I didn't mean to hurt you. You live with him, don't you — Coniston?"

"Yes," replied Cynthia, not knowing whether to laugh or cry.

"I've heard about Coniston. It must be quite a romance in itself to live all the year round in such a beautiful place and to make your own clothes. Yours become you very well," said Miss Duncan, "although I don't know why. They're not at all in style, and yet they give you quite an air of distinction. I wish I could live in Coniston for a year, anyway, and write a book about you. My brother and Bob Worthington went out there one night and serenaded you, didn't they?"

"Yes," said Cynthia, that peculiar flash coming into her eyes again, "and I think it was very foolish of them."

"Do you?" exclaimed Miss Duncan, in surprise; "I wish somebody would serenade me. I think it was the most romantic thing Bob ever did. He's wild about you, and so is Somers — they have both told me so in confidence."

Cynthia's face was naturally burning now.

"If it were true," she said, "they wouldn't have told you about it."

"I suppose that's so," said Miss Duncan, thoughtfully, "only you're very clever to have seen it. Now that I know you, I think you a more remarkable person than ever. You don't seem at all like a country girl, and you don't talk like one."

Cynthia laughed outright. She could not help liking Janet Duncan, mere flesh and blood not being proof against such compliments.

"I suppose it's because my father was an educated man," she said; "he taught me to read and speak when I was young."

"Why, you *are* just like a person out of a novel! Who was your father?"

"He kept the store at Coniston," answered Cynthia,

smiling a little sadly. She would have liked to have added that William Wetherell would have been a great man if he had had health, but she found it difficult to give out confidences, especially when they were in the nature of surmises.

" Well," said Janet, stoutly, " I think that is more like a story than ever. Do you know," she continued, "'I saw you once at the state capital outside of our grounds the day Bob ran after you. That was when I was in love with him. We had just come back from Europe then, and I thought he was the most wonderful person I had ever seen."

If Cynthia had felt any emotion from this disclosure, she did not betray it. Janet, moreover, was not looking for it.

" What made you change your mind? " asked Cynthia, biting her lip.

" Oh, Bob hasn't the temperament," said Janet, making use of a word that she had just discovered ; " he's too practical — he never does or says the things you want him to. He's just been out West with us on a trip, and he was always looking at locomotives and brakes and grades and bridges and all such tiresome things. I should like to marry a poet," said Miss Duncan, dreamily ; " I know they want me to marry Bob, and Mr. Worthington wants it. I'm sure of that. But he wouldn't at all suit me."

If Cynthia had been able to exercise an equal freedom of speech, she might have been impelled to inquire what young Mr. Worthington's views were in the matter. As it was, she could think of nothing appropriate to say, and just then four people entered the room and came towards them. Two of these were Janet's mother and father, and the other two were Mr. Worthington, the elder, and the Honorable Heth Sutton. Mrs. Duncan, whom Janet did not at all resemble, was a person who naturally commanded attention. She had strong features, and a very decided, though not disagreeable, manner.

"I couldn't imagine what had become of you, Janet," she said, coming forward and throwing off her lace shawl. " Whom have you found — a school friend ? "

υ

"No, Mamma," said Janet, "this is Cynthia Wetherell."

"Oh," said Mrs. Duncan, looking very hard at Cynthia in a near-sighted way, and not knowing in the least who she was; "you haven't seen Senator and Mrs. Meade, have you, Janet? They were to be here at eight o'clock."

"No," said Janet, turning again to Cynthia and scarcely hearing the question.

"Janet hasn't seen them, Dudley," said Mrs. Duncan, going up to Mr. Worthington, who was pulling his chop whiskers by the door. "Janet has discovered such a beautiful creature," she went on, in a voice which she did not take the trouble to lower. "Do look at her, Alexander. And you, Mr. Sutton — who are such a bureau of useful information, do tell me who she is. Perhaps she comes from your part of the country — her name's Wetherell."

"Wetherell? Why, of course I know her," said Mr. Sutton, who was greatly pleased because Mrs. Duncan had likened him to an almanac: greatly pleased this evening in every respect, and even the diamond in his bosom seemed to glow with a brighter fire. He could afford to be generous to-night, and he turned to Mr. Worthington and laughed knowingly. "She's the ward of our friend Jethro," he explained.

"What is she?" demanded Mrs. Duncan, who knew and cared nothing about politics; "a country girl, I suppose."

"Yes," replied Mr. Sutton, "a country girl from a little village not far from Clovelly. A good girl, I believe, in spite of the atmosphere in which she has been raised."

"It's really wonderful, Mr. Sutton, how you seem to know every one in your district, including the women and children," said the lady; "but I suppose you wouldn't be where you are if you didn't."

The Honorable Heth cleared his throat.

"Wetherell," Mr. Duncan was saying, staring at Cynthia through his spectacles, "where have I heard that name?"

He must suddenly have remembered, and recalled also

that he and his ally Worthington had been on opposite sides in the Woodchuck Session, for he sat down abruptly beside the door, and remained there for a while. For Mr. Duncan had never believed Mr. Merrill's explanation concerning poor William Wetherell's conduct.

"Pretty, ain't she?" said Mr. Sutton to Mr. Worthington. "Guess she's more dangerous than Jethro, now that we've clipped his wings a little." The congressman had heard of Bob's infatuation.

Isaac D. Worthington, however, was in a good humor this evening, and was moved by a certain curiosity to inspect the girl. Though what he had seen and heard of his son's conduct with her had annoyed him, he did not regard it seriously.

"Aren't you going to speak to your constituent, Mr. Sutton?" said Mrs. Duncan, who was bored because her friends had not arrived; "a congressman ought to keep on the right side of the pretty girls, you know."

It hadn't occurred to the Honorable Heth to speak to his constituent. The ways of Mrs. Duncan sometimes puzzled him, and he could not see why that lady and her daughter seemed to take more than a passing interest in the girl. But if they could afford to notice her, certainly he could, so he went forward graciously and held out his hand to Cynthia, interrupting Miss Duncan in the middle of a discourse upon her diary.

"How do you do, Cynthia?" said Mr. Sutton. Had he been in Coniston, he would have said, "How be you?"

Cynthia took the hand, but did not rise, somewhat to Mr. Sutton's annoyance. A certain respect was due to a member of Congress and the Rajah of Clovelly.

"How do you do, Mr. Sutton?" said Cynthia, very coolly.

"I like her," remarked Mrs. Duncan to Mr. Worthington.

"This is a splendid trip for you, eh, Cynthia?" Mr. Sutton persisted, with a praiseworthy determination to be pleasant.

"It has turned out to be so, Mr. Sutton," replied Cynthia. This was not precisely the answer Mr. Sutton expected, and to tell the truth, he didn't know quite what to make of it.

"A great treat to see Washington and New York, isn't it?" said Mr. Sutton, kindly, "a great treat for a Coniston girl. I suppose you came through New York and saw the sights?"

"Is there another way to get to Washington?" asked Cynthia.

Mrs. Duncan nudged Mr. Worthington and drew a little nearer, while Mr. Sutton began to wish he had not been lured into the conversation. Cynthia had been very polite, but there was something in the quiet manner in which the girl's eyes were fixed upon him that made him vaguely uneasy. He could not back out with dignity, and he felt himself on the verge of becoming voluble. Mr. Sutton prided himself on never being voluble.

"Why, no," he answered, "we have to go to New York to get anywhere in these days." There was a slight pause. "Uncle Jethro taking you and Mr. Prescott on a little pleasure trip?" He had not meant to mention Jethro's name, but he found himself, to his surprise, a little at a loss for a subject.

"Well, partly a pleasure trip. It's always a pleasure for Uncle Jethro to do things for others," said Cynthia, quietly, "although people do not always appreciate what he does for them."

The Honorable Heth coughed. He was now very uncomfortable, indeed. How much did this astounding young person know, whom he had thought so innocent?

"I didn't discover he was in town until I ran across him in the corridor this evening. Should have liked to have introduced him to some of the Washington folks — some of the big men, although not many of 'em are here," Mr. Sutton ran on, not caring to notice the little points of light in Cynthia's eyes. (The idea of Mr. Sutton introducing Uncle Jethro to anybody!) "I haven't seen Ephraim Prescott. It must be a great treat for him, too, to get away on a little trip and see his army friends. How is he?"

"He's very happy," said Cynthia.

"Happy!" exclaimed Mr. Sutton. "Oh, yes, of course, Ephraim's always happy, in spite of his troubles and his rheumatism. I always liked Ephraim Prescott."

Cynthia did not answer this remark at all, and Mr. Sutton suspected strongly that she did not believe it, therefore he repeated it.

"I always liked Ephraim. I want you to tell Jethro that I'm downright sorry I couldn't get him that Brampton postmastership."

"I'll tell him that you are sorry, Mr. Sutton," replied Cynthia, gravely, "but I don't think it'll do any good."

Not do any good! What did the girl mean? Mr. Sutton came to the conclusion that he had been condescending enough, that somehow he was gaining no merit in Mrs. Duncan's eyes by this kindness to a constituent. He buttoned up his coat rather grandly.

"I hope you won't misunderstand me, Cynthia," he said. "I regret extremely that my sense of justice demanded that I should make David Wheelock postmaster at Brampton, and I have made him so."

It was now Cynthia's turn to be amazed.

"But," she exclaimed, "but Cousin Ephraim is postmaster of Brampton."

Mr. Sutton started violently, and that part of his face not hidden by his whiskers seemed to pale, and Mr. Worthington, usually self-possessed, took a step forward and seized him by the arm.

"What does this mean, Sutton?" he said.

Mr. Sutton pulled himself together, and glared at Cynthia.

"I think you are mistaken," said he, "the congressman of the district usually arranges these matters, and the appointment will be sent to Mr. Wheelock to-morrow."

"But Cousin Ephraim already has the appointment," said Cynthia; "it was sent to him this afternoon, and he is up in his room now writing to thank the President for it."

"What in the world's the matter?" cried Mrs. Duncan, in astonishment.

Cynthia's simple announcement had indeed caused something of a panic among the gentlemen present. Mr. Duncan had jumped up from his seat beside the door, and Mr. Worthington, his face anything but impassive, tightened his hold on the congressman's arm.

"Good God, Sutton!" he exclaimed, "can this be true?"

As for Cynthia, she was no less astonished than Mrs. Duncan by the fact that these rich and powerful gentlemen were so excited over a little thing like the postmastership of Brampton. But Mr. Sutton laughed; it was not hearty, but still it might have passed muster for a laugh.

"Nonsense," he exclaimed, making a fair attempt to regain his composure, "the girl's got it mixed up with something else — she doesn't know what she's talking about."

Mrs. Duncan thought the girl did look uncommonly as if she knew what she was talking about, and Mr. Duncan and Mr. Worthington had some such impression, too, as they stared at her. Cynthia's eyes flashed, but her voice was no louder than before.

"I am used to being believed, Mr. Sutton," she said, "but here's Uncle Jethro himself. You might ask him."

They all turned in amazement, and one, at least, in trepidation, to perceive Jethro Bass standing behind them with his hands in his pockets, as unconcerned as though he were under the butternut tree in Coniston.

"How be you, Heth?" he said. "Er — still got that appointment p-practically in your pocket?"

"Uncle Jethro," said Cynthia, "Mr. Sutton does not believe me when I tell him that Cousin Ephraim has been made postmaster of Brampton. He would like to have you tell him whether it is so or not."

But this, as it happened, was exactly what the Honorable Heth did not want to have Jethro tell him. How he got out of the parlor of the Willard House he has not to this day a very clear idea. As a matter of fact, he followed Mr. Worthington and Mr. Duncan, and they made their exit by the farther door. Jethro did not appear to take any notice of their departure.

"Janet," said Mrs. Duncan, "I think Senator and Mrs. Meade must have gone to our sitting room." Then, to Cynthia's surprise, the lady took her by the hand. "I can't imagine what you've done, my dear," she said pleasantly, "but I believe that you are capable of taking care of yourself, and I like you."

Thus it will be seen that Mrs. Duncan was an independent person. Sometimes heiresses are apt to be.

"And I like you, too," said Janet, taking both of Cynthia's hands, "and I hope to see you very, very often."

Jethro looked after them.

"Er — the women folks seem to have some sense," he said. Then he turned to Cynthia. "B-be'n havin' some fun with Heth, Cynthy?" he inquired.

"I haven't any respect for Mr. Sutton," said Cynthia, indignantly; "it serves him right for presuming to think that he could give a post-office to any one."

Jethro made no remark concerning this presumption on the part of the congressman of the district. Cynthia's indignation against Mr. Sutton was very real, and it was some time before she could compose herself sufficiently to tell Jethro what had happened. His enjoyment as he listened may be imagined; but presently he forgot this, and became aware that something really troubled her.

"Uncle Jethro," she asked suddenly, "why do they treat me as they do?"

He did not answer at once. This was because of a pain around his heart — had she known it. He had felt that pain before.

"H-how do they treat you, Cynthy?"

She hesitated. She had not yet learned to use the word *patronize* in the social sense, and she was at a loss to describe the attitude of Mrs. Duncan and her daughter, though her instinct had registered it. She was at a loss to account for Mr. Worthington's attitude, too. Mr. Sutton's she bitterly resented.

"Are they your enemies?" she demanded.

Jethro was in real distress.

"If they are," she continued, "I won't speak to them

again. If they can't treat me as — as your daughter ought to be treated, I'll turn my back on them. I am —. I am just like your daughter — am I not, Uncle Jethro? "

He put out his hand and seized hers roughly, and his voice was thick with suffering.

" Yes, Cynthy," he said, " you — you're all I've got in the world."

She squeezed his hand in return.

" I know it, Uncle Jethro," she cried contritely, " I oughtn't to have troubled you by asking. You — you have done everything for me, much more than I deserve. And I shan't be hurt after this when people are too small to appreciate how good you are, and how great."

The pain tightened about Jethro's heart — tightened so sharply that he could not speak, and scarcely breathe because of it. Cynthia picked up her novel, and set the bookmark.

" Now that Cousin Eph is provided for, let's go back to Coniston, Uncle Jethro." A sudden longing was upon her for the peaceful life in the shelter of the great ridge, and she thought of the village maples all red and gold with the magic touch of the frosts. " Not that I haven't enjoyed my trip," she added; " but we are so happy there."

He did not look at her, because he was afraid to.

" C-Cynthy," he said, after a little pause, " th-thought we'd go to Boston."

" Boston, Uncle Jethro ! "

" Er — to-morrow — at one — to-morrow — like to go to Boston ? "

" Yes," she said thoughtfully, " I remember parts of it. The Common, where I used to walk with Daddy, and the funny old streets that went uphill. It will be nice to go back to Coniston that way — over Truro Pass in the train."

That night a piece of news flashed over the wires to New England, and the next morning a small item appeared in the *Newcastle Guardian* to the effect that one Ephraim Prescott had been appointed postmaster at

Brampton. Copied in the local papers of the state, it caused some surprise in Brampton, to be sure, and excitement in Coniston. Perhaps there were but a dozen men, however, who saw its real significance, who knew through this item that Jethro Bass was still supreme — that the railroads had failed to carry this first position in their war against him.

It was with a light heart the next morning that Cynthia packed the little leather trunk which had been her father's. Ephraim was in the corridor regaling his friend, Mr. Beard, with that wonderful encounter with General Grant which sounded so much like a Fifth Reader anecdote of a chance meeting with royalty. Jethro's room was full of visiting politicians. So Cynthia, when she had finished her packing, went out to walk about the streets alone, scanning the people who passed her, looking at the big houses, and wondering who lived in them. Presently she found herself, in the middle of the morning, seated on a bench in a little park, surrounded by colored mammies and children playing in the paths. It seemed a long time since she had left the hills, and this glimpse of cities had given her many things to think and dream about. Would she always live in Coniston? Or was her future to be cast among those who moved in the world and helped to sway it? Cynthia felt that she was to be of these, though she could not reason why, and she told herself that the feeling was foolish. Perhaps it was that she knew in the bottom of her heart that she had been given a spirit and intelligence to cope with a larger life than that of Coniston. With a sense that such imaginings were vain, she tried to think what she would do if she were to become a great lady like Mrs. Duncan.

She was aroused from these reflections by a distant glimpse, through the trees, of Mr. Robert Worthington. He was standing quite alone on the edge of the park, his hands in his pockets, staring at the White House. Cynthia half rose, and then sat down and looked at him again. He wore a light gray, loose-fitting suit and a straw hat, and she could not but acknowledge that there was something stalwart and clean and altogether appealing in him. She wondered, indeed, why he now failed to appeal to Miss Duncan, and she began to doubt the sincerity of that young lady's statements. Bob certainly was not romantic, but he was a man — or would be very soon.

Cynthia sat still, although her impulse was to go away. She scarcely analyzed her feeling of wishing to avoid him. It may not be well, indeed, to analyze them on paper too closely. She had an instinct that only pain could come from frequent meetings, and she knew now what but a week ago was a surmise, that he belonged to the world of which she had been dreaming — Mrs. Duncan's world. Again, there was that mysterious barrier between them of which she had seen so many evidences. And yet she sat still on her bench and looked at him.

Presently he turned, slowly, as if her eyes had compelled his. She sat still — it was too late, then. In less than a minute he was standing beside her, looking down at her with a smile that had in it a touch of reproach.

"How do you do, Mr. Worthington?" said Cynthia, quietly.

"Mr. Worthington!" he cried, "you haven't called me that before."

"We are not children any more," she said.

"What difference does that make?"

"A great deal," said Cynthia, not caring to define it.

"Cynthia," said Mr. Worthington, sitting down on the bench and facing her, "do you think you've treated me just right?"

"Of course I do," she said, "or I should have treated you differently."

Bob ignored such quibbling.

"Why did you run away from that baseball game in Brampton? And why couldn't you have answered my letter yesterday, if it were only a line? And why have you avoided me here in Washington?"

It is very difficult to answer for another questions which one cannot answer for one's self.

"I haven't avoided you," said Cynthia.

"I've been looking for you all over town this morning," said Bob, with pardonable exaggeration, "and I believe that idiot Somers has, too."

"Then why should you call him an idiot?" Cynthia flashed.

Bob laughed.

"How you do catch a fellow up!" said he, admiringly. "We both found out you'd gone out for a walk alone."

"How did you find it out?"

"Well," said Bob, hesitating, "we asked the colored doorkeeper."

"Mr. Worthington," said Cynthia, with an indignation that made him quail, "do you think it right to ask a doorkeeper to spy on my movements?"

"I'm sorry, Cynthia," he gasped, "I — I didn't think of it that way — and he won't tell. Desperate cases require desperate remedies, you know."

But Cynthia was not appeased.

"If you wanted to see me," she said, "why didn't you send your card to my room, and I would have come to the parlor."

"But I did send a note, and waited around all day."

How was she to tell him that it was to the tone of the note she objected — to the hint of a clandestine meeting? She turned the light of her eyes full upon him.

"Would you have been content to see me in the parlor?" she asked. "Did you mean to see me there?"

"Why, yes," said he; "I would have given my head to see you anywhere, only —"

"Only what?"

"Duncan might have come in and spoiled it."

"Spoiled what?"

Bob fidgeted.

"Look here, Cynthia," he said, "you're not stupid — far from it. Of course you know a fellow would rather talk to you alone."

"I should have been very glad to have seen Mr. Duncan, too."

"You would, would you!" he exclaimed. "I shouldn't have thought that."

"Isn't he your friend?" asked Cynthia.

"Oh, yes," said Bob, "and one of the best in the world. Only — I shouldn't have thought you'd care to talk to him." And he looked around, for fear the vigilant Mr. Duncan was already in the park and had discovered them. Cynthia smiled, and immediately became grave again.

"So it was only on Mr. Duncan's account that you didn't ask me to come down to the parlor?" she said.

Bob was in a quandary. He was a truthful person, and he had learned something of the world through his three years at Cambridge. He had seen many young women, and many kinds of them. But the girl beside him was such a mixture of innocence and astuteness that he was wholly at a loss how to deal with her — how to parry her searching questions.

"Naturally I wanted to have you all to myself," he said; "you ought to know that."

Cynthia did not commit herself on this point. She wished to go mercilessly to the root of the matter, but the notion of what this would imply prevented her. Bob took advantage of her silence.

"Everybody who sees you falls a victim, Cynthia," he went on; "Mrs. Duncan and Janet lost their hearts. You ought to have heard them praising you at breakfast." He paused abruptly, thinking of the rest of that conversation, and laughed. Bob seemed fated to commit himself that day. "I heard the way you handled Heth Sutton," he said, plunging in. "I'll bet he felt as if he'd been dropped out of the third-story window," and Bob laughed again. "I'd have given a thousand dollars to have been there. Somers and I went out to supper with a classmate who lives in Washington, in that house over there," and he pointed casually to one of the imposing mansions fronting on the park. Mrs. Duncan said she'd never heard anybody lay it on the way you did. I don't believe you half know what happened, Cynthia. You made a ten-strike."

"A ten-strike?" she repeated.

"Well," he said, "you not only laid out Heth, but my

father and Mr. Duncan, too.   Mrs. Duncan laughed at
'em — she isn't afraid of anything.   But they didn't say
a word all through breakfast.   I've never seen my father
so mad.   He ought to have known better than to run up
against Uncle Jethro."

"How did they run up against Uncle Jethro?" asked
Cynthia, now keenly interested.

"Don't you know?" exclaimed Bob, in astonishment.

"No," said Cynthia, "or I shouldn't have asked."

"Didn't Uncle Jethro tell you about it?"

"He never tells me anything about his affairs," she
answered.

Bob's astonishment did not wear off at once.   Here was
a new phase, and he was very hard put.   He had heard,
casually, a good deal of abuse of Jethro and his methods
in the last two days.

"Well," he said, "I don't know anything about politics.
I don't know myself why father and Mr. Duncan were
so eager for this postmastership.   But they were.   And
I heard them say something about the President going
back on them when they had telegraphed from Chicago
and come to see him here.   And maybe they didn't let
Heth in for it.   It seems Uncle Jethro only had to walk
up to the White House.   They ought to have sense enough
to know that he runs the state.   But what's the use of
wasting time over this business?" said Bob.   "I told
you I was going to Brampton before the term begins
just to see you, didn't I?"

"Yes, but I didn't believe you," said Cynthia.

"Why not?" he demanded.

"Because it's my nature, I suppose," she replied.

This was too much for Bob, exasperated though he was,
and he burst into laughter.

"You're the queerest girl I've ever known," he said.
Not a very original remark.

"That must be saying a great deal," she answered.

"Why?"

"You must have known many."

"I have," he admitted, "and none of 'em, no matter

how much they'd knocked about, were able to look out for themselves any better than you."

"Not even Cassandra Hopkins?" Cynthia could not resist saying. She saw that she had scored; his expressions registered his sensations so accurately.

"What do you know about her?" he said.

"Oh," said Cynthia, mysteriously, "I heard that you were very fond of her at Andover."

Bob could not help pluming himself a little. He thought the fact that she had mentioned the matter a flaw in Cynthia's armor, as indeed it was. And yet he was not proud of the Cassandra Hopkins episode in his career.

"Cassandra is one of the institutions at Andover," said he; "most fellows have to take a course in Cassandra to complete their education."

"Yours seems to be very complete," Cynthia retorted.

"Great Scott!" he exclaimed, looking at her, "no wonder you made mince-meat of the Honorable Heth. Where did you learn it all, Cynthia?"

Cynthia did not know. She merely wondered where she would be if she hadn't learned it. Something told her that if it were not for this anchor she would be drifting out to sea: might, indeed, soon be drifting out to sea in spite of it. It was one thing for Mr. Robert Worthington, with his numerous resources, to amuse himself with a girl in her position; it would be quite another thing for the girl. She got to her feet and held out her hand to him.

"Good-by," she said.

"Good-by?"

"We are leaving Washington at one o'clock, and Uncle Jethro will be worried if I am not in time for dinner."

"Leaving at one! That's the worst luck I've had yet. But I'm going back to the hotel myself."

Cynthia didn't see how she was to prevent him walking with her. She would not have admitted to herself that she had enjoyed this encounter, since she was trying so hard not to enjoy it. So they started together out of the park.   Bob, for a wonder, was silent awhile, glancing now and then at her profile.   He knew that he had a great deal to say, but he couldn't decide exactly what it was to be.   This is often the case with young men in his state of mind: in fact, to be paradoxical again, he might hardly be said at this time to have had a state of mind.   He lacked both an attitude and a policy.

"If you see Duncan before I do, let me know," he remarked finally.

Cynthia bit her lip.   "Why should I?" she asked.

"Because we've only got five minutes more alone together, at best.   If we see him in time, we can go down a side street."

"I think it would be hard to get away from Mr. Duncan if we met him — even if we wanted to," she said, laughing outright.

"You don't know how true that is," he replied, with feeling.

"That sounds as though you'd tried it before."

He paid no attention to this thrust.

"I shan't see you again till I get to Brampton," he said; "that will be a whole week.   And then," he ventured to look at her, "I shan't see you until the Christmas holidays.   You might be a little kind, Cynthia.   You know I've — I've always thought the world of you.   I don't know how I'm going to get through the three months without seeing you."

"You managed to get through a good many years," said Cynthia, looking at the pavement.

"I know," he said; "I was sent away to school and college, and our lives separated."

"Yes, our lives separated," she assented.

"And I didn't know you were going to be like — like this," he went on, vaguely enough, but with feeling.

"Like what?"

"Like — well, I'd rather be with you and talk to you than any girl I ever saw.   I don't care who she is," Bob declared, "or how much she may have travelled."   He was running into deep water.   "Why are you so cold, Cynthia?

Why can't you be as you used to be? You used to like
me well enough."

"And I like you now," answered Cynthia. They were
very near the hotel by this time.

"You talk as if you were ten years older than I," he
said, smiling plaintively.

She stopped and turned to him, smiling. They had
reached the steps.

"I believe I am, Bob," she replied. "I haven't seen
much of the world, but I've seen something of its troubles.
Don't be foolish. If you're coming to Brampton just to
see me, don't come. Good-by." And she gave him her
hand frankly.

"But I will come to Brampton," he cried, taking her
hand and squeezing it. "I'd like to know why I shouldn't
come."

As Cynthia drew her hand away a gentleman came out
of the hotel, paused for a brief moment by the door and
stared at them, and then passed on without a word or
a nod of recognition. It was Mr. Worthington. Bob
looked after his father, and then glanced at Cynthia.
There was a trifle more color in her cheeks, and her head
was raised a little, and her eyes were fixed upon him
gravely.

"You should know why not," she said, and before he
could answer her she was gone into the hotel. He did not
attempt to follow her, but stood where she had left him in
the sunlight.

He was aroused by the voice of the genial colored doorkeeper.

"Wal, suh, you found the lady, Mistah Wo'thington.
Thought you would, suh. T'other young gentleman come
in while ago — looked as if he was feelin' powerful bad,
Mistah Wo'thington."

CHAPTER VII

AN AMAZING ENCOUNTER

WHEN they reached Boston, Cynthia felt almost as if she were home again, and Ephraim declared that he had had the same feeling when he returned from the war. Though it be the prosperous capital of New England, it is a city of homes, and the dwellers of it have held stanchly to the belief of their forefathers that the home is the very foundation-rock of the nation. Held stanchly to other beliefs, too: that wealth carries with it some little measure of responsibility. The stranger within the gates of that city feels that if he falls, a heedless world will not go charging over his body: that a helping hand will be stretched out, — a helping and a wise hand that will inquire into the circumstances of his fall — but still a human hand.

They were sitting in the parlor of the Tremont House that morning with the sun streaming in the windows, waiting for Ephraim.

"Uncle Jethro," Cynthia asked, abruptly, "did you ever know my mother?"

Jethro started, and looked at her quickly.

"W-why, Cynthy?" he asked.

"Because she grew up in Coniston," answered Cynthia. "I never thought of it before, but of course you must have known her."

"Yes, I knew her," he said.

"Did you know her well?" she persisted.

Jethro got up and went over to the window, where he stood with his back toward her.

"Yes, Cynthy," he answered at length.

"Why haven't you ever told me about her?" asked Cynthia. How was she to know that her innocent questions tortured him cruelly; that the spirit of the Cynthia who had come to him in the tannery house had haunted him all his life, and that she herself, a new Cynthia, was still that spirit? The bygone Cynthia had been much in his thoughts since they came to Boston.

"What was she like?"

"She — she was like you, Cynthy," he said, but he did not turn round. "She was a clever woman, and a good woman, and — a lady, Cynthy."

The girl said nothing for a while, but she tingled with pleasure because Jethro had compared her to her mother. She determined to try to be like that, if he thought her so.

"Uncle Jethro," she said presently, "I'd like to go to see the house where she lived."

"Er — Ephraim knows it," said Jethro.

So when Ephraim came the three went over the hill, past the State House which Bulfinch set as a crown on the crest of it looking over the sweep of the Common, and on into the maze of quaint, old-world streets on the slope beyond : streets with white porticos, and violet panes in the windows. They came to an old square hidden away on a terrace of the hill, and after that the streets grew narrower and dingier. Ephraim, whose memory never betrayed him, hobbled up to a shabby house in the middle of one of these blocks and rang the bell.

"Here's where I found Will when I come back from the war," he said, and explained the matter in full to the slatternly landlady who came to the door. She was a good-natured woman, who thought her boarder would not mind, and led the way up the steep stairs to the chamber over the roofs where Wetherell and Cynthia had lived and hoped and worked together; where he had written those pages by which, with the aid of her loving criticism, he had thought to become famous. The room was as bare now as it had been then, and Ephraim, poking his stick through a hole in the carpet, ventured the assertion that even that had not been changed. Jethro, staring out over the chimney tops, passed his hand across his eyes. Cynthia Ware had come to this!

"I found him right here in that bed," Ephraim was saying, and he poked the bottom boards, too. "The same bed. Had a shock when I saw him. Callate he wouldn't have lived two months if the war hadn't bust up and I hadn't come along."

"Oh, Cousin Eph!" exclaimed Cynthia.

The old soldier turned and saw that there were tears in her eyes. But, stranger than that, Cynthia saw that there were tears in his own. He took her gently by the arm and led her down the stairs again, she supporting him, and Jethro following.

That same morning, Jethro, whose memory was quite as good as Ephraim's, found a little shop tucked away in Cornhill which had been miraculously spared in the advance of prosperity. Mr. Judson's name, however, was no longer in quaint lettering over the door. Standing before it, Jethro told the story in his droll way, of a city clerk and a country bumpkin, and Cynthia and Ephraim both laughed so heartily that the people who were passing turned round to look at them and laughed too. For the three were an unusual group, even in Boston. It was not until they were seated at dinner in the hotel, Ephraim with his napkin tucked under his chin, that Jethro gave them the key to the characters in this story.

"And who was the locket for, Uncle Jethro?" demanded Cynthia.

Jethro, however, shook his head, and would not be induced to tell.

They were still so seated when Cynthia perceived coming toward them through the crowded dining room a merry, middle-aged gentleman with a bald head. He seemed to know everybody in the room, for he was kept busy nodding right and left at the tables until he came to theirs. He was Mr. Merrill, who had come to see her father in Coniston, and who had spoken so kindly to her on that occasion.

"Well, well, *well*," he said; "Jethro, you'll be the death of me yet. 'Don't write — send,' eh? Well, as long as you sent word you were here, I don't complain. So you licked 'em again, eh — down in Washington? Never had a doubt but what you would. Is this the new postmaster? How are you, Mr. Prescott — *and* Cynthia — a young lady! Bless my soul," said Mr. Merrill, looking her over as he shook her hand. "What have you done to her, Jethro? What kind of beauty powder do they use in Coniston?"

Mr. Merrill took the seat next to her and continued to talk, scattering his pleasantries equally among the three, patting her arm when her own turn came. She liked Mr. Merrill very much; he seemed to her (as, indeed, he was) honest and kind-hearted. Cynthia was not lacking in a proper appreciation of herself — that may have been discovered. But she was puzzled to know why this gentleman should make it a point to pay such particular attention to a young country girl. Other railroad presidents whom she could name had not done so. She was thinking of these things, rather than listening to Mr. Merrill's conversation, when the sound of Mr. Worthington's name startled her.

"Well, Jethro," Mr. Merrill was saying, "you certainly nipped this little game of Worthington's in the bud. Thought he'd take you in the rear by going to Washington, did he? Ha, ha! I'd like to know how you did it. I'll get you to tell me to-night — see if I don't. You're all coming in to supper to-night, you know, at seven o'clock."

Ephraim laid down his knife and fork for the first time. Were the wonders of this journey never to cease? And Jethro, once in his life, looked nervous.

"Er — er — Cynthy'll go, Steve — Cynthy'll go."

"Yes, Cynthy'll go," laughed Mr. Merrill, "and you'll go, and Ephraim'll go." Although he by no means liked everybody, as would appear at first glance, Mr. Merrill had a way of calling people by their first names when he did fancy them.

"Er — Steve," said Jethro, "what would your wife say if I was to drink coffee out of my saucer?"

"Let's see," said Mr. Merrill, grave for once. "What's the punishment for that in my house? I know what she'd do if you didn't drink it. What do you think she'd do, Cynthy?"

"Ask him what was the matter with it," said Cynthia, promptly.

"Well, Cynthy," said he, "I know why these old fellows take you round with 'em. To take care of 'em, eh? They're not fit to travel alone."

And so it was settled, after much further argument, that they were all to sup at Mr. Merrill's house, Cynthia stoutly maintaining that she would not desert them. And then Mr. Merrill, having several times repeated the street and number, went back to his office. There was much mysterious whispering between Ephraim and Jethro in the hotel parlor after dinner, while Cynthia was turning over the leaves of a magazine, and then Ephraim proposed going out to see the sights.

"Where's Uncle Jethro going?" she asked.

"He'll meet us," said Ephraim, promptly, but his voice was not quite steady.

"Oh, Uncle Jethro!" cried Cynthia, "you're trying to get out of it. You remember you promised to meet us in Washington."

"Guess he'll keep this app'intment," said Ephraim, who seemed to be full of a strange mirth that bubbled over, for he actually winked at Jethro.

Cynthia's mind flew to Bunker Hill and the old North Church, but they went first to Faneuil Hall. Presently they found themselves among the crowd in Washington Street, where Ephraim confessed the trepidation which he felt over the coming supper party: a trepidation greater, so he declared many times, than he had ever experienced before any of his battles in the war. He stopped once or twice in the eddy of the crowd to glance up at the numbers, and finally came to a halt before the windows of a large dry-goods store.

"I guess I ought to buy a new shirt for this occasion, Cynthy," he said, staring hard at the articles of apparel displayed there. "Let's go in."

Cynthia laughed outright, since Ephraim could not by any chance have worn any of the articles in question.

"Why, Cousin Ephraim," she exclaimed, "you can't buy gentlemen's things here."

"Oh, I guess you can," said Ephraim, and hobbled confidently in at the doorway. There we will leave him for a while conversing in an undertone with a floor-walker, and follow Jethro. He, curiously enough, had some fifteen minutes before gone in at the same doorway, questioned the same floor-walker, and he found himself in due time walking amongst a bewildering lot of models on the third floor, followed by a giggling saleswoman.

"What kind of a dress do you want, sir?" asked the saleslady, — for we are impelled to call her so.

"S-silk cloth," said Jethro.

"What shades of silk would you like, sir?"

"Shades? shades? What do you mean by shades?"

"Why, colors," said the saleslady, giggling openly.

"Green," said Jethro, with considerable emphasis.

The saleslady clapped her hand over her mouth and led the way to another model.

"You don't call that green — do you? That's not green enough."

They inspected another dress, and then another and another, — not all of them were green, — Jethro expressing very decided if not expert views on each of them. At last he paused before two models at the far end of the room, passing his hand repeatedly over each as he had done so often with the cattle of Coniston.

"These two pieces same kind of goods?" he demanded.

"Yes."

"Er — this one is a little shinier than that one?"

"Perhaps the finish is a little higher," ventured the saleslady.

"Sh-shinier," said Jethro.

"Yes, shinier, if you please to call it so."

" W-what would you call it ? "

By this time the saleslady had become quite hysterical, and altogether incapable of performing her duties. Jethro looked at her for a moment in disgust, and in his predicament cast around for another to wait on him. There was no lack of these, at a safe distance, but they all seemed to be affected by the same mania. Jethro's eye alighted upon the back of another customer. She was, apparently, a respectable-looking lady of uncertain age, and her own attention was so firmly fixed in the contemplation of a model that she had not remarked the merriment about her, nor its cause. She did not see Jethro, either, as he strode across to her. Indeed, her first intimation of his presence was a dig in her arm. The lady turned, gave a gasp of amazement at the figure confronting her, and proceeded to annihilate it with an eye that few women possess.

" H-how do, Ma'am," he said. Had he known anything about the appearance of women in general, he might have realized that he had struck a tartar. This lady was at least sixty-five, and probably unmarried. Her face, though not at all unpleasant, was a study in character-development: she wore ringlets, a peculiar bonnet of a bygone age, and her clothes had certain eccentricities which, for lack of knowledge, must be omitted. In short, the lady was no fool, and not being one she glanced at the giggling group of saleswomen and — wonderful to relate — they stopped giggling. Then she looked again at Jethro — and gave him a smile. One of superiority, no doubt, but still a smile.

" How do you do, sir ? "

" T-trying to buy a silk cloth gown for a woman. There's two over here I fancied a little. Er — thought perhaps you'd help me."

" Where are the dresses ? " she demanded abruptly.

Jethro led the way in silence until they came to the models. She planted herself in front of them and looked them over swiftly but critically.

" What is the age of the lady ? "

"W-what difference does that make?" said Jethro, whose instinct was against committing himself to strangers.

"Difference!" she exclaimed sharply, "it makes a considerable difference. Perhaps not to you, but to the lady. What coloring is she?"

"C-coloring? She's white."

His companion turned her back on him.

"What size is she?"

"A-about that size," said Jethro, pointing to a model.

"About! about!" she ejaculated, and then she faced him. "Now look here, my friend," she said vigorously, "there's something very mysterious about all this. You look like a good man, but you may be a very wicked one for all I know. I've lived long enough to discover that appearances, especially where your sex is concerned, are deceitful. Unless you are willing to tell me who this lady is for whom you are buying silk dresses, and what your relationship is to her, I shall leave you. And mind, no evasions. I can detect the truth pretty well when I hear it."

Unexpected as it was, Jethro gave back a step or two before this onslaught of feminine virtue, and the movement did not tend to raise him in the lady's esteem. He felt that he would rather face General Grant a thousand times than this person. She was, indeed, preparing to sweep away when there came a familiar tap-tap behind them on the bare floor, and he turned to behold Ephraim hobbling toward them with the aid of his green umbrella, Cynthia by his side.

"Why, it's Uncle Jethro," cried Cynthia, looking at him and the lady in astonishment, and then with equal astonishment at the models. "What in the world are you doing here?" Then a light seemed to dawn on her. "You frauds! So this is what you were whispering about! This is the way Cousin Ephraim buys his shirts!"

"C-Cynthy," said Jethro, apologetically, "d-don't you think you ought to have a nice city dress for that supper party?"

" So you're ashamed of my country clothes, are you ? " she asked gayly.

" W-want you to have the best, Cynthy," he replied. " M-meant to have it all chose and bought when you come, but I got into a kind of argument with this lady."

" Argument ! " exclaimed the lady. But she did not seem displeased. She had been staring very fixedly at Cynthia. " My dear," she continued kindly, " you look like some one I used to know a long, long time ago, and I'll be glad to help you. Your uncle may be sensible enough in other matters, but I tell him frankly he is out of place here. Let him go away and sit down somewhere with the other gentleman, and we'll get the dress between us, if he'll tell us how much to pay."

" P-pay anything, so's you get it," said Jethro.

" Uncle Jethro, do you really want it so much ? "

It must not be thought that Cynthia did not wish for a dress, too. But the sense of dependence on Jethro and the fear of straining his purse never quite wore off. So Jethro and Ephraim took to a bench at some distance, and at last a dress was chosen — not one of the gorgeous models Jethro had picked out, but a pretty, simple, girlish gown which Cynthia herself had liked and of which the lady highly approved. Not content with helping to choose it, the lady must satisfy herself that it fit, which it did perfectly. And so Cynthia was transformed into a city person, though her skin glowed with a health with which few city people are blessed.

" My dear," said the lady, still staring at her, " you look very well. I should scarcely have supposed it." Cynthia took the remark in good part, for she thought the lady a character, which she was. " I hope you will remember that we women were created for a higher purpose than mere beauty. The Lord gave us brains, and meant that we should use them. If you have a good mind, as I believe you have, learn to employ it for the betterment of your sex, for the time of our emancipation is at hand." Having delivered this little lecture, the lady continued to stare at her with keen eyes. " You look very much like some one I used to love when I was younger. What is your name?"

"Cynthia Wetherell."

"Cynthia Wetherell? Was your mother Cynthia Ware, from Coniston?"

"Yes," said Cynthia, amazed.

In an instant the strange lady had risen and had taken Cynthia in her embrace, new dress and all.

"My dear," she said, "I thought your face had a familiar look. It was your mother I knew and loved. I'm Miss Lucretia Penniman."

Miss Lucretia Penniman! Could this be, indeed, the authoress of the "Hymn to Coniston," of whom Brampton was so proud? The Miss Lucretia Penniman who sounded the first clarion note for the independence of American women, the friend of Bryant and Hawthorne and Longfellow? Cynthia had indeed heard of her. Did not all Brampton point to the house which had held the Social Library as to a shrine?

"Cynthia," said Miss Lucretia, "I have a meeting now of a girls' charity to which I must go, but you will come to me at the offices of the *Woman's Hour* to-morrow morning at ten. I wish to talk to you about your mother and yourself."

Cynthia promised, provided they did not leave for Coniston earlier, and in that event agreed to write. Whereupon Miss Lucretia kissed her again and hurried off to her meeting. On the way back to the Tremont House Cynthia related excitedly the whole circumstance to Jethro and Ephraim. Ephraim had heard of Miss Lucretia, of course. Who had not? But he did not read the *Woman's Hour*. Jethro was silent. Perhaps he was thinking of that fresh summer morning, so long ago, when a girl in a gig had overtaken him in the cañon made by the Brampton road through the woods. The girl had worn a poke bonnet, and was returning a book to this same Miss Lucretia Penniman's Social Library. And the book was the "Life of Napoleon Bonaparte."

"Uncle Jethro, shall we still be in Boston to-morrow morning?" Cynthia asked.

He roused himself.

" Yes," he said, " yes."

" When are you going home ? "

He did not answer this simple question, but countered.

" Hain't you enjoyin' yourself, Cynthy ? "

" Of course I am," she declared. But she thought it strange that he would not tell her when they would be in Coniston.

Ephraim did buy a new shirt, and also (in view of the postmastership in his pocket) a new necktie, his old one being slightly frayed.

The grandeur of the approaching supper party and the fear of Mrs. Merrill hung very heavy over him ; nor was Jethro's mind completely at rest. Ephraim even went so far as to discuss the question as to whether Mr. Merrill had not surpassed his authority in inviting him, and fully expected to be met at the door by that gentleman uttering profuse apologies, which Ephraim was quite prepared and willing to take in good faith.

Nothing of the kind happened, however. Mr. Merrill's railroad being a modest one, his house was modest likewise. But Ephraim thought it grand enough, and yet acknowledged a homelike quality in its grandeur. He began by sitting on the edge of the sofa and staring at the cut-glass chandelier, but in five minutes he discovered with a shock of surprise that he was actually leaning back, describing in detail how his regiment had been cheered as they marched through Boston. And incredible as it may seem, the person whom he was entertaining in this manner was Mrs. Stephen Merrill herself. Mrs. Merrill was as tall as Mr. Merrill was short. She wore a black satin dress with a big cameo brooch pinned at her throat, her hair was gray, and her face almost masculine until it lighted up with a wonderfully sweet smile. That smile made Ephraim and Jethro feel at home ; and Cynthia, too, who liked Mrs. Merrill the moment she laid eyes on her.

Then there were the daughters, Jane and Susan, who welcomed her with a hospitality truly amazing for city people. Jane was big-boned like her mother, but Susan was short and plump and merry like her father. Susan talked and laughed, and Jane sat and listened and smiled, and Cynthia could not decide which she liked the best. And presently they all went into the dining room to supper, where there was another chandelier over the table. There was also real silver, which shone brilliantly on the white cloth — but there was nothing to eat.

"Do tell us another story, Mr. Prescott," said Susan, who had listened to his last one.

The sight of the table, however, had for the moment upset Ephraim.

"Get Jethro to tell you how he took dinner with Jedge Binney," he said.

This suggestion, under the circumstances, might not have been a happy one, but its lack of appropriateness did not strike Jethro either. He yielded to the demand.

"Well," he said, "I supposed I was goin' to set down same as I would at home, where we put the vittles on the table. W-wondered what I was goin' to eat — wahn't nothin' but a piece of bread on the table. S-sat there and watched 'em — nobody ate anything. Presently I found out that Binney's wife ran her house same as they run hotels. Pretty soon a couple of girls come in and put down some food and took it away again before you had a chance. A-after a while we had coffee, and when I set my cup on the table, I noticed Mis' Binney looked kind of cross and began whisperin' to the girls. One of 'em fetched a small plate and took my cup and set it on the plate. That was all right. I used the plate.

"Well, along about next summer Binney had to come to Coniston to see me on a little matter and fetched his wife. Listy, my wife, was alive then. I'd made up my mind that if I could ever get Mis' Binney to eat at my place I would, so I asked 'em to stay to dinner. When we set down, I said : 'Now, Mis' Binney, you and the Judge take right hold, and anything you can't reach, speak out and we'll wait on you.' And Mis' Binney?

"'Yes,' she said. She was a little mite scared, I guess. B-begun to suspect somethin'.

" ' Mis' Binney,' said I, ' y-you can set your cup and sarcer where you've a mind to.' O-ought to have heard the Judge laugh. Says he to his wife: ' Fanny, I told you Jethro'd get even with you some time for that sarcer business.' "

This story, strange as it may seem, had a great success at Mr. Merrill's table. Mr. Merrill and his daughter Susan shrieked with laughter when it was finished, while Mrs. Merrill and Jane enjoyed themselves quite as much in their quiet way. Even the two neat Irish maids, who were serving the supper very much as poor Mis' Binney's had been served, were fain to leave the dining room abruptly, and one of them disgraced herself at sight of Jethro when she came in again, and had to go out once more. Mrs. Merrill insisted that Jethro should pour out his coffee in what she was pleased to call the old-fashioned way. All of which goes to prove that table-silver and cut-glass chandeliers do not invariably make their owners heartless and inhospitable. And Ephraim, whose plan of campaign had been to eat nothing to speak of and have a meal when he got back to the hotel, found that he wasn't hungry when he arose from the table.

There was much bantering of Jethro by Mr. Merrill, which the ladies did not understand — talk of a mighty coalition of the big railroads which was to swallow up the little railroads. Fortunately, said Mr. Merrill, humorously, fortunately they did not want *his* railroad. Or unfortunately, which was it? Jethro didn't know. He never laughed at anybody's jokes. But Cynthia, who was listening with one ear while Susan talked into the other, gathered that Jethro had been struggling with the railroads, and was sooner or later to engage in a mightier struggle with them. How, she asked herself in her innocence, was any one, even Uncle Jethro, to struggle with a railroad? Many other people in these latter days have asked themselves that very question.

All together the evening at Mr. Merrill's passed off so quickly and so happily that Ephraim was dismayed when he discovered that it was ten o'clock, and he began to

make elaborate apologies to the ladies. But Jethro and
Mr. Merrill were still closeted together in the dining
room : once Mrs. Merrill had been called to that conference, and had returned after a while to take her place
quietly again among the circle of Ephraim's listeners.
Now Mr. Merrill came out of the dining room alone.

"Cynthia," he said, and his tone was a little more grave
than usual, "your Uncle Jethro wants to speak to you."

Cynthia rose, with a sense of something in the air which
concerned her, and went into the dining room. Was it
the light falling from above that brought out the lines
of his face so strongly? Cynthia did not know, but she
crossed the room swiftly and sat down beside him.

"What is it, Uncle Jethro?"

"C-Cynthy," he said, putting his hand over hers on the
table, "I want you to do something for me — er — for
me," he repeated, emphasizing the last word.

"I'll do anything in the world for you, Uncle Jethro,"
she answered ; "you know that. What — what is it?"

"L-like Mr. Merrill, don't you?"

"Yes, indeed."

"L-like Mrs. Merrill — like the gals — don't you?"

"Very much," said Cynthia, perplexedly.

"Like 'em enough to — to live with 'em a winter?"

"Live with them a winter!"

"C-Cynthy, I want you should stay in Boston this
winter and go to a young ladies' school."

It was out. He had said it, though he never quite
knew where he had found the courage.

"Uncle Jethro!" she cried. She could only look at
him in dismay, but the tears came into her eyes and
sparkled.

"You — you'll be happy here, Cynthy. It'll be a change
for you. And I shan't be so lonesome as you'd think.
I'll — I'll be busy this winter, Cynthy."

"You know that I wouldn't leave you, Uncle Jethro,"
she said reproachfully. "I should be lonesome, if you
wouldn't. You would be lonesome — you know you
would be."

"You'll do this for me, Cynthy. S-said you would, didn't you — said you would?"

"Why do you want me to do this?"

"W-want you to go to school for a winter, Cynthy. Shouldn't think I'd done right by you if I didn't."

"But I have been to school. Daddy taught me a lot, and Mr. Satterlee has taught me a great deal more. I know as much as most girls of my age, and I will study so hard in Coniston this winter, if that is what you want. I've never neglected my lessons, Uncle Jethro."

"'Tain't book-larnin' — 'tain't what you'd get in book-larnin' in Boston, Cynthy."

"What, then?" she asked.

"Well," said Jethro, "they'd teach you to be a lady, Cynthy."

"A lady!"

"Your father come of good people, and — and your mother was a lady. I'm only a rough old man, Cynthy, and I don't know much about the ways of fine folks. But you've got it in ye, and I want you should be equal to the best of 'em. You can. And I shouldn't die content unless I'd felt that you'd had the chance. Er — Cynthy — will you do it for me?"

She was silent a long while before she turned to him, and then the tears were running very swiftly down her cheeks.

"Yes, I will do it for you," she answered. "Uncle Jethro, I believe you are the best man in the world."

"D-don't say that, Cynthy — d-don't say that," he exclaimed, and a sharp agony was in his voice. He got to his feet and went to the folding doors and opened them. "Steve!" he called, "Steve!"

"S-says she'll stay, Steve."

Mr. Merrill had come in, followed by his wife. Cynthia saw them but dimly through her tears. And while she tried to wipe the tears away she felt Mrs. Merrill's arm about her, and heard that lady say: —

"We'll try to make you very happy, my dear, and send you back safely in the spring."

CHAPTER VIII

CYNTHIA LEARNS HOW TO BE FASHIONABLE

An attempt will be made in these pages to set down such incidents which alone may be vital to this chronicle, now so swiftly running on. The reasons why Mr. Merrill was willing to take Cynthia into his house must certainly be clear to the reader. In the first place, he was under very heavy obligations to Jethro Bass for many favors; in the second place, Mr. Merrill had a real affection for Jethro, which, strange as it may seem to some, was quite possible; and in the third place, Mr. Merrill had taken a fancy to Cynthia, and he had never forgotten the unintentional wrong he had done William Wetherell. Mr. Merrill was a man of impulses, and generally of good impulses. Had he not himself urged upon Jethro the arrangement, it would never have come about. Lastly, he had invited Cynthia to his house that his wife might inspect her, and Mrs. Merrill's verdict had been instant and favorable — a verdict not given in words. A single glance was sufficient, for these good people so understood each other that Mrs. Merrill had only to raise her eyes to her husband's, and this she did shortly after the supper party began; while she was pouring the coffee, to be exact. Thus the compact that Cynthia was to spend the winter in their house was ratified.

There was, first of all, the parting with Jethro and the messages with which he and Ephraim were laden for the whole village and town of Coniston. It was very hard, that parting, and need not be dwelt upon. Ephraim waved his blue handkerchief as the train pulled out, but Jethro stood on the platform, silent and motionless: more eloquent in his sorrow — so Mr. Merrill thought — than any human being he had ever known. Mr. Merrill wondered if Jethro's sorrow were caused by this parting alone; he believed it was not, and suddenly guessed at the true note of it. Having come by chance upon the answer to the riddle, Mr. Merrill stood still with his hand on the carriage door and marvelled that he had not seen it all sooner. He was a man to take to heart the troubles of his friends. A subtle change had indeed come over Jethro, and he was not the same man Mr. Merrill had known for many years. Would others, the men with whom Jethro contended and the men he commanded, mark this change? And what effect would it have on the conflict for the mastery of a state which was to be waged from now on?

"Father," said his daughter Susan, "if you don't get in and close the door, we'll drive off and leave you standing on the sidewalk."

Thus Cynthia went to her new friends in their own carriage. Mrs. Merrill was goodness itself, and loved the girl for what she was. How, indeed, was she to help loving her? Cynthia was scrupulous in her efforts to give no trouble, and yet she never had the air of a dependent or a beneficiary; but held her head high, and when called upon gave an opinion as though she had a right to it. The very first morning Susan, who was prone to be late to breakfast, came down in a great state of excitement and laughter.

"What do you think Cynthia's done, Mother?" she cried. "I went into her room a while ago, and it was all swept and aired, and she was making up the bed."

"That's an excellent plan," said Mrs. Merrill, "to-morrow morning you three girls will have a race to see who makes up her room first."

It is needless to say that the race at bed-making never came off, Susan and Jane having pushed Cynthia into a corner as soon as breakfast was over, and made certain forcible representations which she felt bound to respect, and a treaty was drawn up and faithfully carried out

x

between the three, that she was to do her own room if necessary to her happiness. The chief gainer by the arrangement was the chambermaid.

Odd as it may seem, the Misses Merrill lived amicably enough with Cynthia. It is a difficult matter to force an account of the relationship of five people living in one house into a few pages, but the fact that the Merrills had large hearts makes this simpler. There are few families who can accept with ease the introduction of a stranger into their midst, even for a time, and there are fewer strangers who can with impunity be introduced. The sisters quarrelled among themselves as all sisters will, and sometimes quarrelled with Cynthia. But oftener they made her the arbiter of their disputes, and asked her advice on certain matters. Especially was this true of Susan, whom certain young gentlemen from Harvard College called upon more or less frequently, and Cynthia had all of Susan's love affairs — including the current one — by heart in a very short time.

As for Cynthia, there were many subjects on which she had to take the advice of the sisters. They did not criticise the joint creations of herself and Miss Sukey Kittredge as frankly as Janet Duncan had done; but Jethro had left in Mrs. Merrill's hands a certain sufficient sum for new dresses for Cynthia, and in due time the dresses were got and worn. To do them justice, the sisters were really sincere in their rejoicings over the very wonderful transformation which they had been chiefly instrumental in effecting.

It is not a difficult task to praise a heroine, and one that should be indulged in but charily. But let some little indulgence be accorded this particular heroine by reason of the life she had led, and the situation in which she now found herself: a poor Coniston girl, dependent on one who was not her father, though she loved him as a father; beholden to these good people who dwelt in a world into which she had no reasonable expectations of entering, and which, to tell the truth, she now feared.

It was inevitable that Cynthia should be brought into

contact with many friends and relations of the family. Some of these noticed and admired her; others did neither; others gossiped about Mrs. Merrill behind her back at her own dinners and sewing circles and wondered what folly could have induced her to bring the girl into her house. But Mrs. Merrill, like many generous people who do not stop to calculate a kindness, was always severely criticised.

And then there were Jane's and Susan's friends, in and out of Miss Sadler's school. For Mrs. Merrill's influence had been sufficient to induce Miss Sadler to take Cynthia as a day scholar with her own daughters. This, be it known, was a great concession on the part of Miss Sadler, who regarded Cynthia's credentials as dubious enough; and her young ladies were inclined to regard them so, likewise. Some of these young ladies came from other cities, — New York and Philadelphia and elsewhere, — and their fathers and mothers were usually people to be mentioned as a matter of course — were, indeed, frequently so mentioned by Miss Sadler, especially when a visitor called at the school.

"Isabel, I saw that your mother sailed for Europe yesterday," or, "Sally, your father tells me he is building a gallery for his collection." Then to the visitor, "You know the Broke house in Washington Square, of course."

Of course the visitor did. But Sally or Isabel would often imitate Miss Sadler behind her back, showing how well they understood her snobbishness.

Miss Sadler was by no means the type which we have come to recognize in the cartoons as the Boston schoolma'am. She was a little, round person with thin lips and a sharp nose all out of character with her roundness, and bright eyes like a bird's. To do her justice, so far as instruction went, her scholars were equally well cared for, whether they hailed from Washington Square or Washington Court House. There were, indeed, none from such rural sorts of places — except Cynthia. But Miss Sadler did not take her hand on the opening day — or afterward — and ask her about Uncle Jethro. Oh, no. Miss Sadler

Florence Scovel Shinn

"'You know the Broke house in Washington Square, of course.'"

had no interest for great men who did not sail for Europe
or add picture galleries on to their houses. Cynthia
laughed, a little bitterly, perhaps, at the thought of a picture gallery being added to the tannery house. And she
told herself stoutly that Uncle Jethro was a greater man
than any of the others, even if Miss Sadler did not see fit
to mention him. So she had her first taste of a kind of
wormwood that is very common in the world, though it
did not grow in Coniston.

For a while after Cynthia's introduction to the school
she was calmly ignored by many of the young ladies there,
and once openly — snubbed, to use the word in its most
disagreeable sense. Not that she gave any of them any
real cause to snub her. She did not intrude her own
affairs upon them, but she was used to conversing kindly
with the people about her as equals, and for this offence, on
the third day, Miss Sally Broke snubbed her. It is hard
not to make a heroine of Cynthia, not to be able to relate
that she instantly put Miss Sally's nose out of joint.
Susan Merrill tried to do that, and failed signally, for Miss
Sally's nose was not easily dislodged. Susan fought more
than one of Cynthia's battles. As a matter of fact, Cynthia did not know that she had been affronted until that
evening. She did not tell her friends how she spent the
night yearning fiercely for Coniston and Uncle Jethro,
at times weeping for them, if the truth be told; how she
had risen before the dawn to write a letter, and to lay
some things in the rawhide trunk. The letter was never
sent, and the packing never finished. Uncle Jethro wished
her to stay and to learn to be a lady, and stay she would,
in spite of Miss Broke and the rest of them. She went to
school the next day, and for many days and weeks thereafter, and held communion with the few alone who chose
to treat her pleasantly. Unquestionably this is making
a heroine of Cynthia.

If young men are cruel in their schools, what shall be
written of young women ? It would be better to say that
both are thoughtless. Miss Sally Broke, strange as it
may seem, had a heart, and many of the other young

ladies whose fathers sailed for Europe and owned picture galleries; but these young ladies were absorbed, especially after vacation, in affairs of which a girl from Coniston had no part. Their friends were not her friends, their amusements not her amusements, and their talk not her talk. But Cynthia watched them, as was her duty, and gradually absorbed many things which are useful if not essential — outward observances of which the world takes cognizance, and which she had been sent there by Uncle Jethro to learn. Young people of Cynthia's type and nationality are the most adaptable in the world.

Before the December snows set in Cynthia had made one firm friend, at least, in Boston, outside of the Merrill family. That friend was Miss Lucretia Penniman, editress of the *Woman's Hour*. Miss Lucretia lived in the queerest and quaintest of the little houses tucked away under the hill, with the back door a story higher than the front, an arrangement which in summer enabled the mistress to walk out of her sitting-room windows into a little walled garden. In winter that sitting room was the sunniest, cosiest room in the city, and Cynthia spent many hours there, reading or listening to the wisdom that fell from the lips of Miss Lucretia or her guests. The sitting room had uneven, yellow-white panelling that fairly shone with enamel, mahogany bookcases filled with authors who had chosen to comply with Miss Lucretia's somewhat rigorous censorship; there was a table laden with such magazines as had to do with the uplifting of a sex, a delightful wavy floor covered with a rose carpet ; and, needless to add, not a pin or a pair of scissors out of place in the whole apartment.

There is no intention of enriching these pages with Miss Lucretia's homilies. Their subject-matter may be found in the files of the *Woman's Hour*. She did not always preach, although many people will not believe this statement. Miss Lucretia, too, had a heart, though she kept it hidden away, only to be brought out on occasions when she was sure of its appreciation, and she grew strangely interested in this self-contained girl from Con-

iston whose mother she had known. Miss Lucretia
understood Cynthia, who also was the kind who kept
her heart hidden, the kind who conceal their troubles and
sufferings because they find it difficult to give them out.
So Miss Lucretia had Cynthia to take supper with her at
least once in the week, and watched her quietly, and let
her speak of as much of her life as she chose — which was
not much, at first. But Miss Lucretia was content to
wait, and guessed at many things which Cynthia did not
tell her, and made some personal effort, unknown to Cynthia, to find out other things. It will be said that she
had designs on the girl. If so, they were generous
designs; and perhaps it was inevitable that Miss Lucretia
should recognize in every young woman of spirit and
brains a possible recruit for the cause.

It has now been shown in some manner and as briefly
as possible how Cynthia's life had changed, and what it
had become. We have got her partly through the winter, and find her still dreaming of the sparkling snow
on Coniston and of the wind whirling it on clear, cold
days like smoke among the spruces; of Uncle Jethro
sitting by his stove through the long evenings all alone;
of Rias in his store and Moses Hatch and Lem Hallowell,
and Cousin Ephraim in his new post-office. Uncle Jethro
wrote for the first time in his life — letters : short letters,
but in his own handwriting, and deserving of being read
for curiosity's sake if there were time. The wording was
queer enough and guarded enough, but they were charged
with a great affection which clung to them like lavender.
And Cynthia kept them every one, and read them over
on such occasions when she felt that she could not live
another minute out of sight of her mountain.

Such was the state of affairs one gray afternoon in
December when Cynthia, who was sitting in Mrs. Merrill's
parlor, suddenly looked up from her book to discover that
two young men were in the room. The young men were
apparently quite as much surprised as she, and the parlor
maid stood grinning behind them.

"Tell Miss Susan and Miss Jane, Ellen," said Cynthia,

preparing to depart. One of the young men she recognized from a photograph on Susan's bureau. He was, for the time being, Susan's. His name, although it does not matter much, was Morton Browne, and he would have been considerably astonished if he had guessed how much of his history Cynthia knew. It was Mr. Browne's habit to take Susan for a walk as often as propriety permitted, and on such occasions he generally brought along a good-natured classmate to take care of Jane. This, apparently, was one of the occasions. Mr. Browne was tall and dark and generally good-looking, while his friends were usually distinguished for their good nature. Mr. Browne stood between her and the door and looked at her rather fixedly. Then he said : —

"Excuse me."

A great many friendships, and even love affairs, have been inaugurated by just such an opening.

"Certainly," said Cynthia, and tried to pass out. But Mr. Browne had no intention of allowing her to do so if he could help it.

"I hope I am not intruding," he said politely.

"Oh, no," answered Cynthia, wondering how she could get by him.

"Were you waiting for Miss Merrill?"

"Oh, no," said Cynthia again.

The other young man turned his back and became absorbed in the picture of a lion getting ready to tear a lady to pieces. But Mr. Browne was of that mettle which is not easily baffled in such matters. He introduced himself, and desired to know whom he had the honor of addressing. Cynthia could not but enlighten him. Mr. Browne was greatly astonished, and showed it.

"So you are the mysterious young lady who has been staying here in the house this winter," he exclaimed, as though it were a marvellous thing. "I have heard Miss Merrill speak of you. She admires you very much. Is it true that you come from — Coniston?"

"Yes," she said.

"Let me see — where is Coniston?" inquired Mr. Browne.

"Do you know where Brampton is?" asked Cynthia. "Coniston is near Brampton."

"Brampton!" exclaimed Mr. Browne, "I have a classmate who comes from Brampton — Bob Worthington. You must know Bob, then."

Yes, Cynthia knew Mr. Worthington.

"His father's got a mint of money, they say. I've been told that old Worthington was the whole show up in those parts. Is that true?"

"Not quite," said Cynthia.

Not quite! Mr. Morton Browne eyed her in surprise, and from that moment she began to have decided possibilities. Just then Jane and Susan entered arrayed for the walk, but Mr. Browne showed himself in no hurry to depart: began to speak, indeed, in a deprecating way about the weather, appealed to his friend, Mr. King, if it didn't look remarkably like rain, or hail, or snow. Susan sat down, Jane sat down, Mr. Browne and his friend prepared to sit down when Cynthia moved toward the door.

"You're not going, Cynthia!" cried Susan, in a voice that may have had a little too much eagerness in it. "You must stay and help us entertain Mr. Browne." (Mr. King, apparently, was not to be entertained.) "We've tried so hard to make her come down when people called, Mr. Browne, but she never would."

Cynthia was not skilled in the art of making excuses. She hesitated for one, and was lost. So she sat down, as far from Mr. Browne as possible, next to Jane. In a few minutes Mr. Browne was seated beside her, and how he accomplished this manœuvre Cynthia could not have said, so skilfully and gradually was it done. For lack of a better subject he chose Mr. Robert Worthington. Related, for Cynthia's delectation, several of Bob's escapades in his freshman year: silly escapades enough, but very bold and daring and original they sounded to Cynthia, who listened (if Mr. Browne could have known it) with almost breathless interest, and forgot all about poor Susan talking to Mr. King. Did Mr. Worthington still while away his

evenings stealing barber poles and being chased around
Cambridge by irate policemen? Mr. Browne laughed at
the notion. O dear, no! seniors never descended to that.
Had not Miss Wetherell heard the song wherein seniors
were designated as grave and reverend? Yes, Miss Wetherell had heard the song. She did not say where, or how.
Mr. Worthington, said his classmate, had become very
serious-minded this year. Was captain of the base-ball
team and already looking toward the study of law.

"Study law!" exclaimed Cynthia, "I thought he would
go into his father's mills."

"Do you know Bob very well?" asked Mr. Browne.

She admitted that she did not.

"He's been away from Brampton a good deal, of course,"
said Mr. Browne, who seemed pleased by her admission.
To do him justice, he would not undermine a classmate,
although he had other rules of conduct which might eventu
ally require a little straightening out. "Worthy's a first-
rate fellow, a little quick-tempered, perhaps, and inclined
to go his own way. He's got a good mind, and he's taken
to using it lately. He has come pretty near being suspended once or twice."

Cynthia wanted to ask what "suspended" was. It
sounded rather painful. But at this instant there was the
rattle of a latch key at the door, and Mr. Merrill walked
in.

"Well, well," he said, spying Cynthia, "so you have
got Cynthia to come down and entertain the young men
at last."

"Yes," said Susan, "we have got Cynthia to come down
at last."

Susan did not go to Cynthia's room that night to chat,
as usual, and Mr. Morton Browne's photograph was mysteriously removed from the prominent position it had
occupied. If Susan had carried out a plan which she
conceived in a moment of folly of placing that photograph on Cynthia's bureau, there would undoubtedly have
been a quarrel. Cynthia's own feelings — seeing that
Mr. Browne had not dazzled her — were not enviable.

But she held her peace, which indeed was all she could do, and the next time Mr. Browne called, though he took care to mention her name particularly at the door, she would not go down to entertain him : though Susan implored and Jane appealed, she would not go down.   Mr. Browne called several times again, with the same result.   Cynthia was inexorable — she would have none of him.   Then Susan forgave her.   There was no quarrel, indeed, but there was a reconciliation, which is the best part of a quarrel.   There were tears, of Susan's shedding ; there was a character-sketch of Mr. Browne, of Susan's drawing, and that gentleman flitted lightly out of Susan's life.

Some ten days subsequent to this reconciliation Ellen, the parlor maid, brought up a card to Cynthia's room. The card bore the name of Mr. Robert Worthington. Cynthia stared at it, and bent it in her fingers, while Ellen explained how the gentleman had begged that she might see him.   To tell the truth, Cynthia had wondered more than once why he had not come before, and smiled when she thought of all the assurances of undying devotion she had heard in Washington.   After all, she reflected, why should she not see him — once ?   He might give her news of Brampton and Coniston.   Thus willingly deceiving herself, she told Ellen that she would go down : much to the girl's delight, for Cynthia was a favorite in the house.

As she entered the parlor Mr. Worthington was standing in the window.   When he turned and saw her he started to come forward in his old impetuous way, and stopped and looked at her in surprise.   She herself did not grasp the reason for this.

"Can it be possible," he said, "can it be possible that this is my friend from the country? "   And he took her hand with the greatest formality, pressed it the least little bit, and released it.   "How do you do, Miss Wetherell ?   Do you remember me ? "

"How do you do — Bob," she answered, laughing in spite of herself at his banter.   "You haven't changed, anyway."

"It was Mr. Worthington in Washington," said he.

"Now it is ' Bob ' and 'Miss Wetherell.' Rank patronage! How did you do it, Cynthia ? "

" You are like all men," said Cynthia, " you look at the clothes, and not the woman. They are not very fine clothes; but if they were much finer, they wouldn't change me."

" Then it must be Miss Sadler."

" Miss Sadler would willingly change me — if she could," said Cynthia, a little bitterly. " How did you find out I was at Miss Sadler's ? "

" Morton Browne told me yesterday," said Bob. " I felt like punching his head."

" What did he tell you ? " she asked with some concern.

" He said that you were here, visiting the Merrills, among other things, and said that you knew me."

The " other things " Mr. Browne had said were interesting, but flippant. He had seen Bob at a college club and declared that he had met a witch of a country girl at the Merrills. He couldn't make her out, because she had refused to see him every time he called again. He had also repeated Cynthia's remark about Bob's father not being quite the biggest man in his part of the country, and ventured the surmise that she was the daughter of a rival mill owner.

" Why didn't you let me know you were in Boston ? " said Bob, reproachfully.

" Why should I ? " asked Cynthia, and she could not resist adding, " Didn't you find it out when you went to Brampton — to see me ? "

" Well," said he, getting fiery red, " the fact is — I didn't go to Brampton."

" I'm glad you were sensible enough to take my advice, though I suppose that didn't make any difference. But — from the way you spoke, I should have thought nothing could have kept you away."

" To tell you the truth," said Bob, " I'd promised to visit a fellow named Broke in my class, who lives in New York. And I couldn't get out of it. His sister, by the way, is in Miss Sadler's. I suppose you know her. But if I'd thought you'd see me, I should have gone to Brampton, anyway. You were so down on me in Washington."

" It was very good of you to take the trouble to come to see me here. There must be a great many girls in Boston you have to visit."

He caught the little note of coolness in her voice. Cynthia was asking herself whether, if Mr. Browne had not seen fit to give a good report of her, he would have come at all. He would have come, certainly. It is to be hoped that Bob Worthington's attitude up to this time toward Cynthia has been sufficiently defined by his conversation and actions. There had been nothing serious about it. But there can be no question that Mr. Browne's openly expressed admiration had enhanced her value in his eyes.

"There's no girl in Boston that I care a rap for," he said.

" I'm relieved to hear it," said Cynthia, with feeling.

" Are you really ? "

" Didn't you expect me to be, when you said it ? "

He laughed uncomfortably.

" You've learned more than one thing since you've been in the city," he remarked, " I suppose there are a good many fellows who come here all the time."

" Yes, there are," she said demurely.

" Well," he remarked, " you've changed a lot in three months. I always thought that, if you had a chance, there'd be no telling where you'd end up."

"That doesn't sound very complimentary," said Cynthia. She had, indeed, changed. " In what terrible place do you think I'll end up ? "

" I suppose you'll marry one of these Boston men."

" Oh," she laughed, " that wouldn't be so terrible, would it ? "

" I believe you're engaged to one of 'em now," he remarked, looking very hard at her.

" If you believed that, I don't think you would say it," she answered.

" I can't make you out. You used to be so frank with

me, and now you're not at all so. Are you going to Coniston for the holidays?"

Her face fell at the question.

"Oh, Bob," she cried, surprising him utterly by a glimpse of the real Cynthia, "I wish I were — I wish I were! But I don't dare to."

"Don't dare to?"

"If I went, I should never come back — never. I should stay with Uncle Jethro. He's so lonesome up there, and I'm so lonesome down here, without him. And I promised him faithfully I'd stay a whole winter at school in Boston."

"Cynthia," said Bob, in a strange voice as he leaned toward her, "do you — do you care for him as much as all that?"

"Care for him?" she repeated.

"Care for — for Uncle Jethro?"

"Of course I care for him," she cried, her eyes flashing at the thought. "I love him better than anybody in the world. Certainly no one ever had better reason to care for a person. My father failed when he came to Coniston — he was not meant for business, and Uncle Jethro took care of him all his life, and paid his debts. And he has taken care of me and given me everything that a girl could wish. Very few people know what a fine character Uncle Jethro has," continued Cynthia, carried away as she was by the pent-up flood of feeling within her. "I know what he has done for others, and I should love him for that even if he never had done anything for me."

Bob was silent. He was, in the first place, utterly amazed at this outburst, revealing as it did a depth of passionate feeling in the girl which he had never suspected, and which thrilled him. It was unlike her, for she was usually so self-repressed; and, being unlike her, accentuated both sides of her character the more.

But what was he to say of the defence of Jethro Bass? Bob was not a young man who had pondered much over the problems of life, because these problems had hitherto never touched him. But now he began to perceive, dimly, things that might become the elements of a tragedy, even as Mr. Merrill had perceived them some months before. Could a union endure between so delicate a creature as the girl before him and Jethro Bass? Could Cynthia ever go back to him again, and live with him happily, without seeing many things which before were hidden by reason of her youth and innocence?

Bob had not been nearly four years at college without learning something of the world; and it had not needed the lecture from his father, which he got upon leaving Washington, to inform him of Jethro's political practices. He had argued soundly with his father on that occasion, having the courage to ask Mr. Worthington in effect whether he did not sanction his underlings to use the same tools as Jethro used. Mr. Worthington was righteously angry, and declared that Jethro had inaugurated those practices in the state, and had to be fought with his own weapons. But Mr. Worthington had had the sense at that time not to mention Cynthia's name. He hoped and believed that that affair was not serious, and merely a boyish fancy — as indeed it was.

It remains to be said, however, that the lecture had not been without its effect upon Bob. Jethro Bass, after all, was — Jethro Bass. All his life Bob had heard him familiarly and jokingly spoken of as the boss of the state, and had listened to the tales, current in all the country towns, of how Jethro had outwitted this man or that. Some of them were not refined tales. Jethro Bass as the boss of the state — with the tolerance with which the public in general regard politics — was one thing. Bob was willing to call him " Uncle Jethro," admire his great strength and shrewdness, and declare that the men he had outwitted had richly deserved it. But Jethro Bass as the ward of Cynthia Wetherell was quite another thing.

It was not only that Cynthia had suddenly and inevitably become a lady. That would not have mattered, for such as she would have borne Coniston and the life of Coniston cheerfully. But Bob reflected, as he walked back to his rooms in the dark through the snow-laden streets, that Cynthia, young though she might be, possessed principles from which no love would sway her a hair's breadth. How, indeed, was she to live with Jethro once her eyes were opened?

The thought made him angry, but returned to him persistently during the days that followed, — in the lecture room, in the gymnasium, in his own study, where he spent more time than formerly. By these tokens it will be perceived that Bob, too, had changed a little. And the sight of Cynthia in Mrs. Merrill's parlor had set him to thinking in a very different manner than the sight of her in Washington had affected him.

Bob had managed to shift the subject from Jethro, not without an effort, though he had done it in that merry, careless manner which was so characteristic of him. He had talked of many things, — his college life, his friends, — and laughed at her questions about his freshman escapades. But when at length, at twilight, he had risen to go, he had taken both her hands and looked down into her face with a very different expression than she had seen him wear before — a much more serious expression, which puzzled her. It was not the look of a lover, nor yet that of a man who imagines himself in love. With either of these her instinct would have told her how to deal. It was more the look of a friend, with much of the masculine spirit of protection in it.

"May I come to see you again?" he asked.

Gently she released her hands, and she did not answer at once. She went to the window, and stared across the sloping street at the grilled railing before the big house opposite, thinking. Her reason told her that he should not come, but her spirit rebelled against that reason. It was a pleasure to see him, so she freely admitted to herself. Why should she not have that pleasure? If the truth be told, she had argued it all out before, when she had wondered whether he would come. Mrs. Merrill, she thought, would not object to his coming. But—there was the question she had meant to ask him.

"Bob," she said, turning to him, "Bob, would your father want you to come?"

It was growing dark, and she could scarcely see his face. He hesitated, but he did not attempt to evade the question.

"No, he would not," he answered. And added, with a good deal of force and dignity: "I am of age, and can choose my own friends. I am my own master. If he knew you as I knew you, he would look at the matter in a different light."

Cynthia felt that this was not quite true. She smiled a little sadly.

"I am afraid you don't know me very well, Bob." He was about to protest, but she went on, bravely, "Is it because he has quarrelled with Uncle Jethro?"

"Yes," said Bob. She was making it terribly hard for him, sparing indeed neither herself nor him.

"If you come here to see me, it will cause a quarrel between you and your father. I — I cannot do that."

"There is nothing wrong in my seeing you," said Bob, stoutly; "if he cares to quarrel with me for that, I cannot help it. If the people I choose for my friends are good people, he has no right to an objection, even though he is my father."

Cynthia had never come so near real admiration for him as at that moment.

"No, Bob, you must not come," she said. "I will not have you quarrel with him on my account."

"Then I will quarrel with him on my own account," he had answered. "Good-by. You may expect me this day week."

He went into the hall to put on his overcoat. Cynthia stood still on the spot of the carpet where he had left her. He put his head in at the door.

"This day week," he said.

"Bob, you must not come," she answered. But the street door closed after him as he spoke.

CHAPTER IX

IN WHICH MR. MERRILL ABANDONS A HABIT

"You must not come." Had Cynthia made the prohibition strong enough? Ought she not to have said, "If you do come, I will not see you"? Her knowledge of the motives of the men and women in the greater world was largely confined to that which she had gathered from novels — not trashy novels, but those by standard authors of English life. And many another girl of nineteen has taken a novel for a guide when she has been suddenly confronted with the first great problem outside of her experience. Somebody has declared that there are only seven plots in the world. There are many parallels in English literature to Cynthia's position, — so far as she was able to define that position, — the wealthy young peer, the parson's or physician's daughter, and the worldly, inexorable parents who had other plans.

Cynthia was, of course, foolish. She would not look ahead, yet there was the mirage in the sky when she allowed herself to dream. It can truthfully be said that she was not in love with Bob Worthington. She felt, rather than knew, that if love came to her the feeling she had for Jethro Bass — strong though that was — would be as nothing to it. The girl felt the intensity of her nature, and shrank from it when her thoughts ran that way, for it frightened her.

"Mrs. Merrill," she said, a few days later, when she found herself alone with that lady, "you once told me you would have no objection if a friend came to see me here."

"None whatever, my dear," answered Mrs. Merrill. "I have asked you to have your friends here."

Mrs. Merrill knew that a young man had called on Cynthia. The girls had discussed the event excitedly, had teased Cynthia about it ; they had discovered, moreover, that the young man had not been a tiller of the soil or a clerk in a country store. Ellen, with the enthusiasm of her race, had painted him in glowing colors — but she had neglected to read the name on his card.

"Bob Worthington came to see me last week, and he wants to come again. He lives in Brampton," Cynthia explained, "and is at Harvard College."

Mrs. Merrill was decidedly surprised. She went on with her sewing, however, and did not betray the fact. She knew of Dudley Worthington as one of the richest and most important men in his state ; she had heard her husband speak of him often ; but she had never meddled with politics and railroad affairs.

"By all means let him come, Cynthia," she replied.

When Mr. Merrill got home that evening she spoke of the matter to him.

"Cynthia is a strange character," she said. "Sometimes I can't understand her — she seems so much older than our girls, Stephen. Think of her keeping this to herself for four days !"

Mr. Merrill laughed, but he went off to a little writing room he had and sat for a long time looking into the glowing coals. Then he laughed again. Mr. Merrill was a philosopher. After all, he could not forbid Dudley Worthington's son coming to his house, nor did he wish to.

That same evening Cynthia wrote a letter and posted it. She found it a very difficult letter to write, and almost as difficult to drop into the mail-box. She reflected that the holidays were close at hand, and then he would go to Brampton and forget, even as he had forgotten before. And she determined when Wednesday afternoon came around that she would take a long walk in the direction of Brookline. Cynthia loved these walks, — for she sadly missed the country air, — and they had kept the color in her cheeks and the courage in her heart that winter. She had amazed the Merrill girls by the distances she covered, and on more than one occasion she had trudged many miles to a spot from which there was a view of Blue Hills. They reminded her faintly of Coniston.

Who can speak or write with any certainty of the feminine character, or declare what unexpected twists perversity and curiosity may give to it? Wednesday afternoon came, and Cynthia did not go to Brookline. She put on her coat, and took it off again. Would he dare to come in the face of the mandate he had received? If he did come, she wouldn't see him. Ellen had received her orders.

At four o'clock the doorbell rang, and shortly thereafter Ellen appeared, simpering and apologetic enough, with a card. She had taken the trouble to read it this time. Cynthia was angry, or thought she was, and her cheeks were very red.

" I told you to excuse me, Ellen. Why did you let him in ? "

" Miss Cynthia, darlin'," said Ellen, " if it was made of flint I was, wouldn't he bring the tears out of me with his wheedlin' an' coaxin' ? An' him such a fine young gintleman ! And whin he took to commandin' like, sure I couldn't say no to him at all at all. ' Take the card to her, Ellen,' he says — didn't he know me name ! — ' an' if she says she won't see me, thin I won't trouble her more.' Thim were his words, Miss."

There he was before the fire, his feet slightly apart and his hands in his pockets, waiting for her. She got a glimpse of him standing thus, as she came down the stairs. It was not the attitude of a culprit. Nor did he bear the faintest resemblance to a culprit as he came up to her in the doorway. The chief recollection she carried away of that moment was that his teeth were very white and even when he smiled. He had the impudence to smile. He had the impudence to seize one of her hands in his, and to hold aloft a sheet of paper in the other.

" What does this mean ? " said he.

" What do you think it means ? " retorted Cynthia, with dignity.

"'An' him such a fine young gintleman!'"

"A summons to stay away," said Bob, thereby more or less accurately describing it. "What would you have thought of me if I had not come?"

Cynthia was not prepared for any such question as this. She had meant to ask the questions herself. But she never lacked for words to protect herself.

"I'll tell you what I think of you for coming, Bob, for insisting upon seeing me as you did," she said, remembering with shame Ellen's account of that proceeding. "It was very unkind and very thoughtless of you."

"Unkind?" Thus she succeeded in putting him on the defensive.

"Yes, unkind, because I know it is best for you not to come to see me, and you know it, and yet you will not help me when I try to do what is right. I shall be blamed for these visits," she said. The young ladies in the novels always were. But it was a serious matter for poor Cynthia, and her voice trembled a little. Her troubles seemed very real.

"Who will blame you?" asked Bob, though he knew well enough. Then he added, seeing that she did not answer: "I don't at all agree with you that it is best for me not to see you. I know of nobody in the world it does me more good to see than yourself. Let's sit down and talk it all over," he said, for she still remained standing uncompromisingly by the door.

The suspicion of a smile came over Cynthia's face. She remembered how Ellen had been wheedled. Her instinct told her that now was the time to make a stand or never.

"It wouldn't do any good, Bob," she replied, shaking her head; "we talked it all over last week."

"Not at all," said he, "we only touched upon a few points last week. We ought to thrash it out. Various aspects of the matter have occurred to me which I ought to call to your attention."

He could not avoid this bantering tone, but she saw that he was very much in earnest, too. He realized the necessity of winning, likewise, and he had got in and meant to stay.

" I don't want to argue," said Cynthia.   " I've thought it all out."

" So have I," said Bob.   " I haven't thought of anything else, to speak of.   And by the way," he declared, shaking the envelope, " I never got a colder and more formal letter in my life.   You must have taken it from one of Miss Sadler's copy books."

" I'm sorry I haven't been able to equal the warmth of your other correspondents," said Cynthia, smiling at the mention of Miss Sadler.

" You've got a good many degrees yet to go," he replied.

" I have no idea of doing so," said Cynthia.

If Cynthia had lured him there, and had carefully thought out a plan of fanning his admiration into a flame, she could not have done better than to stand obstinately by the door.   Nothing appeals to a man like resistance : resistance for a principle appealed to Bob, although he did not care a fig about that particular principle.   In his former dealings with young women — and they had not been few — the son of Dudley Worthington had encountered no resistance worth the mentioning.   He looked at the girl before him, and his blood leaped at the thought of a conquest over her.   She was often demure, but behind that demureness was firmness : she was mistress of herself, and yet possessed a marvellous vitality.

" And now," said Cynthia, " don't you think you had better go ? "

Go ! He laughed outright. Never ! He would sit down under that fortress, and some day he meant to scale the walls.   Like John Paul Jones, he had not yet begun to fight.   But he did not sit down just yet, because Cynthia remained standing.

" I'm here now," he said, " what's the good of going away ?   I might as well stay the rest of the afternoon."

" You will find a photograph album on the table," said Cynthia, " with pictures of all the Merrill family and their friends and relations."

In spite of the threat this remark conveyed, he could

not help laughing at it.   Mrs. Merrill in her sitting room
heard the laugh, and felt that she would like Bob Worthington.

"It's a heavy album, Cynthia," he said; "perhaps you
would hold up one side of it."

It was Cynthia's turn to laugh.   She could not decide
whether he were a man or a boy.   Sometimes, she had to
admit, he was very much of a man.

" Where are you going ? " he cried.

" Upstairs, of course," she answered.

This was really alarming.   But fate thrust a final
weapon into his hands.

" All right," said he, " I'll look at the album.   What
time does Mr. Merrill get home ? "

" About six," answered Cynthia.   " Why ? "

" When he comes," said Bob, " I shall put on my most
disconsolate expression.   He'll ask me what I'm doing,
and I'll tell him you went upstairs at half-past four
and haven't come down.   He'll sympathize, I'll bet anything."

Whether Bob were really capable of doing this, Cynthia
could not tell.   She believed he was.   Perhaps she really
did not intend to go upstairs just then.   To his intense
relief she seated herself on a straight-backed chair near
the door, although she had the air of being about to get
up again at any minute.   It was not a surrender, not at
all — but a parley, at least.

" I really want to talk to you seriously, Bob," she said, and
her voice was serious.   " I like you very much — I always
have — and I want you to listen seriously.   All of us
have friends.   Some people — you, for instance — have a
great many.   We have but one father."   Her voice failed
a little at the word.   " No friend can ever be the same to
you as your father, and no friendship can make up what
his displeasure will cost you.   I do not mean to say that
I shan't always be your friend, for I shall be."

Young men seldom arrive at maturity by gradual steps
— something sets them thinking, a week passes, and suddenly the world has a different aspect.   Bob had thought

much of his father during that week, and had considered their relationship very carefully.   He had a few precious memories of his mother before she had been laid to rest under that hideous and pretentious monument in the Brampton hill cemetery.   How unlike her was that monument!   Even as a young boy, when on occasions he had wandered into the cemetery, he used to stand before it with a lump in his throat and bitter resentment in his heart, and once he had shaken his fist at it.   He had grown up out of sympathy with his father, but he had never until now began to analyze the reasons for it.   His father had given him everything except that communion of which Cynthia spoke so feelingly.   Mr. Worthington had acted according to his lights : of all the people in the world he thought first of his son.   But his thoughts and care had been alone of what the son would be to the world: how that son would carry on the wealth and greatness of Isaac D. Worthington.

Bob had known this before, but it had had no such significance for him then as now.   He was by no means lacking in shrewdness, and as he had grown older he had perceived clearly enough Mr. Worthington's reasons for throwing him socially with the Duncans.   Mr. Worthington had never been a plain-spoken man, but he had as much as told his son that it was decreed that he should marry the heiress of the state.   There were other plans connected with this.   Mr. Worthington meant that his son should eventually own the state itself, for he saw that the man who controlled the highways of a state could snap his fingers at governor and council and legislature and judiciary: could, indeed, do more — could own them even more completely than Jethro Bass now owned them, and without effort.   The dividends would do the work: would canvass the counties and persuade this man and that with sufficient eloquence.   By such tokens it will be seen that Isaac D. Worthington is destined to become great, though the greatness will be akin to that possessed by those gentlemen who in past ages had built castles across the highway between Venice and the

North Sea. All this was in store for Bob Worthington, if he could only be brought to see it. These things would be given him, if he would but confine his worship to the god of wealth.

We are running ahead, however, of Bob's reflections in Mr. Merrill's parlor in Mount Vernon Street, and the ceremony of showing him the cities of his world from Brampton hill was yet to be gone through. Bob knew his father's plans only in a general way, but in the past week he had come to know his father with a fair amount of thoroughness. If Isaac D. Worthington had but chosen a worldly wife, he might have had a more worldly son. As it was, Bob's thoughts were a little bitter when Cynthia spoke of his father, and he tried to think instead what his mother would have him do. He could not, indeed, speak of Mr. Worthington's shortcomings as he understood them, but he answered Cynthia vigorously enough — even if his words were not as serious as she desired.

" I tell you I am old enough to judge for myself, Cynthia," said he, " and I intend to judge for myself. I don't pretend to be a paragon of virtue, but I have a kind of a conscience which tells me when I am doing wrong, if I listen to it. I have not always listened to it. It tells me I'm doing right now, and I mean to listen to it."

Cynthia could not but think there was very little self-denial attached to this. Men are not given largely to self-denial.

" It is easy enough to listen to your conscience when you think it impels you to do that which you want to do, Bob," she answered, laughing at his argument in spite of herself.

" Are you wicked ? " he demanded abruptly.

" Why, no, I don't think I am," said Cynthia, taken aback. But she corrected herself swiftly, perceiving his bent. " I should be doing wrong to let you come here."

He ignored the qualification.

" Are you vain and frivolous ? "

She remembered that she had looked in the glass before she had come down to him, and bit her lip.

"Are you given over to idle pursuits, to leading young men from their occupations and duties?"

"If you've come here to recite the Blue Laws," said she, laughing again, "I have something better to do than to listen to them."

"Cynthia," he cried, "I'll tell you what you are. I'll draw your character for you, and then, if you can give me one good reason why I should not associate with you, I'll go away and never come back."

"That's all very well," said Cynthia, "but suppose I don't admit your qualifications for drawing my character. And I don't admit them, not for a minute."

"I will draw it," said he, standing up in front of her. "Oh, confound it!"

This exclamation, astonishing and out of place as it was, was caused by a ring at the doorbell. The ring was followed by a whispering and giggling in the hall, and then by the entrance of the Misses Merrill into the parlor. Curiosity had been too strong for them. Susan was human, and here was the opportunity for a little revenge. In justice to her, she meant the revenge to be very slight.

"Well, Cynthia, you should have come to the concert," she said; "it was fine, wasn't it, Jane? Is this Mr. Worthington? How do you do. I'm Miss Susan Merrill, and this is Miss Jane Merrill."

Susan only intended to stay a minute, but how was Bob to know that? She was tempted into staying longer. Bob lighted the gas, and she inspected him and approved. Her approval increased when he began to talk to her in his bantering way, as if he had known her always. Then, when she was fully intending to go, he rose to take his leave.

"I'm awfully glad to have met you at last," he said to Susan, "I've heard so much about you." His leave-taking of Jane was less effusive, and then he turned to Cynthia and took her hand. "I'm going to Brampton on Friday," he said, "for the holidays. I wish you were going."

"We couldn't think of letting her go, Mr. Worthington," cried Susan, for the thought of the hills had made

Cynthia incapable of answering. "We're only to have her for one short winter, you know."

"Yes, I know," said Mr. Worthington, gravely. "I'll see old Ephraim, and tell him you're well, and what a marvel of learning you've become. And — and I'll go to Coniston if that will please you."

"Oh, no, Bob, you mustn't do anything of the kind," answered Cynthia, trying to keep back the tears. "I — I write to Uncle Jethro very often. Good-by. I hope you will enjoy your holidays."

"I'm coming to see you the minute I get back and tell you all about everybody," said he.

How was she to forbid him to come before Susan and Jane! She could only be silent.

"Do come, Mr. Worthington," said Susan, warmly, wondering at Cynthia's coldness and, indeed, misinterpreting it. "I am sure she will be glad to see you. And we shall always make you welcome, at any rate."

As soon as he was out of the door, Susan became very repentant, and slipped her hand about Cynthia's waist.

"We shouldn't have come in at all if we had known he would go so soon, indeed we shouldn't, Cynthia." And seeing that Cynthia was still silent, she added: "I wouldn't do such a mean thing, Cynthia, I really wouldn't. Won't you believe me and forgive me?"

Cynthia scarcely heard her at first. She was thinking of Coniston mountain, and how the sun had just set behind it. The mountain would be ultramarine against the white fields, and the snow on the hill pastures to the east stained red as with wine. What would she not have given to be going back to-morrow — yes, with Bob. She confessed — though startled by the very boldness of the thought — that she would like to be going there with Bob. Susan's appeal brought her back to Boston and the gas-lit parlor.

"Forgive you, Susan! There's nothing to forgive. I wanted him to go."

"You wanted him to go?" repeated Susan, amazed. She may be pardoned if she did not believe this, but a

"'I'm coming to see you the minute I get back.'"

glance at Cynthia's face scarcely left a room for doubt. "Cynthia Wetherell, you're the strangest girl I've ever known in all my life. If I had a — a friend" (Susan had another word on her tongue) "if I had such a friend as Mr. Worthington, I shouldn't be in a hurry to let him leave me. Of course," she added, "I shouldn't let him know it."

Cynthia's heart was very heavy during the next few days, heavier by far than her friends in Mount Vernon Street imagined. They had grown to love her almost as one of themselves, and because of the sympathy which comes of such love they guessed that her thoughts would be turning homeward at Christmastide. At school she had listened, perforce, to the festival plans of thirty girls of her own age; to accounts of the probable presents they were to receive, the cost of some of which would support a family in Coniston for several months; to arrangements for visits, during which there were to be theatre-parties and dances and other gayeties. Cynthia could not help wondering, as she listened in silence to this talk, whether Uncle Jethro had done wisely in sending her to Miss Sadler's; whether she would not have been far happier if she had never known about such things.

Then came the last day of school, which began with leave-takings and embraces. There were not many who embraced Cynthia, though, had she known it, this was largely her own fault. Poor Cynthia! how was she to know it? Many more of them than she imagined would have liked to embrace her had they believed that the embrace would be returned. Secretly they had grown to admire this strange, dark girl, who was too proud to bend for the good opinion of any one — even of Miss Sally Broke. Once during the term Cynthia had held some of them in the hollow of her hand, and had incurred the severe displeasure of Miss Sadler by refusing to tell what she knew of certain mischief-makers.

Now, Miss Sadler was going about among them in the school parlor saying good-by, sending particular remembrances to such of the fathers and mothers as she thought worthy of that honor ; kissing some, shaking hands with all.   It was then that a dramatic incident occurred — dramatic for a girls' school, at least. Cynthia deliberately turned her back on Miss Sadler and looked out of the window.   The chatter in the room was hushed, and for a moment a dangerous wrath flamed in Miss Sadler's eyes. Then she passed on with a smile, to send most particular messages to the mother of Miss Isabel Burrage.

Some few moments afterward Cynthia felt a touch on her arm, and turned to find herself confronted by Miss Sally Broke.   Unfortunately there is not much room for Miss Broke in this story, although she may appear in another one yet to be written. She was extremely good-looking, with real golden hair and mischievous blue eyes. She was, in brief, the leader of Miss Sadler's school.

" Cynthia," she said, " I was rude to you when you first came here, and I'm sorry for it.   I want to beg your pardon." And she held out her hand.

There was a moment's suspense for those watching to see if Cynthia would take it. She did take it.

" I'm sorry, too," said Cynthia, simply, " I couldn't see what I'd done to offend you. Perhaps you'll explain now."

Miss Broke blushed violently, and for an instant looked decidedly uncomfortable.   Then she burst into laughter, — merry, irresistible laughter that carried all before it.

" I was a snob, that's all," said she, " just a plain, low-down snob.   You don't understand what that means, because you're not one."   (Cynthia did understand, never-theless.) "But I like you, and I want you to be my friend. Perhaps when I get to know you better, you will come home with me sometime for a visit."

Go home with her for a visit to that house in Washington Square with the picture gallery !

" I want to say that I'd give my head to have been able to turn my back on Miss Sadler as you did," continued Miss Broke ; " if you ever want a friend, remember Sally Broke."

Some of Cynthia's trouble, at least, was mitigated by

this episode; and Miss Broke having led the way, Miss
Broke's followers came shyly, one by one, with proffers of
friendship. To the good-hearted Merrill girls the walk
home that day was a kind of a triumphal march, a victory
over Miss Sadler and a vindication of their friend. Mrs.
Merrill, when she heard of it, could not find it in her heart
to reprove Cynthia. Miss Sadler had got her just deserts.
But Miss Sadler was not a person who was likely to forget
such an incident. Indeed, Mrs. Merrill half expected to
receive a note before the holidays ended that Cynthia's
presence was no longer desired at the school. No such
note came, however.

If one had to be away from home on Christmas, there
could surely be no better place to spend that day than in
the Merrill household. Cynthia remembers still, when that
blessed season comes around, how each member of the
family vied with the others to make her happy; how they
showered presents on her, and how they strove to include
her in the laughter and jokes at the big family dinner.
Mr. Merrill's brother was there with his wife, and Mrs.
Merrill's aunt and her husband, and two broods of cousins.
It may be well to mention that the Merrill relations, like
Sally Broke, had overcome their dislike for Cynthia.

There were eatables from Coniston on that board. A
turkey sent by Jethro for which, Mr. Merrill declared,
the table would have to be strengthened; a saddle of ven-
ison — Lem Hallowell having shot a deer on the mountain
two Sundays before; and mince-meat made by Amanda
Hatch herself. Other presents had come to Cynthia from
the hills : a gorgeous copy of Mr. Longfellow's poems
from Cousin Ephraim, and a gold locket from Uncle
Jethro. This locket was the precise counterpart (had she
but known it) of a silver one bought at Mr. Judson's shop
many years before, though the inscription " Cynthy, from
Uncle Jethro," was within. Into the other side exactly
fitted that daguerreotype of her mother which her father
had given her when he died. The locket had a gold
chain with a clasp, and Cynthia wore it hidden beneath
her gown — too intimate a possession to be shown.

There was still another and very mysterious present, this being a huge box of roses, addressed to Miss Cynthia Wetherell, which was delivered on Christmas morning. If there had been a card, Susan Merrill would certainly have found it. There was no card. There was much pretended speculation on the part of the Merrill girls as to the sender, sly reference to Cynthia's heightened color, and several attempts to pin on her dress a bunch of the flowers, and Susan declared that one of them would look stunning in her hair. They were put on the dining-room table in the centre of the wreath of holly, and under the mistletoe which hung from the chandelier. Whether Cynthia surreptitiously stole one has never been discovered.

So Christmas came and went: not altogether unhappily, deferring for a day at least the knotty problems of life. Although Cynthia accepted the present of the roses with such magnificent unconcern, and would not make so much as a guess as to who sent them, Mr. Robert Worthington was frequently in her thoughts. He had declared his intention of coming to Mount Vernon Street as soon as the holidays ended, and had been cordially invited by Susan to do so. Cynthia took the trouble to procure a Harvard catalogue from the library, and discovered that he had many holidays yet to spend. She determined to write another letter, which he would find in his rooms when he returned. Just what terrible prohibitory terms she was to employ in that letter Cynthia could not decide in a moment, nor yet in a day, or a week. She went so far as to make several drafts, some of which she destroyed for the fault of leniency, and others for that of severity. What was she to say to him? She had expended her arguments to no avail. She could wound him, indeed, and at length made up her mind that this was the only resource left her, although she would thereby wound herself more deeply. When she had arrived at this decision, there remained still more than a week in which to compose the letter.

On the morning after New Year's, when the family were

2 A

assembled around the breakfast table, Mrs. Merrill remarked that her husband was neglecting a custom which had been his for many years.

" Didn't the newspaper come, Stephen? " she asked.

Mr. Merrill had read it.

" Read it! " repeated his wife, in surprise, " you haven't been down long enough to read a column."

" It was full of trash," said Mr. Merrill, lightly, and began on his usual jokes with the girls. But Mrs. Merrill was troubled. She thought his jokes not as hearty as they were wont to be, and disquieting surmises of business worries filled her mind. The fact that he beckoned her into his writing room as soon as breakfast was over did not tend to allay her suspicions. He closed and locked the door after her, and taking the paper from a drawer in his desk bade her read a certain article in it.

The article was an arraignment of Jethro Bass — and a terrible arraignment indeed. Step by step it traced his career from the beginning, showing first of all how he had debauched his own town of Coniston ; how, enlarging on the same methods, he had gradually extended his grip over the county and finally over the state; how he had bought and sold men for his own power and profit, deceived those who had trusted in him, corrupted governors and legislators, congressmen and senators, and even justices of the courts; how he had trafficked ruthlessly in the enterprises of the people. Instance upon instance was given, and men of high prominence from whom he had received bribes were named, not the least important of these being the Honorable Alva Hopkins of Gosport.

Mrs. Merrill looked up from the paper in dismay.

" It's copied from the *Newcastle Guardian*," she said, for lack of immediate power to comment. " Isn't the *Guardian* the chief paper in that state? "

" Yes, Worthington's bought it, and he instigated the article, of course. I've been afraid of this for a long time, Carry," said Mr. Merrill, pacing up and down. " There's a bigger fight than they've ever had coming on up there, and this is the first gun. Worthington, with

Duncan behind him, is trying to get possession of and consolidate all the railroads in the western part of that state. If he succeeds, it will mean the end of Jethro's power. But he won't succeed."

"Stephen," said his wife, " do you mean to say that Jethro Bass will try to defeat this consolidation simply to keep his power?"

"Well, my dear," answered Mr. Merrill, still pacing, "two wrongs don't make a right, I admit. I've known these things a long time, and I've thought about them a good deal. But I've had to run along with the tide, or give place to another man who would, and — and starve."

Mrs. Merrill's eyes slowly filled with tears.

"Stephen," she began, "do you mean to say —?" There she stopped, utterly unable to speak. He ceased his pacing and sat down beside her and took her hand.

"Yes, my dear, I mean to say I've submitted to these things. God knows whether I've been right or wrong, but I have. I've often thought I'd be happier if I resigned my office as president of my road and became a clerk in a store. I don't attempt to excuse myself, Carry, but my sin has been in holding on to my post. As long as I remain president I have to cope with things as I find them."

Mr. Merrill spoke thickly, for the sight of his wife's tears wrung his heart.

"Stephen," she said, " when we were first married and you were a district superintendent, you used to tell me everything."

Stephen Merrill was a man, and a good man, as men go. How was he to tell her the degrees by which he had been led into his present situation? How was he to explain that these degrees had been so gradual that his conscience had had but a passing wrench here and there? Politics being what they were, progress and protection had to be obtained in accordance with them, and there was a duty to the holders of bonds and stocks.

His wife had a question on her lips, a question for which

she had to summon all her courage.   She chose that form
for it which would hurt him least.

"Mr. Worthington is going to try to change these
things?"

Mr. Merrill roused himself at the words, and his eyes
flashed.   He became a different man.

"Change them!" he cried bitterly, "change them for
the worse, if he can.   He will try to wrest the power
from Jethro Bass.   I don't defend him.   I don't defend
myself.   But I like Jethro Bass.   I won't deny it.   He's
human, and I like him, and whatever they say about him
I know that he's been a true friend to me.   And I tell
you as I hope for happiness here and hereafter, that if
Worthington succeeds in what he is trying to do, if the
railroads win in this fight, there will be no mercy for the
people of that state.   I'm a railroad man myself, though I
have no interest in this affair.   My turn may come later.
Will come later, I suppose.   Isaac D. Worthington has a
very little heart or soul or mercy himself ; but the corporation which he means to set up will have none at all.   It
will grind the people and debase them and clog their
progress a hundred times more than Jethro Bass has done.
Mark my words, Carry.   I'm running ahead of the times
a little, but I can see it all as clearly as if it existed now."

Mrs. Merrill went about her duties that morning with
a heavy heart, and more than once she paused to wipe
away a tear that would have fallen on the linen she was
sorting.   At eleven o'clock the doorbell rang, and Ellen
appeared at the entrance to the linen closet with a card
in her hand.   Mrs. Merrill looked at it with a flurry of
surprise.   It read : —

MISS LUCRETIA PENNIMAN

The Woman's Hour

CHAPTER X

IT was certainly affinity that led Miss Lucretia to choose the rosewood sofa of a bygone age, which was covered with horsehair. Miss Lucretia's features seemed to be constructed on a larger and more generous principle than those of women are nowadays. Her face was longer. With her curls and her bonnet and her bombazine, — which she wore in all seasons, — she was in complete harmony with the sofa. She had thrown aside the storm cloak which had become so familiar to pedestrians in certain parts of Boston.

"My dear Miss Penniman," said Mrs. Merrill, "I am delighted and honored. I scarcely hoped for such a pleasure. I have so long admired you and your work, and I have heard Cynthia speak of you so kindly."

"It is very good of you to say so, Mrs. Merrill," answered Miss Lucretia, in her full, deep voice. It was by no means an unpleasant voice. She settled herself, though she sat quite upright, in the geometrical centre of the horsehair sofa, and cleared her throat. "To be quite honest with you, Mrs. Merrill," she continued, "I came upon a particular errand, though I believe it would not be a perversion of the truth if I were to add that I have had for a month past every intention of paying you a friendly call."

Good Mrs. Merrill's breath was a little taken away by this extremely scrupulous speech. She also began to feel a misgiving about the cause of the visit, but she managed to say something polite in reply.

"I have come about Cynthia," announced Miss Lucretia, without further preliminaries.

357

" About Cynthia ? " faltered Mrs. Merrill.

Miss Lucretia opened a reticule at her waist and drew
forth a newspaper clipping, which she unfolded and handed
to Mrs. Merrill.

" Have you seen this ? " she demanded.

Mrs. Merrill took it, although she guessed very well
what it was, glanced at it with a shudder, and handed it
back.

" Yes, I have read it," she said.

" I have come to ask you, Mrs. Merrill," said Miss
Lucretia, "if it is true."

Here was a question, indeed, for the poor lady to answer!
But Mrs. Merrill was no coward.

" It is partly true, I believe."

" Partly ? " said Miss Lucretia, sharply.

" Yes, partly," said Mrs. Merrill, rousing herself for the
trial ; " I have never yet seen a newspaper article which
was wholly true."

" That is because newspapers are not edited by women,"
observed Miss Lucretia. " What I wish you to tell me,
Mrs. Merrill, is this : how much of that article is true,
and how much of it is false ? "

" Really, Miss Penniman," replied Mrs. Merrill, with
spirit, " I don't see why you should expect me to know."

" A woman should take an intelligent interest in her
husband's affairs, Mrs. Merrill. I have long advocated it
as an entering wedge."

" An entering wedge! " exclaimed Mrs. Merrill, who had
never read a page of the *Woman's Hour*.

" Yes. Your husband is the president of a railroad, I
believe, which is largely in that state. I should like to
ask him whether these statements are true in the main.
Whether this Jethro Bass is the kind of man they declare
him to be."

Mrs. Merrill was in a worse quandary than ever. Her
own spirits were none too good, and Miss Lucretia's eye,
in its search for truth, seemed to pierce into her very soul.
There was no evading that eye. But Mrs. Merrill did what
few people would have had the courage or good sense to do.

"That is a political article, Miss Penniman," she said, "inspired by a bitter enemy of Jethro Bass, Mr. Worthington, who has bought the newspaper from which it was copied. For that reason, I was right in saying that it is partly true. You nor I, Miss Penniman, must not be the judges of any man or woman, for we know nothing of their problems or temptations. God will judge them. We can only say that they have acted rightly or wrongly according to the light that is in us. You will find it difficult to get a judgment of Jethro Bass that is not a partisan judgment, and yet I believe that that article is in the main a history of the life of Jethro Bass. A partisan history, but still a history. He has unquestionably committed many of the acts of which he is accused."

Here was talk to make the author of the "Hymn to Coniston" sit up, if she hadn't been sitting up already.

"And don't you condemn him for those acts?" she gasped.

"Ah," said Mrs. Merrill, thinking of her own husband. Yesterday she would certainly have condemned Jethro Bass. But now! "I do not condemn anybody, Miss Penniman."

Miss Lucretia thought this extraordinary, to say the least.

"I will put the question in another way, Mrs. Merrill," said she. "Do you think this Jethro Bass a proper guardian for Cynthia Wetherell?"

To her amazement Mrs. Merrill did not give her an instantaneous answer to this question. Mrs. Merrill was thinking of Jethro's love for the girl, manifold evidences of which she had seen, and her heart was filled with a melting pity. It was such a love, Mrs. Merrill knew, as is not given to many here below. And there was Cynthia's love for him. Mrs. Merrill had suffered that morning thinking of this tragedy also.

"I do not think he is a proper guardian for her, Miss Penniman."

It was then that the tears came to Mrs. Merrill's eyes, for there is a limit to all human endurance. The sight of

these caused a remarkable change in Miss Lucretia, and
she leaned forward and seized Mrs. Merrill's arm.

"My dear," she cried, "my dear, what are we to do?
Cynthia can't go back to that man. She loves him, I
know, she loves him as few girls are capable of loving.
But when she finds out what he is! When she finds
out how he got the money to support her father!"
Miss Lucretia fumbled in her reticule and drew forth
a handkerchief and brushed her own eyes — eyes which
a moment ago were so piercing. "I have seen many young
women," she continued; "but I have known very few
who were made of as fine a fibre and who have such
principles as Cynthia Wetherell."

"That is very true," assented Mrs. Merrill, too much
cast down to be amazed by this revelation of Miss
Lucretia's weakness.

"But what are we to do?" insisted that lady; "who
is to tell her what he is? How is it to be kept from
her, indeed?"

"Yes," said Mrs. Merrill, "there will be more articles.
Mr. Merrill says so. It seems there is to be a great political struggle in that state."

"Precisely," said Miss Lucretia, sadly. "And whoever tells the girl will forfeit her friendship. I — I am
very fond of her," and here she applied again to the
reticule.

"Whom would she believe?" asked Mrs. Merrill,
whose estimation of Miss Lucretia was increasing by
leaps and bounds.

"Precisely," agreed Miss Lucretia. "But she must
hear about it sometime."

"Wouldn't it be better to let her hear?" suggested
Mrs. Merrill; "we cannot very well soften that shock.
I talked the matter over a little with Mr. Merrill, and
he thinks that we must take time over it, Miss Penniman.
Whatever we do, we must not act hastily."

"Well," said Miss Lucretia, "as I said, I am very fond
of the girl, and I am willing to do my duty, whatever it
may be. And I also wished to say, Mrs. Merrill, that

I have thought about another matter very carefully.
I am willing to provide for the girl. I am getting too
old to live alone. I am getting too old, indeed, to do
my work properly, as I used to do it. I should like
to have her to live with me."

"She has become as one of my own daughters," said
Mrs. Merrill. Yet she knew that this offer of Miss
Lucretia's was not one to be lightly set aside, and that
it might eventually be the best solution of the problem.
After some further earnest discussion it was agreed between them that the matter was, if possible, to be kept
from Cynthia for the present, and when Miss Lucretia
departed Mrs. Merrill promised her an early return of her
call.

Mrs. Merrill had another talk with her husband, which
lasted far into the night. This talk was about Cynthia
alone, and the sorrow which threatened her. These good
people knew that it would be no light thing to break the
faith of such as she, and they made her troubles their
own.

Cynthia little guessed as she exchanged raillery with
Mr. Merrill the next morning that he had risen fifteen minutes earlier than usual to search his newspaper through.
He would read no more at breakfast, so he declared in
answer to his daughters' comments : it was a bad habit
which did not agree with his digestion. It was something new for Mr. Merrill to have trouble with his
digestion.

There was another and scarcely less serious phase of
the situation which Mr. and Mrs. Merrill had yet to discuss between them — a phase of which Miss Lucretia
Penniman knew nothing.

The day before Miss Sadler's school was to reopen —
nearly a week before the Harvard term was to commence
— a raging, wet snowstorm came charging in from the
Atlantic. Snow had no terrors for a Coniston person, and
Cynthia had been for her walk. Returning about five
o'clock, she was surprised to have the door opened for her
by Susan herself.

"What a picture you are in those furs!" she cried, with an intention which for the moment was lost upon Cynthia. "I thought you would never come. You must have walked to Dedham this time. Who do you think is here? Mr. Worthington."

"Mr. Worthington!"

"I have been trying to entertain him, but I am afraid I have been a very poor substitute. However, I have persuaded him to stay for supper."

"It needed but little persuasion," said Bob, appearing in the doorway. All the snowstorms of the wide Atlantic could not have brought such color to her cheeks. Cynthia, for all her confusion at the meeting, had not lost her faculty of observation. He seemed to have changed again, even during the brief time he had been absent. His tone was grave.

"He needs to be cheered up, Cynthia," Susan went on, as though reading her thoughts. "I have done my best, without success. He won't confess to me that he has come back to make up some of his courses. I don't mind owning that I've got to finish a theme to be handed in to-morrow."

With these words Susan departed, and left them standing in the hall together. Bob took hold of Cynthia's jacket and helped her off with it. He could read neither pleasure nor displeasure in her face, though he searched it anxiously enough. It was she who led the way into the parlor and seated herself, as before, on one of the uncompromising, straight-backed chairs. Whatever inward tremors the surprise of this visit had given her, she looked at him clearly and steadily, completely mistress of herself, as ever.

"I thought your holidays did not end until next week," she said.

"They do not."

"Then why are you here?"

"Because I could not stay away, Cynthia," he answered. It was not the manner in which he would have said it a month ago. There was a note of intense earnestness in his voice now, and to it she could make no light reply. Confronted again with an unexpected situation, she could not decide at once upon a line of action.

"When did you leave Brampton?" she asked, to gain time. But with the words her thoughts flew to the hill country.

"This morning," he said, "on the early train. They have three feet of snow up there." He, too, seemed glad of a respite from something. "They're having a great fuss in Brampton about a new teacher for the village school. Miss Goddard has got married. Did you know Miss Goddard, the lanky one with the glasses?"

"Yes," said Cynthia, beginning to be amused at the turn the conversation was taking.

"Well, they can't find anybody smart enough to replace Miss Goddard. Old Ezra Graves, who's on the prudential committee, told Ephraim they ought to get you. I was in the post-office when they were talking about it. Just see what a reputation for learning you have in Brampton!"

Cynthia was plainly pleased by the compliment.

"How is Cousin Eph?" she asked.

"Happy as a lark," said Bob, "the greatest living authority in New England on the Civil War. He's made the post-office the most popular social club I ever saw. If anybody's missing in Brampton, you can nearly always find them in the post-office. But I smiled at the notion of your being a schoolma'am."

"I don't see anything so funny about it," replied Cynthia, smiling too. "Why shouldn't I be? I should like it."

"You were made for something different," he answered quietly.

It was a subject she did not choose to discuss with him, and dropped her lashes before the plainly spoken admiration in his eyes. So a silence fell between them, broken only by the ticking of the agate clock on the mantel and the music of sleigh-bells in a distant street. Presently the sleigh-bells died away, and it seemed to Cynthia that the sound of her own heart-beats must be louder than the ticking of the clock. Her tact had suddenly deserted her, without reason, and she did not dare to glance again at Bob as he sat under the lamp. That minute — for it was a full minute — was charged with a presage which she could not grasp. Cynthia's instincts were very keen. She understood, of course, that he had cut short his holiday to come to see her, and she might have dealt with him had that been all. But — through that sixth sense with which some women are endowed — she knew that something troubled him. He, too, had never yet been at a loss for words.

The silence forced him to speak first, and he tried to restore the light tone to the conversation.

"Cousin Ephraim gave me a piece of news," he said. "Ezra Graves got it, too. He told us you were down in Boston at a fashionable school. Cousin Ephraim knows a thing or two. He says he always callated you were cut out for a fine lady."

"Bob," said Cynthia, nerving herself for the ordeal, "did you tell Cousin Ephraim you had seen me?"

"I told him and Ezra that I had been a constant and welcome visitor at this house."

"Did you tell your father that you had seen me?"

This was too serious a question to avoid.

"No, I did not. There was no reason why I should have."

"There was every reason," said Cynthia, "and you know it. Did you tell him why you came to Boston to-day?"

"No."

"Why does he think you came?"

"He doesn't think anything about it," said Bob. "He went off to Chicago yesterday to attend a meeting of the board of directors of a western railroad."

"And so," she said reproachfully, "you slipped off as soon as his back was turned. I would not have believed that of you, Bob. Do you think that was fair to him or me?"

Bob Worthington sprang to his feet and stood over her. She had spoken to a boy, but she had aroused a man, and she felt an amazing thrill at the result. The muscles in his face tightened, and deepened the lines about his mouth, and a fire was lighted about his eyes.

"Cynthia," he said slowly, "even you shall not speak to me like that. If I had believed it were right, if I had believed that it would have done any good to you or me, I should have told my father the moment I got to Brampton. In affairs of this kind — in a matter of so much importance in my life," he continued, choosing his words carefully, "I am likely to know whether I am doing right or wrong. If my mother were alive, I am sure that she would approve of this — this friendship."

Having got so far, he paused. Cynthia felt that she was trembling, as though the force and feeling that was in him had charged her also.

"I did not intend to come so soon," he went on, "but — I had a reason for coming. I knew that you did not want me."

"You know that that is not true, Bob," she faltered. His next words brought her to her feet.

"Cynthia," he said, in a voice shaken by the intensity of his passion, "I came because I love you better than all the world — because I always will love you so. I came to protect you, and care for you whatever happens. I did not mean to tell you so, now. But it cannot matter, Cynthia!"

He seized her, roughly indeed, in his arms, but his very roughness was a proof of the intensity of his love. For an instant she lay palpitating against him, and as long as he lives he will remember the first exquisite touch of her firm but supple figure and the marvellous communion of her lips. A current from the great store that was in her, pent up and all unknown, ran through him, and then she had struggled out of his arms and fled, leaving him standing alone in the parlor.

It is true that such things happen, and no man or woman may foretell the day or the hour thereof. Cynthia fled up the stairs, miraculously arriving unnoticed at her own room, and locked the door and flung herself on the bed.

Tears came — tears of shame, of joy, of sorrow, of rejoicing, of regret; tears that burned, and yet relieved her, tears that pained while they comforted. Had she sinned beyond the pardon of heaven, or had she committed a supreme act of right? One moment she gloried in it, and the next upbraided herself bitterly. Her heart beat with tumult, and again seemed to stop. Such, though the words but faintly describe them, were her feelings, for thoughts were still to emerge out of chaos. Love comes like a flame to few women, but so it came to Cynthia Wetherell, and burned out for a while all reason.

Only for a while. Generations which had practised self-restraint were strong in her — generations accustomed, too, to thinking out, so far as in them lay, the logical consequences of their acts; generations ashamed of these very instants when nature has chosen to take command. After a time had passed, during which the world might have shuffled from its course, Cynthia sat up in the darkness. How was she ever to face the light again? Reason had returned.

So she sat for another space, and thought of what she had done — thought with a surprising calmness now which astonished her. Then she thought of what she would do, for there was an ordeal still to be gone through. Although she shrank from it, she no longer lacked the courage to endure it. Certain facts began to stand out clearly from the confusion. The least important and most immediate of these was that she would have to face him, and incidentally face the world in the shape of the Merrill family, at supper. She rose mechanically and lighted the gas and bathed her face and changed her gown. Then she heard Susan's voice at the door.

" Cynthia, what in the world are you doing? "

Cynthia opened the door and the sisters entered. Was it possible that they did not read her terrible secret in her face? Apparently not. Susan was busy commenting on the qualities and peculiarities of Mr. Robert Worthington, and showering upon Cynthia a hundred questions which she answered she knew not how; but neither Susan nor Jane, wonderful as it may seem, betrayed any suspicion. Did he send the flowers? Cynthia had not asked him. Did he want to know whether she read the newspapers? He had asked Susan that, before Cynthia came. Susan was ready to repeat the whole of her conversation with him. Why did he seem so particular about newspapers? Had he notions that girls ought not to read them?

The significance of Bob's remarks about newspapers was lost upon Cynthia then. Not till afterward did she think of them, or connect them with his unexpected visit. Then the supper bell rang, and they went downstairs.

The reader will be spared Mr. Worthington's feelings after Cynthia left him, although they were intense enough, and absorbing and far-reaching enough. He sat down on a chair and buried his head in his hands. His impulse had been to leave the house and return again on the morrow, but he remembered that he had been asked to stay for supper, and that such a proceeding would cause comment. At length he got up and stood before the fire, his thoughts still above the clouds, and it was thus that Mr. Merrill found him when he entered.

"Good evening," said that gentleman, genially, not knowing in the least who Bob was, but prepossessed in his favor by the way he came forward and shook his hand and looked him clearly in the eye.

"I'm Robert Worthington, Mr. Merrill," said he.

"Eh!" Mr. Merrill gasped, "eh! Oh, certainly, how do you do, Mr. Worthington?" Mr. Merrill would have been polite to a tax collector or a sheriff. He separated the office from the man, which ought not always to be done. "I'm glad to see you, Mr. Worthington. Well, well, bad storm, isn't it? I had an idea the college didn't open until next week."

"Mr. Worthington's going to stay for supper, Papa," said Susan, entering.

"Good!" cried Mr. Merrill. "Capital! You won't miss the old folks after supper, will you, girls? Your mother wants me to go to a whist party."

"It can't be helped, Carry," said Mr. Merrill to his

wife, as they walked up the hill to a neighbor's that evening.

"He's in love with Cynthia," said Mrs. Merrill, somewhat sadly; "it's as plain as the nose on your face, Stephen."

"That isn't very plain. Suppose he is! You can dam a mountain stream, but you can't prevent it reaching the sea, as we used to say when I was a boy in Edmundton. I like Bob," said Mr. Merrill, with his usual weakness for Christian names, "and he isn't any more like Dudley Worthington than I am. If you were to ask me, I'd say he couldn't do a better thing than marry Cynthia."

"Stephen!" exclaimed Mrs. Merrill. But in her heart she thought so, too. "What will Mr. Worthington say when he hears the young man has been coming to our house to see her?"

Mr. Merrill had been thinking of that very thing, but with more amusement than concern.

To return to Mr. Merrill's house, the three girls and the one young man were seated around the fire, and their talk, merrily as it had begun, was becoming minute by minute more stilted. This was largely the fault of Susan, who would not be happy until she had taken Jane upstairs and left Mr. Worthington and Cynthia together. This matter had been arranged between the sisters before supper. Susan found her opening at last, and upbraided Jane for her unfinished theme; Jane, having learned her lesson well, accused Susan. But Cynthia, who saw through the ruse, declared that both themes were finished. Susan, naturally indignant at such ingratitude, denied this. The manœuvre, in short, was executed very clumsily and very obviously, but executed nevertheless — the sisters marching out of the room under a fire of protests. The reader, too, will no doubt think it a very obvious manœuvre, but some things are managed badly in life as well as in books.

Cynthia and Bob were left alone: left, moreover, in mortal terror of each other. It is comparatively easy to open the door of a room and rush into a lady's arms —

if the lady be willing and alone. But to be abandoned, as Susan had abandoned them, and with such obvious intent, creates quite a different atmosphere. Bob had dared to hope for such an opportunity : had made up his mind during supper, while striving to be agreeable, just what he would do if the opportunity came. Instead, all he could do was to sit foolishly in his chair and look at the coals, not so much as venturing to turn his head until the sound of footsteps had died away on the upper floors. It was Cynthia who broke the silence and took command — a very different Cynthia from the girl who had thrown herself on the bed not three hours before. She did not look at him, but stared with determination into the fire.

" Bob, you must go," she said.

" Go ! " he cried. Her voice loosed the fetters of his passion, and he dared to seize the hand that lay on the arm of her chair. She did not resist this.

" Yes, you must go. You should not have stayed for supper."

" Cynthia," he said, " how can I leave you ? I will not leave you."

" But you can and must," she replied.

" Why ? " he asked, looking at her in dismay.

" You know the reason," she answered.

" Know it ? " he cried. " I know why I should stay. I know that I love you with my whole heart and soul. I know that I love you as few men have ever loved — and that you are the one woman among millions who can inspire such a love."

" No, Bob, no," she said, striving hard to keep her head, withdrawing her hand that it might not betray the treason of her lips. Aware, strange as it may seem, of the absurdity of the source of what she was to say, for a trace of a smile was about her mouth as she gazed at the coals. " You will get over this. You are not yet out of college, and many such fancies happen there."

For the moment he was incapable of speaking, incapable of finding an answer sufficiently emphatic. How was he to tell her of the rocks upon which his love was built ?

2 B

How was he to declare that the very perils which threatened her had made a man of him, with all of a man's yearning to share these perils and shield her from them? How was he to speak at all of those perils? He did not declaim, yet when he spoke, an enduring sincerity which she could not deny was in his voice.

"You know in your heart that what you say is not true, Cynthia. Whatever happens, I shall always love you."

Whatever happens! She shuddered at the words, reminding her as they did of all her vague misgivings and fears.

"Whatever happens!" she found herself repeating them involuntarily.

"Yes, whatever happens I will love you truly and faithfully. I will never desert you, never deny you, as long as I live. And you love me, Cynthia," he cried, "you love me, I know it."

"No, no," she answered, her breath coming fast. He was on his feet now, dangerously near her, and she rose swiftly to avoid him. She turned her head, that he might not read the denial in her eyes, and yet had to look at him again, for he was coming toward her quickly. "Don't touch me," she said, "don't touch me."

He stopped, and looked at her so pitifully that she could scarce keep back her tears.

"You do love me," he repeated.

So they stood for a moment, while Cynthia made a supreme effort to speak calmly.

"Listen, Bob," she said at last, "if you ever wish to see me again, you must do as I say. You must write to your father, and tell him what you have done and — and what you wish to do. You may come to me and tell me his answer, but you must not come to me before." She would have said more, but her strength was almost gone. Yes, and more would have implied a promise or a concession. She would not bind herself even by a hint. But of this she was sure : that she would not be the means of wrecking his opportunities. "And now — you must go."

He stayed where he was, though his blood leaped within

him, his admiration and respect for the girl outran his passion. Robert Worthington was a gentleman.

" I will do as you say, Cynthia," he answered, " but I am doing it for you. Whatever my father's reply may be will not change my love or my intentions. For I am determined that you shall be my wife."

With these words, and one long, lingering look, he turned and left her. He had lacked the courage to speak of his father's bitterness and animosity. Who will blame him ? Cynthia thought none the less of him for not telling her. There was, indeed, no need now to describe Dudley Worthington's feelings.

When the door had closed she stole to the window, and listened to his footfalls in the snow until she heard them no more.

CHAPTER XI

IN WHICH MISS SADLER WRITES A LETTER

THE next morning Cynthia's heart was heavy as she greeted her new friends at Miss Sadler's school. Life had made a woman of her long ago, while these girls had yet been in short dresses, and now an experience had come to her which few, if any, of these could ever know. It was of no use for her to deny to herself that she loved Bob Worthington — loved him with the full intensity of the strong nature that was hers. To how many of these girls would come such a love? and how many would be called upon to make such a renunciation as hers had been? No wonder she felt out of place among them, and once more the longing to fly away to Coniston almost overcame her. Jethro would forgive her, she knew, and stretch out his arms to receive her, and understand that some trouble had driven her to him.

She was aroused by some one calling her name — some one whose voice sounded strangely familiar. Cynthia was perhaps the only person in the school that day who did not know that Miss Janet Duncan had entered it. Miss Sadler certainly knew it, and asked Miss Duncan very particularly about her father and mother and even her brother. Miss Sadler knew, even before Janet's unexpected arrival, that Mr. and Mrs. Duncan had come to Boston after Christmas, and had taken a large house in the Back Bay in order to be near their son at Harvard. Mrs. Duncan was, in fact, a Bostonian, and more at home there than at any other place.

Miss Sadler observed with a great deal of astonishment the warm embrace that Janet bestowed on Cynthia. The occurrence started in Miss Sadler a train of thought, as a result of which she left the drawing-room where these reunions were held, and went into her own private study to write a note. This she addressed to Mrs. Alexander Duncan, at a certain number on Beacon Street, and sent it out to be posted immediately. In the meantime, Janet Duncan had seated herself on the sofa beside Cynthia, not having for an instant ceased to talk to her. Of what use to write a romance, when they unfolded themselves so beautifully in real life! Here was the country girl she had seen in Washington already in a fine way to become the princess, and in four months! Janet would not have thought it possible for any one to change so much in such a time. Cynthia listened, and wondered what language Miss Duncan would use if she knew how great and how complete that change had been. Romances, Cynthia thought sadly, were one thing to theorize about and quite another thing to endure — and smiled at the thought. But Miss Duncan had no use for a heroine without a heart-ache.

It is not improbable that Miss Janet Duncan may appear with Miss Sally Broke in another volume. The style of her conversation is known, and there is no room to repro-duce it here. She, too, had a heart, but she was a young woman given to infatuations, as Cynthia rightly guessed. Cynthia must spend many afternoons at her house — lunch with her, drive with her. For one omission Cynthia was thankful : she did not mention Bob Worthington's name. There was the romance under Miss Duncan's nose, and she did not see it. It is frequently so with romancers.

Cynthia's impassiveness, her complete poise, had fasci-nated Miss Duncan with the others. Had there been nothing beneath that exterior, Janet would never have guessed it, and she would have been quite as happy. Cynthia saw very clearly that Mr. Worthington or no other man or woman could force Bob to marry Janet.

The next morning, in such intervals as her studies per-mitted, Janet continued her attentions to Cynthia. That same morning she had brought a note from her father to

Miss Sadler, of the contents of which Janet knew nothing.
Miss Sadler retired into her study to read it, and two
newspaper clippings fell out of it under the paper-cutter.
This was the note : —

"MY DEAR MISS SADLER : Mrs. Duncan has referred
your note to me, and I enclose two clippings which speak
for themselves.   Miss Wetherell, I believe, stands in the
relation of ward to the person to whom they refer, and
her father was a sort of political assistant to this person.
Although, as you say, we are from that part of the
country " (Miss Sadler had spoken of the Duncans as the
people of importance there), "it was by the merest accident that Miss Wetherell's connection with this Jethro
Bass was brought to my notice.
                    "Sincerely yours,
                              "ALEXANDER DUNCAN."

It is pleasant to know that there were people in the
world who could snub Miss Sadler ; and there could be no
doubt, from the manner in which she laid the letter down
and took up the clippings, that Miss Sadler felt snubbed :
equally, there could be no doubt that the revenge would
fall on other shoulders than Mr. Duncan's.   And when
Miss Sadler proceeded to read the clippings, her hair
would have stood on end with horror had it not been so
efficiently plastered down.   Miss Sadler seized her pen,
and began a letter to Mrs. Merrill.   Miss Sadler's knowledge of the proprieties — together with other qualifications — had made her school what it was.   No Cynthia
Wetherells had ever before entered its sacred portals, or
should again.

The first of these clippings was the article containing
the arraignment of Jethro Bass which Mr. Merrill had
shown to his wife, and which had been the excuse for
Miss Penniman's call.   The second was one which Mr.
Duncan had clipped from the *Newcastle Guardian* of the
day before, and gave, from Mr. Worthington's side, a

very graphic account of the conflict which was to tear the
state asunder. The railroads were tired of paying toll to
the chief of a band of thieves and cutthroats, to a man
who had long throttled the state which had nourished
him, to — in short, to Jethro Bass. Miss Sadler was not
much interested in the figures and metaphors of political
compositions. Right had found a champion — the article
continued — in Mr. Isaac D. Worthington of Brampton,
president of the Truro Road and owner of large hold-
ings elsewhere. Mr. Worthington, backed by other
respectable property interests, would fight this monster
of iniquity to the death, and release the state from his
thraldom. Jethro Bass, the article alleged, was already
about his abominable work — had long been so — as in
mockery of that very vigilance which is said to be the
price of liberty. His agents were busy in every town of
the state, seeing to it that the slaves of Jethro Bass should
be sent to the next legislature.

And what was this system which he had built up
among these rural communities? It might aptly be
called the System of Mortgages. The mortgage — dread
name for a dreadful thing — was the chief weapon of the
monster. Even as Jethro Bass held the mortgages of
Coniston and Tarleton and round about, so his lieutenants held mortgages in every town and hamlet of the
state. What was a poor farmer to do? His choice was
not between right and wrong, but between a roof over
the heads of his wife and children and no roof. He must
vote for the candidate of Jethro Bass and corruption or
become a homeless wanderer. How the gentleman and
his other respectable backers were to fight the system the
article did not say. Were they to buy up all the mortgages? As a matter of fact, they intended to buy up enough
of these to count, but to mention this would be to betray
the methods of Mr. Worthington's reform. The first bitter frontier fighting between the advance cohorts of the
new giant and the old — the struggle for the caucuses and
the polls — had begun. Miss Sadler cared but little and
understood less of all this matter. She lingered over the

sentences which described Jethro Bass as a monster of iniquity, as a pariah with whom decent men would have no
intercourse, and in the heat of her passion that one who
had touched him had gained admittance to the most exclusive school for young ladies in the country she wrote
a letter.

Miss Sadler wrote the letter, and three hours later tore
it up and wrote another and more diplomatic one. Mrs.
Merrill, though not by any means of the same importance
as Mrs. Duncan, was not a person to be wantonly offended,
and might — knowing nothing about the monster — in
the goodness of her heart have taken the girl into her
house. Had it been otherwise, surely Mrs. Merrill would
not have had the effrontery! She would give Mrs. Merrill
a chance. The bell of release from studies was ringing
as she finished this second letter, and Miss Sadler in her
haste forgot to enclose the clippings. She ran out in time
to intercept Susan Merrill at the door, and to press into
her hands the clippings and the note, with a request to
take both to her mother.

Although the Duncans dined in the evening, the Merrills had dinner at half-past one in the afternoon, when
the girls returned from school. Mr. Merrill usually came
home, but he had gone off somewhere for this particular
day, and Mrs. Merrill had a sewing circle. The girls sat
down to dinner alone. When they got up from the table,
Susan suddenly remembered the note which she had left
in her coat pocket. She drew out the clippings with it.

" I wonder what Miss Sadler is sending mamma clippings
for," she said. " Why, Cynthia, they're about your uncle.
Look ! "

And she handed over the article headed " Jethro Bass."
Jane, who had quicker intuitions than her sister, would
have snatched it from Cynthia's hand, and it was a long
time before Susan forgave herself for her folly. Thus
Miss Sadler had her revenge.

It is often mercifully ordained that the mightiest blows
of misfortune are tempered for us. During the winter
evenings in Coniston, Cynthia had read little newspaper

attacks on Jethro, and scorned them as the cowardly
devices of enemies. They had been, indeed, but guarded
and covert allusions — grimaces from a safe distance.
Cynthia's first sensation as she read was anger — anger
so intense as to send all the blood in her body rushing
to her head. But what was this? " Right had found a
champion at last " in — in *Isaac D. Worthington!* That
was the first blow, and none but Cynthia knew the weight
of it. It sank but slowly into her consciousness, and
slowly the blood left her face, slowly but surely : left
it at length as white as the lace curtain of the window
which she clutched in her distress. Words which somebody had spoken were ringing in her ears. *Whatever
happens!* " Whatever happens I will never desert you,
never deny you, as long as I live." This, then, was what
he had meant by newspapers, and why he had come to
her !

The sisters, watching her, cried out in dismay. There
was no need to tell them that they were looking on at a
tragedy, and all the love and sympathy in their hearts
went out to her.

" Cynthia! Cynthia! What is it? " cried Susan, who,
thinking she would faint, seized her in her arms. " What
have I done? "

Cynthia did not faint, being made of sterner substance.
Gently, but with that inexorable instinct of her kind
which compels them to look for reliance within themselves even in the direst of extremities, Cynthia released
herself from Susan's embrace and put a hand to her
forehead.

" Will you leave me here a little while — alone? " she
said.

It was Jane now who drew Susan out and shut the door
of the parlor after them. In utter misery they waited on
the stairs while Cynthia fought out her battle for herself.

When they were gone she sank down into the big chair
under the reading lamp — the very chair in which he had
sat only two nights before. She saw now with a terrible
clearness the thing which for so long had been but a vague

premonition of disaster, and for a while she forgot the clippings. And when after a space the touch of them in her hand brought them back to her remembrance, she lacked the courage to read them through. But not for long. Suddenly her fear of them gave place to a consuming hatred of the man who had inspired these articles: of Isaac D. Worthington, for she knew that he must have inspired them. And then she began again to read them.

Truth, though it come perverted from the mouth of an enemy, has in itself a note to which the soul responds, let the mind deny as vehemently as it will. Cynthia read, and as she read her body was shaken with sobs, though the tears came not. Could it be true? Could the least particle of the least of these fearful insinuations be true? Oh, the treason of those whispers in a voice that was surely not her own, and yet which she could not hush! Was it possible that such things could be printed about one whom she had admired and respected above all men — nay, whom she had so passionately adored from childhood? A monster of iniquity, a pariah! The cruel, bitter calumny of those names! Cynthia thought of his goodness and loving kindness and his charity to her and to many others. His charity! The dreaded voice repeated that word, and sent a thought that struck terror into her heart: Whence had come the substance of that charity? Then came another word — mortgage. There it was on the paper, and at sight of it there leaped out of her memory a golden-green poplar shimmering against the sky and the distant blue billows of mountains in the west. She heard the high-pitched voice of a woman speaking the word, and even then it had had a hateful sound, and she heard herself asking, "Uncle Jethro, what is a mortgage?" He had struck his horse with the whip.

Loyal though the girl was, the whispers would not hush, nor the doubts cease to assail her. What if ever so small a portion of this were true? Could the whole of this hideous structure, tier resting upon tier, have been reared without something of a foundation? Fiercely though she told herself she would believe none of it, fiercely though she hated Mr. Worthington, fervently though she repeated aloud that her love for Jethro and her faith in him had not changed, the doubts remained. Yet they remained unacknowledged.

An hour passed. It was a thing beyond belief that one hour could have held such a store of agony. An hour passed, and Cynthia came dry-eyed from the parlor. Susan and Jane, waiting to give her comfort when she was recovered a little from this unknown but overwhelming affliction, were fain to stand mute when they saw her: to pay a silent deference to one whom sorrow had lifted far above them and transfigured. That was the look on Cynthia's face. She went up the stairs, and they stood in the hall not knowing what to do, whispering in awe-struck voices. They were still there when Cynthia came down again, dressed for the street. Jane seized her by the hand.

" Where are you going, Cynthia ?" she asked.

" I shall be back by five," said Cynthia.

She went up the hill, and across to old Louisburg Square, and up the hill again. The weather had cleared, the violet-paned windows caught the slanting sunlight and flung it back across the piles of snow. It was a day for wedding-bells. At last Cynthia came to a queerly fashioned little green door that seemed all askew with the slanting street, and rang the bell, and in another moment was standing on the threshold of Miss Lucretia Penniman's little sitting room. To Miss Lucretia, at her writing table, one glance was sufficient. She rose quickly to meet the girl, kissed her unresponsive cheek, and led her to a chair. Miss Lucretia was never one to beat about the bush, even in the gravest crises.

" You have read the articles," she said.

Read them ! During her walk hither Cynthia had been incapable of thought, but the epithets and arraignments and accusations, the sentences and paragraphs, were printed now upon her brain, never, she believed, to be effaced. Every step of the way she had been unconsciously repeating them.

" Have you read them ? " asked Cynthia.

" Yes, my dear."

" Has everybody read them ? " Did the whole world, then, know of her shame ?

" I am glad you came to me, my dear," said Miss Lucretia, taking her hand. "Have you talked of this to any one else ? "

" No," said Cynthia, simply.

Miss Lucretia was puzzled. She had not looked for apathy, but she did not know all of Cynthia's troubles. She wondered whether she had misjudged the girl, and was misled by her attitude.

" Cynthia," she said, with a briskness meant to hide emotion (for Miss Lucretia had emotions), "I am a lonely old woman, getting too old, indeed, to finish the task of my life. I went to see Mrs. Merrill the other day to ask her if she would let you come and live with me. Will you ? "

Cynthia shook her head.

" No, Miss Lucretia, I cannot," she answered.

" I won't press it on you now," said Miss Lucretia.

" I cannot, Miss Lucretia. I'm going to Coniston."

" Going to Coniston ! " exclaimed Miss Lucretia.

The name of that place — magic name once so replete with visions of happiness and content — seemed to recall Cynthia's spirit from its flight. Yes, the spirit was there, for it flashed in her eyes as she turned and looked into Miss Lucretia's face.

" Are these the articles you read ? " she asked, taking the clippings from her muff.

Miss Lucretia put on her spectacles.

" I have seen both of them," she said.

" And do you believe what they say about — about Jethro Bass ? "

Poor Miss Lucretia ! For once in her life she was at a loss. She, too, paid a deference to that face, young as it was. She had robbed herself of sleep trying to make up her mind what she would say upon such an occasion if it came. A wonderful virgin faith had to be shattered, and was she to be the executioner? She loved the girl with that strange, intense affection which sometimes comes to the elderly and the lonely, and she had prayed that this cup might pass from her. Was it possible that it was her own voice using very much the same words for which she had rebuked Mrs. Merrill?

"Cynthia," she said, "those articles were written by politicians, in a political controversy. No such articles can ever be taken literally."

"Miss Lucretia, do you believe what it says about Jethro Bass?" repeated Cynthia.

How was she to avoid those eyes? They pierced into her soul, even as her own had pierced into Mrs. Merrill's. Oh, Miss Lucretia, who pride yourself on your plain speaking, that you should be caught quibbling! Miss Lucretia blushed for the first time in many years, and into her face came the light of battle.

"I am a coward, my dear. I deserve your rebuke. To the best of my knowledge and belief, and so far as I can judge from the inquiries I have undertaken, Jethro Bass has made his living and gained and held his power by the methods described in those articles."

Miss Lucretia took off her spectacles and wiped them. She had committed a fine act of courage.

Cynthia stood up.

"Thank you," she said, "that is what I wanted to know."

"But—" cried Miss Lucretia, in amazement and apprehension, "but what are you going to do?"

"I am going to Coniston," said Cynthia, "to ask him if those things are true."

"To ask him!"

"Yes. If he tells me they are true, then I shall believe them."

"If he tells you?" Miss Lucretia gasped. Here was a courage of which she had not reckoned. "Do you think he will tell you?"

"He will tell me, and I shall believe him, Miss Lucretia."

"You are a remarkable girl, Cynthia," said Miss Lucretia, involuntarily. Then she paused for a moment. "Sup-

pose he tells you they are true? You surely can't live
with him again, Cynthia."

"Do you suppose I am going to desert him, Miss Lucretia?" she asked. "He loves me, and — and I love
him." This was the first time her voice had faltered.
"He kept my father from want and poverty, and he has
brought me up as a daughter. If his life has been as you
say, I shall make my own living!"

"How?" demanded Miss Lucretia, the practical part of
her coming uppermost.

"I shall teach school. I believe I can get a position,
in a place where I can see him often. I can break his
heart, Miss Lucretia, I — I can bring sadness to myself,
but I will not desert him."

Miss Lucretia stared at her for a moment, not knowing
what to say or do. She perceived that the girl had a
spirit as strong as her own : that her plans were formed,
her mind made up, and that no arguments could change
her.

"Why did you come to me?" she asked irrelevantly.

"Because I thought that you would have read the
articles, and I knew if you had, you would have taken
the trouble to inform yourself of the world's opinion."

Again Miss Lucretia stared at her.

"I will go to Coniston with you," she said, "at least
as far as Brampton."

Cynthia's face softened a little at the words.

"I would rather go alone, Miss Lucretia," she answered
gently, but with the same firmness. "I — I am very
grateful to you for your kindness to me in Boston. I
shall not forget it — or you. Good-by, Miss Lucretia."

But Miss Lucretia, sobbing openly, gathered the girl in
her arms and pressed her. Age was coming on her indeed,
that she should show such weakness. For a long time
she could not trust herself to speak, and then her words
were broken. Cynthia must come to her at the first sign
of doubt or trouble : this, Miss Lucretia's house, was to
be a refuge in any storm that life might send — and Miss
Lucretia's heart. Cynthia promised, and when she went

out at last through the little door her own tears were
falling, for she loved Miss Lucretia.

Cynthia was going to Coniston. That journey was as
fixed, as inevitable, as things mortal can be. She would
go to Coniston unless she perished on the way. No loving
entreaties, no fears of Mrs. Merrill or her daughters, were
of any avail. Mrs. Merrill, too, was awed by the vastness
of the girl's sorrow, and wondered if her own nature were
small by comparison. She had wept, to be sure, at her
husband's confession, and lain awake over it in the night
watches, and thought of the early days of their marriage.

And then, Mrs. Merrill told herself, Cynthia would
have to talk with Mr. Merrill. How was he to come
unscathed out of that ? There was pain and bitterness in
that thought, and almost resentment against Cynthia,
quivering though she was with sympathy for the girl. For
Mrs. Merrill, though the canker remained, had already
pardoned her husband and had asked the forgiveness of
God for that pardon. On other occasions, in other crises,
she had waited and watched for him in the parlor window,
and to-night she was at the door before his key was in the
lock, while he was still stamping the snow from his boots.
She drew him into the room and told him what had happened.

" Oh, Stephen," she cried, " what are you going to say
to her ? "

What, indeed ? His wife had sorrowed, but she had
known the obstacles and perils by which he had been beset. But what was he to say to Cynthia ? Her very
name had grown upon him, middle-aged man of affairs
though he was, until the thought of it summoned up in
his mind a figure of purity, and of the strength which was
from purity. He would not have believed it possible that
the country girl whom they had taken into their house
three months before should have wrought such an influence
over them all.

Even in the first hour of her sorrow which she had
spent that afternoon in the parlor, Cynthia had thought
of Mr. Merrill. He could tell her whether those accusa-

tions were true or false, for he was a friend of Jethro's. Her natural impulse — the primeval one of a creature which is hurt — had been to hide herself ; to fly to her own room, and perhaps by nightfall the courage would come to her to ask him the terrible questions. He was a friend of Jethro's. An illuminating flash revealed to her the meaning of that friendship — if the accusations were true. It was then she had thought of Miss Lucretia Penniman, and somehow she had found the courage to face the sunlight and go to her. She would spare Mr. Merrill.

But had she spared him ? Sadly the family sat down to supper without her, and after supper Mr. Merrill sent a message to his club that he could not attend a committee meeting there that evening. He sat with his wife in the little writing room, he pretending to read and she pretending to sew, until the silence grew too oppressive, and they spoke of the matter that was in their hearts. It was one of the bitterest evenings in Mr. Merrill's life, and there is no need to linger on it. They talked earnestly of Cynthia, and of her future. But they both knew why she did not come down to them.

" So she is really going to Coniston," said Mr. Merrill.

" Yes," answered Mrs. Merrill, " and I think she is doing right, Stephen."

Mr. Merrill groaned. His wife rose and put her hand on his shoulder.

" Come, Stephen," she said gently, " you will see her in the morning."

" I will go to Coniston with her," he said.

" No," replied Mrs. Merrill, " she wants to go alone. And I believe it is best that she should."

CHAPTER XII

GREAT afflictions generally bring in their train a host of smaller sorrows, each with its own little pang. One of these sorrows had been the parting with the Merrill family. Under any circumstance it was not easy for Cynthia to express her feelings, and now she had found it very difficult to speak of the gratitude and affection which she felt. But they understood — dear, good people that they were : no eloquence was needed with them. The ordeal of breakfast over, and the tearful " God bless you, Miss Cynthia," of Ellen the parlor-maid, the whole family had gone with her to the station. For Susan and Jane had spent their last day at Miss Sadler's school.

Mr. Merrill had sent for the conductor and bidden him take care of Miss Wetherell, and recommend her in his name to a conductor on the Truro Road. The man took off his cap to Mr. Merrill and called him by name and promised. It was a dark day, and long after the train had pulled out Cynthia remembered the tearful faces of the family standing on the damp platform of the station. As they fled northward through the flat river-meadows, the conductor would have liked to talk to her of Mr. Merrill ; there were few employees on any railroad who did not know the genial and kindly president of the Grand Gulf and sympathize with his troubles. But there was a look on the girl's face that forbade intrusion. Passengers stared at her covertly, as though fascinated by that look, and some tried to fathom it. But her eyes were firmly fixed upon a point far beyond their vision. The car stopped many times, and flew on again, but nothing seemed to break her absorption.

At last she was aroused by the touch of the conductor on her sleeve. The people were beginning to file out of the car, and the train was under the shadow of the snow-covered sheds in the station of the state capital. Cynthia recognized the place, though it was cold and bare and very different in appearance from what it had been on the summer's evening when she had come into it with her father. That, in effect, had been her first glimpse of the world, and well she recalled the thrill it had given her. The joy of such things was gone now, the rapture of holidays and new sights. These were over, so she told herself. Sorrow had quenched the thrills forever.

The kind conductor led her to the eating room, and when she would not eat his concern grew greater than ever. He took a strange interest in this young lady who had such a face and such eyes. He pointed her out to his friend the Truro conductor, and gave him some sandwiches and fruit which he himself had bought, with instructions to press them on her during the afternoon.

Cynthia could not eat. She hated this place, with its memories. Hated it, too, as a mart where men were bought and sold, for the wording of those articles ran in her head as though some priest of evil were chanting them in her ears. She did not remember then the sweeter aspect of the old town, its pretty homes set among their shaded gardens — homes full of good and kindly people. State House affairs were far removed from most of these, and the sickness and corruption of the body politic. And this political corruption, had she known it, was no worse than that of the other states in the wide Union : not so bad, indeed, as many, though this was small comfort. No comfort at all to Cynthia, who did not think of it.

After a while she rose and followed the new conductor to the Truro train, glad to leave the capital behind her. She was going to the hills — to the mountains. They, in truth, could not change, though the seasons passed over them, hot and cold, wet and dry. They were immutable in their goodness. Presently she saw them, the lower ones : the waters of the little stream beside her broke the black bonds of ice and raced over the rapids; the engine was puffing and groaning on the grade. Then the sun crept out, slowly, from the indefinable margin of vapor that hung massed over the low country.

Yes, she had come to the hills. Up and up climbed the train, through the little white villages in the valley nooks, banked with whiter snow; through the narrow gorges, — sometimes hanging over them, — under steep granite walls seared with ice-filled cracks, their brows hung with icicles.

Truro Pass is not so high as the Brenner, but it has a grand, wild look in winter, remote as it is from the haunts of men. A fitting refuge, it might be, for a great spirit heavy with the sins of the world below. Such a place might have been chosen, in the olden time, for a monastery — a gray fastness built against the black forest over the crag looking down upon the green clumps of spruces against the snow. Some vague longing for such a refuge was in Cynthia's heart as she gazed upon that silent place, and then the waters had already begun to run westward — the waters of Tumble Down brook, which flowed into Coniston Water above Brampton. The sun still had more than two hours to go on its journey to the hill crests when the train pulled into Brampton station. There were but a few people on the platform, but the first face she saw as she stepped from the car was Lem Hallowell's. It was a very red face, as we know, and its owner was standing in front of the Coniston stage, on runners now. He stared at her for an instant, and no wonder, and then he ran forward with outstretched hands.

"Cynthy — Cynthy Wetherell!" he cried. "Great Godfrey!"

He got so far, he seized her hands, and then he stopped, not knowing why. There were many more ejaculations and welcomes and what not on the end of his tongue. It was not that she had become a lady — a lady of a type he had never before seen. He meant to say that, too, in his own way, but he couldn't. And that transformation would have bothered Lem but little. What was the change, then? Why was he in awe of her — he, Lem

Hallowell, who had never been in awe of any one? He
shook his head, as though openly confessing his inability
to answer that question. He wanted to ask others, but
they would not come.

"Lem," she said, "I am so glad you are here."

"Climb right in, Cynthy. I'll git the trunk." There
it lay, the little rawhide one before him on the boards, and
he picked it up in his bare hands as though it had been a
paper parcel. It was a peculiarity of the stage driver that
he never wore gloves, even in winter, so remarkable was
the circulation of his blood. After the trunk he deposited,
apparently with equal ease, various barrels and boxes, and
then he jumped in beside Cynthia, and they drove down
familiar Brampton Street, as wide as a wide river; past
the meeting-house with the terraced steeple; past the post-
office, — Cousin Ephraim's post-office, — where Lem gave
her a questioning look — but she shook her head, and he
did not wait for the distribution of the last mail that day;
past the great mansion of Isaac D. Worthington, where
the iron mastiffs on the lawn were up to their muzzles in
snow. After that they took the turn to the right, which
was the road to Coniston.

Well-remembered road, and in winter or summer, Cynthia knew every tree and farmhouse beside it. Now it
consisted of two deep grooves in the deep snow; that was
all, save for a curving turnout here and there for team to
pass team. Well-remembered scene! How often had
Cynthia looked upon it in happier days! Such a crust
was on the snow as would bear a heavy man, and the
pasture hillocks were like glazed cakes in the window
of a baker's shop. Never had the western sky looked so
yellow through the black columns of the pine trunks.
A lonely, beautiful road it was that evening.

For a long time the silence of the great hills was broken
only by the sweet jingle of the bells on the shaft. Many
a day, winter and summer, Lem had gone that road alone,
whistling, and never before heeding that silence. Now it
seemed to symbolize a great sorrow: to be in subtle harmony with that of the girl at his side. What that sorrow

was he could not guess. The good man yearned to comfort her, and yet he felt his comfort too humble to be noticed by such sorrow. He longed to speak, but for the first time in his life feared the sound of his own voice. Cynthia had not spoken since she left the station, had not looked at him, had not asked for the friends and neighbors whom she had loved so well — had not asked for Jethro! Was there any sorrow on earth to be felt like that? And was there one to feel it?

At length, when they reached the great forest, Lem Hallowell knew that he must speak or cry aloud. But what would be the sound of his voice — after such an age of disuse? Could he speak at all? Broken and hoarse and hideous though the sound might be, he must speak. And hoarse and broken it was. It was not his own, but still it was a voice.

"Folks — folks'll be surprised to see you, Cynthy."

No, he had not spoken at all. Yes, he had, for she answered him.

"I suppose they will, Lem."

"Mighty glad to have you back, Cynthy. We think a sight of you. We missed you."

"Thank you, Lem."

"Jethro hain't lookin' for you by any chance, be he?"

"No," she said. But the question startled her. Suppose he had not been at home! She had never once thought of that. Could she have borne to wait for him?

After that Lem gave it up. He had satisfied himself as to his vocal powers, but he had not the courage even to whistle. The journey to Coniston was faster in the winter, and at the next turn of the road the little village came into view. There it was, among the snows. The pain in Cynthia's heart, so long benumbed, quickened when she saw it. How write of the sharpness of that pain to those who have never known it? The sight of every gable brought its agony, — the store with the checker-paned windows, the harness shop, the meeting-house, the white parsonage on its little hill. Rias Richardson ran out of the store in his carpet slippers, bareheaded in the cold, and gave one shout. Lem heeded him not; did not stop there as usual, but drove straight to the tannery house and pulled up under the butternut tree. Milly Skinner ran out on the porch, and gave one long look, and cried: —

"Good Lord, it's Cynthy!"

"Where's Jethro?" demanded Lem.

Milly did not answer at once. She was staring at Cynthia.

"He's in the tannery shed," she said, "choppin' wood." But still she kept her eyes on Cynthia's face. "I'll fetch him."

"No," said Cynthia, "I'll go to him there."

She took the path, leaving Millicent with her mouth open, too amazed to speak again, and yet not knowing why.

In the tannery shed! Would Jethro remember what happened there almost six and thirty years before? Would he remember how that other Cynthia had come to him there, and what her appeal had been?

Cynthia came to the doors. One of these was open now — both had been closed that other evening against the storm of sleet — and she caught a glimpse of him standing on the floor of chips and bark — tan-bark no more. Cynthia caught a glimpse of him, and love suddenly welled up into her heart as waters into a spring after a drought. He had not seen her, not heard the sound of the sleigh-bells. He was standing with his foot upon the sawbuck and the saw across his knee, he was staring at the woodpile, and there was stamped upon his face a look which no man or woman had ever seen there, a look of utter loneliness and desolation, a look as of a soul condemned to wander forever through the infinite, cold spaces between the worlds — alone.

Cynthia stopped at sight of it. What had been her misery and affliction compared to this? Her limbs refused her, though she knew not whether she would have fled or rushed into his arms. How long she stood thus, and he stood, may not be said, but at length he put down his foot and took the saw from his knee, his eyes fell upon her, and his lips spoke her name.

"Cynthy!"

Speechless, she ran to him and flung her arms about his neck, and he dropped the saw and held her tightly — even as he had held that other Cynthia in that place in the year gone by. And yet not so. Now he clung to her with a desperation that was terrible, as though to let go of her would be to fall into nameless voids beyond human companionship and love. But at last he did release her, and stood looking down into her face, as if seeking to read a sentence there.

And how was she to pronounce that sentence ! Though her faith might be taken away, her love remained, and grew all the greater because he needed it. Yet she knew that no subterfuge or pretence would avail her to hide why she had come. She could not hide it. It must be spoken out now, though death was preferable.

And he was waiting. Did he guess? She could not tell. He had spoken no word but her name. He had expressed no surprise at her appearance, asked no reasons for it. Superlatives of suffering or joy or courage are hard to convey — words fall so far short of the feeling. And Cynthia's pain was so far beyond tears.

" Uncle Jethro," she said, " yesterday something — something happened. I could not stay in Boston any longer."

He nodded.

" I had to come to you. I could not wait."

He nodded again.

" I — I read something." To take a white-hot iron and sear herself would have been easier than this.

" Yes," he said.

She felt that the look was coming again — the look which she had surprised in his face. His hands dropped lifelessly from her shoulders, and he turned and went to the door, where he stood with his back to her, silhouetted against the eastern sky all pink from the reflection of sunset. He would not help her. Perhaps he could not. The things were true. There had been a grain of hope within her, ready to sprout.

" I read two articles from the *Newcastle Guardian* — about you — about your life."

"Yes," he said. But he did not turn.

"How you had — how you had earned your living. How you had gained your power," she went on, her pain lending to her voice an exquisite note of many modulations.

"Yes — Cynthy," he said, and still stared at the eastern sky.

She took two steps toward him, her arms outstretched, her fingers opening and closing. And then she stopped.

"I would believe no one," she said, "I will believe no one — until — unless you tell me. Uncle Jethro," she cried in agony, "Uncle Jethro, tell me that those things are not true!"

She waited a space, but he did not stir. There was no sound, save the song of Coniston Water under the shattered ice.

"Won't you speak to me?" she whispered. "Won't you tell me that they are not true?"

His shoulders shook convulsively. O for the right to turn to her and tell her that they were lies! He would have bartered his soul for it. What was all the power in the world compared to this priceless treasure he had lost? Once before he had cast it away, though without meaning to. Then he did not know the eternal value of love — of such love as those two women had given him. Now he knew that it was beyond value, the one precious gift of life, and the knowledge had come too late. Could he have saved his life if he had listened to that other Cynthia?

"Won't you tell me that they are not true?"

Even then he did not turn to her, but he answered. Curious to relate, though his heart was breaking, his voice was steady — steady as it always had been.

"I — I've seen it comin', Cynthy," he said. "I never knowed anything I was afraid of before — but I was afraid of this. I knowed what your notions of right and wrong was — your — your mother had them. They're the principles of good people. I — I knowed the day would come when you'd ask, but I wanted to be happy as long as I could. I hain't been happy, Cynthy. But you was right when you said I'd tell you the truth. S-so I will. I guess them things which you speak about are true — the way I got where I am, and the way I made my livin'. They — they hain't put just as they'd ought to be, perhaps, but that's the way I done it in the main."

It was thus that Jethro Bass met the supreme crisis of his life. And who shall say he did not meet it squarely and honestly? Few men of finer fibre and more delicate morals would have acquitted themselves as well. That was a Judgment Day for Jethro; and though he knew it not, he spoke through Cynthia to his Maker, confessing his faults freely and humbly, and dwelling on the justness of his punishment; putting not forward any good he may have done, nor thinking of it, nor seeking excuse because of the light that was in him. Had he been at death's door in the face of nameless tortures, no man could have dragged such a confession from him. But a great love had been given him, and to that love he must speak the truth, even at the cost of losing it.

But he was not to lose it. Even as he was speaking a thrill of admiration ran through Cynthia, piercing her sorrow. The superb strength of the man was there in that simple confession, and it is in the nature of woman to admire strength. He had fought his fight, and gained, and paid the price without a murmur, seeking no palliation. Cynthia had not come to that trial — so bitter for her — as a judge. If the reader has seen youth and innocence sitting in the seat of justice, with age and experience at the bar, he has mistaken Cynthia. She came to Coniston inexorable, it is true, because hers was a nature impelled to do right though it perish. She did not presume to say what Jethro's lights and opportunities might have been. Her own she knew, and by them she must act accordingly.

When he had finished speaking, she stole silently to his side and slipped her hand in his. He trembled violently at her touch.

"Uncle Jethro," she said in a low tone, "I love you." At the words he trembled more violently still.

"No, no, Cynthy," he answered thickly, "don't say

that — I — I don't expect it, Cynthy, I know you can't —
'twouldn't be right, Cynthy. I hain't fit for it."

"Uncle Jethro," she said, "I love you better than I
have ever loved you in my life."

Oh, how welcome were the tears! and how human!
He turned, pitifully incredulous, wondering that she
should seek by deceit to soften the blow; he saw them
running down her cheeks, and he believed. Yes, he believed, though it seemed a thing beyond belief. Unworthy,
unfit though he were, she loved him. And his own love
as he gazed at her, sevenfold increased as it had been by
the knowledge of losing her, changed in texture from
homage to worship — nay, to adoration. His punishment
would still be heavy; but whence had come such a wondrous gift to mitigate it?

"Oh, don't you believe me?" she cried, "can't you see
that it is true?"

And yet he could only hold her there at arm's length
with that new and strange reverence in his face. He
was not worthy to touch her, but still she loved him.

The flush had faded from the eastern sky, and the
faintest border of yellow light betrayed the ragged out-
lines of the mountain as they walked together to the
tannery house.

Millicent, in the kitchen, was making great preparations
— for Millicent. Miss Skinner was a person who had
hitherto laid it down as a principle of life to pay deference
or do honor to no human made of mere dust, like herself.
Millicent's exception, if Cynthia had thought about it, was
a tribute of no mean order. Cynthia, alas, did not think
about it: she did not know that, in her absence, the fire
had not been lighted in the evening, Jethro supping on
crackers and milk and Milly partaking of the evening
meal at home. Moreover, Miss Skinner had an engagement with a young man. Cynthia saw the fire, and threw
off her sealskin coat which Mr. and Mrs. Merrill had given
her for Christmas, and took down the saucepan from the
familiar nail on which it hung. It was a miraculous fact,
for which she did not attempt to account, that she was

almost happy: happy, indeed, in comparison to that which had been her state since the afternoon before. Millicent snatched the saucepan angrily from her hand.

"What be you doin', Cynthy?" she demanded.

Such was Miss Skinner's little way of showing deference. Though deference is not usually vehement, Miss Skinner's was very real, nevertheless.

"Why, Milly, what's the matter?" exclaimed Cynthia, in astonishment.

"You hain't a-goin' to do any cookin', that's all," said Milly, very red in the face.

"But I've always helped," said Cynthia. "Why not?"

Why not? A tribute was one thing, but to have to put the reasons for that tribute into words was quite another.

"Why not?" cried Milly, "because you hain't a-goin' to, that's all."

Strange deference! But Cynthia turned and looked at the girl with a little, sad smile of comprehension and affection. She took her by the shoulders and kissed her.

Whereupon a most amazing thing happened — Millicent burst into tears — wild, ungovernable tears they were.

"Because you hain't a-goin' to," she repeated, her words interspersed with violent sobs. "You go 'way, Cynthy," she cried, "git out!"

"Milly," said Cynthia, shaking her head, "you ought to be ashamed of yourself." But they were not words of reproof. She took a little lamp from the shelf, and went up the narrow stairs to her own room in the gable, where Lemuel had deposited the rawhide trunk.

Though she had had nothing all day, she felt no hunger, but for Milly's sake she tried hard to eat the supper when it came. Before it had fairly begun Moses Hatch had arrived, with Amandy and Eben; and Rias Richardson came in, and other neighbors, to say a word of welcome: to hear (if the truth be not too disparaging to their characters) the reasons for her sudden appearance, and such news of her Boston experiences as she might choose to give them. They had learned from Lem Hallowell that Cynthia had returned a lady: a real lady, not a sham

one who relied on airs and graces, such as had come to
Coniston the summer before to look for a summer place
on the painter's recommendation. Lem was not a gossip,
in the disagreeable sense of the term, and he had not said
a word to his neighbors of his feelings on that terrible
drive from Brampton. Knowing that some blow had fallen
upon Cynthia, he would have spared her these visits if
he could. But Lem was wise and kind, so he merely
said that she had returned a lady.

And they had found a lady. As they stood or sat
around the kitchen (Eben and Rias stood), Cynthia talked
to them — about Coniston : rather, be it said, that they
talked about Coniston in answer to her questions. The
sledding had been good ; Moses had hauled so many thousand feet of lumber to Brampton ; Sam Price's woman
(she of Harwich) had had a spell of sciatica ; Chester
Perkins's bull had tossed his brother-in-law, come from
Iowy on a visit, and broke his leg ; yes, Amandy guessed
her dyspepsy was somewhat improved since she had tried
Graham's Golden Remedy — it made her feel real light-
hearted ; Eben (blushing furiously) was to have the
Brook Farm in the spring; there was a case of spotted
fever in Tarleton.

Yes, Lem Hallowell had been right, Cynthia was a lady,
but not a mite stuck up. What was the difference in her ?
Not her clothes, which she wore as if she had been used
to them all her life. Poor Cynthia, the clothes were simple
enough. Not her manner, which was as kind and sweet
as ever. What was it that compelled their talk about
themselves, that made them refrain from asking those
questions about Boston, and why she had come back ?
Some such query was running in their minds as they
talked, while Jethro, having finished his milk and crackers,
sat silent at the end of the table with his eyes upon her.
He rose when Mr. Satterlee came in.

Mr. Satterlee looked at her, and then he went quietly
across the room and kissed her. But then Mr. Satterlee
was the minister. Cynthia thought his hair a little
thinner and the lines in his face a little deeper. And

Mrs. Samuel Price.

Mr. Satterlee thought — perhaps he was the only one of the visitors who guessed why she had come back. He laid his thin hand on her head, as though in benediction, and sat down beside her.

"And how is the learning, Cynthia?" he asked.

Now, indeed, they were going to hear something at last. An intuition impelled Cynthia to take advantage of that opportunity.

"The learning has become so great, Mr. Satterlee," she said, "that I have come back to try to make some use of it. It shall be wasted no more."

She did not dare to look at Jethro, but she was aware that he had sat down abruptly. What sacrifice will not a good woman make to ease the burden of those whom she loves! And Jethro's burden would be heavy enough. Such a woman will speak almost gayly, though her heart be heavy. But Cynthia's was lighter now than it had been.

"I was always sure you would not waste your learning, Cynthia," said Mr. Satterlee, gravely; "that you would make the most of the advantages God has given you."

"I am going to try, Mr. Satterlee. I cannot be content in idleness. I was wasting time in Boston, and I — I was not happy so far away from you all — from Uncle Jethro. Mr. Satterlee, I am going to teach school. I have always wanted to, and now I have made up my mind to do it."

This was Jethro's punishment. But had she not lightened it for him a little by choosing this way of telling him that she could not eat his bread or partake of his bounty? Though by reason of that bounty she was what she was, she could not live and thrive on it longer, coming as it did from such a source. Mr. Satterlee might perhaps surmise the truth, but the town and village would think her ambition a very natural one; certainly no better time could have been chosen to announce it.

"To teach school." She was sure now that Mr. Satterlee knew and approved, and perceived something, at least, of her little ruse. He was a man whose talents fitted him for a larger flock than he had at Coniston, but he possessed neither the graces demanded of city ministers nor the power of pushing himself. Never was a more retiring man. The years she had spent in his study had not gone for nothing, for he who has cherished the bud can predict what the flower will be, and Mr. Satterlee knew her spiritually better than any one else in Coniston. He had heard of her return, and had walked over to the tannery house full of fears, the remembrance of those expressions of simple faith in Jethro coming back to his mind. Had the revelation which he had so long expected come at last? and how had she taken it? would it embitter her? The good man believed that it would not, and now he saw that it had not, and rejoiced accordingly.

"To teach school," he said. "I expected that you would wish to, Cynthia. It is a desire that most of us have, who like books and what is in them. I should have taught school if I had not become a minister. It is a high calling, and an absorbing one, to develop the minds of the young." Mr. Satterlee was often a little discursive, though there was reason for it on this occasion, and Moses Hatch half closed his eyes and bowed his head a little out of sheer habit at the sound of the minister's voice. But he raised it suddenly at the next words. "I was in Brampton yesterday, and saw Mr. Graves, who is on the prudential committee of that district. You may not have heard that Miss Goddard has left. They have not yet succeeded in filling her place, and I think it more than likely that you can get it."

Cynthia glanced at Jethro, but the habit of years was so strong in him that he gave no sign.

"Do you think so, Mr. Satterlee?" she said gratefully. "I had heard of the place, and hoped for it, because it is near enough for me to spend the Saturdays and Sundays with Uncle Jethro. And I meant to go to Brampton to-morrow to see about it."

"I will go with you," said the minister; "I have business in Brampton to-morrow." He did not mention that this was the business.

When at length they had all departed, Jethro rose and

went about the house making fast the doors, as was his custom, while Cynthia sat staring through the bars at the dying embers in the stove. He knew now, and it was inevitable that he should know, what she had made up her mind to do. It had been decreed that she, who owed him everything, should be made to pass this most dreadful of censures upon his whole life. Oh, the cruelty of that decree!

How, she mused, would it affect him? Had the blow been so great that he would relinquish those practices which had become a lifelong habit with him? Would he (she caught her breath at this thought) — would he abandon that struggle with Isaac D. Worthington in which he was striving to maintain the mastery of the state by those very practices? Cynthia hated Mr. Worthington. The term is not too strong, and it expresses her feeling. But she would have got down on her knees on the board floor of the kitchen that very night and implored Jethro to desist from that contest, if she could. She remembered how, in her innocence, she had believed that the people had given Jethro his power, — in those days when she was so proud of that very power, — now she knew that he had wrested it from them. What more supreme sacrifice could he make than to relinquish it! Ah, there was a still greater sacrifice that Jethro was to make, had she known it.

He came and stood over her by the stove, and she looked up into his face with these yearnings in her eyes. Yes, she would have thrown herself on her knees, if she could. But she could not. Perhaps he would abandon that struggle. Perhaps — perhaps his heart was broken. And could a man with a broken heart still fight on? She took his hand and pressed it against her face, and he felt that it was wet with her tears.

"B-better go to bed now, Cynthy," he said; "m-must be worn out — m-must be worn out."

He stooped and kissed her on the forehead. It was thus that Jethro Bass accepted his sentence.

CHAPTER XIII

CYNTHIA BECOMES A TEACHER

AT sunrise, in that Coniston hill-country, it is the western hills which are red, and a distant hillock on the meadow farm which was soon to be Eben's looked like the daintiest conical cake with pink icing as Cynthia surveyed the familiar view the next morning. There was the mountain, the pastures on the lower slopes all red, too, and higher up the dark masses of bristling spruce and pine and hemlock mottled with white where the snow-covered rocks showed through.

Sunrise in January is not very early, and sunrise at any season is not early for Coniston. Cynthia sat at her window, and wondered whether that beautiful landscape would any longer be hers. Her life had grown up on it; but now her life had changed. Would the beauty be taken from it, too? Almost hungrily she gazed at the scene. She might look upon it again — many times, perhaps — but a conviction was strong in her that its daily possession would now be only a memory.

Mr. Satterlee was as good as his word, for he was seated in the stage when it drew up at the tannery house, ready to go to Brampton. And as they drove away Cynthia took one last look at Jethro standing on the porch. It seemed to her that it had been given her to feel all things, and to know all things : to know, especially, this strange man, Jethro Bass, as none other knew him, and to love him as none other loved him. The last severe wrench was come, and she had left him standing there alone in the cold, divining what was in his heart as though it were in her own. How worthless was this mighty power which he had gained, how hateful, when he could not bestow the smallest fragment of it upon one whom he loved? Some one has described hell as disqualification in the face of opportunity. Such was Jethro's torment that morning as he saw her drive away, the minister in the place where he should have been, at her side, and he, Jethro Bass, as helpless as though he had indeed been in the pit among the flames. Had the prudential committee at Brampton promised the appointment ten times over, he might still have obtained it for her by a word. And he must not speak even that word. Who shall say that a large part of the punishment of Jethro Bass did not come to him in the life upon this earth?

Some such thoughts were running in Cynthia's head as they jingled away to Brampton that dazzling morning. Perhaps the stage driver, too, who knew something of men and things and who meddled not at all, had made a guess at the situation. He thought that Cynthia's spirits seemed lightened a little, and he meant to lighten them more; so he joked as much as his respect for his passengers would permit, and told the news of Brampton. Not the least of the news concerned the first citizen of that place. There was a certain railroad in the West which had got itself much into Congress, and much into the newspapers, and Isaac D. Worthington had got himself into that railroad : was gone West, it was said on that business, and might not be back for many weeks. And Lem Hallowell remembered when Mr. Worthington was a slim-chested young man wandering up and down Coniston Water in search of health. Good Mr. Satterlee, thinking this a safe subject, allowed himself to be led into a discussion of the first citizen's career, which indeed had something fascinating in it.

Thus they jingled into Brampton Street and stopped before the cottage of Judge Graves — a courtesy title. The judge himself came to the door and bestowed a pronounced bow on the minister, for Mr. Satterlee was honored in Brampton. Just think of what Ezra Graves might have looked like, and you have him. He greeted Cynthia, too, with a warm welcome — for Ezra Graves, — and ushered them into a best parlor which was reserved for ministers and funerals and great occasions in general, and actually raised the blinds. Then Mr. Satterlee, with much hemming and hawing, stated the business which had brought them, while Cynthia looked out of the window.

Mr. Graves sat and twirled his lean thumbs. He went so far as to say that he admired a young woman who scorned to live in idleness, who wished to impart the learning with which she had been endowed. Fifteen applicants were under consideration for the position, and the prudential committee had so far been unable to declare that any of them were completely qualified. (It was well named, that prudential committee!) Mr. Graves, further-more, volunteered that he had expressed a wish to Colonel Prescott (Oh, Ephraim, you too have got a title with your new honors!), to Colonel Prescott and others, that Miss Wetherell might take the place. The middle term opened on the morrow, and Miss Bruce, of the Worthington Free Library, had been induced to teach until a successor could be appointed, although it was most inconvenient for Miss Bruce.

Could Miss Wetherell start in at once, provided the committee agreed? Cynthia replied that she would like nothing better. There would be an examination before Mr. Errol, the Brampton Superintendent of Schools. In short, owing to the pressing nature of the occasion, the judge would take the liberty of calling the committee together immediately. Would Mr. Satterlee and Miss Wetherell make themselves at home in the parlor?

It very frequently happens that one member of a com-mittee is the brain, and the other members form the body of it. It was so in this case. Ezra Graves typified all of prudence there was about it, — which, it must be admitted, was a great deal. He it was who had weighed in the balance the fifteen applicants and found them wanting. Another member of the committee was that comfortable Mr. Dodd, with the tuft of yellow beard, the hardware

dealer whom we have seen at the baseball game. Mr.
Dodd was not a person who had opinions unless they were
presented to him from certain sources, and then he had
been known to cling to them tenaciously. It is sufficient to
add that, when Cynthia Wetherell's name was mentioned to
him, he remembered the girl to whom Bob Worthington
had paid such marked attentions on the grand stand. He
knew literally nothing else about Cynthia. Judge Graves,
apparently, knew all about her ; this was sufficient, at that
time, for Mr. Dodd ; he was sick and tired of the whole
affair, and if, by the grace of heaven, an applicant had
been sent who conformed with Judge Graves's multitude
of requirements, he was devoutly thankful. The other
member, Mr. Hill, was a feed and lumber dealer, and
not a very good one, for he was always in difficulties ;
certain scholarly attainments were attributed to him, and
therefore he had been put on the committee. They met
in Mr. Dodd's little office back of the store, and in five
minutes Cynthia was a schoolmistress, subject to examination by Mr. Errol.

Just a word about Mr. Errol. He was a retired lawyer,
with some means, who took an interest in town affairs to
occupy his time. He had a very delicate wife, whom he
had been obliged to send South at the beginning of the
winter. There she had for a while improved, but had
been taken ill again, and two days before Cynthia's appointment he had been summoned to her bedside by a
telegram. Cynthia could go into the school, and her
examination would take place when Mr. Errol returned.

All this was explained by the judge when, half an hour
after he had left them, he returned to the best parlor.
Miss Wetherell would, then, be prepared to take the
school the following morning. Whereupon the judge
shook hands with her, and did not deny that he had been
instrumental in the matter.

"And, Mr. Satterlee, I am so grateful to you," said
Cynthia, when they were in the street once more.

"My dear Cynthia, I did nothing," answered the
minister, quite bewildered by the quick turn affairs had

taken; "it is your own good reputation that got you the place."

Nevertheless Mr. Satterlee had done his share in the matter. He had known Mr. Graves for a long time, and better than any other person in Brampton. Mr. Graves remembered Cynthia Ware, and indeed had spoken to Cynthia that day about her mother. Mr. Graves had also read poor William Wetherell's contributions to the *Newcastle Guardian*, and he had not read that paper since they had ceased. From time to time Mr. Satterlee had mentioned his pupil to the judge, whose mind had immediately flown to her when the vacancy occurred. So it all came about.

"And now," said Mr. Satterlee, "what will you do, Cynthia? We've got the good part of a day to arrange where you will live, before the stage returns."

"I won't go back to-night, I think," said Cynthia, turning her head away; "if you would be good enough to tell Uncle Jethro to send my trunk and some other things."

"Perhaps that is just as well," assented the minister, understanding perfectly. "I have thought that Miss Bruce might be glad to board you," he continued, after a pause. "Let us go to see her."

"Mr. Satterlee," said Cynthia, "would you mind if we went first to see Cousin Ephraim?"

"Why, of course, we must see Ephraim," said Mr. Satterlee, briskly. So they walked on past the mansion of the first citizen, and the new block of stores which the first citizen had built, to the old brick building which held the Brampton post-office, and right through the door of the partition into the sanctum of the postmaster himself, which some one had nicknamed the Brampton Club. On this occasion the postmaster was seated in his shirt sleeves by the stove, alone, his listeners being conspicuously absent. Cynthia, who had caught a glimpse of him through the little mail-window, thought he looked very happy and comfortable.

"Great Tecumseh!" he cried, — an exclamation he

reserved for extraordinary occasions, — "if it hain't Cynthy ! "

He started to hobble toward her, but Cynthia ran to him.

" Why," said he, looking at her closely after the greeting was over, " you be changed, Cynthy. Mercy, I don't know as I'd have dared done that if I'd seed you first. What have you b'en doin' to yourself ? You must have seed a whole lot down there in Boston. And you're a full-blown lady, too."

" Oh, no, I'm not, Cousin Eph," she answered, trying to smile.

" Yes, you be," he insisted, still scrutinizing her, vainly trying to account for the change. Tact, as we know, was not Ephraim's strong point. Now he shook his head. " You always was beyond me. Got a sort of air about you, and it grows on you, too. Wouldn't be surprised," he declared, speaking now to the minister, " wouldn't be a mite surprised to see her in the White House, some day."

" Now, Cousin Eph," said Cynthia, coloring a little, " you mustn't talk nonsense. What have you done with your coat ? You have no business to go without it with your rheumatism."

" It hain't b'en so bad since Uncle Sam took me over again, Cynthy," he answered, " with nothin' to do but sort letters in a nice hot room." The room was hot, indeed. " But where did you come from ? "

" I grew tired of being taught, Cousin Eph. I — I've always wanted to teach. Mr. Satterlee has been with me to see Mr. Graves, and they've given me Miss Goddard's place. I'm coming to Brampton to live, to-day."

" Great Tecumseh ! " exclaimed Ephraim again, overpowered by the news. " I want to know ! What does Jethro say to that ? "

" He — he is willing," she replied in a low voice.

" Well," said Ephraim, " I always thought you'd come to it. It's in the blood, I guess — teachin'. Your mother had it too. I'm kind of sorry for Jethro, though, so I be. But I'm glad for myself, Cynthy. So you're comin' to Brampton to live with me ! "

" I was going to ask Miss Bruce to take me in," said Cynthia.

" No you hain't, anything of the kind," said Ephraim, indignantly. " I've got a little house up the street, and a room all ready for you."

" Will you let me share expenses, Cousin Eph ? "

" I'll let you do anything you want," said he, " so's you come. Don't you think she'd ought to come and take care of an old man, Mr. Satterlee?"

Mr. Satterlee turned. He had been contemplating, during this conversation, a life-size print of General Grant under two crossed flags, that was hung conspicuously on the wall.

" I do not think you could do better, Cynthia," he answered, smiling. The minister liked Ephraim, and he liked a little joke, occasionally. He felt that one would not be particularly out of place just now; so he repeated, " I do not think you could do better than to accept the offer of Colonel Prescott."

Ephraim grew very red, as was his wont when twitted about his new title. He took things literally.

" I hain't a colonel, no more than you be, Mr. Satterlee. But the boys down here will have it so."

Three days later, by the early train which leaves the state capital at an unheard-of hour in the morning, a young man arrived in Brampton. His jaw seemed squarer than ever to the citizens who met the train out of curiosity, and to Mr. Dodd, who was expecting a pump; and there was a set look on his face like that of a man who is going into a race or a fight. Mr. Dodd, though astonished, hastened toward him.

" Well, this is unexpected, Bob," said he. " How be you? Harvard College failed up ? "

For Mr. Dodd never let slip a chance to assure a member of the Worthington family of his continued friendship.

" How are you, Mr. Dodd ? " answered Bob, nodding at him carelessly, and passing on. Mr. Dodd did not dare to follow. What was young Worthington doing in Bramp-

ton, and his father in the West on that railroad business ?
Filled with curiosity, Mr. Dodd forgot his pump, but Bob
was already striding into Brampton Street, carrying his
bag. If he had stopped for a few moments with the
hardware dealer, or chatted with any of the dozen people
who bowed and stared at him, he might have saved himself a good deal of trouble. He turned in at the Worthington mansion, and rang the bell, which was answered by
Sarah, the housemaid.

"Mr. Bob ! " she exclaimed.

"Where's Mrs. Holden ? " he asked.

Mrs. Holden was the elderly housekeeper. She had
gone, unfortunately, to visit a bereaved relative ; unfortunately for Bob, because she, too, might have told him
something.

"Get me some breakfast, Sarah. Anything," he commanded, "and tell Silas to hitch up the black trotters to
my cutter."

Sarah, though in consternation, did as she was bid.
The breakfast was forthcoming, and in half an hour Silas
had the black trotters at the door. Bob got in without a
word, seized the reins, the cutter flew down Brampton
Street (observed by many of the residents thereof) and
turned into the Coniston road. Silas said nothing. Silas,
as a matter of fact, never did say anything. He had been
the Worthington coachman for five and twenty years, and
he was known in Brampton as Silas the Silent. Young
Mr. Worthington had no desire to talk that morning.

The black trotters covered the ten miles in much quicker
time than Lem Hallowell could do it in his stage, but the
distance seemed endless to Bob. It was not much more
than half an hour after he had left Brampton Street, however, that he shot past the store, and by the time Rias
Richardson in his carpet slippers reached the platform the
cutter was in front of the tannery house, and the trotters,
with their sides smoking, were pawing up the snow under
the butternut tree.

Bob leaped out, hurried up the path, and knocked at
the door. It was opened by Jethro Bass himself.

" How do you do, Mr. Bass," said the young man, gravely, and he held out his hand. Jethro gave him such a scrutinizing look as he had given many a man whose business he cared to guess, but Bob looked fearlessly into his eyes. Jethro took his hand.

"C-come in," he said.

Bob went into that little room where Jethro and Cynthia had spent so many nights together, and his glance flew straight to the picture on the wall, — the portrait of Cynthia Wetherell in crimson and seed pearls, so strangely set amidst such surroundings. His glance went to the portrait, and his feet followed, as to a lodestone. He stood in front of it for many minutes, in silence, and Jethro watched him. At last he turned.

" Where is she ? " he asked.

It was a queer question, and Jethro's answer was quite as lacking in convention.

" G-gone to Brampton — gone to Brampton."

" Gone to Brampton ! Do you mean to say — ? What is she doing there ? " Bob demanded.

" Teachin' school," said Jethro; " g-got Miss Goddard's place."

Bob did not reply for a moment. The little schoolhouse was the only building in Brampton he had glanced at as he came through. Mrs. Merrill had told him that she might take that place, but he had little imagined she was already there on her platform facing the rows of shining little faces at the desks. He had deemed it more than possible that he might see Jethro at Coniston, but he had not taken into account that which he might say to him. Bob had, indeed, thought of nothing but Cynthia, and of the blow that had fallen upon her. He had tried to realize the multiple phases of the situation which confronted him. Here was the man who, by the conduct of his life, had caused the blow ; he, too, was her benefactor ; and again, this same man was engaged in the bitterest of conflicts with his father, Isaac D. Worthington, and it was this conflict which had precipitated that blow. Bob could not have guessed, by looking at Jethro Bass, how great was the sorrow which had fallen upon him. But Bob knew that Jethro hated his father, must hate him now, because of Cynthia, with a hatred given to few men to feel. He thought that Jethro would crush Mr. Worthington and ruin him if he could; and Bob believed he could.

What was he to say? He did not fear Jethro, for Bob Worthington had courage enough; but these things were running in his mind, and he felt the power of the man before him, as all men did. Bob went to the window and came back again. He knew that he must speak.

"Mr. Bass," he said at last, "did Cynthia ever mention me to you?"

"No," said Jethro.

"Mr. Bass, I love her. I have told her so, and I have asked her to be my wife."

There was no need, indeed, to have told Jethro this. The shock of that revelation had come to him when he had seen the trotters, had been confirmed when the young man had stood before the portrait. Jethro's face might have twitched when Bob stood there with his back to him.

Jethro could not speak. Once more there had come to him a moment when he would not trust his voice to ask a question. He dreaded the answer, though none might have surmised this. He knew Cynthia. He knew that, when she had given her heart, it was for all time. He dreaded the answer, because it might mean that her sorrow was doubled.

"I believe," Bob continued painfully, seeing that Jethro would say nothing, "I believe that Cynthia loves me. I should not dare to say it or to hope it, without reason. She has not said so, but —" the words were very hard for him, yet he stuck manfully to the truth; "but she told me to write to my father and let him know what I had done, and not to come back to her until I had his answer. This," he added, wondering that a man could listen to such a thing without a sign, "this was before — before she had any idea of coming home."

Yes, Cynthia did love him. There was no doubt about it

in Jethro's mind.   She would not have bade Bob write to his father if she had not loved him.   Still Jethro did not speak, but by some intangible force compelled Bob to go on.

"I shall write to my father as soon as he comes back from the West, but I wish to say to you, Mr. Bass, that whatever his answer contains, I mean to marry Cynthia. Nothing can shake me from that resolution.   I tell you this because my father is fighting you, and you know what he will say."   (Jethro knew Dudley Worthington well enough to appreciate that this would make no particular difference in his opposition to the marriage except to make that opposition more vehement.)   "And because you do not know me," continued Bob.   "When I say a thing, I mean it.   Even if my father cuts me off and casts me out, I will marry Cynthia.   Good-by, Mr. Bass."

Jethro took the young man's hand again.   Bob imagined that he even pressed it — a little — something he had never done before.

"Good-by, Bob."

Bob got as far as the door.

"Er — go back to Harvard, Bob?"

"I intend to, Mr. Bass."

"Er — Bob?"

"Yes?"

"D-don't quarrel with your father — don't quarrel with your father."

"I shan't be the one to quarrel, Mr. Bass."

"Bob — hain't you pretty young — pretty young?"

"Yes," said Bob, rather unexpectedly, "I am."   Then he added, "I know my own mind."

"P-pretty young.   Don't want to get married yet awhile — do you?"

"Yes, I do," said Bob, "but I suppose I shan't be able to."

"Er — wait awhile, Bob.   Go back to Harvard. W-wouldn't write that letter if I was you."

"But I will.   I'll not have him think I'm ashamed of what I've done.   I'm proud of it, Mr. Bass."

In the eyes of Coniston, which had been waiting for his

reappearance, Bob Worthington jumped into the sleigh and drove off. He left behind him Jethro Bass, who sat in his chair the rest of the morning with his head bent in revery so deep that Millicent had to call him twice to his simple dinner. Bob left behind him, too, a score of rumors, sprung full grown into life with his visit. Men and women an incredible distance away heard them in an incredible time : those in the village found an immediate pretext for leaving their legitimate occupation and going to the store, and a gathering was in session there when young Mr. Worthington drove past it on his way back. Bob thought little about the rumors, and not thinking of them it did not occur to him that they might affect Cynthia. The only person then in Coniston whom he thought about was Jethro Bass. Bob decided that his liking for Jethro had not diminished, but rather increased ; he admired Jethro for the advice he had given, although he did not mean to take it. And for the first time he pitied him.

Bob did not know that rumor, too, was spreading in Brampton. He had his dinner in the big walnut dining room all alone, and after it he smoked his father's cigars and paced up and down the big hall, watching the clock. For he could not go to her in the school hours. At length he put on his hat and hurried out, crossing the parklike enclosure in the middle of the street ; bowed at by Mr. Dodd, who always seemed to be on hand, and others, and nodding absently in return. Concealment was not in Bob Worthington's nature. He reached the post-office, where the partition door was open, and he walked right into a comparatively full meeting of the Brampton Club. Ephraim sat in their midst, and for once he was not telling war stories. He was silent. And the others fell suddenly silent, too, at Bob's entrance.

"How do you do, Mr. Prescott?" he said, as Ephraim struggled to his feet. "How is the rheumatism?"

"How be you, Mr. Worthington?" said Ephraim ; "this is a kind of a surprise, hain't it?" Ephraim was getting used to surprises. "Well, it is good-natured of you to come in and shake hands with an old soldier."

" Don't mention it, Mr. Prescott," answered honest Bob, a little abashed, " I should have done so anyway, but the fact is, I wanted to speak to you a moment in private."

" Certain," said Ephraim, glancing helplessly around him, " jest come out front." That space, where the public were supposed to be, was the only private place in the Brampton post-office. But the members of the Brampton Club could take a hint, and with one consent began to make excuses. Bob knew them all from boyhood and spoke to them all. Some of them ventured to ask him if Harvard had bust up.

" Where does Cynthia live ? " he demanded, coming straight to the point.

Ephraim stared at him for a moment in a bewildered fashion, and then a light began to dawn on him.

" Lives with me," he answered. He was quite as ashamed, for Bob's sake, as if he himself had asked the question, and he went on talking to cover that embarrassment. " It's made some difference, too, sence she come. House looks like a different place. Afore she come I cooked with a kit, same as I used to in the harness shop. I l'arned it in the army. Cynthy's got a stove."

It was not the way Ephraim would have gone about a love affair, had he had one. Sam Price's were the approved methods in that section of the country, though Sam had overdone them somewhat. It was an unheard-of thing to ask a man right out like that where a girl lived.

" Much obliged," said Bob, and was gone. Ephraim raised his hands in despair, and hobbled to the little window to get a last look at him. Where were the proprieties in these days ? The other aspect of the affair, what Mr. Worthington would think of it when he returned, did not occur to the innocent mind of the old soldier until people began to talk about it that afternoon. Then it worried him into another attack of rheumatism.

Half of Brampton must have seen Bob Worthington march up to the little yellow house which Ephraim had rented from John Billings. It had four rooms around the big chimney in the middle, and that was all. Simple as it was, an architect would have said that its proportions were nearly perfect. John Billings had it from his Grandfather Post, who built it, and though Brampton would have laughed at the statement, Isaac D. Worthington's mansion was not to be compared with it for beauty. The old cherry furniture was still in it, and the old wall papers and the panelling in the little room to the right which Cynthia had made into a sitting room.

Half of Brampton, too, must have seen Cynthia open the door and Bob walk into the entry. Then the door was shut. But it had been held open for an appreciable time, however, — while you could count twenty, — because Cynthia had not the power to close it. For a while she could only look into his eyes, and he into hers. She had not seen him coming, she had but answered the knock. Then, slowly, the color came into her cheeks, and she knew that she was trembling from head to foot.

"Cynthia," he said, "mayn't I come in?"

She did not answer, for fear her voice would tremble, too. And she could not send him away in the face of all Brampton. She opened the door a little wider, a very little, and he went in. Then she closed it, and for a moment they stood facing each other in the entry, which was lighted only by the fan-light over the door, Cynthia with her back against the wall. He spoke her name again, his voice thick with the passion which had overtaken him like a flood at the sight of her — a passion to seize her in his arms, and cherish and comfort and protect her forever and ever. All this he felt and more as he looked into her face and saw the traces of her great sorrow there. He had not thought that that face could be more beautiful in its strength and purity, but it was even so.

"Cynthia — my love!" he cried, and raised his arms. But a look as of a great fear came into her eyes, which for one exquisite moment had yielded to his own; and her breath came quickly, as though she were spent — as indeed she was. So far spent that the wall at her back was grateful.

"No!" she said; "no — you must not — you must

not — you must not!" Again and again she repeated the words, for she could summon no others. They were a mandate — had he guessed it — to herself as to him. For the time her brain refused its functions, and she could think of nothing but the fact that he was there, beside her, ready to take her in his arms. How she longed to fly into them, none but herself knew — to fly into them as into a refuge secure against the evil powers of the world. It was not reason that restrained her then, but something higher in her, that restrained him likewise. Without moving from the wall she pushed open the door of the sitting room.

"Go in there," she said.

He went in as she bade him and stood before the flickering logs in the wide and shallow chimney-place — logs that seemed to burn on the very hearth itself, and yet the smoke rose unerring into the flue. No stove had ever desecrated that room. Bob looked into the flames and waited, and Cynthia stood in the entry fighting this second great battle which had come upon her while her forces were still spent with that other one. Woman in her very nature is created to be sheltered and protected ; and the yearning in her, when her love is given, is intense as nature itself to seek sanctuary in that love. So it was with Cynthia leaning against the entry wall, her arms full length in front of her, and her hands clasped as she prayed for strength to withstand the temptation. At last she grew calmer, though her breath still came deeply, and she went into the sitting room.

Perhaps he knew, vaguely, why she had not followed him at once. He had grown calmer himself, calmer with that desperation which comes to a man of his type when his soul and body are burning with desire for a woman. He knew that he would have to fight for her with herself. He knew now that she was too strong in her position to be carried by storm, and the interval had given him time to collect himself. He did not dare at first to look up from the logs, for fear he should forget himself and be defeated instantly.

"I have been to Coniston, Cynthia," he said.

"Yes."

"I have been to Coniston this morning, and I have seen Mr. Bass, and I have told him that I love you, and that I will never give you up. I told you so in Boston, Cynthia," he said ; "I knew that this — this trouble would come to you. I would have given my life to have saved you from it — from the least part of it. I would have given my life to have been able to say 'it shall not touch you.' I saw it flowing in like a great sea between you and me, and yet I could not tell you of it. I could not prepare you for it. I could only tell you that I would never give you up, and I can only repeat that now."

"You must, Bob," she answered, in a voice so low that it was almost a whisper ; "you must give me up."

"I would not," he said, "I would not if the words were written on all the rocks of Coniston Mountain. I love you."

"Hush," she said gently. "I have to say some things to you. They will be very hard to say, but you must listen to them."

"I will listen," he said doggedly ; "but they will not affect my determination."

"I am sure you do not wish to drive me away from Brampton," she continued, in the same low voice, "when I have found a place to earn my living near — near Uncle Jethro."

These words told him all he had suspected — almost as much as though he had been present at the scene in the tannery shed in Coniston. She knew now the life of Jethro Bass, but he was still "Uncle Jethro" to her. It was even as Bob had supposed, — that her affection once given could not be taken away.

"Cynthia," he said, "I would not by an act or a word annoy or trouble you. If you bade me, I would go to the other side of the world to-morrow. You must know that. But I should come back again. You must know that, too. I should come back again for you."

"Bob," she said again, and her voice faltered a very

little now, "you must know that I can never be your wife."

"I do not know it," he exclaimed, interrupting her vehemently, "I will not know it."

"Think," she said, "think! I must say what I have to say, however it hurts me. If it had not been for — for your father, those things never would have been written. They were in his newspaper, and they express his feelings toward — toward Uncle Jethro."

Once the words were out, she marvelled that she had found the courage to pronounce them.

"Yes," he said, "yes, I know that, but listen — "

"Wait," she went on, "wait until I have finished. I am not speaking of the pain I had when I read these things, I — I am not speaking of the truth that may be in them — I have learned from them what I should have known before, and felt, indeed, that your father will never consent to — to a marriage between us."

"And if he does not," cried Bob, "if he does not, do you think that I will abide by what he says, when my life's happiness depends upon you, and my life's welfare? I know that you are a good woman, and a true woman, that you will be the best wife any man could have. Though he is my father, he shall not deprive me of my soul, and he shall not take my life away from me."

As Cynthia listened she thought that never had words sounded sweeter than these — no, and never would again. So she told herself as she let them run into her heart to be stored among the treasures there. She believed in his love — believed in it now with all her might. (Who, indeed, would not?) She could not demean herself now by striving to belittle it or doubt its continuance, as she had in Boston. He was young, yes; but he would never be any older than this, could never love again like this. So much was given her, ought she not to be content? Could she expect more?

She understood Isaac Worthington, now, as well as his son understood him. She knew that, if she were to yield to Bob Worthington, his father would disown and disin-

2 E

herit him. She looked ahead into the years as a woman will, and allowed herself for the briefest of moments to wonder whether any happiness could thrive in spite of the violence of that schism — any happiness for him. She would be depriving him of his birthright, and it may be that those who are born without birthrights often value them the most. Cynthia saw these things, and more, for those who sit at the feet of sorrow soon learn the world's ways. She saw herself pointed out as the woman whose designs had beggared and ruined him in his youth, and (agonizing and revolting thought!) the name of one would be spoken from whom she had learned such craft. Lest he see the scalding tears in her eyes, she turned away — and conquered them. What could she do? Where should she hide her love that it might not be seen of men? And how, in truth, could she tell him these things?

"Cynthia," he went on, seeing that she did not answer, and taking heart, "I will not say a word against my father. I know you would not respect me if I did. We are different, he and I, and find happiness in different ways." Bob wondered if his father had ever found it. "If I had never met you and loved you, I should have refused to lead the life my father wishes me to lead. It is not in me to do the things he will ask. I shall have to carve out my own life, and I feel that I am as well able to do it as he was. Percy Broke, a classmate of mine and my best friend, has a position for me in a locomotive works in which his father is largely interested. We are going in together, the day after we graduate; it is all arranged, and his father has agreed. I shall work very hard, and in a few years, Cynthia, we shall be together, never to part again. Oh, Cynthia," he cried, carried away by the ecstasy of this dream which he had summoned up, "why do you resist me? I love you as no man has ever loved," he exclaimed, with scornful egotism and contempt of those who had made the world echo with that cry through the centuries, "and you love me! Ah, do you think I do not see it — cannot feel it? You love me — tell me so."

He was coming toward her, and how was she to prevent

his taking her by storm? That was his way, and well she knew it. In her dreams she had felt herself lifted and borne off, breathless in his arms, to Elysium. Her breath was going now, her strength was going, and yet she made him pause by the magic of a word. A concession was in that word, but one could not struggle so piteously and concede nothing.

"Bob," she said, "do you love me?"

Love her! If there was a love that acknowledged no bounds, that was confined by no superlatives, it was his. He began to speak, but she interrupted him with a wild passion that was new to her. As he sat in the train on his way back to Cambridge through the darkening afternoon, the note of it rang in his ears and gave him hope — yes, and through many months afterward.

"If you love me I beg, I implore, I beseech you in the name of that love — for your sake and my sake, to leave me. Oh, can you not see why you must go?"

He stopped, even as he had before in the parlor in Mount Vernon Street. He could but stop in the face of such an appeal — and yet the blood beat in his head with a mad joy.

"Tell me that you love me, — once," he cried, — "once, Cynthia."

"Do — do not ask me," she faltered. "Go."

Her words were a supplication, not a command. And in that they were a supplication he had gained a victory. Yes, though she had striven with all her might to deny, she had bade him hope. He left her without so much as a touch of the hand, because she had wished it. And yet she loved him! Incredible fact! Incredible conjury which made him doubt that his feet touched the snow of Brampton Street, which blotted, as with a golden glow, the faces and the houses of Brampton from his sight. He saw no one, though many might have accosted him. That part of him which was clay, which performed the menial tasks of his being, had kindly taken upon itself to fetch his bag from the house to the station, and to board the train.

Ah, but Brampton had seen him!

CHAPTER XIV

IN WHICH THE LORD OF BRAMPTON RETURNS

GREAT events, like young Mr. Worthington's visit to Brampton, are all very well for a while, but they do not always develop with sufficient rapidity to satisfy the audiences of the drama. Seven days were an interlude quite long enough in which to discuss every phase and bearing of this opening scene, and after that the play in all justice ought to move on. But there it halted — for a while — and the curtain obstinately refused to come up. If the inhabitants of Brampton had only known that the drama, when it came, would be well worth waiting for, they might have been less restless.

It is unnecessary to enrich the pages of this folio with all the footnotes and remarks of the sages of Brampton. These can be condensed into a paragraph or two — and we can ring up the curtain when we like on the next scene, for which Brampton had to wait considerably over a month. There is to be no villain in this drama with the face of an Abbé Maury like the seven cardinal sins. Comfortable-looking Mr. Dodd of the prudential committee, with his chin-tuft of yellow beard, is cast for the part of the villain, but will play it badly; he would have been better suited to a comedy part.

Young Mr. Worthington left Brampton on the five o'clock train, and at six Mr. Dodd met his fellow-member of the committee, Judge Graves.

"Called a meetin'?" asked Mr. Dodd, pulling the yellow tuft.

"What for?" said the judge, sharply.

"What be you a-goin' to do about it?" said Mr. Dodd.

"Do about what?" demanded the judge, looking at the hardware dealer from under his eyebrows.

Mr. Dodd knew well enough that this was not ignorance on the part of Mr. Graves, whose position in the matter had been very well defined in the two sentences he had spoken. Mr. Dodd perceived that the judge was trying to get him to commit himself, and would then proceed to annihilate him. He, Levi Dodd, had no intention of walking into such a trap.

"Well," said he, with a final tug at the tuft, "if that's the way you feel about it."

"Feel about what?" said the judge, fiercely.

"Callate you know best," said Mr. Dodd, and passed on up the street. But he felt the judge's gimlet eyes boring holes in his back. The judge's position was very fine, no doubt — for the judge. All of which tends to show that Levi Dodd had swept his mind, and that it was ready now for the reception of — an opinion.

Six weeks or more, as has been said, passed before the curtain rose again, but the snarling trumpets of the orchestra played a fitting prelude. Cynthia's feelings and Cynthia's life need not be gone into during this interval: knowing her character, they may well be imagined. They were trying enough, but Brampton had no means of guessing them. During the weeks she came and went between the little house and the little school, putting all the strength that was in her into her duties. The Prudential Committee, which sometimes sat on the platform, could find no fault with the performance of these duties, or with the capability of the teacher, and it is not going too far to state that the children grew to love her better than Miss Goddard had been loved. It may be declared that children are the fittest citizens of a republic, because they are apt to make up their own minds on any subject without regard to public opinion. It was so with the scholars of Brampton village lower school: they grew to love the new teacher, careless of what the attitude of their elders might be, and some of them could have been seen almost any day walking home with her down the street.

As for the attitude of the elders — there was none. Before assuming one they had thought it best, with characteristic caution, to await the next act in the drama. There were ladies in Brampton whose hearts prompted them, when they called on the new teacher, to speak a kindly word of warning and advice; but somehow, when they were seated before her in the little sitting room of the John Billings house, their courage failed them. There was something about this daughter of the Coniston storekeeper and ward of Jethro Bass that made them pause. So much for the ladies of Brampton. What they said among themselves would fill a chapter, and more.

There was, at this time, a singular falling-off in the attendance of the Brampton Club. Ephraim sat alone most of the day in his Windsor chair by the stove, pretending to read newspapers. But he did not mention this fact to Cynthia. He was more lonesome than ever on the Saturdays and Sundays which she spent with Jethro Bass.

Jethro Bass! It is he who might be made the theme of the music of the snarling trumpets. What was he about during those six weeks? That is what the state at large was beginning to wonder, and the state at large was looking on at a drama, too. A rumor reached the capital and radiated thence to every city and town and hamlet, and was followed by other rumors like confirmations. Jethro Bass, for the first time in a long life of activity, was inactive: inactive, too, at this most critical period of his career, the climax of it, with a war to be waged which for bitterness and ferocity would have no precedent; with the town meetings at hand, where the frontier fighting was to be done, and no quarter given. Lieutenants had gone to Coniston for further orders and instructions, and had come back without either. Achilles was sulking in the tannery house — some said a broken Achilles. Not a word could be got out of him, or the sign of an intention. Jake Wheeler moped through the days in Rias Richardson's store, too sore at heart to speak to any man, and could have wept if tears had been a relief to him. No more blithe errands over the mountain to Clovelly and elsewhere, though Jake knew the issue now and itched for the battle, and the vassals of the hill-Rajah under a jubilant Bijah Bixby were arming cap-a-pie. Lieutenant-General-and-Senator Peleg Hartington of Brampton, in his office over the livery stable, shook his head like a mournful stork when questioned by brother officers from afar. Operations were at a standstill, and the sinews of war relaxed. Rural givers of mortgages, who had not had the opportunity of selling them or had feared to do so, began (*mirabile dictu*) to express opinions. Most ominous sign of all — the proprietor of the Pelican Hotel had confessed that the Throne Room had not been engaged for the coming session.

Was it possible that Jethro Bass lay crushed under the weight of the accusations which had been printed, and were still being printed, in the *Newcastle Guardian?* He did not answer them, or retaliate in other newspapers, but Jethro Bass had never made use of newspapers in this way. Still, nothing ever printed about him could be compared with those articles. Had remorse suddenly overtaken him in his old age? Such were the questions people were asking all over the state — people, at least, who were interested in politics, or in those operations which went by the name of politics : yes, and many private citizens — who had participated in politics only to the extent of voting for such candidates as Jethro in his wisdom had seen fit to give them, read the articles and began to say that boss domination was at an end. A new era was at hand, which they fondly (and very properly) believed was to be a golden era. It was, indeed, to be a golden era — until things got working ; and then the gold would cease. The *Newcastle Guardian*, with unconscious irony, proclaimed the golden era ; and declared that its columns, even in other days and under other ownership, had upheld the wisdom of Jethro Bass. And he was still a wise man, said the *Guardian*, for he had had sense enough to give up the fight.

Had he given up the fight? Cynthia fervently hoped

and prayed that he had, but she hoped and prayed in silence. Well she knew, if the event in the tannery shed had not made him abandon his affairs, no appeal could do so. Her happiest days in this period were the Saturdays and Sundays spent with him in Coniston, and as the weeks went by she began to believe that the change, miraculous as it seemed, had indeed taken place. He had given up his power. It was a pleasure that made the weeks bearable for her. What did it matter whether he had made the sacrifice for the sake of his love for her? He had made it.

On these Saturdays and Sundays they went on long drives together over the hills, while she talked to him of her life in Brampton or the books she was reading, and of those she had chosen for him to read. Sometimes they did not turn homeward until the delicate tracery of the branches on the snow warned them of the rising moon. Jethro was often silent for hours at a time, but it seemed to Cynthia that it was the silence of peace — of a peace he had never known before. There came no newspapers to the tannery house now: during the mid-week he read the books of which she had spoken — William Wetherell's books; or sat in thought, counting, perhaps, the days until she should come again. And the joy of those days for him was more pathetic than much that is known to the world as sorrow.

And what did Coniston think? Coniston, indeed, knew not what to think, when, little by little, the great men ceased to drive up to the door of the tannery house, and presently came no more. Coniston sank then from its proud position as the real capital of the state to a lonely hamlet among the hills. Coniston, too, was watching the drama, and had had a better view of the stage than Brampton, and saw some reason presently for the change in Jethro Bass. Not that Mr. Satterlee told, but such evidence was bound, in the end, to speak for itself. The *Newcastle Guardian* had been read and debated at the store — debated with some heat by Chester Perkins and other mortgagors; discussed, nevertheless, in a political rather than a moral light. Then Cynthia had returned home, her face had awed them by its sorrow, and she had begun to earn her own living. Then the politicians had ceased to come. The credit belongs to Rias Richardson for having been the first to piece these three facts together, causing him to burn his hand so severely on the stove that he had to carry it bandaged in soda for a week. Cynthia Wetherell had reformed Jethro.

Though the village loved and revered Cynthia, Coniston as a whole did not rejoice in that reform. The town had fallen from its mighty estate, and there were certain envious ones who whispered that it had remained for a young girl who had learned city ways to twist Jethro around her finger; that she had made him abandon his fight with Isaac D. Worthington because Mr. Worthington had a son — but there is no use writing such scandal. Stripped of his power — even though he stripped himself — Jethro began to lose their respect, a trait tending to prove that the human race may have had wolves for ancestors as well as apes. People had small opportunity, however, of showing a lack of respect to his person, for in these days he noticed no one and spoke to none.

When the lion is crippled, the jackals begin to range. A jackal reconnoitred the lair to see how badly the lion was crippled, and conceived with astounding insolence the plan of capturing the lion's quarry. This jackal, who was an old one, well knew how to round up a quarry, and fled back over the hills to consult with a bigger jackal, his master. As a result, two days before March town-meeting day, Mr. Bijah Bixby paid a visit to the Harwich bank and went among certain Coniston farmers looking over the sheep, his clothes bulging out in places when he began, and seemingly normal enough when he had finished. History repeats itself, even among lions and jackals. Thirty-six years before there had been a town-meeting in Coniston and a surprise. Established Church, decent and orderly selectmen and proceedings had been toppled over that day, every outlying farm sending its representative through the sleet to do it. And now retribution was

at hand. This March-meeting day was mild, the grass
showing a green color on the south slopes where the snow
had melted, and the outlying farmers drove through mud-
holes up to the axles. Drove, albeit, in procession along
the roads, grimly enough, and the sheds Jock Hallowell
had built around the meeting-house could not hold the
horses ; they lined the fences and usurped the hitching
posts of the village street, and still they came. Their
owners trooped with muddy boots into the meeting-house,
and when the moderator rapped for order the Chairman
of the Board of Selectmen, Jethro Bass, was not in his
place ; never, indeed, would be there again. Six and
thirty years he had been supreme in that town — long
enough for any man. The beams and king posts would
know him no more. Mr. Amos Cuthbert was elected
Chairman, not without a gallant and desperate but un-
supported fight of a minority led by Mr. Jake Wheeler,
whose loyalty must be taken as a tribute to his species.
Farmer Cuthbert was elected, and his mortgage was not
foreclosed ! Had it been, there was more money in the
Harwich bank.

There was no telegraph to Coniston in these days, and
so Mr. Sam Price, with his horse in a lather, might have
been seen driving with unseemly haste toward Brampton,
where in due time he arrived. Half an hour later there
was excitement at Newcastle, sixty-five miles away, in the
office of the *Guardian*, and the next morning the excitement had spread over the whole state.

Jethro Bass was dethroned in Coniston — discredited
in his own town !

And where was Jethro? Did his heart ache, did he
bow his head as he thought of that supremacy, so hardly
won, so superbly held, gone forever? Many were the
curious eyes on the tannery house that day, and for days
after, but its owner gave no signs of concern. He read
and thought and chopped wood in the tannery shed as
usual. Never, I believe, did man, shorn of power, accept
his lot more quietly. His struggle was over, his battle
was fought, a greater peace than he had ever thought to

Florence Scovel Shinn.

"Trooped with muddy boots into the meeting-house."

hope for was won. For the opinion and regard of the world he had never cared. A greater reward awaited him, greater than any knew — the opinion and regard and the praise of one whom he loved beyond all the world. On Friday she came to him, on Friday at sunset, for the days were growing longer, and that was the happiest sunset of his life. She said nothing as she raised her face to his and kissed him and clung to him in the little parlor, but he knew, and he had his reward. So much for earthly power !

Cynthia brought the little rawhide trunk this time, and came to Coniston for the March vacation — a happy two weeks that was soon gone. Happy by comparison, that is, with what they both had suffered, and a haven of rest after the struggle and despair of the wilderness. The bond between them had, in truth, never been stronger, for both the young girl and the old man had denied themselves the thing they held most dear. Jethro had taken refuge and found comfort in his love. But Cynthia! Her greatest love had now been bestowed elsewhere.

If there were letters for the tannery house, Milly Skinner, who made it a point to meet the stage, brought them. And there were letters during Cynthia's sojourn, — many of them, bearing the Cambridge postmark. One evening it was Jethro who laid the letter on the table beside her as she sat under the lamp. He did not look at her or speak, but she felt that he knew her secret — felt that he deserved to have from her own lips what he had been too proud — yes — and too humble to ask. Whose sympathy could she be sure of, if not of his ? Still she had longed to keep this treasure to herself. She took the letter in her hand.

"I do not answer them, Uncle Jethro, but — I cannot prevent his writing them," she faltered. She did not confess that she kept them, every one, and read them over and over again ; that she had grown, indeed, to look forward to them as to a sustenance. "I — I do love him, but I will not marry him."

Yes, she could be sure of Jethro's sympathy, though he

could not express it in words. Yet she had not told him
for this. She had told him, much as the telling had hurt
her, because she feared to cut him more deeply by her
silence.

It was a terrible moment for Jethro, and never had he
desired the gift of speech as now. Had it not been for
him, Cynthia might have been Robert Worthington's wife.
He sat down beside her and put his hand over hers that
lay on the letter in her lap. It was the only answer he
could make, but perhaps it was the best, after all. Of
what use were words at such a time !

Four days afterward, on a Monday morning, she went
back to Brampton to begin the new term.

That same Monday a circumstance of no small importance took place in Brampton — nothing less than the
return, after a prolonged absence in the West and elsewhere, of its first citizen. Isaac D. Worthington was
again in residence. No bells were rung, indeed, and no
delegation of citizens as such, headed by the selectmen,
met him at the station ; and other feudal expressions of
fealty were lacking. No staff flew Mr. Worthington's
arms ; nevertheless the lord of Brampton was in his castle
again, and Brampton felt that he was there. He arrived
alone, wearing the silk hat which had become habitual
with him now, and stepping into his barouche at the
station had been driven up Brampton Street behind his
grays, looking neither to the right nor left. His reddish
chop whiskers seemed to cling a little more closely to his
face than formerly, and long years of compression made
his mouth look sterner than ever. A hawk-like man, Isaac
Worthington, to be reckoned with and feared, whether in
a frock coat or in breastplate and mail.

His seneschal, Mr. Flint, was awaiting him in the
library. Mr. Flint was large and very ugly, big-boned,
smooth-shaven, with coarse features all askew, and a
large nose with many excrescences, and thick lips. He
was forty-two. From a foreman of the mills he had risen,
step by step, to his present position, which no one seemed
able to define. He was, indeed, a seneschal. He managed

the mills in his lord's absence, and — if the truth be told
— in his presence ; knotty questions of the Truro Railroad
were brought to Mr. Flint and submitted to Mr. Worthington, who decided them, — with Mr. Flint's advice ;
and, within the last three months, Mr. Flint had invaded
the realm of politics, quietly, as such a man would, under
the cover of his patron's name and glory. Mr. Flint it
was who had bought the *Newcastle Guardian*, who went
occasionally to Newcastle and spoke a few effective words
now and then to the editor; and, if the truth will out,
Mr. Flint had largely conceived that scheme about the
railroads which was to set Mr. Worthington on the throne
of the state, although the scheme was not now being
carried out according to Mr. Flint's wishes. Mr. Flint
was, in a sense, a Bismarck, but he was not as yet all-
powerful. Sometimes his august master or one of his
fellow petty sovereigns would sweep Mr. Flint's plans
into the waste basket, and then Mr. Flint would be content to wait. To complete the character sketch, Mr.
Flint was not above hanging up his master's hat and coat,
which he did upon the present occasion, and went up to
Mr. Worthington's bedroom to fetch a pocket handkerchief out of the second drawer. He even knew where the
handkerchiefs were kept. Lucky petty sovereigns sometimes possess Mr. Flints to make them emperors.

The august personage seated himself briskly at his desk.

" So that scoundrel Bass is actually discredited at last,"
he said, blowing his nose in the pocket handkerchief Mr.
Flint had brought him. " I lose patience when I think
how long we've stood the rascal in this state. I knew the
people would rise in their indignation when they learned
the truth about him."

Mr. Flint did not answer this. He might have had
other views.

" I wonder we did not think of it before," Mr. Worthington continued. " A very simple remedy, and only re-
quiring a little courage and—and — " (Mr. Worthington
was going to say money, but thought better of it) "and the
chimera disappears. I congratulate you, Flint."

"Congratulate yourself," said Mr. Flint; "that would not have been my way."

"Very well, I congratulate myself," said the august personage, who was in too good a humor to be put out by the rejection of a compliment. "You remember what I said: the time was ripe, just publish a few biographical articles telling people what he was, and Jethro Bass would snuff out like a candle. Mr. Duncan tells me the town-meeting results are very good all over the state. Even if we hadn't knocked out Jethro Bass, we'd have a fair majority for our bill in the next legislature."

"You know Bass's saying," answered Mr. Flint, "You can hitch that kind of a hoss, but they won't always 'stay hitched.'"

"I know, I know," said Mr. Worthington; "don't croak, Flint. We can buy more hitch ropes, if necessary. Well, what's the outlay up to the present? Large, I suppose. Well, whatever it is, it's small compared to what we'll get for it." He laughed a little and rubbed his hands, and then he remembered that capacity in which he stood before the world. Yes, and he stood before himself in the same capacity. Isaac Worthington may have deceived himself, but he may or may not have been a hero to his seneschal. "We have to fight fire with fire," he added, in a pained voice. "Let me see the account."

"I have tabulated the expense in the different cities and towns," answered Mr. Flint; "I will show you the account in a little while. The expenses in Coniston were somewhat greater than the size of the town justified, perhaps. But Sutton thought —"

"Yes, yes," interrupted Mr. Worthington, "if it had cost as much to carry Coniston as Newcastle, it would have been worth it — for the moral effect alone."

Moral effect! Mr. Flint thought of Mr. Bixby with his bulging pockets going about the hills, and smiled at the manner in which moral effects are sometimes obtained.

"Any news, Flint?"

No news yet, Mr. Flint might have answered. In a few minutes there might be news, and plenty of it, for it

lay ready to be hatched under Mr. Worthington's eye.
A letter in the bold and upright hand of his son was on
the top of the pile, placed there by Mr. Flint himself, who
had examined Mr. Worthington's face closely when he
came in to see how much he might know of its contents.
He had decided that Mr. Worthington was in too good
a humor to know anything of them.   Mr. Flint had not
steamed the letter open, and read the news ; but he
could guess at them pretty shrewdly, and so could have
the biggest fool in Brampton.   That letter contained the
opening scene of the next act in the drama.

Mr. Worthington cut the envelope and began to read,
and while he did so Mr. Flint, who was not afraid of man
or beast, looked at him.   It was a manly and straight-
forward letter, and Mr. Worthington, no matter what
his opinions on the subject were, should have been proud
of it.   Bob announced, first of all, that he was going to
marry Cynthia Wetherell ; then he proceeded with praiseworthy self-control (for a lover) to describe Cynthia's
character and attainments : after which he stated that
Cynthia had refused him — twice, because she believed
that Mr. Worthington would oppose the marriage, and
had declared that she would never be the cause of a
breach between father and son.   Bob asked for his father's
consent, and hoped to have it, but he thought it only
right to add that he had given his word and his love,
and did not mean to retract either.   He spoke of his
visit to Brampton, and explained that Cynthia was teach-
ing school there, and urged his father to see her before he
made a decision.   Mr. Worthington read it through to
the end, his lips closing tighter and tighter until his
mouth was but a line across his face.   There was pain
in the face, too, the kind of pain which anger sends, and
which comes with the tottering of a pride that is false.
Of what gratification now was the overthrow of Jethro
Bass ?

He stared at the letter for a moment after he had finished it, and his face grew a dark red.   Then he seized
the paper and tore it slowly, deliberately, into bits.

Dudley Worthington was not thinking then — not he! — of the young man in the white beaver who had called at the Social Library many years before to see a young woman whose name, too, had been Cynthia. He was thinking, in fact, for he was a man to think in anger, whether it were not possible to remove this Cynthia from the face of the earth — at least to a place beyond his horizon and that of his son. Had he worn the chain mail instead of the frock coat he would have had her hung outside the town walls.

"Good God!" he exclaimed. And the words sounded profane indeed as he fixed his eyes upon Mr. Flint. "You knew that Robert had been to Brampton?"

"Yes," said Flint, "the whole village knew it."

"Good God!" cried Mr. Worthington again, "why was I not informed of this? Why was I not warned of this? Have I no friends? Do you pretend to look after my interests and not take the trouble to write me on such a subject?"

"Do you think I could have prevented it?" asked Mr. Flint, very calmly.

"You allow this — this woman to come here to Brampton and teach school in a place where she can further her designs? What were you about?"

"When the prudential committee appointed her, nothing of this was known, Mr. Worthington."

"Yes, but now — now! What are you doing, what are they doing to allow her to remain? Who are on that committee?"

Mr. Flint named the men. They had been reëlected, as usual, at the recent town-meeting. Mr. Errol, who had also been reëlected, had returned but had not yet issued the certificate or conducted the examination.

"Send for them, have them here at once," commanded Mr. Worthington, without listening to this.

"If you take my advice, you will do nothing of the kind," said Mr. Flint, who, as usual, had the whole situation at his fingers' ends. He had taken the trouble to inform himself about the girl, and he had discovered,

2 F

shrewdly enough, that she was the kind which might be led, but not driven. If Mr. Flint's advice had been listened to, this story might have had quite a different ending. But Mr. Flint had not reached the stage where his advice was always listened to, and he had a maddened man to deal with now. At that moment, as if fate had determined to intervene, the housemaid came into the room.

"Mr. Dodd to see you, sir," she said.

"Show him in," shouted Mr. Worthington; "show him in!"

Mr. Dodd was not a man who could wait for a summons which he had felt in his bones was coming. He was ordinarily, as we have seen, officious. But now he was thoroughly frightened. He had seen the great man in the barouche as he drove past the hardware store, and he had made up his mind to go up at once, and have it over with. His opinions were formed now. He put a smile on his face when he was a foot outside of the library door.

"This is a great pleasure, Mr. Worthington, a great pleasure, to see you back," he said, coming forward. "I callated —"

But the great man sat in his chair, and made no attempt to return the greeting.

"Mr. Dodd, I thought you were my friend," he said.

Mr. Dodd went all to pieces at this reception.

"So I be, Mr. Worthington — so I be," he cried. "That's why I'm here now. I've b'en a friend of yours ever since I can remember — never fluctuated. I'd rather have chopped my hand off than had this happen — so I would. If I could have foreseen what she was, she'd never have had the place, as sure as my name's Levi Dodd."

If Mr. Dodd had taken the trouble to look at the seneschal's face, he would have seen a well-defined sneer there.

"And now that you know what she is," cried Mr. Worthington, rising and smiting the pile of letters on his desk, "why do you keep her there an instant?"

Mr. Dodd stopped to pick up the letters, which had

flown over the floor.   But the great man was now in the full tide of his anger.

"Never mind the letters," he shouted ; "tell me why you keep her there."

"We callated we'd wait and see what steps you'd like taken," said the trembling townsman.

"Steps !   Steps !   Good God !   What kind of man are you to serve in such a place when you allow the professed ward of Jethro Bass — of Jethro Bass, the most notoriously depraved man in this state, to teach the children of this town.   Steps !   How soon can you call your committee together ? "

"Right away," answered Mr. Dodd, breathlessly.   He would have gone on to exculpate himself, but Mr. Worthington's inexorable finger was pointing at the door.

"If you are a friend of mine," said that gentleman, " and if you have any regard for the fair name of this town, you will do so at once."

Mr. Dodd departed precipitately, and Mr. Worthington began to pace the room, clasping his hands now in front of him, now behind him, in his agony : repeating now and again various appellations which need not be printed here, which he applied in turn to the prudential committee, to his son, and to Cynthia Wetherell.

" I'll run her out of Brampton," he said at last.

"If you do," said Mr. Flint, who had been watching him apparently unmoved, "you may have Jethro Bass on your back."

"Jethro Bass ? " shouted Mr. Worthington, with a laugh that was not pleasant to hear, "Jethro Bass is as dead as Julius Cæsar."

It was one thing for Mr. Dodd to promise so readily a meeting of the committee, and quite another to decide how he was going to get through the affair without any more burns and scratches than were absolutely necessary. He had reversed the usual order, and had been in the fire — now he was going to the frying-pan.   He stood in the street for some time, pulling at his tuft, and then made his way to Mr. Jonathan Hill's feed store.   Mr. Hill was

reading " Sartor Resartus " in his little office, the tempera-
ture of which must have been 95°, and Mr. Dodd was perspiring when he got there.

" It's come," said Mr. Dodd, sententiously.

"What's come ? " inquired Mr. Hill, mildly.

" Isaac D.'s come, that's what," said Mr. Dodd.   "I
hain't b'en sleepin' well of nights, lately. I can't think
what we was about, Jonathan, puttin' that girl in the
school.   We'd ought to've knowed she wahn't fit."

" What's the matter with her ? " inquired Mr. Hill.

" Matter with her ! " exclaimed his fellow-committee-
man, " she lives with Jethro Bass — she's his ward."

" Well, what of it ? " said Mr. Hill, who never bothered
himself about gossip or newspapers, or indeed about anything not between the covers of a book, except when he
couldn't help it.

"Good God ! " exclaimed Mr. Dodd, "he's the most
notorious, depraved man in the state. Hain't we got to
look out for the fair name of Brampton ? "

Mr. Hill sighed and closed his book.

" Well," he said, " I'd hoped we were through with that.
Let's go up and see what Judge Graves says about it."

" Hold on," said Mr. Dodd, seizing the feed dealer by
the coat, " we've got to get it fixed in our minds what
we're goin' to do, first.   We can't allow no notorious
people in our schools. We've got to stand up to the jedge,
and tell him so. We app'inted her on his recommendation,
you know."

" I like the girl," replied Mr. Hill ; " I don't think we
ever had a better teacher. She's quiet, and nice appearin',
and attends to her business."

Mr. Dodd pulled his tuft, and cocked his head.

" Mr. Worthington holds a note of yours, don't he,
Jonathan ? "

Mr. Hill reflected. He said he thought perhaps Mr.
Worthington did.

" Well," said Mr. Dodd, " I guess we might as well go
along up to the jedge now as any time."

But when they got there Mr. Dodd's knock was so timid

that he had to repeat it before the judge came to the door and peered at them over his spectacles.

"Well, gentlemen, what can I do for you?" he asked, severely, though he knew well enough. He had not been taken by surprise many times during the last forty years. Mr. Dodd explained that they wished a little meeting of the committee. The judge ushered them into his bed-room, the parlor being too good for such an occasion.

"Now, gentlemen," said he, "let us get down to business. Mr. Worthington arrived here to-day, he has seen Mr. Dodd, and Mr. Dodd has seen Mr. Hill. Mr. Worthington is a political opponent of Jethro Bass, and wishes Miss Wetherell dismissed. Mr. Dodd and Mr. Hill have agreed, for various reasons which I will spare you, that Miss Wetherell should be dismissed. Have I stated the case, gentlemen, or have I not?"

Mr. Graves took off his spectacles and wiped them, looking from one to the other of his very uncomfortable fellow-members. Mr. Hill did not attempt to speak; but Mr. Dodd, who was not sure now that this was not the fire and the other the frying-pan, pulled at his tuft until words came to him.

"Jedge," he said finally, "I must say I'm a mite surprised. I must say your language is unwarranted."

"The truth is never unwarranted," said the judge.

"For the sake of the fair name of Brampton," began Mr. Dodd, "we cannot allow —"

"Mr. Dodd," interrupted the judge, "I would rather have Mr. Worthington's arguments from Mr. Worthington himself, if I wanted them at all. There is no need of prolonging this meeting. If I were to waste my breath until six o'clock, it would be no use. I was about to say that your opinions were formed, but I will alter that, and say that your minds are fixed. You are determined to dismiss Miss Wetherell. Is it not so?"

"I wish you'd hear me, Jedge," said Mr. Dodd, desperately.

"Will you kindly answer me *yes* or *no* to that question," said the judge; "my time is valuable."

"Well, if you put it that way, I guess we are agreed that she hadn't ought to stay. Not that I've anything against her personally—"

"All right," said the judge, with a calmness that made them tremble. They had never bearded him before. "All right, you are two to one and no certificate has been issued. But I tell you this, gentlemen, that you will live to see the day when you will bitterly regret this injustice to an innocent and a noble woman, and Isaac D. Worthington will live to regret it. You may tell him I said so. Good day, gentlemen."

They rose.

"Jedge," began Mr. Dodd again, "I don't think you've been quite fair with us."

"Fair!" repeated the judge, with unutterable scorn. "Good day, gentlemen." And he slammed the door behind them.

They walked down the street some distance before either of them spoke.

"Goliah," said Mr. Dodd, at last, "did you ever hear such talk? He's got the drattedest temper of any man I ever knew, and he never callates to make a mistake. It's a little mite hard to do your duty when a man talks that way."

"I'm not sure we've done it," answered Mr. Hill.

"Not sure!" ejaculated the hardware dealer, for he was now far enough away from the judge's house to speak in his normal tone, "and she connected with that depraved—"

"Hold on," said Mr. Hill, with an astonishing amount of spirit for him, "I've heard that before."

Mr. Dodd looked at him, swallowed the wrong way and began to choke.

"You hain't wavered, Jonathan?" he said, when he got his breath.

"No, I haven't," said Mr. Hill, sadly; "but I wish to hell I had."

Mr. Dodd looked at him again, and began to choke again. It was the first time he had known Jonathan Hill to swear.

" You're a-goin' to stick by what you agreed — by your principles ? "

" I'm going to stick by my bread and butter," said Mr. Hill, " not by my principles. I wish to hell I wasn't."

And so saying that gentleman departed, cutting diagonally across the street through the snow, leaving Mr. Dodd still choking and pulling at his tuft. This third and totally unexpected shaking-up had caused him to feel somewhat deranged internally, though it had not altered the opinions now so firmly planted in his head. After a few moments, however, he had collected himself sufficiently to move on once more, when he discovered that he was repeating to himself, quite unconsciously, Mr. Hill's profanity " I wish to hell I wasn't." The iron mastiffs glaring at him angrily out of the snow banks reminded him that he was in front of Mr. Worthington's door, and he thought he might as well go in at once and receive the great man's gratitude. He certainly deserved it. But as he put his hand on the bell Mr. Worthington himself came out of the house, and would actually have gone by without noticing Mr. Dodd if he had not spoken.

" I've got that little matter fixed, Mr. Worthington," he said, "called the committee, and we voted to discharge the — the young woman." No, he did not deliver Judge Graves's message.

" Very well, Mr. Dodd," answered the great man, passing on so that Mr. Dodd was obliged to follow him in order to hear, " I'm glad you've come to your senses at last. Kindly step into the library and tell Miss Bruce from me that she may fill the place to-morrow."

" Certain," said Mr. Dodd, with his hand to his chin. He watched the great man turn in at his bank in the new block, and then he did as he was bid.

By the time school was out that day the news had leaped across Brampton Street and spread up and down both sides of it that the new teacher had been dismissed. The story ran fairly straight — there were enough clews, certainly. The great man's return, the visit of Mr. Dodd, the call on Judge Graves, all had been marked. The

fiat of the first citizen had gone forth that the ward of
Jethro Bass must be got rid of; the designing young
woman who had sought to entrap his son must be punished
for her amazing effrontery.

Cynthia came out of school happily unaware that her
name was on the lips of Brampton: unaware, too, that the
lord of the place had come into residence that day. She
had looked forward to living in the same town with Bob's
father as an evil which was necessary to be borne, as one
of the things which are more or less inevitable in the
lives of those who have to make their own ways in the
world. The children trooped around her, and the little
girls held her hand, and she talked and laughed with
them as she came up the street in the eyes of Brampton,
— came up the street to the block of new buildings where
the bank was. Stepping out of the bank, with that
businesslike alertness which characterized him, was the
first citizen — none other. He found himself entangled
among the romping children and — horror of horrors —
he bumped against the schoolmistress herself! Worse than
this, he had taken off his hat and begged her pardon before
he looked at her and realized the enormity of his mistake.
And the schoolmistress had actually paid no attention to
him, but with merely heightened color had drawn the
children out of his way and passed on without a word.
The first citizen, raging inwardly, but trying to appear
unconcerned, walked rapidly back to his house. On the
street of his own town, before the eyes of men, he had been
snubbed by a school-teacher. And such a school-teacher!

Mr. Worthington, as he paced his library burning with
the shame of this occurrence, remembered that he had had
to glance at her twice before it came over him who she
was. His first sensation had been astonishment. And now,
in spite of his bitter anger, he had to acknowledge that
the face had made an impression on him — a fact that only
served to increase his rage. A conviction grew upon him
that it was a face which his son, or any other man, would
not be likely to forget. He himself could not forget it.

In the meantime Cynthia had reached her home, her

cheeks still smarting, conscious that people had stared at her. This much, of course, she knew — that Brampton believed Bob Worthington to be in love with her: and the knowledge at such times made her so miserable that the thought of Jethro's isolation alone deterred her from asking Miss Lucretia Penniman for a position in Boston. For she wrote to Miss Lucretia about her life and her reading, as that lady had made her promise to do. She sat down now at the cherry chest of drawers that was also a desk, to write: not to pour out her troubles, for she never had done that, — but to calm her mind by drawing little character sketches of her pupils. But she had only written the words, "My dear Miss Lucretia," when she looked out of the window and saw Judge Graves coming up the path, and ran to open the door for him.

"How do you do, Judge?" she said, for she recognized Mr. Graves as one of her few friends in Brampton. "I have sent to Boston for the new reader, but it has not come."

The judge took her hand and pressed it and led her into the little sitting room. His face was very stern, but his eyes, which had flung fire at Mr. Dodd, looked at her with a vast compassion. Her heart misgave her.

"My dear," he said, — it was long since the judge had called any woman "my dear," — "I have bad news for you. The committee have decided that you cannot teach any longer in the Brampton school."

"Oh, Judge," she answered, trying to force back the tears which would come, "I have tried so hard. I had begun to believe that I could fill the place."

"Fill the place!" cried the judge, startling her with his sudden anger. "No woman in the state can fill it better than you."

"Then why am I dismissed?" she asked breathlessly.

The judge looked at her in silence, his blue lips quivering. Sometimes even he found it hard to tell the truth. And yet he had come to tell it, that she might suffer less. He remembered the time when Isaac D. Worthington had done him a great wrong.

"You are dismissed," he said, "because Mr. Worthington has come home, and because the two other members of the committee are dogs and cowards." Mr. Graves never minced matters when he began, and his voice shook with passion. "If Mr. Errol had examined you, and you had your certificate, it might have been different. Errol is not a sycophant. Worthington does not hold his mortgage."

"Mortgage!" exclaimed Cynthia. The word always struck terror to her soul.

"Mr. Worthington holds Mr. Hill's mortgage," said Mr. Graves, more than ever beside himself at the sight of her suffering. "That man's tyranny is not to be borne. We will not give up, Cynthia. I will fight him in this matter if it takes my last ounce of strength, so help me God!"

Mortgage! Cynthia sank down in the chair by the desk. In spite of the misery the news had brought, the thought that his father, too, who was fighting Jethro Bass as a righteous man, dealt in mortgages and coerced men to do his will, was overwhelming. So she sat for a while staring at the landscape on the old wall paper.

"I will go to Coniston to-night," she said at last.

"No," cried the judge, seizing her shoulder in his excitement, "no. Do you think that I have been your friend — that I am your friend?"

"Oh, Judge Graves —"

"Then stay here, where you are. I ask it as a favor to me. You need not go to the school to-morrow — indeed, you cannot. But stay here for a day or two at least, and if there is any justice left in a free country, we shall have it. Will you stay, as a favor to me?"

"I will stay, since you ask it," said Cynthia. "I will do what you think right."

Her voice was firmer than he expected — much firmer. He glanced at her quickly, with something very like admiration in his eye.

"You are a good woman, and a brave woman," he said, and with this somewhat surprising tribute he took his departure instantly.

Cynthia was left to her thoughts, and these were harassing and sorrowful enough. One idea, however, persisted through them all. Mr. Worthington, whose power she had lived long enough in Brampton to know, was an unjust man and a hypocrite. That thought was both sweet and bitter: sweet, as a retribution; and bitter, because he was Bob's father. She realized, now, that Bob knew these things, and she respected and loved him the more, if that were possible, because he had refrained from speaking of them to her. And now another thought came, and though she put it resolutely from her, persisted. Was she not justified now in marrying him? The reasoning was false, so she told herself. She had no right to separate Bob from his father, whatever his father might be. Did not she still love Jethro Bass? Yes, but he had renounced his ways. Her heart swelled gratefully as she spoke the words to herself, and she reflected that he, at least, had never been a hypocrite.

Of one thing she was sure, now. In the matter of the school she had right on her side, and she must allow Judge Graves to do whatever he thought proper to maintain that right. If Isaac D. Worthington's character had been different, this would not have been her decision. Now she would not leave Brampton in disgrace, when she had done nothing to merit it. Not that she believed that the judge would prevail against such mighty odds. So little did she think so that she fell, presently, into a despondency which in all her troubles had not overtaken her — the despondency which comes even to the pure and the strong when they feel the unjust strength of the world against them. In this state her eyes fell on the letter she had started to Miss Lucretia Penniman, and in desperation she began to write.

It was a short letter, reserved enough, and quite in character. It was right that she should defend herself, which she did with dignity, saying that she believed the committee had no fault to find with her duties, but that Mr. Worthington had seen fit to bring influence to bear upon them because of her connection with Jethro Bass.

It was not the whole truth, but Cynthia could not bring
herself to write of that other reason. At the end she
asked, very simply, if Miss Lucretia could find her
something to do in Boston in case her dismissal became certain. Then she put on her coat, and walked to the post-
office to post the letter, for she resolved that there could
be no shame without reason for it. There was a little
more color in her cheeks, and she held her head high, preparing to be slighted. But she was not slighted, and got
more salutations, if anything, than usual. She was, indeed, in the right not to hide her head, and policy alone
would have forbade it, had Cynthia thought of policy.

CHAPTER XV

CONTAINING A DRAMATIC CLIMAX

PUBLIC opinion is like the wind — it bloweth where it listeth. It whistled around Brampton the next day, whirling husbands and wives apart, and families into smithereens. Brampton had a storm all to itself — save for a sympathetic storm raging in Coniston — and all about a school-teacher.

Had Cynthia been a certain type of woman, she would have had all the men on her side and all of her own sex against her. It is a decided point to be recorded in her favor that she had among her sympathizers as many women as men. But the excitement of a day long remembered in Brampton began, for her, when a score or more of children assembled in front of the little house, tramping down the snow on the grass plots, shouting for her to come to school with them. Children give no mortgages, or keep no hardware stores.

Cynthia, trying to read in front of the fire, was all in a tremble at the sound of the high-pitched little voices she had grown to love, and she longed to go out and kiss them, every one. Her nature, however, shrank from any act which might appear dramatic or sensational. She could not resist going to the window and smiling at them, though they appeared but dimly — little dancing figures in a mist. And when they shouted, the more she shook her head and put her finger to her lips in reproof and vanished from their sight. Then they trooped sadly on to school, resolved to make matters as disagreeable as possible for poor Miss Bruce, who had not offended in any way.

"Then they trooped sadly on to school."

Two other episodes worthy of a place in this act of the drama occurred that morning, and one had to do with Ephraim. Poor Ephraim! His way had ever been to fight and ask no questions, and in his journey through the world he had gathered but little knowledge of it. He had limped home the night before in a state of anger of which Cynthia had not believed him capable, and had reappeared in the sitting room in his best suit of blue.

"Where are you going, Cousin Eph?" Cynthia had asked suspiciously.

"Never you mind, Cynthy."

"But I do mind," she said, catching hold of his sleeve. "I won't let you go until you confess."

"I'm a-goin' to tell Isaac Worthington what I think of him, that's whar I'm a-goin'," cried Ephraim—"what I always hev thought of him sence he sent a substitute to the war an' acted treasonable here to home talkin' ag'in' Lincoln."

"Oh, Cousin Eph, you mustn't," said Cynthia, clinging to him with all her strength in her dismay. It had taken every whit of her influence to persuade him to relinquish his purpose. Cynthia knew very well that Ephraim meant to lay hands on Mr. Worthington, and it would indeed have been a disastrous hour for the first citizen if the old soldier had ever got into his library. Cynthia pointed out, as best she might, that it would be an evil hour for her, too, and that her cause would be greatly injured by such a proceeding; she knew very well that it would ruin Ephraim, but he would not have listened to such an argument.

The next thing he wished to do was to go to Coniston and rouse Jethro. Cynthia's heart stood still when he proposed this, for it touched upon her greatest fear, — which had impelled her to go to Coniston. But she had hoped and believed that Jethro, knowing her feelings, would do nothing — since for her sake he had chosen to give up his power. Now an acute attack of rheumatism had come to her rescue, and she succeeded in getting Ephraim off to bed, swathed in bandages.

The next morning he had insisted upon hobbling away to the post-office, where in due time he was discovered by certain members of the Brampton Club nailing to the wall a new engraving of Abraham Lincoln, and draping it with a little silk flag he had bought in Boston. By which it will be seen that a portion of the Club were coming back to their old haunt. This portion, it may be surmised, was composed of such persons alone as were likely to be welcomed by the postmaster. Some of these had grievances against Mr. Worthington or Mr. Flint; others, in more prosperous circumstances, might have been moved by envy of these gentlemen; still others might have been actuated largely by righteous resentment at what they deemed oppression by wealth and power. These members who came that morning comprised about one-fourth of those who formerly had been in the habit of dropping in for a chat, and their numbers were a fair indication of the fact that those who from various motives took the part of the school-teacher in Brampton were as one to three.

It is not necessary to repeat their expressions of indignation and sympathy. There was a certain Mr. Gamaliel Ives in the town, belonging to an old Brampton family, who would have been the first citizen if that other first citizen had not, by his rise to wealth and power, so completely overshadowed him. Mr. Ives owned a small mill on Coniston Water below the town. He fairly bubbled over with civic pride, and he was an authority on all matters pertaining to Brampton's history. He knew the "Hymn to Coniston" by heart. But we are digressing a little. Mr. Ives, like that other Gamaliel of old, had exhorted his fellow-townsmen to wash their hands of the controversy. But he was an intimate of Judge Graves, and after talking with that gentleman he became a partisan overnight; and when he had stopped to get his mail he had been lured behind the window by the debate in progress. He was in the midst of some impromptu remarks when he recognized a certain brisk step behind him, and — Isaac D. Worthington himself entered the sanctum!

It must be explained that Mr. Worthington sometimes

had an important letter to be registered which he carried
to the post-office with his own hands. On such occasions
— though not a member of the Brampton Club — he
walked, as an overlord will, into any private place he
chose, and recognized no partitions or barriers. Now
he handed the letter (addressed to a certain person in
Cambridge, Massachusetts) to the postmaster.

" You will kindly register that and give me a receipt,
Mr. Prescott," he said.

Ephraim turned from his contemplation of the features
of the martyred President, and on his face was something
of the look it might have worn when he confronted his
enemies over the logworks at Five Forks. No, for there
was a vast contempt in his gaze now, and he had had no
contempt for the Southerners, and would have shaken hands
with any of them the moment the battle was over. Mr.
Worthington, in spite of himself, recoiled a little before
that look, fearing, perhaps, physical violence.

" I hain't a-goin' to hurt you, Mr. Worthington,"
Ephraim said, "but I am a-goin' to ask you to git out in
front, and mighty quick. If you hev any business with
the postmaster, there's the window," and Ephraim pointed
to it with his twisted finger.   " I don't allow nobody but
my friends here, Mr. Worthington, and people I respect."

Mr. Worthington looked — well, eye-witnesses give
various versions as to how he looked. All agree that his
lip trembled ; some say his eyes watered : at any rate, he
quailed, stood a moment undecided, and then swung on
his heel and walked to the partition door. At this safe
distance he turned.

" Mr. Prescott," he said, his voice quivering with passion and perhaps another emotion, " I will make it my
duty to report to the postmaster-general the manner in
which this office is run. Instead of attending to your
business, you make the place a resort for loafers and idlers.
Good morning, sir."

Ten minutes later Mr. Flint himself came to register
the letter. But it was done at the window, and the loafers and idlers were still there.

2 G

The curtain had risen again, indeed, and the action was
soon fast enough for the most impatient that day. No
sooner had the town heard with bated breath of the ex-
pulsion of the first citizen from the inner sanctuary of the
post-office, than the news of another event began to go
the rounds. Mr. Worthington had other and more important things to think about than minor postmasters,
and after his anger and — yes, and momentary fear had
subsided, he forgot the incident except to make a mental
note to remember to deprive Mr. Prescott of his postmastership, which he believed could be done readily
enough now that Jethro Bass was out of the way. Then
he had stepped into the bank, which he had come to regard
as his own bank, as he regarded most institutions in Brampton. He had, in the old days, been president of it, as we
know. He stepped into the bank, and then — he stepped
out again.

Most people have experienced that sickly feeling of the
diaphragm which sometimes comes from a sudden shock.
Mr. Worthington had it now as he hurried up the street,
and he presently discovered that he was walking in the
direction opposite to that of his own home. He crossed
the street, made a pretence of going into Mr. Goldthwaite's
drug store, and hurried back again. When he reached
his own library, he found Mr. Flint busy there at his desk.
Mr. Flint rose. Mr. Worthington sat down and began to
pull the papers about in a manner which betrayed to his
seneschal (who knew every mood of his master) mental
perturbation.

"Flint," he said at last, striving his best for an indiffer-
ent accent, "Jethro Bass is here — I ran across him just
now drawing money in the bank."

"I could have told you that this morning," answered
Mr. Flint. "Wheeler, who runs errands for him in Conis-
ton, drove him in this morning, and he's been with Peleg
Hartington for two hours over Sherman's livery stable."

An interval of silence followed, during which Mr.
Worthington shuffled with his letters and pretended to
read them.

" Graves has called a mass meeting to-night, I understand," he remarked in the same casual way. ;" The man's
a demagogue, and mad as a loon. I believe he sent back
one of our passes once, didn't he ? I suppose Bass has
come in to get Hartington to work up the meeting. They'll
be laughed out of the town hall, or hissed out."

" I guess you'll find Bass has come down for something
else," said Mr. Flint, looking up from a division report.

" What do you mean ? " demanded Mr. Worthington,
changing his attitude to one of fierceness. But he was well
aware that whatever tone he took with his seneschal, he
never fooled him.

" I mean what I told you yesterday," said Flint, " that
you've stirred up the dragon."

Even Mr. Flint did not know how like a knell his words
sounded in Isaac Worthington's ears.

" Nonsense ! " he cried, " you're talking nonsense, Flint.
We maimed him too thoroughly for that. He hasn't
power enough left to carry his own town."

" All right," said the seneschal.

" What do you mean by that ? " said his master, with
extreme irritation.

" I mean what I said yesterday, that we haven't maimed
him at all. He had his own reasons for going into his
hole, and he never would have come out again if you hadn't
goaded him. Now he's out, and we'll have to step around
pretty lively, I can tell you, or he'll maim us."

All of which goes to show that Mr. Flint had some
notion of men and affairs. He became, as may be predicted, the head of many material things in later days,
and he may sometime reappear in company with other
characters in this story.

The sickly feeling in Mr. Worthington's diaphragm had
now returned.

" I think you will find you are mistaken, Flint," he
said, attempting dignity now. " Very much mistaken."

" Very well," said Flint, " perhaps I am. But I believe
you'll find he left for the capital on the eleven o'clock,
and if you take the trouble to inquire from Redding you

will probably learn that the Throne Room is bespoken for the session."

All of that which Mr. Flint had predicted turned out to be true. The dragon had indeed waked up. It all began with the news Milly Skinner had got from the stage driver, imparted to Jethro as he sat reading about Hiawatha. And terrible indeed had been that awakening. This dragon did not bellow and roar and lash his tail when he was roused, but he stood up, and there seemed to emanate from him a fire which frightened poor Milly Skinner, upset though she was by the news of Cynthia's dismissal. O, wondrous and paradoxical might of love, which can tame the most powerful of beasts, and stir them again into furies by a touch!

Coniston was the first to tremble, as though the forces stretching themselves in the tannery house were shaking the very ground, and the name of Jethro Bass took on once more, as by magic, a terrible meaning. When Vesuvius is silent, pygmies may make faces on the very lip of the crater, and they on the slopes forget the black terror of the fiery hail. Jake Wheeler himself, loyal as he was, did not care to look into the crater now that he was summoned; but a force pulled him all the way to the tannery house. He left behind him an awe-stricken gathering at the store, composed of inhabitants who had recently spoken slightingly of the volcano.

We are getting a little mixed in our metaphors between lions and dragons and volcanoes, and yet none of them are too strong to represent Jethro Bass when he heard that Isaac Worthington had had the teacher dismissed from Brampton lower school. He did not stop to reason then that action might distress her. The beast in him awoke again; the desire for vengeance on a man whom he had hated most of his life, and who now had dared to cause pain to the woman whom he loved with all his soul, and even idolized, was too great to resist. He had no thought of resisting it, for the waters of it swept over his soul like the Atlantic over a lost continent. He would crush Isaac Worthington if it took the last breath from his body.

Jake went to the tannery house and received his orders — orders of which he made a great mystery afterward at the store, although they consisted simply of directions to be prepared to drive Jethro to Brampton the next morning. But the look of the man had frightened Jake. He had never seen vengeance so indelibly written on that face, and he had never before realized the terrible power of vengeance. Mr. Wheeler returned from that meeting in such a state of trepidation that he found it necessary to accompany Rias to a certain keg in the cellar ; after which he found his tongue. His description of Jethro's appearance awed his hearers, and Jake declared that he would not be in Isaac Worthington's shoes for all of Isaac Worthington's money. There were others right here in Coniston, Jake hinted, who might now find it convenient to emigrate to the far West.

Jethro's face had not changed when Jake drove him out of Coniston the next morning. Good Mr. Satterlee saw it, and felt that the visit he had wished to make would have been useless ; Mr. Amos Cuthbert and Mr. Sam Price saw it, from a safe distance within the store, and it is a fact that Mr. Price seriously thought of taking Mr. Wheeler's advice about a residence in the West ; Mr. Cuthbert, of a sterner nature, made up his mind to be hung and quartered. A few minutes before Jethro walked into his office over the livery stable, Senator Peleg Hartington would have denied, with that peculiar and mournful scorn of which he was master, that Jethro Bass could ever again have any influence over him. Peleg was, indeed, at that moment preparing, in his own way, to make overtures to the party of Isaac D. Worthington. Jethro walked into the office, leaving Jake below with Mr. Sherman ; and Senator Hartington was very glad he had not made the overtures. And when he accompanied Jethro to the station when he left for the capital, the senator felt that the eyes of men were upon him.

And Cynthia? Happily, Cynthia passed the day in ignorance that Jethro had gone through Brampton.

Ephraim, though he knew of it, did not speak of it when he came home to his dinner ; Mr. Graves had called, and informed her of the meeting in the town hall that night.

" It is our only chance," he said obdurately, in answer to her protests. " We must lay the case before the people of Brampton. If they have not the courage to right the wrong, and force your reinstatement through public opinion, there is nothing more to be done."

To Cynthia, the idea of having a mass meeting concerning herself was particularly repellent.

" Oh, Judge Graves ! " she cried, " if there isn't any other way, please drop the matter. There are plenty of teachers who will — be acceptable to everybody."

" Cynthia," said the judge, " I can understand that this publicity is very painful to you. I beg you to remember that we are contending for a principle. In such cases the individual must be sacrificed to the common good."

" But I cannot go to the meeting — I cannot."

" No," said the judge ; " I don't think that will be necessary."

After he was gone, she could think of nothing but the horror of having her name — yes, and her character — discussed in that public place ; and it seemed to her, if she listened, she could hear a clatter of tongues throughout the length of Brampton Street, and that she must fain stop her ears or go mad. The few ladies who called during the day out of kindness or curiosity, or both, only added to her torture. She was not one who could open her heart to acquaintances : the curious ones got but little satisfaction, and the kind ones thought her cold, and they did not perceive that she was really grateful for their little attentions. Gratitude, on such occasions, does not always consist in pouring out one's troubles in the laps of visitors.

So the visitors went home, wondering whether it were worth while after all to interest themselves in the cause of such a self-contained and self-reliant young woman. In spite of all her efforts, Cynthia had never wholly succeeded in making most of the Brampton ladies believe that she did not secretly deem herself above them.   They belonged to a reserved race themselves ; but Cynthia had a reserve which was even different from their own.

As night drew on the predictions of Mr. Worthington seemed likely to be fulfilled, and it looked as if Judge Graves would have a useless bill to pay for gas in the new town hall. The judge had never been a man who could compel a following, and he had no magnetism with which to lead a cause : the town tradesmen, especially those in the new brick block, would be chary as to risking the displeasure of their best customer.   At half-past seven Mr. Graves came in, alone, and sat on the platform staring grimly at his gas.   Is there a lecturer, or a playwright, or a politician, who has not, at one time or another, been in the judge's place ?   Who cannot sympathize with him as he watched the thin and hesitating stream of people out of the corner of his eye as they came in at the door ?   The judge despised them with all his soul, but it is human nature not to wish to sit in a hall or a theatre that is three-quarters empty.

At sixteen minutes to eight a mild excitement occurred, an incident of some significance which served to detain many waverers.   Senator Peleg Hartington walked up the aisle, and the judge rose and shook him by the hand, and as *Deacon* Hartington he was invited to sit on the platform.   The senator's personal influence was not to be ignored ; and it had sufficed to carry his district in the last election against the Worthington forces, in spite of the abdication of Jethro Bass.   Mr. Page, the editor of the *Clarion*, Senator Hartington's organ, was also on the platform.   But where was Mr. Ives ?   Where was that Gamaliel who had been such a warm partisan in the post-office that morning ?

" Saw him outside the hall — wahn't but ten minutes ago," said Deacon Hartington, sadly ; " thought he was a-comin' in."

Eight o'clock came, and no Mr. Ives ; ten minutes past — fifteen minutes past.   If the truth must be told, Mr. Ives had been on the very threshold of the hall, and one

glance at the poor sprinkling of people there had decided
him.   Mr. Ives had a natural aversion to being laughed
at, and as he walked back on the darker side of the street
he wished heartily that he had stuck to his original
Gamaliel-advocacy of no interference, of allowing the
Supreme Judge to decide.   Such opinions were inevitably just, Mr. Ives was well aware, though not always
handed down immediately.   If he were to humble the first
citizen, Mr. Ives reflected that a better opportunity might
present itself.   The whistle of the up-train served to
strengthen his resolution, for he was reminded thereby
that his mill often had occasion to ask favors of the Truro
Railroad.

In the meantime it was twenty minutes past eight in the
town hall, and Mr. Graves had not rapped for order.
Deacon Hartington sat as motionless as a stork on the borders of a glassy lake at sunrise, the judge had begun seriously to estimate the gas bill, and Mr. Page had chewed
up the end of a pencil.   There was one, at least, in the
audience of whom the judge could be sure.   A certain old
soldier in blue sat uncompromisingly on the front bench
with his hands crossed over the head of his stick ; but the
ladies and gentlemen nearest the door were beginning to
vanish, one by one, silently as ghosts, when suddenly
the judge sat up.   He would have rubbed his eyes, had he
been that kind of a man.   Four persons had entered the
hall — he was sure of it — and with no uncertain steps
as if frightened by its emptiness.   No, they came boldly.
And after them trooped others, and still others were heard
in the street beyond, not whispering, but talking in the unmistakable tones of people who had more coming behind
them.   Yes, and more came.   It was no illusion, or delu-
sion : there they were filling the hall as if they meant to
stay, and buzzing with excitement.   The judge was quivering with excitement now, but he, too, was only a spectator
of the drama.   And what a drama, with a miracle-play for
Brampton !

Mr. Page rose from his chair and leaned over the edge
of the platform that something might be whispered in his

CONTAINING A DRAMATIC CLIMAX 457

ear. The news, whatever it was, was apparently electrify-
ing, and after the first shock he turned to impart it to Mr.
Graves ; but turned too late, for the judge had already
rapped for order and was clearing his throat. He could
not account for this extraordinary and unlooked-for audience, among whom he spied many who had thought it
wiser not to protest against the dictum of the first citizen,
and many who had professed to believe that the teacher's
connection with Jethro Bass was a good and sufficient
reason for dismissal. The judge was prepared to take
advantage of the tide, whatever its cause.

"Ladies and gentlemen," he said, "I take the liberty of
calling this meeting to order. And before a chairman be
elected, I mean to ask your indulgence to explain my purposes in requesting the use of this hall to-night. In our
system of government, the inalienable and most precious
gift — "

Whatever the gift was, the judge never explained. He
paused at the words, and repeated them, and stopped altogether because no one was paying any attention to him.
The hall was almost full, the people had risen, with a hum,
and as one man had turned toward the door. Mr. Gamaliel
Ives was triumphantly marching down the aisle, and with
him was — well, another person. Nay, personage would
perhaps be the better word.

Let us go back for a moment. There descended from
that train of which we have heard the whistle a lady with
features of no ordinary moulding, with curls and a string
bonnet and a cloak that seemed strangely to harmonize
with the lady's character. She had the way of one in authority, and Mr. Sherman himself ran to open the door of
his only closed carriage, and the driver galloped off with her
all the way to the Brampton House. Once there, the lady
seized the pen as a soldier seizes the sword, and wrote her
name in most uncompromising characters on the register,
Miss Lucretia Penniman, Boston. Then she marched up
to her room.

Miss Lucretia Penniman, author of the "Hymn to Coniston," in the reflected glory of whose fame Brampton had

shone for thirty years! Whose name was lauded and
whose poem was recited at every Fourth of July celebration, that the very children might learn it and honor its com-
poser! Stratford-on-Avon is not prouder of Shakespeare
than Brampton of Miss Lucretia, and now she was come
back, unheralded, to her birthplace. Mr. Raines, the clerk,
looked at the handwriting on the book, and would not believe his own sight until it was vouched for by sundry
citizens who had followed the lady from the station — on
foot. And then there was a to-do.

Send for Mr. Gamaliel Ives; send for Miss Bruce, the
librarian; send for Mr. Page, editor of the *Clarion*, and
notify the first citizen. He, indeed, could not be sent for,
but had he known of her coming he would undoubtedly
have had her met at the portals and presented with the
keys in gold. Up and down the street flew the news which
overshadowed and blotted out all other, and the poor little
school-teacher was forgotten.

One of these notables was at hand, though he did not
deserve to be. Mr. Gamaliel Ives sent up his card to Miss
Lucretia, and was shown deferentially into the parlor, where
he sat mopping his brow and growing hot and cold by
turns. How would the celebrity treat him? The celebrity herself answered the question by entering the room
in such stately manner as he had expected, to the rustle of
the bombazine. Whereupon Mr. Ives bounced out of his
chair and bowed, though his body was not formed to bend
that way.

"Miss Penniman," he exclaimed, "what an honor for
Brampton! And what a pleasure, the greater because so
unexpected! How cruel not to have given us warning,
and we could have greeted you as your great fame deserves!
You could never take time from your great duties to accept
the invitations of our literary committee, alas! But now
that you are here, you will find a warm welcome, Miss
Penniman. How long it has been — thirty years, — you
see I know it to a day, thirty years since you left us.
Thirty years, I may say, we have kept burning the vestal
fire in your worship, hoping for this hour."

Miss Lucretia may have had her own ideas about the propriety of the reference to the vestal fire.

" Gamaliel," she said sharply, " straighten up and don't talk nonsense to me.   I've had you on my knee, and I knew your mother and father."

Gamaliel did straighten up, as though Miss Lucretia had applied a lump of ice to the small of his back.   So it is when the literary deities, vestal or otherwise, return to their Stratfords.   There are generally surprises in store for the people they have had on their knees, and for others.

" Gamaliel," said Miss Lucretia, " I want to see the prudential committee for the village district."

" The prudential committee !"   Mr. Ives fairly shrieked the words in his astonishment.

" I tried to speak plainly," said Miss Lucretia.   " Who are on that committee ? "

" Ezra Graves," said Mr. Ives, as though mechanically compelled, for his head was spinning round.   " Ezra Graves always has run it, until now.   But he's in the town hall."

" What's he doing there ? "

Mr. Ives was no fool.   Some inkling of the facts began to shoot through his brain, and he saw his chance.

" He called a mass meeting to protest against the dismissal of a teacher."

" Gamaliel," said Miss Lucretia, " you will conduct me to that meeting.   I will get my cloak."

Mr. Ives wasted no time in the interval, and he fairly ran out into the office.   Miss Lucretia Penniman was in town, and would attend the mass meeting.   Now, indeed, it was to be a mass meeting.   Away flew the tidings, broadcast, and people threw off their carpet slippers and dressing gowns, and some who had gone to bed got up again.   Mr. Dodd heard it, and changed his shoes three times, and his intentions three times three.   Should he go, or should he not ?   Already he heard in imagination the first distant note of the populace, and he was not of the metal to defend a Bastille or a Louvre for his royal master with the last drop of his blood.

In the meantime Gamaliel Ives was conducting Miss

Lucretia toward the town hall, and speaking in no measured
tones of indignation of the cringing, truckling qualities of
that very Mr. Dodd. The injustice to Miss Wetherell,
which Mr. Ives explained as well as he could, made his
blood boil: so he declared.

And now we are back again at the meeting, when the
judge, with his hand on his Adam's apple, is pronouncing
the word "gift." Mr. Ives is triumphantly marching down
the aisle, escorting the celebrity of Brampton to the platform, and quite aware of the heart burnings of his fellow-
citizens on the benches. And Miss Lucretia, with that
stern composure with which celebrities accept public situ-
ations, follows up the steps as of right and takes the chair he
assigns her beside the chairman. The judge, still grasping
his Adam's apple, stares at the newcomer in amazement,
and recognizes her in spite of the years, and trembles.
Miss Lucretia Penniman! Blücher was not more welcome
to Wellington, or Lafayette to Washington, than was Miss
Lucretia to Ezra Graves as he turned his back on the audience and bowed to her deferentially. Then he turned again,
cleared his throat once more to collect his senses, and was
about to utter the familiar words, "We have with us to-
night," when they were taken out of his mouth — taken out
of his mouth by one who had in all conscience stolen
enough thunder for one man, — Mr. Gamaliel Ives.

"Mr. Chairman," said Mr. Ives, taking a slight dropping
of the judge's lower jaw for recognition, "and ladies and
gentlemen of Brampton. It is our great good fortune to
have with us to-night, most unexpectedly, one of whom
Brampton is, and for many years has been, justly proud."
(Cheers.) "One whose career Brampton has followed with
a mother's eyes and with a mother's heart. One who has
chosen a broader field for the exercise of those great powers
with which Nature endowed her than Brampton could give.
One who has taken her place among the luminaries of literature of her time." (Cheers.) "One who has done
more than any other woman of her generation toward the
uplifting of the sex which she honors." (Cheers and clap-
ping of hands.) "And one who, though her lot has fallen

among the great, has not forgotten the home of her childhood.   For has she not written those beautiful lines which
we all know by heart?

> ' Ah, Coniston ! Thy lordly form I see
> Before mine eyes in exile drear.'

" Mr. Chairman and fellow-townsmen and women, I have
the extreme honor of introducing to you one whom we all
love and revere, the author of the ' Hymn to Coniston,' the
editor of the *Woman's Hour*, Miss Lucretia Penniman."
(Loud and long-continued applause.)

Well might Brampton be proud, too, of Gamaliel Ives,
president of its literary club, who could make such a speech
as this on such short notice.   If the truth be told, the
literary club had sent Miss Lucretia no less than seven
invitations, and this was the speech Mr. Ives had intended
to make on those seven occasions.   It was unquestionably a
neat speech, and Judge Graves or no other chairman should
cheat him out of making it.   Mr. Ives, with a wave of his
hand toward the celebrity, sat down by no means dissatis-
fied with himself.   What did he care how the judge glared.
He did not see how stiffly Miss Lucretia sat in her chair.
She could not take him on her knee then, but she would
have liked to.

Miss Lucretia rose, and stood quite as stiffly as she had
sat, and the judge rose, too.   He was very angry, but this
was not the time to get even with Mr. Ives.   As it turned
out, he did not need to bother about getting even.

" Ladies and gentlemen," said he, " in the absence of any
other chairman I take pleasure in introducing to you Miss
Lucretia Penniman."

More applause was started, but Miss Lucretia put a stop
to it by the lifting of a hand.   Then there was a breathless
silence.   Then she cast her eyes around the hall, as though
daring any one to break that silence, and finally they rested
upon Mr. Ives.

" Mr. Chairman," she said, with an inclination toward
the judge, " my friends — for I hope you will be my friends
when I have finished " (Miss Lucretia made it quite clear

"How stiffly Miss Lucretia sat in her chair."

by her tone that it entirely depended upon them whether they would be or not), "I understood when I came here that this was to be a mass meeting to protest against an injustice, and not a feast of literature and oratory, as Gamaliel Ives seems to suppose."

She paused, and when the first shock of amazement was past an audible titter ran through the audience, and Mr. Ives squirmed visibly.

"Am I right, Mr. Chairman?" asked Miss Lucretia.

"You are unquestionably right, Miss Penniman," answered the chairman, rising, "unquestionably."

"Then I will proceed," said Miss Lucretia. "I wrote the 'Hymn to Coniston' many years ago, when I was younger, and yet it is true that I have always remembered Brampton with kindly feelings. The friends of our youth are dear to us. We look indulgently upon their failings, even as they do on ours. I have scanned the faces here in the hall to-night, and there are some that have not changed beyond recognition in thirty years. Ezra Graves I remember, and it is a pleasure to see him in that chair." (Mr. Graves inclined his head, reverently. None knew how the inner man exulted.) "But there was one who was often in Brampton in those days," Miss Lucretia continued, "whom we all loved and with whom we found no fault, and I confess that when I have thought of Brampton I have oftenest thought of her. Her name," said Miss Lucretia, her hand now in the reticule, "her name was Cynthia Ware."

There was a decided stir among the audience, and many leaned forward to catch every word.

"Even old people may have an ideal," said Miss Lucretia, "and you will forgive me for speaking of mine. Where should I speak of it, if not in this village, among those who knew her and among their children? Cynthia Ware, although she was younger than I, has been my ideal, and is still. She was the daughter of the Rev. Samuel Ware of Coniston, and a descendant of Captain Timothy Prescott, whom General Stark called 'Honest Tim.' She was, to me, all that a woman should be, in intellect, in her scorn of all that is ignoble and false, and in her loyalty to her friends." Here the handkerchief came out of the reticule. "She went to Boston to teach school, and some time afterward I was offered a position in New York, and I never saw her again. But she married in Boston a man of learning and literary attainments, though his health was feeble and he was poor, William Wetherell." (Another stir.) "Mr. Wetherell was a gentleman — Cynthia Ware could have married no other — and he came of good and honorable people in Portsmouth. Very recently I read a collection of letters which he wrote to the *Newcastle Guardian*, which some of you may know. I did not trust my own judgment as to those letters, but I took them to an author whose name is known wherever English is spoken, but which I will not mention. And the author expressed it as his opinion, in writing to me, that William Wetherell was undoubtedly a genius of a high order, and that he would have been so recognized if life had given him a chance. Mr. Wetherell, after his wife died, was taken in a dying condition to Coniston, where he was forced, in order to earn his living, to become the storekeeper there. But he took his books with him, and found time to write the letters of which I have spoken, and to give his daughter an early education such as few girls have.

"My friends, I am rejoiced to see that the spirit of justice and the sense of right are as strong in Brampton as they used to be — strong enough to fill this town hall to overflowing because a teacher has been wrongly — yes, and iniquitously — dismissed from the lower school." (Here there was a considerable stir, and many wondered whether Miss Lucretia was aware of the irony in her words.) "I say wrongly and iniquitously, because I have had the opportunity in Boston this winter of learning to know and love that teacher. I am not given to exaggeration, my friends, and when I tell you that I know her, that her character is as high and pure as her mother's, I can say no more. I am here to tell you this to-night because I do not believe you know her as I do. During the seventy years

I have lived I have grown to have but little faith in outward demonstration, to believe in deeds and attainments
rather than expressions.   And as for her fitness to teach,
I believe that even the prudential committee could find
no fault with that."   (I wonder whether Mr. Dodd was in
the back of the hall.)   "I can find no fault with it.   I
am constantly called upon to recommend teachers, and I
tell you I should have no hesitation in sending Cynthia
Wetherell to a high school, young as she is.

"And now, my friends, why was she dismissed?   I have
heard the facts, though not from her.   Cynthia Wetherell
does not know that I have come to Brampton, unless somebody has told her, and did not know that I was coming.
I have heard the facts, and I find it difficult to believe that
so great a wrong could be attempted against a woman,
and if the name of Cynthia Wetherell had meant no more
to me than the letters in it I should have travelled twice
as far as Brampton, old as I am, to do my utmost to right
that wrong.   I give you my word of honor that I have
never been so indignant in my life.   I do not come here to
stir up enmities among you, and I will mention no more
names.   I prefer to believe that the prudential committee
of this district has made a mistake, the gravity of which
they must now realize, and that they will reinstate Cynthia
Wetherell to-morrow.   And if they should not of their
own free will, I have only to look around this meeting to
be convinced that they will be compelled to.   Compelled
to, my friends, by the sense of justice and the righteous
indignation of the citizens of Brampton."

Miss Lucretia sat down, her strong face alight with the
spirit that was in her.   Not the least of the compelling
forces in this world is righteous anger, and when it is exercised by a man or a woman whose life has been a continual
warfare against the pests of wrong, it is well-nigh irresistible.
While you could count five seconds the audience sat silent,
and then began such tumult and applause as had never
been seen in Brampton — all started, so it is said, by an
old soldier in the front row with his stick.   Isaac D. Worthington, sitting alone in the library of his mansion, heard it,

2 H

and had no need to send for Mr. Flint to ask what it was, or who it was had fired the Third Estate. And Mr. Dodd heard it. He may have been in the hall, but now he sat at home, seeing visions of the lantern, and he would have fled to the palace had he thought to get any sympathy from his sovereign. No, Mr. Dodd did not hold the Bastille or even fight for it. Another and a better man gave up the keys, for heroes are sometimes hidden away in meek and retiring people who wear spectacles and have a stoop to their shoulders. Long before the excitement died away a dozen men were on their feet shouting at the chairman, and among them was the tall, stooping man with spectacles. He did not shout, but Judge Graves saw him and made up his mind that this was the man to speak. The chairman raised his hand and rapped with his gavel, and at length he had obtained silence.

"Ladies and gentlemen," he said, "I am going to recognize Mr. Hill of the prudential committee, and ask him to step up on the platform."

There fell another silence, as absolute as the first, when Mr. Hill walked down the aisle and climbed the steps. Indeed, people were stupefied, for the feed dealer was a man who had never opened his mouth in town-meeting; who had never taken an initiative of any kind; who had allowed other men to take advantage of him, and had never resented it. And now he was going to speak. Would he defend the prudential committee, or would he declare for the teacher? Either course, in Mr. Hill's case, required courage, and he had never been credited with any. If Mr. Hill was going to speak at all, he was going to straddle.

He reached the platform, bowed irresolutely to the chairman, and then stood awkwardly with one knee bent, peering at his audience over his glasses. He began without any address whatever.

"I want to say," he began in a low voice, "that I had no intention of coming to this meeting. And I am going to confess — I am going to confess that I was afraid to come." He raised his voice a little defiantly at the words, and paused. One could almost hear the people breathing. "I was afraid to come for fear that I should do the very thing I am going to do now. And yet I was impelled to come. I want to say that my conscience has not been clear since, as a member of the prudential committee, I gave my consent to the dismissal of Miss Wetherell. I know that I was influenced by personal and selfish considerations which should have had no weight. And after listening to Miss Penniman I take this opportunity to declare, of my own free will, that I will add my vote to that of Judge Graves to reinstate Miss Wetherell."

Mr. Hill bowed slightly, and was about to descend the steps when the chairman, throwing parliamentary dignity to the winds, arose and seized the feed dealer's hand. And the people in the hall almost as one man sprang to their feet and cheered, and some — Ephraim Prescott among these — even waved their hats and shouted Mr. Hill's name. A New England audience does not frequently forget itself, but there were few present who did not understand the heroism of the man's confession, who were not carried away by the simple and dramatic dignity of it. He had no need to mention Mr. Worthington's name, or specify the nature of his obligations to that gentleman. In that hour Jonathan Hill rose high in the respect of Brampton, and some pressed into the aisle to congratulate him on his way back to his seat. Not a few were grateful to him for another reason. He had relieved the meeting of the necessity of taking any further action : of putting their names, for instance, in their enthusiasm to a paper which the first citizen might see.

Judge Graves, whose sense of a climax was acute, rapped for order.

"Ladies and gentlemen," he said, in a voice not wholly free from emotion, "you will all wish to pay your respects to the famous lady who is with us. I see that the Rev. Mr. Sweet is present, and I suggest that we adjourn, after he has favored us with a prayer."

As the minister came forward, Deacon Hartington dropped his head and began to flutter his eyelids. The

Rev. Mr. Sweet prayed, and so was brought to an end the most exciting meeting ever held in Brampton town hall.

But Miss Lucretia did not like being called " a famous lady."

CHAPTER XVI

MISS LUCRETIA QUOTES GENESIS

WHILE Miss Lucretia was standing, unwillingly enough, listening to the speeches that were poured into her ear by various members of the audience, receiving the incense and myrrh to which so great a celebrity was entitled, the old soldier hobbled away to his little house as fast as his three legs would carry him. Only one event in his life had eclipsed this in happiness — the interview in front of the White House. He rapped on the window with his stick, thereby frightening Cynthia half out of her wits as she sat musing sorrowfully by the fire.

"Cousin Ephraim," she said, taking off his corded hat, "what in the world's the matter with you?"

"You're a schoolmarm again, Cynthy."

"Do you mean to say —?"

"Miss Lucretia Penniman done it."

"Miss Lucretia Penniman!" Cynthia began to think his rheumatism was driving him out of his mind.

"You bet. 'Long toward the openin' of the engagement there wahn't scarcely anybody thar but me, and they was a-goin'. But they come fast enough when they l'arned she was in town, and she blew 'em up higher'n the Petersburg crater. Great Tecumseh, there's a woman! Next to General Grant, I'd sooner shake her hand than anybody's livin'."

"Do you mean to say that Miss Lucretia is in Brampton and spoke at the mass meeting?"

"Spoke!" exclaimed Ephraim, "callate she did — some. Tore 'em all up. They'd a hung Isaac D. Worthington or Levi Dodd if they'd a had 'em thar."

Cynthia, striving to be calm herself, got him into a chair and took his stick and straightened out his leg, and then Ephraim told her the story, and it lost no dramatic effect in his telling. He would have talked all night. But at length the sound of wheels was heard in the street, Cynthia flew to the door, and a familiar voice came out of the darkness.

"You need not wait, Gamaliel. No, thank you, I think I will stay at the hotel."

Gamaliel was still protesting when Miss Lucretia came in and seized Cynthia in her arms, and the door was closed behind her.

"Oh, Miss Lucretia, why did you come?" said Cynthia, "if I had known you would do such a thing, I should never have written that letter. I have been sorry to-day that I did write it, and now I'm sorrier than ever."

"Aren't you glad to see me?" demanded Miss Lucretia.

"Miss Lucretia!"

"What are friends for?" asked Miss Lucretia, patting her hand. "If you had known how I wished to see you, Cynthia, and I thought a little trip would be good for such a provincial Bostonian as I am. Dear, dear, I remember this house. It used to belong to Gabriel Post in my time, and right across from it was the Social Library, where I have spent so many pleasant hours with your mother. And this is Ephraim Prescott. I thought it was, when I saw him sitting in the front row, and I think he must have been very lonesome there at one time."

"Yes, ma'am," said Ephraim, giving her his gnarled fingers; "I was just sayin' to Cynthy that I'd rather shake your hand than anybody's livin' exceptin' General Grant."

"And I'd rather shake yours than the General's," said Miss Lucretia, for the *Woman's Hour* had taken the opposition side in a certain recent public question concerning women.

"If you'd a fit with him, you wouldn't say that, Miss Lucrety."

"I haven't a word to say against his fighting qualities," she replied.

"Guess the General might say the same of you," said

Ephraim. "If you'd a b'en a man, I callate you'd a come out of the war with two stars on your shoulder. Godfrey, Miss Lucrety, you'd ought to've b'en a man."

"A man!" cried Miss Lucretia, "and 'stars on my shoulder'! I think this kind of talk has gone far enough, Ephraim Prescott."

"Cousin Eph," said Cynthia, laughing, "you're no match for Miss Lucretia, and it's long past your bedtime."

"A man!" repeated Miss Lucretia, after he had retired, and after Cynthia had tried to express her gratitude and had been silenced. They sat side by side in front of the chimney. "I suppose he meant that as a compliment. I never yet saw the man I couldn't back down, and I haven't any patience with a woman who gives in to them." Miss Lucretia poked vigorously a log which had fallen down, as though that were a man, too, and she was putting him back in his proper place.

Cynthia, strange to say, did not reply to this remark.

"Cynthia," said Miss Lucretia, abruptly, "you don't mean to say that you are in love!"

Cynthia drew a long breath, and grew as red as the embers.

"Miss Lucretia!" she exclaimed, in astonishment and dismay.

"Well," Miss Lucretia said, "I should have thought you could have gotten along, for a while at least, without anything of that kind. My dear," she said leaning toward Cynthia, "who is he?"

Cynthia turned away. She found it very hard to speak of her troubles, even to Miss Lucretia, and she would have kept this secret even from Jethro, had it been possible.

"You must let him know his place," said Miss Lucretia, "and I hope he is in some degree worthy of you."

"I do not intend to marry him," said Cynthia, with her head still turned away.

It was now Miss Lucretia who was silent.

"I came near getting married once," she said presently, with characteristic abruptness.

"You!" cried Cynthia, looking around in amazement.

"You see, I am franker than you, my dear — though I never told any one else. I believe you can keep a secret."

"Of course I can. Who — was it any one in Brampton, Miss Lucretia?" The question was out before Cynthia realized its import. She was turning the tables with a vengeance.

"It was Ezra Graves," said Miss Lucretia.

"Ezra Graves!" And then Cynthia pressed Miss Lucretia's hand in silence, thinking how strange it was that both of them should have been her champions that evening.

Miss Lucretia poked the fire again.

"It was shortly after that, when I went to Boston, that I wrote the 'Hymn to Coniston.' I suppose we must all be fools once or twice, or we should not be human."

"And — weren't you ever — sorry?" asked Cynthia.

Again there was a silence.

"I could not have done the work I have had to do in the world if I had married. But I have often wondered whether that work was worth the while. Such a feeling must come over all workers, occasionally. Yes," said Miss Lucretia, "there have been times when I have been sorry, my dear, though I have never confessed it to another soul. I am telling you this for your own good — not mine. If you have the love of a good man, Cynthia, be careful what you do with it."

The tears had come into Cynthia's eyes.

"I should have told you, Miss Lucretia," she faltered. "If I could have married him, it would have been easier."

"Why can't you marry him?" demanded Miss Lucretia, sharply — to hide her own emotion.

"His name," said Cynthia, "is Bob Worthington."

"Isaac Worthington's son?"

"Yes."

Another silence, Miss Lucretia being utterly unable to say anything for a space.

"Is he a good man?"

Cynthia was on the point of indignant protest, but she stopped herself in time.

" I will tell you what he has done," she answered, " and then you shall judge for yourself."

And she told Miss Lucretia, simply, all that Bob had done, and all that she herself had done.

" He is like his mother, Sarah Hollingsworth; I knew her well," said Miss Lucretia. " If Isaac Worthington were a man, he would be down on his knees begging you to marry his son. He tried hard enough to marry your own mother."

" My mother ! " exclaimed Cynthia, who had never believed that rumor.

" Yes," said Miss Lucretia, " and you may think your stars he didn't succeed. I mistrusted him when he was a young man, and now I know that he hasn't changed. He is a coward and a hypocrite."

Cynthia could not deny this.

" And yet," she said, after a moment's silence, " I am sure you will say that I have been right. My own conscience tells me that it is wrong to deprive Bob of his inheritance, and to separate him from his father, whatever his father may be."

" We shall see what happens in five years," said Miss Lucretia.

" Five years ! " said Cynthia, in spite of herself.

" Jacob served seven for Rachel," answered Miss Lucretia; " that period is scarcely too short to test a man, and you are both young."

" No," said Cynthia, " I cannot marry him, Miss Lucretia. The world would accuse me of design, and I feel that I should not be happy. I am sure that he would never reproach me, even if things went wrong, but — the day might come when — when he would wish that it had been otherwise."

Miss Lucretia kissed her.

" You are very young, my dear," she repeated, "and none of us may say what changes time may bring forth. And now I must go."

Cynthia insisted upon walking with her friend down the street to the hotel — an undertaking that was without danger in Brampton. And it was only a step, after all. A late moon floated in the sky, throwing in relief the shadow of the Worthington mansion against the white patches of snow. A light was still burning in the library.

The next morning after breakfast Miss Lucretia appeared at the little house, and informed Cynthia that she would walk to school with her.

"But I have not yet been notified by the Committee," said Cynthia. There was a knock at the door, and in walked Judge Ezra Graves. Miss Lucretia may have blushed, but it is certain that Cynthia did. Never had she seen the judge so spick and span, and he wore the broadcloth coat he usually reserved for Sundays. He paused at the threshold, with his hand on his Adam's apple.

"Good morning, ladies," he said, and looked shyly at Miss Lucretia and cleared his throat, and spoke with the elaborate decorum he used on occasions, "Miss Penniman, I wish to thank you again for your noble action of last evening."

"Don't 'Miss Penniman' me, Ezra Graves," retorted Miss Lucretia; "the only noble action I know of was poor Jonathan Hill's — unless it was paying for the gas."

This was the way in which Miss Lucretia treated her lover after thirty years! Cynthia thought of what the lady had said to her a few hours since, by this very fire, and began to believe she must have dreamed it. Fires look very differently at night — and sometimes burn brighter then. The judge parted his coat tails, and seated himself on the wooden edge of a cane-bottomed chair.

"Lucretia," he said, "you haven't changed."

"You have, Ezra," she replied, looking at the Adam's apple.

"I'm an old man," said Ezra Graves.

Cynthia could not help thinking that he was a very different man, in Miss Lucretia's presence, than when at the head of the prudential committee.

"Ezra," said Miss Lucretia, "for a man you do very well."

The judge smiled.

" Thank you, Lucretia," said he.   He seemed to appreciate the full extent of the compliment.

" Judge Graves," said Cynthia, " I can tell you how good
you are, at least, and thank you for your great kindness to
me, which I shall never forget."

She took his withered hands from his knees and pressed
them.   He returned the pressure, and then searched his
coat tails, found a handkerchief, and blew his nose violently.

" I merely did my duty, Miss Wetherell," he said.   " I
would not wilfully submit to a wrong."

" You called me ' Cynthia' yesterday."

" So I did," he answered, " so I did."   Then he looked
at Miss Lucretia.

" Ezra," said that lady, smiling a little, " I don't believe
you have changed, after all."

What she meant by that nobody knows.

" I had thought, Cynthia," said the judge, " that it might
be more comfortable for you to have me go to the school
with you.   That is the reason for my early call."

" Judge Graves, I do appreciate your kindness," said
Cynthia; " I hope you won't think I'm rude if I say I'd
rather go alone."

" On the contrary, my dear," replied the judge, " I think
I can understand and esteem your feeling in the matter,
and it shall be as you wish."

" Then I think I had better be going," said Cynthia.
The judge rose in alarm at the words, but she put her hand
on his shoulder.   " Won't you sit down and stay," she
begged, " you haven't seen Miss Lucretia for how many
years, — thirty, isn't it?"

Again he glanced at Miss Lucretia, uncertainly.   " Sit
down, Ezra," she commanded, " and for goodness' sake
don't be afraid of the cane bottom.   You won't go through
it.   I should like to talk to you, and most of the gossips
of our day are dead.   I shall stay in Brampton to-day,
Cynthia, and eat supper with you here this evening."

Cynthia, as she went out of the door, wondered what
they would talk about.   Then she turned toward the
school.   It was not the March wind that burned her cheeks;

as she thought of the mass meeting the night before, which
was all about her, she wished she might go to school that
morning through the woods and pasture lots rather than
down Brampton Street. What — what would Bob say
when he heard of the meeting? Would he come again to
Brampton? If he did, she would run away to Boston
with Miss Lucretia. Every day it had been a trial to pass
the Worthington house, but she could not cross the wide
street to avoid it. She hurried a little, unconsciously,
when she came to it, for there was Mr. Worthington on
the steps talking to Mr. Flint. How he must hate her
now, Cynthia reflected! He did not so much as look
up when she passed.

The other citizens whom she met made up for Mr.
Worthington's coldness, and gave her a hearty greeting,
and some stopped to offer their congratulations. Cynthia
did not pause to philosophize: she was learning to accept
the world as it was, and hurried swiftly on to the little
schoolhouse. The children saw her coming, and ran to
meet her and escorted her triumphantly in at the door.
Of their welcome she could be sure. Thus she became
again teacher of the lower school.

How the judge and Miss Lucretia got along that morning, Cynthia never knew. Miss Lucretia spent the day in
her old home, submitting to hero-worship, and attended an
evening party in her honor at Mr. Gamaliel Ives's house —
a mansion not so large as the first citizen's, though it had
two bay-windows and was not altogether unimposing. The
first citizen, needless to say, was not there, but the rest of
the élite attended. Mr. Ives will tell you all about the
entertainment if you go to Brampton, but the real reason
Miss Lucretia consented to go was to please Lucy Baird,
who was Gamaliel's wife, and to chat with certain old
friends whom she had not seen. The next morning she
called at the school to bid Cynthia good-by, and to whisper
something in her ear which made her very red before all
the scholars. She shook her head when Miss Lucretia
said it, for it had to do with an incident in the 29th chapter
of Genesis.

"To chat with certain old friends."

477

While Jonathan Hill was being made a hero of in the little two-by-four office of the feed store the morning after the mass meeting (though nobody offered to take over his mortgage), Mr. Dodd was complaining to his wife of shooting pains, and "callated" he would stay at home that day.

"Shootin' fiddlesticks!" said Mrs. Dodd. "Get along down to the store and face the music, Levi Dodd. You'd have had shootin' pains if you'd a went to the meetin'."

"I might stop by at Mr. Worthington's house and explain how powerless I was —"

"For goodness' sake git out, Levi. I guess he knows how powerless you are with your shootin' pains. If you only could forget Isaac D. Worthington for three minutes, you wouldn't have 'em."

Mr. Dodd's two clerks saw him enter the store by the back door and he was very much interested in the new ploughs which were piled up in crates outside of it. Then he disappeared into his office and shut the door, and supposedly became very much absorbed in book-keeping. If any one called, he was out — any one. Plenty of people did call, but he was not disturbed — until ten o'clock. Mr. Dodd had a very sensitive ear, and he could often recognize a man by his step, and this man he recognized.

"Where's Mr. Dodd?" demanded the owner of the step, indignantly.

"He's out, Mr. Worthington. Anything I can do for you, Mr. Worthington?"

"You can tell him to come up to my house the moment he comes in."

Unfortunately Mr. Dodd in the office had got into a strained position. He found it necessary to move a little; the day-book fell heavily to the floor, and the perspiration popped out all over his forehead. Come out, Levi Dodd. The Bastille is taken, but there are other fortresses still in the royal hands where you may be confined.

"Who's in the office?"

"I don't know, sir," answered the clerk, winking at his companion, who was sorting nails.

In three strides the great man had his hand on the office door and had flung it open, disclosing the culprit cowering over the day-book on the floor.

"Mr. Dodd," cried the first citizen, "what do you mean by — ?"

Some natures, when terrified, are struck dumb. Mr. Dodd's was the kind which bursts into speech.

"I couldn't help it, Mr. Worthington," he cried, "they would have it. I don't know what got into 'em. They lost their senses, Mr. Worthington, plumb lost their senses. If you'd a b'en there, you might have brought 'em to. I tried to git the floor, but Ezry Graves —"

"Confound Ezra Graves, and wait till I have done, can't you," interrupted the first citizen, angrily. "What do you mean by putting a bath-tub into my house with the tin loose, so that I cut my leg on it?"

Mr. Dodd nearly fainted from sheer relief.

"I'll put a new one in to-day, right now," he gasped.

"See that you do," said the first citizen, "and if I lose my leg, I'll sue you for a hundred thousand dollars."

"I was a-goin' to explain about them losin' their heads at the mass meetin' —"

"Damn their heads!" said the first citizen. "And yours, too," he may have added under his breath as he stalked out. It was not worth a swing of the executioner's axe in these times of war. News had arrived from the state capital that morning of which Mr. Dodd knew nothing. Certain feudal chiefs from the North Country, of whose allegiance Mr. Worthington had felt sure, had obeyed the summons of their old sovereign, Jethro Bass, and had come South to hold a conclave under him at the Pelican. Those chiefs of the North Country, with their clans behind them as one man, what a power they were in the state! What magnificent qualities they had, in battle or strategy, and how cunning and shrewd was their generalship! Year after year they came down from their mountains and fought shoulder to shoulder, and year after year they carried back the lion's share of the spoils between them. The great South, as a whole, was powerless to resist them, for there could be no lasting alliance between Harwich and Brampton and Newcastle and Gosport. Now their king had come back, and the North Country men were rallying again to his standard. No wonder that Levi Dodd's head, poor thing that it was, was safe for a while.

"Organize what you have left, and be quick about it," said Mr. Flint, when the news had come, and they sat in the library planning a new campaign in the face of this evident defection. There was no time to cry over spilt milk or reinstated school-teachers. The messages flew far and wide to the manufacturing towns to range their guilds into line for the railroads. The seneschal wrote the messages, and sent the summons to the sleek men of the cities, and let it be known that the coffers were full and not too tightly sealed, that the faithful should not lack for the sinews of war. Mr. Flint found time, too, to write some carefully worded but nevertheless convincing articles for the *Newcastle Guardian*, very damaging to certain commanders who had proved unfaithful.

"Flint," said Mr. Worthington, when they had worked far into the night, "if Bass beats us, I'm a crippled man."

"And if you postpone the fight now that you have begun it? What then?"

The answer, Mr. Worthington knew, was the same either way. He did not repeat it. He went to his bed, but not to sleep for many hours, and when he came down to his breakfast in the morning, he was in no mood to read the letter from Cambridge which Mrs. Holden had put on his plate. But he did read it, with what anger and bitterness may be imagined. There was the ultimatum, — respectful, even affectionate, but firm. "I know that you will, in all probability, disinherit me as you say, and I tell you honestly that I regret the necessity of quarrelling with you more than I do the money. I do not pretend to say that I despise money, and I like the things that it buys, but the woman I love is more to me than all that you have."

Mr. Worthington laid the letter down, and there came irresistibly to his mind something that his wife had said to him before she died, shortly after they had moved into the mansion. "Dudley, how happy we used to be together before we were rich!" Money had not been everything to Sarah Worthington, either. But now no tender wave of feeling swept over him as he recalled those words. He was thinking of what weapon he had to prevent the marriage beyond that which was now useless — disinheritance. He would disinherit Bob, and that very day. He would punish his son to the utmost of his power for marrying the ward of Jethro Bass. He wondered bitterly, in case a certain event occurred, whether he would have much to alienate.

When Mr. Flint arrived, fresh as usual in spite of the work he had accomplished and the cigars he had smoked the night before, Mr. Worthington still had the letter in his hand, and was pacing his library floor, and broke into a tirade against his son.

"After all I have done for him, building up for him a position and a fortune that is only surpassed by young Duncan's, to treat me in this way, to drag down the name of Worthington in the mire. I'll never forgive him. I'll send for Dixon and leave the money for a hospital in Brampton. Can't you suggest any way out of this, Flint?"

"No," said Flint, "not now. The only chance you have is to ignore the thing from now on. He may get tired of her — I've known such things to happen."

"When she hears that I've disinherited him, she will get tired of him," declared Mr. Worthington.

"Try it and see, if you like," said Flint.

"Look here, Flint, if the woman has a spark of decent feeling, as you seem to think, I'll send for her and tell her that she will ruin Robert if she marries him." Mr. Worthington always spoke of his son as "Robert."

"You ought to have thought of that before the mass meeting. Perhaps it would have done some good then."

"Because this Penniman woman has stirred people up — is that what you mean? I don't care anything about that. Money counts in the long run."

2 1

"If money counted with this school-teacher, it would be a simple matter. I think you'll find it doesn't."

"I've known you to make some serious mistakes," snapped Mr. Worthington.

"Then why do you ask for my advice?"

"I'll send for her, and appeal to her better nature," said Mr. Worthington, with an unconscious and sublime irony.

Flint gave no sign that he heard. Mr. Worthington seated himself at his desk, and after some thought wrote on a piece of note-paper the following lines: "My dear Miss Wetherell, I should be greatly obliged if you would find it convenient to call at my house at eight o'clock this evening," and signed them, "Sincerely Yours." He sealed them up in an envelope and addressed it to Miss Wetherell, at the schoolhouse, and handed it to Mr. Flint. That gentleman got as far as the door, and then he hesitated and turned.

"There is just one way out of this for you, that I can see, Mr. Worthington," he said. "It's a desperate measure, but it's worth thinking about."

"What's that?"

It took some courage, even for Mr. Flint, to make the suggestion.

"The girl's a good girl, well educated, and by no means bad looking. Bob might do a thousand times worse. Give your consent to the marriage, and Jethro Bass will go back to Coniston."

It was wisdom such as few lords get from their seneschals, but Isaac D. Worthington did not so recognize it. His anger rose and took away his breath as he listened to it.

"I will never give my consent to it, never — do you hear? — never. Send that note!" he cried.

Mr. Flint walked out, sent the note, and returned and took his place silently at his own table. He was a man of concentration, and he put his mind on the arguments he was composing to certain political leaders. Mr. Worthington merely pretended to work as he waited for the answer to come back. And presently, when it did come back, he tore it open and read it with an expression not often on his lips. He flung the paper at Mr. Flint.

"Read that," he said.

This is what Mr. Flint read: "Miss Wetherell begs to inform Mr. Isaac D. Worthington that she can have no communication or intercourse with him whatsoever."

Mr. Flint handed it back without a word. His opinion of the school-teacher had risen mightily, but he did not say so. Mr. Worthington took the note, too, without a word. Speech was beyond him, and he crushed the paper as fiercely as he would have liked to have crushed Cynthia, had she been in his hands.

One accomplishment which Cynthia had learned at Miss Sadler's school was to write a letter in the third person, Miss Sadler holding that there were occasions when it was beneath a lady's dignity to write a direct note. And Cynthia, sitting at her little desk in the schoolhouse during her recess, had deemed this one of the occasions. She could not bring herself to write, "My dear Mr. Worthington." Her anger, when the note had been handed to her, was for the moment so great that she could not go on with her classes; but she had controlled it, and compelled Silas to stand in the entry until recess, when she sat with her pen in her hand until that happy notion of the third person occurred to her. And after Silas had gone she sat still, though trembling a little at intervals, picturing with some satisfaction Mr. Worthington's appearance when he received her answer. Her instinct told her that he had received his son's letter, and that he had sent for her to insult her. By sending for her, indeed, he had insulted her irrevocably, and that is why she trembled.

Poor Cynthia! her troubles came thick and fast upon her in those days. When she reached home, there was the letter which Ephraim had left on the table addressed in the familiar, upright handwriting, and when Cynthia saw it, she caught her hand sharply at her breast, as if the pain there had stopped the beating of her heart. Well it was for Bob's peace of mind that he could not see her as she read it, and before she had come to the end there were

drops on the sheets where the purple ink had run. How
precious would have been those drops to him! He would
never give her up. No mandate or decree could separate
them — nothing but death. And he was happier now —
so he told her — than he had been for months: happy in
the thought that he was going out into the world to win
bread for her, as became a man. Even if he had not her
to strive for, he saw now that such was the only course for
him. He could not conform.

It was a manly letter, — how manly Bob himself never
knew. But Cynthia knew, and she wept over it and even
pressed it to her lips — for there was no one to see. Yes,
she loved him as she would not have believed it possible
to love, and she sat through the afternoon reading his
words and repeating them until it seemed that he were
there by her side, speaking them. They came, untram-
melled and undefiled, from his heart into hers.

And now that he had quarrelled with his father for her
sake, and was bent with all the determination of his character upon making his own way in the world, what was
she to do? What was her duty? Not one letter of the
twoscore she had received (so she kept their count from day
to day) — not one had she answered. His faith had indeed
been great. But she must answer this: must write, too,
on that subject of her dismissal, lest it should be wrongly
told him. He was rash in his anger, and fearless; this she
knew, and loved him for such qualities as he had.

She must stay in Brampton and do her work, — so much
was clearly her duty, although she longed to flee from it.
And at last she sat down and wrote to him. Some things
are too sacred to be set forth on a printed page, and this
letter is one of those things. Try as she would, she could
not find it in her heart at such a time to destroy his
hope, — or her own. The hope which she would not acknowledge, and the love which she strove to conceal from
him seeped up between the words of her letter like
water through grains of sand. Words, indeed, are but as
grains of sand to conceal strong feelings, and as Cynthia
read the letter over she felt that every line betrayed her,

and knew that she could compose no lines which would not.

She said nothing of the summons which she had received that morning, or of her answer; and her account of the matter of the dismissal and reinstatement was brief and dignified, and contained no mention of Mr. Worthington's name or agency. It was her duty, too, to rebuke Bob for the quarrel with his father, to point out the folly of it, and the wrong, and to urge him as strongly as she could to retract, though she felt that all this was useless. And then — then came the betrayal of hope. She could not ask him never to see her again, but she did beseech him for her sake, and for the sake of that love which he had declared, not to attempt to see her: not for a year, she wrote, though the word looked to her like eternity. Her reasons, aside from her own scruples, were so obvious, while she taught in Brampton, that she felt that he would consent to banishment — until the summer holidays in July, at least: and then she would be in Coniston, and would have had time to decide upon future steps. A reprieve was all she craved, — a reprieve in which to reflect, for she was in no condition to reflect now. Of one thing she was sure, that it would not be right at this time to encourage him — although she had a guilty feeling that the letter had given him encouragement in spite of all the prohibitions it contained. "If, in the future years," thought Cynthia, as she sealed the envelope, " he persists in his determination, what then?" You, Miss Lucretia, of all people in the world, have planted the seeds with your talk about Genesis!

The letter was signed " One who will always remain your friend, Cynthia Wetherell." And she posted it herself.

When Ephraim came home to supper that evening, he brought the Brampton *Clarion*, just out, and in it was an account of Miss Lucretia Penniman's speech at the mass meeting, and of her visit, and of her career. It was written in Mr. Page's best vein, and so laudatory was it that we shall have to spare Miss Lucretia in not repeating it here: yes, and omit the encomiums, too, on the teacher of the Brampton lower school. Mr. Worthington was not mentioned, and for this, at least, Cynthia drew a long breath of relief, though Ephraim was of the opinion that the first citizen should have been scored as he deserved, and held up to the contempt of his fellow-townsmen. The dismissal of the teacher, indeed, was put down to a regrettable misconception on the part of "one of the prudential committee," who had confessed his mistake in "a manly and altogether praiseworthy speech." The article was as near the truth, perhaps, as the Clarions may come on such matters — which is not very near. Cynthia would have been better pleased if Mr. Page had spared his readers the recital of her qualities, and she did not in the least recognize the paragon whom Miss Lucretia had befriended and defended. She was thankful that Mr. Page did not state that the celebrity had come up from Boston on her account. Miss Penniman had been "actuated by a sudden desire to see once more the beauties of her old home, to look into the faces of the old friends who had followed her career with such pardonable pride." The speech of the president of the literary club, you may be sure, was printed in full, for Mr. Ives himself had taken the trouble to write it out for the editor — by request, of course.

Cynthia turned over the sheet, and read many interesting items: one concerning the beauty and fashion and intellect which attended the party at Mr. Gamaliel Ives's; in the Clovelly notes she saw that Miss Judy Hatch, of Coniston, was visiting relatives there; she learned the output of the Worthington Mills for the past week. Cynthia was about to fold up the paper and send it to Miss Lucretia, whom she thought it would amuse, when her eyes were arrested by the sight of a familiar name.

"Jethro Bass come to life again.

From the *State Tribune*."

That was the heading. "One of the greatest political surprises in many years was the arrival in the capital on Wednesday of Judge Bass, whom it was thought had

permanently retired from politics.   This, at least, seems to
have been the confident belief of a faction in the state who
have at heart the consolidation of certain lines of railroads.
Judge Bass was found by a *Tribune* reporter in the familiar
'Throne Room' at the Pelican, but, as usual, he could not
be induced to talk for publication.   He was in conference
throughout the afternoon with several well-known leaders
from the North Country.   The return of Jethro Bass to
activity seriously complicates the railroad situation, and
many prominent politicians are freely predicting to-night
that, in spite of the town-meeting returns, the proposed bill
for consolidation will not go through.   Judge Bass is a
man of such remarkable personality that he has regained at
a stroke much of the influence that he lost by the sudden
and unaccountable retirement which electrified the state
some months since.   His reappearance, the news of which
was the one topic in all political centres yesterday, is
equally unaccountable.   It is hinted that some action on
the part of Isaac D. Worthington has brought Jethro Bass
to life.   They are known to be bitter enemies, and it is said
that Jethro Bass has but one object in returning to the field
— to crush the president of the Truro Railroad.   Another
theory is that the railroads and interests opposed to the
consolidation have induced Judge Bass to take charge of
their fight for them.   All indications point to the fiercest
struggle the state has ever seen in June, when the Legislature meets.   The *Tribune*, whose sentiments are well
known to be opposed to the iniquity of consolidation, ex-
tends a hearty welcome to the judge.   No state, we believe,
can claim a party leader of a higher order of ability than
Jethro Bass."

Cynthia dropped the paper in her lap, and sat very still.
This, then, was what happened when Jethro had heard of
her dismissal — he had left Coniston without writing her a
word and passed through Brampton without seeing her.
He had gone back to that life which he had abandoned for
her sake ; the temptation had been too strong, the desire
for vengeance too great.   He had not dared to see her.
And yet the love for her which had been strong enough to

make him renounce the homage of men, and even incur their ridicule, had incited him to this very act of vengeance.

What should she do now, indeed? Had those peaceful and happy Saturdays and Sundays in Coniston passed away forever? Should she follow him to the capital and appeal to him? Ah no, she felt that were a useless pain to them both. She believed, now, that he had gone away from her for all time, that the veil of limitless space was set between them. Silently she arose, — so silently that Ephraim, dozing by the fire, did not awake. She went into her own room and wept, and after many hours fell into a dreamless sleep of sheer exhaustion.

*   *   *   *   *   *   *

The days passed, and the weeks; the snow ran from the brown fields, and melted at length even in the moist crotches under the hemlocks of the northern slopes; the robin and bluebird came, the hillsides were mottled with exquisite shades of green, and the scent of fruit blossom and balm of Gilead was in the air. June came as a maiden and grew into womanhood. But Jethro Bass did not return to Coniston.

CHAPTER XVII

WHEN THE PIE WAS OPENED

THE legends which surround the famous war which we
are about to touch upon are as dim as those of Troy or
Tuscany. Decorous chronicles and biographies and mono-
graphs and eulogies exist, bound in leather and stamped
in gold, each lauding its own hero: chronicles written in
really beautiful language, and high-minded and noble, out
of which the heroes come unstained. Horatius holds the
bridge, and not a dent in his armor; and swims the Tiber
without getting wet or muddy. Castor and Pollux fight
in the front rank at Lake Regillus, in the midst of all that
gore and slaughter, and emerge all white and pure at the
end of the day — but they are gods.

Out of the classic wars to which we have referred sprang
the great Roman Republic and Empire, and legend runs into
authentic and written history. Just so, *parva componere
magnis*, out of the cloud-wrapped conflicts of the five railroads of which our own Gaul is composed, emerged one
imperial railroad, authentically and legally written down
on the statute books, for all men to see. We cannot go
behind that statute except to collect the legends and write
homilies about the heroes who held the bridges.

If we were not in mortal terror of the imperial power,
and a little fearful, too, of tiring our readers, we would
write out all the legends we have collected of this first
fight for consolidation, and show the blood, too.

In the statute books of a certain state may be found a
number of laws setting forth the various things that a
railroad or railroads may do, and on the margin of these
pages is invariably printed a date, that being the particular

year in which these laws were passed. By a singular coincidence it is the very year at which we have now arrived in our story. We do not intend to give a map of the state, or discuss the merits or demerits of the consolidation of the Central and the Northwestern and the Truro railroads. Such discussions are not the province of a novelist, and may all be found in the files of the *Tribune* at the State Library. There were, likewise, decisions without number handed down by the various courts before and after that celebrated session, — opinions on the validity of leases, on the extension of railroads, on the rights of individual stockholders — all dry reading enough.

At the risk of being picked to pieces by the corporation lawyers who may read these pages, we shall attempt to state the situation and with all modesty and impartiality — for we, at least, hold no brief. When Mr. Isaac D. Worthington obtained that extension of the Truro Railroad (which we have read about from the somewhat verdant point of view of William Wetherell), that railroad then formed a connection with another road which ran northward from Harwich through another state, and with which we have nothing to do. Having previously purchased a line to the southward from the capital, Mr. Worthington's railroad was in a position to compete with Mr. Duncan's (the " Central ") for Canadian traffic, and also to cut into the profits of the " Northwestern," Mr. Lovejoy's road. In brief, the Truro Railroad found itself very advantageously placed, as Mr. Worthington and Mr. Flint had foreseen. There followed a period of bickering and recrimination, of attempts of the other two railroads to secure representation in the Truro directorate, of suits and injunctions and appeals to the Legislature and I know not what else — in all of which affairs Mr. Bijah Bixby and other gentlemen we could name found both pleasure and remuneration.

Oh, that those halcyon days of the little wars would come again, when a captain could ride out almost any time at the head of his band of mercenaries and see honest fighting and divide honest spoils! There was much knocking about of men and horses, but very little bloodshed, so we are told. Mr. Bixby will sit on the sunny side of his barns in Clovelly and tell you stories of that golden period with tears in his eyes, when he went to conventions with a pocketful of proxies from the river towns, and controlled in the greatest legislative year of all a "block" which included the President of the Senate, for which he got the fabulous sum of ——. He will tell you, but I won't. Mr. Bixby's occupation is gone now. We have changed all that, and we are ruled from imperial Rome. If you don't do right, they cut off your (political) head, and it is of no use to run away, because there is no one to run to.

It was Isaac D. Worthington — or shall we say Mr. Flint? — who was responsible for this pernicious change for the worse, who conceived the notion of leasing for the Truro the Central and the Northwestern, — thus making one railroad out of the three. If such a gigantic undertaking could be got through, Mr. Worthington very rightly deemed that the other railroads of the state would eventually fall like ripe fruit into their caps — owning the ground under the tree, as they would. A movement, which we need not go into, was first made upon the courts, and for a while adverse decisions came down like summer rain. A genius by the name of Jethro Bass had for many years presided (in the room of the governor and council at the State House) at the political birth of justices of the Supreme Court. None of them actually wore livery, but we have seen one of them — a long time ago — in a horse blanket. None of them were favorable to the plans of Mr. Worthington and Mr. Duncan.

We have listened to the firing on the skirmish lines for a long time, and now the real battle is at hand. It is June, and the Legislature is meeting, and Bijah Bixby has come down to the capital at the head of his regiment of mercenaries, of which Mr. Sutton is the honorary colonel; the clans are here from the north, well quartered and well fed; the Throne Room, within the sacred precincts of which we have been before, is occupied. But there is another headquarters now, too, in the Pelican House — a Railroad Room ; larger than the Throne Room, with a bath-room leading out of it. Another old friend of ours, Judge Abner Parkinson of Harwich, he who gave the sardonic laugh when Sam Price applied for the post of road agent, may often be seen in that Railroad Room from now on. The fact is that the judge is about to become famous far beyond the confines of Harwich ; for he, and none other, is the author of the Consolidation Bill itself.

Mr. Flint is the generalissimo of the allied railroads, and sits in his headquarters early and late, going over the details of the campaign with his lieutenants ; scanning the clauses of the bill with Judge Parkinson for the last time, and giving orders to the captains of mercenaries as to the disposition of their forces ; writing out passes for the deserving and the true. For these latter, also, and for the wavering there is a claw-hammer on the marble-topped mantel wielded by Mr. Bijah Bixby, *pro tem* chief of staff — or of the hammer, for he is self-appointed and very useful. He opens the mysterious packing cases which come up to the Railroad Room thrice a week, and there is water to be had in the bath-room — and glasses. Mr. Bixby also finds time to do some of the scouting about the rotunda and lobbies, for which he is justly celebrated, and to drill his regiment every day. The Honorable Heth Sutton, M.C., — who held the bridge in the Woodchuck Session, — is there also, sitting in a corner, swelled with importance, smoking big Florizel cigars which come from — somewhere. There are, indeed, many great and battle-scarred veterans who congregate in that room — too numerous and great to mention ; and saunterers in the Capitol Park opposite know when a council of war is being held by the volumes of smoke which pour out of the window, just as the Romans are made cognizant by the smoking of a chimney of when another notable event takes place.

Who, then, are left to frequent the Throne Room ? Is

that ancient seat of power deserted, and does Jethro Bass sit there alone behind the curtains, in his bitterness, thinking of other bright June days that are gone ?

Of all those who had been amazed when Jethro Bass suddenly emerged from his retirement and appeared in the capital some months before, none were more thunderstruck than certain gentlemen who had been to Coniston repeatedly, but in vain, to urge him to make this very fight. The most important of these had been Mr. Balch, president of the " Down East " Road, and the representatives of two railroads of another state. They had at last offered Jethro fabulous sums to take charge of their armies in the field — sums, at least, that would seem fabulous to many people, and had seemed so to them. When they heard that the lion had roused and shaken himself and had unaccountably come forth of his own accord, they hastened to the state capital to renew their offers. Another shock, but of a different kind, was in store for them. Mr. Balch had not actually driven the pack-mules, laden with treasure, to the door of the Pelican House, where Jethro might see them from his window ; but he requested a private audience, and it was probably accidental that the end of his personal check-book protruded a little from his pocket. He was a big, coarse-grained man, Mr. Balch, who had once been a brakeman, and had risen by what is known as horse sense to the presidency of his road. There was a wonderful sunset beyond the Capitol, but Mr. Balch did not talk about the sunset, although Jethro was watching it from behind the curtains.

" If you are willing to undertake this fight against consolidation," said Mr. Balch, " we are ready to talk business with you."

" D-don't know what you're going to do," answered Jethro ; " I'm going to prevent consolidation, if I can."

" All right," said Balch, smiling. He regarded this reply as one of Jethro's delicate euphemisms. " We're prepared to give that same little retainer."

Jethro did not look up. Mr. Balch went to the table

and seized a pen and filled out a check for an amount that shall be nameless.

"I have made it payable to bearer, as usual," he said, and he handed it to Jethro.

Jethro took it, and absently tore it into little pieces, and threw the pieces on the floor. Mr. Balch watched him in consternation. He began to think the report that Jethro had reached his second childhood was true.

"What in Halifax are you doing, Bass?" he cried.

"W-want to stop this consolidation, don't you — want to stop it?"

"Certainly I do."

"G-goin' to do all you can to stop it — hain't you?"

"Certainly I am."

"I-I'll help you," said Jethro.

"Help us!" exclaimed Balch. "Great Scott, we want you to take charge of it."

"I-I'll do all I can, but I won't guarantee it — w-won't guarantee it," said Jethro.

"We don't ask you to guarantee it. If you'll do all you can, that's enough. You won't take a retainer?"

"W-won't take anything," said Jethro.

"You mean to say you don't want anything for your — for your time and your services if the bill is defeated?"

"T-that's about it, Ed. Little p-private matter with both of us. You don't want consolidation, and I don't. I hain't offered to give you a retainer — have I?"

"No," said the astounded Mr. Balch. He scratched his head and fingered the leaves of his check-book. The captains over the tens and the captains over the hundreds would want little retainers — and who was to pay these?

"How about the boys?" asked Mr. Balch.

"S-still got the same office in the depot — hain't you, Ed, — same office?"

"Yes."

"G-guess the boys hev b'en there before," said Jethro.

Mr. Balch went away, meditating upon those sayings, and took the train for Boston. If he had waked up of a fine morning to find himself at the head of some benevolent and charitable organization, instead of the "Down East" Railroad, he could not have been more astonished than he had been at the unaccountable change of heart of Jethro Bass. He did not know what to make of it, and told his colleagues so ; and at first they feared one of two things, — treachery or lunacy. But a little later a rumor reached Mr. Balch's ears that Jethro's hatred of Isaac D. Worthington was at the bottom of his reappearance in public life, although Jethro himself never mentioned Mr. Worthington's name. Jethro sat in the Throne Room, consulting, directing day after day, and when the Legislature assembled, "the boys" began to call at Mr. Balch's office. But Mr. Balch never again broached the subject of money to Jethro Bass.

We have to sing the song of sixpence for the last time in these pages ; and as it is an old song now, there will be no encores. If you can buy one member of the lower house for ten dollars, how many members can you buy for fifty ? It was no such problem in primary arithmetic that Mr. Balch and his associates had to solve — theirs was in higher mathematics, in permutations and combinations, and in least squares. No wonder the old campaigners speak with tears in their eyes of the days of that ever memorable summer. There were spoils to be picked up in the very streets richer than the sack of the thirty cities ; and as the session wore on it is affirmed by men still living that money rained down in the Capitol Park and elsewhere like manna from the skies, if you were one of a chosen band. If you were, all you had to do was to look in your vest pockets when you took your clothes off in the evening and extract enough legal tender to pay your bill at the Pelican for a week. Mr. Lovejoy having been overheard one day to make a remark concerning the diet of hogs, the next morning certain visitors to the capital were horrified to discover trails of corn leading from the Pelican House to their doorways. Men who had never seen a receiving teller opened bank accounts. No, it was not a problem in simple arithmetic, and Mr. Balch and Mr. Flint, and even Mr. Duncan and

Mr. Worthington, covered whole sheets with figures during the stifling days in July. Some men are so valuable that they can be bought twice, or even three times, and they make figuring complicated.

Jethro Bass did no calculating. He sat behind the curtains, and he must have kept the figures in his head.

The battle had closed in earnest, and for twelve long, sultry weeks it raged with unabated fierceness. Consolidation had a terror for the rural mind, and the state *Tribune* skilfully played its stream upon the constituents of those gentlemen who stood tamely at the Worthington hitching-posts, and the constituents flocked to the capital ; that able newspaper, too, found space to return, with interest, the attacks of Mr. Worthington's organ, the *Newcastle Guardian*. These amenities are much too personal to reproduce here, now that the smoke of battle has rolled away. An epic could be written upon the conflict, if there were space : Canto One, the first position carried triumphantly, though at some expense, by the Worthington forces, who elect the Speaker. That had been a crucial time before the town meetings, when Jethro abdicated. The Worthington Speaker goes ahead with his committees, and it is needless to say that Mr. Chauncey Weed is not made Chairman of the Committee on Corporations. As an offset to this, the Jethro forces gain on the extreme right, where the Honorable Peleg Hartington is made President of the Senate, etc.

For twelve hot weeks, with a public spirit which is worthy of the highest praise, the Committee sit in their shirt sleeves all day long and listen to arguments for and against consolidation; and ask learned questions that startle rural witnesses ; and smoke big Florizel cigars (a majority of them). Judge Abner Parkinson defends his bill, quoting from the Constitution and the Declaration of Independence and the Bible ; a celebrated lawyer from the capital riddles it, using the same authorities, and citing the *Federalist* and the Golden Rule in addition. The Committee sit open-minded, listening with laudable impartiality ; it does not become them to arrive at a hasty decision on a question of such magnitude. In the meantime the House passes an important bill dealing with the bounty on hedgehogs, and there are several card games going on in the cellar, where it is cool.

The governor of the state is a free lance, and may be seen any afternoon walking through the park, consorting with no one. He may be recognized even at a distance by his portly figure, his silk hat, and his dignified mien. Yes, it is an old and valued friend, the Honorable Alva Hopkins, patron of the drama, and sometimes he has a beautiful young woman (still unattached) by his side. He lives in a suite of rooms at the Pelican. It is a well-known fact (among Mr. Worthington's supporters) that the Honorable Alva promised in January, when Mr. Bass retired, to sign the Consolidation Bill, and that he suddenly became open-minded in March, and has remained open-minded ever since, listening gravely to arguments, and giving much study to the subject. He is an executive now, although it is the last year of his term, and of course he is never seen either in the Throne Room or the Railroad Room. And besides, he may become a senator.

August has come, and the forces are spent and panting, and neither side dares to risk the final charge. The reputation of Jethro Bass is at stake. Should he risk and lose, he must go back to Coniston a beaten man, subject to the contempt of his neighbors and his state. People do not know that he has nothing now to go back to, and that he cares nothing for contempt. As he sits in his window day after day he has only one thought and one wish,—to ruin Isaac D. Worthington. And he will do it if he can. Those who know — and among them is Mr. Balch himself — say that Jethro has never conducted a more masterly campaign than this, and that all the others have been mere childish trials of strength compared to it. So he sits there through those twelve weeks while the session slips by, while his opponents grumble, and while even his supporters, eager for the charge, complain. The truth is that in all the years of his activity he has never had such an antagonist as Mr. Flint. Victory hangs

2 k

in the balance, and a false move will throw it to either side.

Victory hangs now, to be explicit, upon two factors. The first and most immediate of these is a certain canny captain of many wars whose regiment is still at the disposal of either army — for a price, a regiment which has hitherto remained strictly neutral. And what a regiment it is! A block of river towns and a senator, and not a casualty since they marched boldly into camp twelve weeks ago. Mr. Balch is getting very much worried about this regiment, and beginning to doubt Jethro's judgment.

"I tell you, Bass," he said one evening, "if you allow him to run around loose much longer, we're lost, that's all there is to it!" (Mr. Balch referred to the captain in question.) "They'll buy up his block at his figure — see if they don't. They're getting desperate. Don't you think I'd better bid him in?"

"B-bid him in if you've a mind to, Ed."

"Look here, Jethro," said Mr. Balch, savagely biting off the end of a cigar, "I'm beginning to think you don't care a continental about this business. Which side are you on, anyway?" The heat and the length and the uncertainty of the struggle were telling on the nerves of the railroad president. "You sit there from morning till night and won't say anything; and now, when there's only one block out, you won't give the word to buy it."

"N-never told you to buy anything, did I — Ed?"

"No," answered Mr. Balch, "you haven't. I don't know what the devil's got into you."

"D-done all the payin' without consultin' me, hain't you, Ed?"

"Yes, I have. What are you driving at?"

"D-done it if I hadn't b'en here, wouldn't you?"

"Yes, and more too," said Mr. Balch.

"W-wouldn't make much difference to you if I wasn't here — would it?"

"Great Scott, Jethro, what do you mean?" cried the railroad president, in genuine alarm; "you're not going to pull out, are you?"

" W-wouldn't make much odds if I did — would it, Ed ? "

" The devil it wouldn't! " exclaimed Mr. Balch. " If you pulled out, we'd lose the North Country, and Peleg, and Gosport, and nobody can tell which way Alva Hopkins will swing. I guess you know what he'll do — you're so d—d secretive I can't tell whether you do or not. If you pulled out, they'd have their bill on Friday."

" H-hain't under any obligations to you, Ed — am I ? "

" No," said Mr. Balch, " but I don't see why you keep harping on that."

" J-just wanted to have it clear," said Jethro, and relapsed into silence.

There was a fireproof carpet on the Throne Room, and Mr. Balch flung down his cigar and stamped on it and went out. No wonder he could not understand Jethro's sudden scruples about money and obligations — about railroad money, that is. Jethro was spending some of his own, but not in the capital, and in a manner which was most effective. In short, at the very moment when Mr. Balch stamped on his cigar, Jethro had the victory in his hands — only he did not choose to say so. He had had a mysterious telegram that day from Harwich, signed by Chauncey Weed, and Mr. Weed himself appeared at the door of Number 7, fresh from his travels, shortly after Mr. Balch had gone out of it. Mr. Weed closed the door gently, and locked it, and sat down in a rocking chair close to Jethro and put his hand over his mouth. We cannot hear what Mr. Weed is saying. All is mystery here, and in order to preserve that mystery we shall delay for a little the few words which will explain Mr. Weed's successful mission.

Mr. Balch, angry and bewildered, descended into the rotunda, where he shortly heard two astounding pieces of news. The first was that the Honorable Heth Sutton had abandoned the Florizel cigars and had gone home to Clovelly. The second, that Mr. Bijah Bixby had resigned the claw-hammer and had ceased to open the packing cases in the Railroad Room. Consternation reigned in that room, so it was said (and this was true). Mr. Worthington and Mr. Duncan and Mr. Lovejoy were closeted there with Mr. Flint, and the door was locked and the transom shut, and smoke was coming out of the windows.

Yes, Mr. Bijah Bixby is the canny captain of whom Mr. Balch spoke : he it is who owns that block of river towns, intact, and the one senator. Impossible ! We have seen him opening the packing cases, we have seen him working for the Worthington faction for the last two years. Mr. Bixby was very willing to open boxes, and to make himself useful and agreeable; but it must be remembered that a good captain of mercenaries owes a sacred duty to his followers. At first Mr. Flint had thought he could count on Mr. Bixby ; after a while he made several unsuccessful attempts to talk business with him ; a particularly difficult thing to do, even for Mr. Flint, when Mr. Bixby did not wish to talk business. Mr. Balch had found it quite as difficult to entice Mr. Bixby away from the boxes and the Railroad Room. The weeks drifted on, until twelve went by, and then Mr. Bixby found himself, with his block of river towns and one senator, in the incomparable position of being the arbiter of the fate of the Consolidation Bill in the House and Senate. No wonder Mr. Balch wanted to buy the services of that famous regiment at any price !

But Mr. Bixby, for once in his life, had waited too long.

When Mr. Balch, rejoicing, but not a little indignant at not having been taken into confidence, ascended to the Throne Room after supper to question Jethro concerning the meaning of the things he had heard, he found Senator Peleg Hartington seated mournfully on the bed, talking at intervals, and Jethro listening.

"Come up and eat out of my hand," said the senator.

"Who ? " demanded Mr. Balch.

"Bije," answered the senator.

"Great Scott, do you mean to say you've got Bixby ? " exclaimed the railroad president. He felt as if he would like to shake the senator, who was so deliberate and mournful in his answers. "What did you pay him ? "

Mr. Hartington appeared shocked by the question.

"Guess Heth Sutton will settle with him," he said.

"Heth Sutton! Why the — why should Heth pay him?"

"Guess Heth'd like to make him a little present, under the circumstances. I was goin' through the barber shop," Mr. Hartington continued, speaking to Jethro and ignoring the railroad president, "and I heard somebody whisperin' my name. Sound came out of that little shampoo closet; went in there and found Bije. 'Peleg,' says he, right into my ear, 'tell Jethro it's all right — you understand. We want Heth to go back — break his heart if he didn't — you understand. If I'd knowed last winter Jethro meant business, I wouldn't hev' helped Gus Flint out. Tell Jethro he can have 'em — you know what I mean.' Bije waited a little mite too long," said the senator, who had given a very fair imitation of Mr. Bixby's nasal voice and manner.

"Well, I'm d—d!" ejaculated Mr. Balch, staring at Jethro. "How did you work it?"

"Sent Chauncey through the deestrict," said Mr. Hartington.

Mr. Chauncey Weed had, in truth, gone through a part of the congressional district of the Honorable Heth Sutton with a little leather bag. Mr. Weed had been able to do some of his work (with the little leather bag) in the capital itself. In this way Mr. Bixby's regiment, of which Mr. Sutton was the honorary colonel, had been attacked in the rear and routed. There was to be a congressional convention that autumn, and a large part of Mr. Sutton's district lay in the North Country, which, as we have seen, was loyal to Jethro to the back bone. The district, too, was largely rural, and therefore anti-consolidation, and the inability of the Worthington forces to get their bill through had made it apparent that Jethro Bass was as powerful as ever. Under these circumstances it had not been very difficult for a gentleman of Mr. Chauncey Weed's powers of persuasion to induce various lieutenants in the district to agree to send delegates to the

coming convention who would be conscientiously opposed
to Mr. Sutton's renomination: hence the departure from
the capital of Mr. Sutton; hence the generous offer of
Mr. Bixby to put his regiment at the disposal of Mr. Bass
— free of charge.

The second factor on which victory hung (we can use
the past tense now) was none other than his Excellency
Alva Hopkins, governor of the state. The bill would never
get to his Excellency now — so people said; would never
get beyond that committee who had listened so patiently
to the twelve weeks of argument. These were only
rumors, after all, for the rotunda never knows positively
what goes on in high circles; but the rotunda does
figuring, too, when at length the problem is reduced to
a simple equation, with Bijah Bixby as x. If it were
true that Bijah had gone over to Jethro Bass, the Consolidation Bill was dead.

CHAPTER XVIII

A BIOGRAPHICAL EPISODE: HITHERTO UNPUBLISHED

When Jethro Bass walked out of the hotel that evening men looked at him, and made way for him, but none spoke to him. There was something in his face that forbade speech. He was a great man once more — a greater man than ever; and he had, if the persistent rumors were true, accomplished an almost incomprehensible feat, even for Jethro Bass. There was another reason, too, why they stared at him. In all those twelve weeks of that most trying of all sessions he had not once gone into the street, and he had been less than ever common in the eyes of men. Twice a day he had descended to the dining room for a simple meal — that was all ; and fewer had gained entrance to Room Number 7 this session than ever before.

There is a river that flows by the capital, a wide and gentle river bordered by green meadows and fringed with willows; higher up, if you go far enough, a forest comes down to the water on the western side. Jethro walked through the hooded bridge, and up the eastern bank until he could see the forest like a black band between the orange sky and the orange river, and there he sat down upon a fallen log on the edge of the bank. But Jethro was thinking of another scene, — of a granite-ribbed pasture on Coniston Mountain that swings in limitless space, from either end of which a man may step off into eternity. William Wetherell, in one of his letters, had described that place as the Threshold of the Nameless Worlds, and so it had seemed to Jethro in the years of his desolation. He was thinking of it now, even as it had been in his mind that winter's evening when Cynthia had come to Coniston and had surprised him with that look of terrible loneliness on his face.

Yes, and he was thinking of Cynthia. When, indeed, had he not been thinking of her? How many times had he rehearsed the events in the tannery house — for they were the events of his life now. The triumphs over his opponents and enemies fell away, and the pride of power. Such had not been his achievements. She had loved him, and no man had reached a higher pinnacle than that.

Why he had forfeited that love for vengeance, he could not tell. The embers of a man's passions will suddenly burst into flame, and he will fiddle madly while the fire burns his soul. He had avenged her as well as himself; but had he avenged her, now that he held Isaac Worthington in his power? By crushing him, had he not added to her trouble and her sorrow? She had confessed that she loved Isaac Worthington's son, and was not he (Jethro) widening the breach between Cynthia and the son by crushing the father? Jethro had not thought of this. But he had thought of her, night and day, as he had sat in his room directing the battle. . Not a day had passed that he had not looked for a letter, hoping against hope. If she had written to him once, if she had come to him once, would he have desisted? He could not say — the fires of hatred had burned so fiercely, and still burned so fiercely, that he clenched his fists when it came over him that Isaac Worthington was at last in his power.

A white line above the forest was all that remained of the sunset when he rose up and took from his coat a silver locket and opened it and held it to the fading light. Presently he closed it again, and walked slowly along the river bank toward the little city twinkling on its hill. He crossed the hooded bridge and climbed the slope, stopping for a moment at a little stationery shop; he passed through the groups which were still loudly discussing this thing he had done, and gained his room and locked the door. Men came to it and knocked and got no answer. The room was in darkness, and the night breeze stirred among the trees in the park and blew in at the window.

At last Jethro got up and lighted the gas and paused at the centre table. He was to violate more than one principle of his life that night, though not without a struggle; and he sat for a long while looking at the blank paper before him. Then he wrote, and sealed the letter — which contained three lines — and pulled the bell cord. The call was answered by a messenger who had been for many years in the service of the Pelican House, and who knew many secrets of the gods. The man actually grew pale when he saw the address on the envelope which was put in his hand and read the denomination of the crisp note under it that was the price of silence.

"F-find the gentleman and give it to him yourself. Er — John?"

"Yes, Mr. Bass?"

"If you don't find him, bring it back."

When the man had gone, Jethro turned down the gas and went again to his chair by the window. For a while voices came up to him from the street, but at length the groups dispersed, one by one, and a distant clock boomed out eleven solemn strokes. Twice the clock struck again, at the half-hour and midnight, and the noises in the house — the banging of doors and the jangling of keys and the hurrying of feet in the corridors — were hushed. Jethro took no thought of these or of time, and sat gazing at the stars in the depths of the sky above the capital dome until a shadow emerged from the black mass of the trees opposite and crossed the street. In a few minutes there were footsteps in the corridor, — stealthy footsteps — and a knock on the door. Jethro got up and opened it, and closed it again and locked it. Then he turned up the gas.

"S-sit down," he said, and nodded his head toward the chair by the table.

Isaac Worthington laid his silk hat on the table, and sat down. He looked very haggard and worn in that light, very unlike the first citizen who had entered Brampton in triumph on his return from the West not many months before. The long strain of a long fight, in which he had risked much for which he had labored a life to gain,

had told on him, and there were crow's-feet at the corners
of his eyes, and dark circles under them. Isaac Worthington had never lost before, and to destroy the fruits of
such a man's ambition is to destroy the man. He was not
as young as he had once been. But now, in the very hour
of defeat, hope had rekindled the fire in the eyes and
brought back the peculiar, tight-lipped, mocking smile to
the mouth. An hour ago, when he had been pacing Alexander Duncan's library, the eyes and the mouth had been
different.

Long habit asserts itself at the strangest moments.
Jethro Bass took his seat by the window, and remained
silent. The clock tolled the half-hour after midnight.

"You wanted to see me," said Mr. Worthington, finally.
Jethro nodded, almost imperceptibly.

"I suppose," said Mr. Worthington, slowly, "I suppose
you are ready to sell out." He found it a little difficult
to control his voice.

"Yes," answered Jethro, "r-ready to sell out."

Mr. Worthington was somewhat taken aback by this
simple admission. He glanced at Jethro sitting motionless
by the window, and in his heart he feared him: he had
come into that room when the gas was low, afraid. Although he would not confess it to himself, he had been
in fear of Jethro Bass all his life, and his fear had been
greater than ever since the March day when Jethro had
left Coniston. And could he have known, now, the fires
of hatred burning in Jethro's breast, Isaac Worthington
would have been in terror indeed.

"What have you got to sell?" he demanded sharply.

"G-guess you know, or you wouldn't have come here."

"What proof have I that you have it to sell?"

Jethro looked at him for an instant.

"M-my word," he said.

Isaac Worthington was silent for a while: he was striving to calm himself, for an indefinable something had
shaken him. The strange stillness of the hour and the
stranger atmosphere which seemed to surround this transaction filled him with a nameless dread. The man in the

window had been his lifelong enemy: more than this, Jethro Bass was not like ordinary men — his ways were enshrouded in mystery, and when he struck, he struck hard. There grew upon Isaac Worthington a sense that this midnight hour was in some way to be the culmination of the long years of hatred between them.

He believed Jethro: he would have believed him even if Mr. Flint had not informed him that afternoon that he was beaten, and bitterly he wished he had taken Mr. Flint's advice many months before. Denunciation sprang to his lips which he dared not utter. He was beaten, and he must pay — the pound of flesh. Isaac Worthington almost thought it would be a pound of flesh.

"How much do you want?" he said.

Again Jethro looked at him.

"B-biggest price you can pay," he answered.

"You must have made up your mind what you want. You've had time enough."

"H-have made up my mind," said Jethro.

"Make your demand," said Mr. Worthington, "and I'll give you my answer."

"B-biggest price you can pay," said Jethro, again.

Mr. Worthington's nerves could stand it no longer.

"Look here," he cried, rising in his chair, "if you've brought me here to trifle with me, you've made a mistake. It's your business to get control of things that belong to other people, and sell them out. I am here to buy. Nothing but necessity brings me here, and nothing but necessity will keep me here a moment longer than I have to stay to finish this abominable affair. I am ready to pay you twenty thousand dollars the day that bill becomes a law."

This time Jethro did not look at him.

"P-pay me now," he said.

"I will pay you the day the bill becomes a law. Then I shall know where I stand."

Jethro did not answer this ultimatum in any manner, but remained perfectly still looking out of the window. Mr. Worthington glanced at him, twice, and got his fingers on the brim of his hat, but he did not pick it up. He

stood so for a while, knowing full well that if he went
out of that room his chance was gone. Consolidation
might come in other years, but he, Isaac Worthington,
would not be a factor in it.

" You don't want a check, do you? " he said at last.

" No — d-don't want a check."

" What in God's name do you want? I haven't got
twenty thousand dollars in currency in my pocket."

" Sit down, Isaac Worthington," said Jethro.

Mr. Worthington sat down — out of sheer astonishment,
perhaps.

" W-want the consolidation — don't you? Want it bad
— don't you? "

Mr. Worthington did not answer. Jethro stood over
him now, looking down at him from the other side of the
narrow table.

" Know Cynthy Wetherell? " he said.

Then Isaac Worthington understood that his premoni-
tions had been real. The pound of flesh was to be demanded, but strangely enough, he did not yet comprehend
the nature of it.

" I know that there is such a person," he answered, for
his pride would not permit him to say more.

" W-what do you know about her? "

Isaac Worthington was bitterly angry — the more so
because he was helpless, and could not question Jethro's
right to ask. What did he know about her? Nothing,
except that she had intrigued to marry his son. Bob's
letter had described her, to be sure, but he could not be
expected to believe that: and he had not heard Miss
Lucretia Penniman's speech. And yet he could not tell
Jethro that he knew nothing about her, for he was shrewd
enough to perceive the drift of the next question.

" Kn-know anything against her? " said Jethro.

Mr. Worthington leaned back in his chair.

" I can't see what Miss Wetherell has to do with the
present occasion," he replied.

" H-had her dismissed by the prudential committee —
had her dismissed — didn't you? "

" They chose to act as they saw fit."

" T-told Levi Dodd to dismiss her — didn't you ? "

That was a matter of common knowledge in Brampton, having leaked out through Jonathan Hill.

" I must decline to discuss this," said Mr. Worthington.

" W-wouldn't if I was you."

" What do you mean ? "

" What I say. T-told Levi Dodd to dismiss her, didn't you ? "

" Yes, I did." Isaac Worthington had lost in self-esteem by not saying so before.

" Why ? Wahn't she honest ? Wahn't she capable ? Wahn't she a lady ? "

" I can't say that I know anything against Miss Wetherell's character, if that's what you mean."

" F-fit to teach — wahn't she — fit to teach ? "

" I believe she has since qualified before Mr. Errol."

" Fit to teach — wahn't fit to marry your son — was she ? "

Isaac Worthington clutched the table and started from his chair. He grew white to his lips with anger, and yet he knew that he must control himself.

" Mr. Bass," he said, " you have something to sell, and I have something to buy — if the price is not ruinous. Let us confine ourselves to that. My affairs and my son's affairs are neither here nor there. I ask you again, how much do you want for this Consolidation Bill ? "

" N-no money will buy it."

" What ! "

" C-consent to this marriage, c-consent to this marriage."

There was yet room for Isaac Worthington to be amazed, and for a while he stared up at Jethro, speechless.

" Is that your price ? " he asked at last.

" Th-that's my price," said Jethro.

Isaac Worthington got up and went to the window and stood looking out above the black mass of trees at the dome outlined against the star-flecked sky. At first his anger choked him, and he could not think ; he had just enough reason left not to walk out of the door. But presently habit asserted itself in him, too, and he began to reflect and calculate in spite of his anger. It is strange that memory plays so small a part in such a man. Before he allowed his mind to dwell on the fearful price, he thought of his ambitions gratified; and yet he did not think then of the woman to whom he had once confided those ambitions — the woman who was the girl's mother. Perhaps Jethro was thinking of her.

It may have been — I know not — that Isaac Worthington wondered at this revelation of the character of Jethro Bass, for it was a revelation. For this girl's sake Jethro was willing to forego his revenge, was willing at the end of his days to allow the world to believe that he had sold out to his enemy, or that he had been defeated by him.

But when he thought of the marriage, Isaac Worthington ground his teeth. A certain sentiment which we may call pride was so strong in him that he felt ready to make almost any sacrifice to prevent it. To hinder it he had quarrelled with his son, and driven him away, and threatened disinheritance. The price was indeed heavy — the heaviest he could pay. But the alternative — was not that heavier? To relinquish his dream of power, to sink for a while into a crippled state; for he had spent large sums, and one of those periodical depressions had come in the business of the mills, and those Western investments were not looking so bright now.

So, with his hands opening and closing in front of him, Isaac Worthington fought out his battle. A terrible war, that, between ambition and pride — a war to the knife. The issue may yet have been undecided when he turned round to Jethro with a sneer which he could not resist.

"Why doesn't she marry him without my consent?"

In a moment Mr. Worthington knew he had gone too far. A certain kind of an eye is an incomparable weapon, and armed men have been cowed by those who possess it, though otherwise defenceless. Jethro Bass had that kind of an eye.

"G-guess you wouldn't understand if I was to tell you," he said.

Mr. Worthington walked to the window again, perhaps to compose himself, and then came back again.

"Your proposition is," he said at length, "that if I give my consent to this marriage, we are to have Bixby and the governor, and the Consolidation Bill will become a law. Is that it?"

"Th-that's it," said Jethro, taking his accustomed seat.

"And this consent is to be given when the bill becomes a law?"

"Given now. T-to-night."

Mr. Worthington took another turn as far as the door, and suddenly came and stood before Jethro.

"Well, I consent."

Jethro nodded toward the table.

"Er — pen and paper there," he said.

"What do you want me to do?" demanded Mr. Worthington.

"W-write to Bob — write to Cynthy. Nice letters."

"This is carrying matters with too high a hand, Mr. Bass. I will write the letters to-morrow morning." It was intolerable that he, the first citizen of Brampton, should have to submit to such humiliation.

"Write 'em now. W-want to see 'em."

"But if I give you my word they will be written and sent to you to-morrow afternoon?"

"T-too late," said Jethro; "sit down and write 'em now."

Mr. Worthington went irresolutely to the table, stood for a minute, and dropped suddenly into the chair there. He would have given anything (except the realization of his ambitions) to have marched out of the room and to have slammed the door behind him. The letter paper and envelopes which Jethro had bought stood in a little pile, and Mr. Worthington picked up the pen. The clock struck two as he wrote the date, as though to remind him that he had written it wrong. If Flint could see him now! Would Flint guess? Would anybody guess? He stared at the white paper, and his rage came on again like a gust of wind, and he felt that he would rather beg in the

streets than write such a thing. And yet — and yet he
sat there. Surely Jethro Bass must have known that he
could have taken no more exquisite vengeance than this,
to compel a man — and such a man — to sit down in the
white heat of passion and write two letters of forgiveness!
Jethro sat by the window, to all appearances oblivious to
the tortures of his victim.

He who has tried to write a note — the simplest note —
when his mind was harassed, will understand something of
Isaac Worthington's sensations. He would no sooner get
an inkling of what his opening sentence was to be than
the flames of his anger would rise and sweep it away.
He could not even decide which letter he was to write
first: to his son, who had defied him and who (the father
knew in his heart) contemned him? or to the school-
teacher, who was responsible for all his misery; who — Mr.
Worthington believed — had taken advantage of his son's
youth by feminine wiles of no mean order so as to gain
possession of him. I can almost bring myself to pity the
first citizen of Brampton as he sits there with his pen
poised over the paper, and his enemy waiting to read
those tender epistles of forgiveness which he has yet to
write. The clock has almost got round to the half-hour
again, and there is only the date — and a wrong one at
that.

" My dear Miss Wetherell, — Circumstances (over which
I have no control?) " — ought he not to call her Cynthia?
He has to make the letter credible in the eyes of the cen-
sor who sits by the window. " My dear Miss Wetherell, —
I have come to the conclusion " — two sheets torn up, or
thrust into Mr. Worthington's pocket. By this time
words have begun to have a colorless look. " My dear
Miss Wetherell, — Having become convinced of the sincere attachment which my son Robert has for you, I am
writing him to-night to give my full consent to his marriage. He has given me to understand that you have
hitherto persistently refused to accept him because I have
withheld that consent, and I take this opportunity of
expressing my admiration of this praiseworthy resolution

on your part." (If this be irony, it is sublime! Perhaps Isaac Worthington has a little of the artist in him, and now that he is in the heat of creation has forgotten the circumstances under which he is composing.) "My son's happiness and career in life are of such moment to me that, until the present, I could not give my sanction to what I at first regarded as a youthful fancy. Now that my son, for your sake, has shown his determination and ability to make his own way in the world" (Isaac Worthington was not a little proud of this) "I have determined that it is wise to withdraw my opposition, and to recall Robert to his proper place, which is near me. I am sure that my feelings in this matter will be clear to you, and that you will look with indulgence upon any acts of mine which sprang from a natural solicitation for the welfare and happiness of my only child. I shall be in Brampton in a day or two, and I shall at once give myself the pleasure of calling on you. Sincerely yours, Isaac D. Worthington."

Perhaps a little formal and pompous for some people, but an admirable and conciliatory letter for the first citizen of Brampton. Written under such trying circumstances, with I know not how many erasures and false starts, it is little short of a marvel in art: neither too much said, nor too little, for a relenting parent of Mr. Worthington's character, and I doubt whether Talleyrand or Napoleon or even Machiavelli himself could have surpassed it. The second letter, now that Mr. Worthington had got into the swing, was more easily written. "My dear Robert" (it said), — "I have made up my mind to give my consent to your marriage to Miss Wetherell, and I am ready to welcome you home, where I trust I shall see you shortly. I have not been unimpressed by the determined manner in which you have gone to work for yourself, but I believe that your place is in Brampton, where I trust you will show the same energy in learning to succeed me in the business which I have founded there as you have exhibited in Mr. Broke's works. Affectionately, your Father."

A very creditable and handsome letter for a forgiving father. When Mr. Worthington had finished it, and had

2 L

addressed both the envelopes, his shame and vexation had, curious to relate, very considerably abated. Not to go too deeply into the somewhat contradictory mental and cardiac processes of Mr. Worthington, he had somehow tricked himself by that magic exercise of wielding his pen into thinking that he was doing a noble and generous action : into believing that in the course of a very few days — or weeks, at the most — he would have recalled his erring son and have given Cynthia his blessing. He would, he told himself, have been forced eventually to yield when that paragon of inflexibility, Bob, dictated terms to him at the head of the locomotive works. Better let the generosity be on his (Mr. Worthington's) side. At all events, victory had never been bought more cheaply. Humiliation, in Mr. Worthington's eyes, had an element of publicity in it, and this episode had had none of that element; and Jethro Bass, moreover, was a highwayman who had held a pistol to his head. In such logical manner he gradually bolstered up again his habitual poise and dignity. Next week, at the latest, men would point to him as the head of the largest railroad interests in the state.

He pushed back his chair, and rose, merely indicating the result of his labors by a wave of his hand. And he stood in the window as Jethro Bass got up and went to the table. I would that I had a pen able to describe Jethro's sensations when he read them. Unfortunately, he is a man with few facial expressions. But I believe that he was artist enough himself to appreciate the perfections of the first citizen's efforts. After a much longer interval than was necessary for their perusal, Mr. Worthington turned.

"G-guess they'll do," said Jethro, as he folded them up. He was too generous not to indulge, for once, in a little well-deserved praise. "Hain't underdone it, and hain't overdone it a mite — hev you? M-man of resource. Callate you couldn't hev beat that if you was to take a week to it."

"I think it only fair to tell you," said Mr. Worthington, picking up his silk hat, "that in those letters I have merely anticipated a very little my intentions in the matter. My son having proved his earnestness, I was about to consent to the marriage of my own accord."

"G-goin' to do it anyway — was you?"

"I had so determined."

"A-always thought you was high-minded," said Jethro.

Mr. Worthington was on the point of giving a tart reply to this, but restrained himself.

"Then I may look upon the matter as settled?" he said. "The Consolidation Bill is to become a law?"

"Yes," said Jethro, "you'll get your bill." Mr. Worthington had got his hand on the knob of the door when Jethro stopped him with a word. He had no facial expressions, but he had an eye, as we have seen — an eye that for the second time appeared terrible to his visitor. "Isaac Worthington," he said, "a-act up to it. No trickery — or look out — look out."

Then, the incident being closed so far as he was concerned, Jethro went back to his chair by the window, but it is to be recorded that Isaac Worthington did not answer him immediately. Then he said : —

"You seem to forget that you are talking to a gentleman."

"That's so," answered Jethro, "so you be."

He sat where he was long after the sky had whitened and the stars had changed from gold to silver and gone out, and the sunlight had begun to glance upon the green leaves of the park. Perhaps he was thinking of the life he had lived, which was spent now : of the men he had ruled, of the victories he had gained from that place which would know him no more. He had won the last and the greatest of his victories there, compared to which the others had indeed been as vanities. Perhaps he looked back over the highway of his life and thought of the woman whom he had loved, and wondered what it had been if she had trod it by his side. Who will judge him? He had been what he had been; and as the Era was, so was he. Verily, one generation passeth away, and another generation cometh.

*   *   *   *   *   *   *

When Mr. Isaac Worthington arrived at Mr. Duncan's house, where he was staying, at three o'clock in the morning, he saw to his surprise light from the library windows lying in bars across the lawn under the trees.   He found Mr. Duncan in that room with Somers, his son, who had just returned from a seaside place, and they were discussing a very grave event.   Miss Janet Duncan had that day eloped with a gentleman who — to judge from the photograph Somers held — was both handsome and romantic-looking.   He had long hair and burning eyes, and a title not to be then verified, and he owned a castle near some place on the peninsula of Italy not on the map.

CHAPTER XIX

WE are back in Brampton, owning, as we do, an annual pass over the Truro Railroad. Cynthia has been there all the summer, and as it is now the first of September, her school has begun again. I do not by any means intend to imply that Brampton is not a pleasant place to spend the summer: the number of its annual visitors is a refutation of that; but to Cynthia the season had been one of great unhappiness. Several times Lem Hallowell had stopped the stage in front of Ephraim's house to beg her to go to Coniston, and Mr. Satterlee had come himself; but she could not have borne to be there without Jethro. Nor would she go to Boston, though urged by Miss Lucretia; and Mrs. Merrill and the girls had implored her to join them at a seaside place on the Cape.

Cynthia had made a little garden behind Ephraim's house, and she spent the summer there with her flowers and her books, many of which Lem had fetched from Coniston. Ephraim loved to sit there of an evening and smoke his pipe and chat with Ezra Graves and the neighbors who dropped in. Among these were Mr. Gamaliel Ives, who talked literature with Cynthia; and Lucy Baird, his wife, who had taken Cynthia under her wing. I wish I had time to write about Lucy Baird. And Mr. Jonathan Hill came — his mortgage not having been foreclosed, after all. When Cynthia was alone with Ephraim she often read to him, — generally from books of a martial flavor, — and listened with an admirable hypocrisy to certain narratives which he was in the habit of telling.

They never spoke of Jethro. Ephraim was not a casuist,

and his sense of right and wrong came largely through his
affections.   It is safe to say that he never made an analysis
of the sorrow which he knew was afflicting the girl, but he
had had a general and most sympathetic understanding of
it ever since the time when Jethro had gone back to the capital; and Ephraim never brought home his *Guardian* or
his *Clarion* now, but read them at the office, that their
contents might not disturb her.

No wonder that Cynthia was unhappy.   The letters
came, almost every day, with the postmark of the town in
New Jersey where Mr. Broke's locomotive works were;
and she answered them now (but oh, how scrupulously!),
though not every day.   If the waters of love rose up
through the grains of sand, it was, at least, not Cynthia's
fault.   Hers were the letters of a friend.   She was reading such and such a book — had he read it?   And he
must not work too hard.   How could her letters be otherwise when Jethro Bass, her benefactor, was at the capital
working to defeat and perhaps to ruin Bob's father? when
Bob's father had insulted and persecuted her?   She ought
not to have written at all; but the lapses of such a heroine are very rare, and very dear.

Yes, Cynthia's life was very bitter that summer, with
but little hope on the horizon of it.   Her thoughts were
divided between Bob and Jethro.   Many a night she lay
awake resolving to write to Jethro, even to go to him, but
when morning came she could not bring herself to do so.
I do not think it was because she feared that he might
believe her appeal would be made in behalf of Bob's father.
Knowing Jethro as she did, she felt that it would be useless, and she could not bear to make it in vain; if the
memory of that evening in the tannery shed would not
serve, nothing would serve.   And again — he had gone to
avenge her.

It was inevitable that she should hear tidings from the
capital.   Isaac Worthington's own town was ringing with
it.   And as week after week of that interminable session
went by, the conviction slowly grew upon Brampton that
its first citizen had been beaten by Jethro Bass.   Some-

thing of Mr. Worthington's affairs was known: the mills, for instance, were not being run to their full capacity. And then had come the definite news that Mr. Worthington was beaten, a local representative having arrived straight from the rotunda. Cynthia overheard Lem Hallowell telling it to Ephraim, and she could not for the life of her help rejoicing, though she despised herself for it. Isaac Worthington was humbled now, and Jethro had humbled him to avenge her. Despite her grief over his return to that life, there was something to compel her awe and admiration in the way he had risen and done this thing after men had fallen from him. Her mother had had something of these same feelings, without knowing why.

People who had nothing but praise for him before were saying hard things about Isaac Worthington that night. When the baron is defeated, the serfs come out of their holes in the castle rock and fling their curses across the moat. Cynthia slept but little, and was glad when the day came to take her to her scholars, to ease her mind of the thoughts which tortured it.

And then, when she stopped at the post-office to speak to Ephraim on her way homeward in the afternoon, she heard men talking behind the partition, and she stood, as one stricken, listening beside the window. Other tidings had come in the shape of a telegram. The first rumor had been false. Brampton had not yet received the details, but the Consolidation Bill had gone into the House that morning, and would be a law before the week was out. A part of it was incomprehensible to Cynthia, but so much she had understood. She did not wait to speak to Ephraim, and she was going out again when a man rushed past her and through the partition door. Cynthia paused instinctively, for she recognized him as one of the frequenters of the station and a bearer of news.

"Jethro's come home, boys," he shouted; "come in on the four o'clock, and went right off to Coniston. Guess he's done for, this time, for certain. Looks it. By Godfrey, he looks eighty! Callate his day's over, from the way the boys talked on the train."

Cynthia lingered to hear no more, and went out, dazed, into the September sunshine. Jethro beaten, and broken, and gone to Coniston. Resolution came to her as she walked. Arriving home, she wrote a little note and left it on the table for Ephraim; and going out again, ran by the back lane to Mr. Sherman's livery stable behind the Brampton House, and in half an hour was driving along that familiar road to Coniston, alone; for she had often driven Jethro's horses, and knew every turn of the way. And as she gazed at the purple mountain through the haze and drank in the sweet scents of the year's fulness, she was strangely happy. There was the village green in the cool evening light, and the flagstaff with its tip silvered by the departing sun. She waved to Rias and Lem and Moses at the store, but she drove on to the tannery house, and hitched the horse at the rough granite post, and went in, and through the house, softly, to the kitchen.

Jethro was standing in the doorway, and did not turn. He may have thought she was Millicent Skinner. Cynthia could see his face. It was older, indeed, and lined and worn, but that fearful look of desolation which she had once surprised upon it, and which she in that instant feared to see, was not there. Jethro's soul was at peace, though Cynthia could not understand why it was so. She stole to him and flung her arms about his neck, and with a cry he seized her and held her against him for I know not how long. Had it been possible to have held her there always, he would never have let her go. At last he looked down into her tear-wet face, into her eyes that were shining with tears.

"D-done wrong, Cynthy."

Cynthia did not answer that, for she remembered how she, too, had exulted when she had believed him to have accomplished Isaac Worthington's downfall. Now that he had failed, and she was in his arms, it was not for her to judge — only to rejoice.

"Didn't look for you to come back — didn't expect it."

"Uncle Jethro!" she faltered. Love for her had made him go, and she would not say that, either.

" D-don't hate me, Cynthy — don't hate me?"

She shook her head.

" Love me — a little?"

She reached up her hands and brushed back his hair, tenderly, from his forehead. Such — a loving gesture — was her answer.

" You are going to stay here always, now," she said, in a low voice, " you are never going away again."

"G-goin' to stay always," he answered. Perhaps he was thinking of the hillside clearing in the forest — who knows! " You'll come — sometime, Cynthy — sometime?"

" I'll come every Saturday and Sunday, Uncle Jethro," she said, smiling up at him. " Saturday is only two days away, now. I can hardly wait."

" Y-you'll come sometime?"

"Uncle Jethro, do you think I'll be away from you, except — except when I have to?"

" C-come and read to me — won't you — come and read?"

" Of course I will!"

" C-call to mind the first book you read to me, Cynthy?"

" It was 'Robinson Crusoe,'" she said.

"'R-Robinson Crusoe.' Often thought of that book. Know some of it by heart. R-read it again, sometime, Cynthy?"

She looked up at him a little anxiously. His eyes were on the great hill opposite, across Coniston Water.

" I will, indeed, Uncle Jethro, if we can find it," she answered.

" Guess I can find it," said Jethro. " R-remember when you saw him makin' a ship?"

"Yes," said Cynthia, " and I had my feet in the pool."

The book had made a profound impression upon Jethro, partly because Cynthia had first read it to him, and partly for another reason. The isolation of Crusoe, depicted by Defoe's genius, had been comparable to his own isolation, and he had pondered upon it much of late. Yes, and upon a certain part of another book which he had read earlier in life: Napoleon had ended his days on St. Helena.

They walked out under the trees to the brookside and

stood listening to the tinkling of the cowbells in the wood-lot beyond. The light faded early on these September evenings, and the smoky mist had begun to rise from the water when they turned back again. The kitchen windows were already growing yellow, and through them the faithful Millicent could be seen bustling about in her preparations for supper. But Cynthia, having accomplished her errand, would not go in. She could not have borne to have any one drive back with her to Brampton then, and she must not be late upon the road.

"I will come Friday evening, Uncle Jethro," she said, as she kissed him and gave one last, lingering look at his face. Had it been possible, she would not have left him, and on her way to Brampton through the gathering darkness she mused anxiously upon that strange calmness he had shown after defeat.

She drove her horse on to the floor of Mr. Sherman's stable, that gentleman himself gallantly assisting her to alight, and walked homeward through the lane. Ephraim had not yet returned from the post-office, which did not close until eight, and Cynthia smiled when she saw the utensils of his cooking-kit strewn on the hearth. In her absence he invariably unpacked and used it, and of course Cynthia at once set herself to cleaning and packing it again. After that she got her own supper — a very simple affair — and was putting the sitting room to rights when Ephraim came thumping in.

"Well, I swan!" he exclaimed when he saw her. "I didn't look for you to come back so soon, Cynthy. Put up the kit — hev you?" He stood in front of the fireplace staring with apparent interest at the place where the kit had been, and added in a voice which he strove to make quite casual, "How be Jethro?"

"He looks older, Cousin Eph," she answered, after a pause, "and I think he is very tired. But he seems — he seems more tranquil and contented than I hoped to find him."

"I want to know," said Ephraim. "I am glad to hear it. Glad you went up, Cynthy — you done right to go.

I'd have gone with you, if you'd only told me. I'll git a chance to go up Sunday."

There was an air of repressed excitement about the veteran which did not escape Cynthia. He held two letters in his hand, and, being a postmaster, he knew the handwriting on both. One had come from that place in New Jersey, and drew no comment. But the other! That one had been postmarked at the capital, and as he had sat at his counter at the post-office waiting for closing time he had turned it over and over with many ejaculations and futile guesses. Past master of dissimulation that he was, he had made up his mind — if he should find Cynthia at home — to lay the letters indifferently on the table and walk into his bedroom. This campaign he now proceeded to carry out.

Cynthia smiled again when he was gone, and shook her head and picked up the letters. Bob's was uppermost and she read that first, without a thought of the other one. And she smiled as she read — for Bob had had a promotion. He was not yet at the head of the locomotive works, he hastened to add, for fear that Cynthia might think that Mr. Broke had resigned the presidency in his favor; and Cynthia never failed to laugh at these little facetious asides. He was now earning the princely sum of ninety dollars a month — not enough to marry on, alas! On Saturday nights he and Percy Broke scrubbed as much as possible of the grime from their hands and faces and went to spend Sunday at Elberon, the Broke place on the Hudson; from whence Miss Sally Broke, if she happened to be at home, always sent Cynthia her love. As Cynthia is still a heroine, I shall not describe how she felt about Sally Broke's love. There was plenty of Bob's own in the letter. Cynthia would not have blamed him if he had fallen in love with Miss Broke. It seemed to her little short of miraculous that, amidst such surroundings, he could be true to her.

After a period which was no briefer than that usually occupied by Bob's letters, Cynthia took the other one from her lap, and stared at it in much perplexity before

she tore it open. We have seen its contents over Mr.
Worthington's shoulder, and our hearts will not stop
beating — as Cynthia's did. She read it twice before the
full meaning of it came to her, and after that she could
not well mistake it, — the language being so admirable
in every way. She sat very still for a long while, and
presently she heard Ephraim go out. But Cynthia did
not move. Mr. Worthington relented and Bob recalled!
The vista of happiness suddenly opened up, widened and
widened until it was too bright for Cynthia's vision, and
she would compel her mind to dwell on another prospect, — that of the father and son reconciled. Although
her temples throbbed, she tried to analyze the letter.
It implied that Mr. Worthington had allowed Bob to
remain away on a sort of probation; it implied that it had
been dictated by a strong paternal love mingled with a
strong paternal justice. And then there was the appeal
to her : " You will look with indulgence upon any acts
of mine which sprang from a natural solicitation for the
welfare and happiness of my only child." A terrible insight
is theirs to whom it is given to love as Cynthia loved.

Suddenly there came a knock which frightened her, for
her mind was running on swiftly from point to point: had,
indeed, flown as far as Coniston by now, and she was thinking of that strange look of peace on Jethro's face which
had troubled her. One letter she thrust into her dress,
but the other she laid aside, and her knees trembled under
her as she rose and went into the entry and raised the
latch and opened the door. There was a moon, and the
figure in the frock coat and the silk hat was the one which
she expected to see. The silk hat came off very promptly.

"I hope I am not disturbing you, Miss Wetherell," said
the owner of it.

" No," answered Cynthia, faintly.

" May I come in ? "

Cynthia held open the door a little wider, and Mr.
Worthington walked in. He seemed very majestic and
out of place in the little house which Gabriel Post had
built, and he carried into it some of the atmosphere of the

walnut and high ceilings of his own mansion. His manner of laying his hat, bottom up, on the table, and of unbuttoning his coat, subtly indicated the honor which he was conferring upon the place. And he eyed Cynthia, standing before him in the lamplight, with a modification of the hawklike look which was meant to be at once condescending and conciliatory. He did not imprint a kiss upon her brow, as some prospective fathers-in-law would have done. But his eyes, perhaps involuntarily, paid a tribute to her personal appearance which heightened her color. She might not, after all, be such a discredit to the Worthington family.

" Won't you sit down ? " she asked.

" Thank you, Cynthia," he said; " I hope I may now be allowed to call you Cynthia ? "

She did not answer him, but sat down herself, and he followed her example, with his eyes still upon her.

" You have doubtless received my letter," began Mr. Worthington. " I only arrived in Brampton an hour ago, but I thought it best to come to you at once, under the circumstances."

" Yes," replied Cynthia, " I received the letter."

" I am glad," said Mr. Worthington. He was beginning to be a little taken aback by her calmness and her apparent absence of joy. It was scarcely the way in which a school-teacher should receive the advances of the first citizen, come to give a gracious consent to her marriage with his son. Had he known it, Cynthia was anything but calm. " I am glad," he said, " because I took pains to explain the exact situation in that letter, and to set forth my own sentiments. I hope you understood them."

" Yes, I understood them," said Cynthia, in a low tone.

This was enigmatical, to say the least. But Mr. Worthington had come with such praiseworthy intentions that he was disposed to believe that the girl was overwhelmed by the good fortune which had suddenly overtaken her. He was therefore disposed to be a little conciliatory.

" My conduct may have appeared harsh to you," he continued. " I will not deny that I opposed the matter at first.

Robert was still in college, and he has a generous, impressionable nature which he inherits from his poor mother — the kind of nature likely to commit a rash act which would ruin his career. I have since become convinced that he has — ahem — inherited likewise a determination of purpose and an ability to get on in the world which I confess I had underestimated. My friend, Mr. Broke, has written me a letter about him, and tells me that he has already promoted him."

"Yes," said Cynthia.

"You hear from him?" inquired Mr. Worthington, giving her a quick glance.

"Yes," said Cynthia, her color rising a little.

"And yet," said Mr. Worthington, slowly, "I have been under the impression that you have persistently refused to marry him."

"That is true," she answered.

"I cannot refrain from complimenting you, Cynthia, upon such rare conduct," said he. "You will be glad to know that it has contributed more than anything else toward my estimation of your character, and has strengthened me in my resolution that I am now doing right. It may be difficult for you to understand a father's feelings. The complete separation from my only son was telling on me severely, and I could not forget that you were the cause of that separation. I knew nothing about you, except — " He hesitated, for she had turned to him.

"Except what?" she asked.

Mr. Worthington coughed. Mr. Flint had told him, that very morning, of her separation from Jethro, and of the reasons which people believed had caused it. Unfortunately, we have not time to go into that conversation with Mr. Flint, who had given a very good account of Cynthia indeed. After all (Mr. Worthington reflected), he had consented to the marriage, and there was no use in bringing Jethro's name into the conversation. Jethro would be forgotten soon.

"I will not deny to you that I had other plans for my son," he said. "I had hoped that he would marry a daughter of a friend of mine. You must be a little indulgent with parents, Cynthia," he added with a little smile, "we have our castles in the air, too. Sometimes, as in this case, by a wise provision of providence they go astray. I suppose you have heard of Miss Duncan's marriage."

"No," said Cynthia.

"She ran off with a worthless Italian nobleman. I believe, on the whole," he said, with what was an extreme complaisance for the first citizen, "that I have reason to congratulate myself upon Robert's choice. I have made inquiries about you, and I find that I have had the pleasure of knowing your mother, whom I respected very much. And your father, I understand, came of very good people, and was forced by circumstances to adopt the means of livelihood he did. My attention has been called to the letters he wrote to the *Guardian*, which I hear have been highly praised by competent critics, and I have ordered a set of them for the files of the library. You yourself, I find, are highly thought of in Brampton " (a not unimportant factor, by the way); "you have been splendidly educated, and are a lady. In short, Cynthia, I have come to give my formal consent to your engagement to my son Robert."

"But I am not engaged to him," said Cynthia.

"He will be here shortly, I imagine," said Mr. Worthington.

Cynthia was trembling more than ever by this time. She was very angry, and she had found it very difficult to repress the things which she had been impelled to speak. She did not hate Isaac Worthington now — she despised him. He had not dared to mention Jethro, who had been her benefactor, though he had done his best to have her removed from the school because of her connection with Jethro.

"Mr. Worthington," she said, " I have not yet made up my mind whether I shall marry your son."

To say that Mr. Worthington's breath was taken away when he heard these words would be to use a mild expression. He doubted his senses.

" What? " he exclaimed, starting forward, " what do you mean ? "

Cynthia hesitated a moment. She was not frightened, but she was trying to choose her words without passion.

" I refused to marry him," she said, " because you withheld your consent, and I did not wish to be the cause of a quarrel between you. It was not difficult to guess your feelings toward me, even before certain things occurred of which I will not speak. I did my best, from the very first, to make Bob give up the thought of marrying me, although I loved and honored him. Loving him as I do, I do not want to be the cause of separating him from his father, and of depriving him of that which is rightfully his. But something is due to myself. If I should ever make up my mind to marry him," continued Cynthia, looking at Mr. Worthington steadfastly, " it will not be because your consent is given or withheld."

" Do you tell me this to my face ? " exclaimed Mr. Worthington, now in a rage himself at such unheard-of presumption.

" To your face," said Cynthia, who got more self-controlled as he grew angry. " I believe that that consent, which you say you have given freely, was wrung from you."

It was unfortunate that the first citizen might not always have Mr. Flint by him to restrain and caution him. But Mr. Flint could have no command over his master's sensations, and anger and apprehension goaded Mr. Worthington to indiscretion.

" Jethro Bass told you this! " he cried out.

" No," Cynthia answered, not in the least surprised by the admission, " he did not tell me — but he will if I ask him. I guessed it from your letter. I heard that he had come back to-day, and I went to Coniston to see him, and he told me — he had been defeated."

Tears came into her eyes at the remembrance of the scene in the tannery house that afternoon, and she knew now why Jethro's face had worn that look of peace. He had made his supreme sacrifice — for her. No, he had told her nothing, and she might never have known. She sat thinking of the magnitude of this thing Jethro had done, and she ceased to speak, and the tears coursed down her cheeks unheeded.

Isaac Worthington had a habit of clutching things when he was in a rage, and now he clutched the arms of the chair. He had grown white. He was furious with her, furious with himself for having spoken that which might be construed into a confession. He had not finished writing the letters before he had stood self-justified, and he had been self-justified ever since. Where now were these arguments so wonderfully plausible? Where were the refutations which he had made ready in case of a barely possible need? He had gone into the Pelican House intending to tell Jethro of his determination to agree to the marriage. That was one. He had done so — that was another — and he had written the letters that Jethro might be convinced of his good will. There were still more, involving Jethro's character for veracity and other things. Summoning these, he waited for Cynthia to have done speaking, but when she had finished — he said nothing. He looked at her, and saw the tears on her face, and he saw that she had completely forgotten his presence.

For the life of him, Isaac Worthington could not utter a word. He was a man, as we know, who did not talk idly, and he knew that Cynthia would not hear what he said; and arguments and denunciations lose their effect when repeated. Again, he knew that she would not believe him. Never in his life had Isaac Worthington been so ignored, so put to shame, as by this school-teacher of Brampton. Before, self-esteem and sophistry had always carried him off between them; sometimes, in truth, with a wound — the wound had always healed. But he had a feeling, to-night, that this woman had glanced into his soul, and had turned away from it. As he looked at her the texture of his anger changed; he forgot for the first time that which he had been pleased to think of as her position in life, and he feared her. He had matched his spirit against hers.

2 M

Before long the situation became intolerable to him, for
Cynthia still sat silent. She was thinking of how she had
blamed Jethro for going back to that life, even though his
love for her had made him do it. But Isaac Worthington
did not know of what she was thinking — he thought only
of himself and his predicament. He could not remain,
and yet he could not go — with dignity. He who had
come to bestow could not depart like a whipped dog.

Suddenly a fear transfixed him: suppose that this
woman, from whom he could not hide the truth, should tell
his son what he had done. Bob would believe her. Could
he, Isaac Worthington, humble his pride and ask her to
keep her suspicions to herself ? He would then be acknowl-
edging that they were more than suspicions. If he did so,
he would have to appear to forgive her in spite of what
she had said to him. And Bob was coming home. Could
he tell Bob that he had changed his mind and withdrawn
his consent to the marriage ? There would be the reason,
and again Bob would believe her. And again, if he with-
drew his consent, there was Jethro to reckon with. Jethro
must have a weapon still, Mr. Worthington thought, although he could not imagine what it might be. As Isaac
Worthington sat there, thinking, it grew clear to him at
last that there was but one exit out of a very desperate
situation.

He glanced at Cynthia again, this time appraisingly.
She had dried her eyes, but she made no effort to speak.
After all, she would make such a wife for his son as few
men possessed. He thought of Sarah Hollingsworth. She
had been a good woman, but there had been many times
when he had deplored — especially in his travels — the lack
of other qualities in his wife. Cynthia, he thought, had
these qualities, — so necessary for the wife of one who
would succeed to power — though whence she had got
them Isaac Worthington could not imagine. She would
become a personage; she was a woman of whom they had
no need to be ashamed at home or abroad. Having completed these reflections, he broke the silence.

"I am sorry that you should have been misled into

thinking such a thing as you have expressed, Cynthia," he said, " but I believe that I can understand something of the feelings which prompted you. It is natural that you should have a resentment against me after everything that has happened. It is perhaps natural, too, that I should lose my temper under the circumstances. Let us forget it. And I trust that in the future we shall grow into the mutual respect and affection which our nearer relationship will demand."

He rose, and took up his hat, and Cynthia rose too. There was something very fine, he thought, about her carriage and expression as she stood in front of him.

" There is my hand," he said, — " will you take it ? "

" I will take it," Cynthia answered, " because you are Bob's father."

And then Mr. Worthington went away.

CHAPTER XX

"TO CHANGE THE NAME, AND NOT THE LETTER"

I AM able to cite one notable instance, at least, to disprove the saying a part of which is written above, and I have yet to hear of a case in which a gentleman ever hesitated a single instant on account of the first letter of a lady's last name. I know, indeed, of an occasion when locomotives could not go fast enough, when thirty miles an hour seemed a snail's pace to a young man who sat by the open window of a train that crept northward on a certain hazy September morning up the beautiful valley of a broad river which we know.

It was after three o'clock before he caught sight of the familiar crest of Farewell Mountain, and the train ran into Harwich. How glad he was to see everybody there, whether he knew them or not! He came near hugging the conductor of the Truro accommodation; who, needless to say, did not ask him for a ticket, or even a pass. And then the young man went forward and almost shook the arms off of the engineer and the fireman, and climbed into the cab, and actually drove the engine himself as far as Brampton, where it arrived somewhat ahead of schedule, — having taken some of the curves and bridges at a speed a little beyond the law. The engineer was richer by five dollars, and the son of a railroad president is a privileged character, anyway.

Yes, here was Brampton, and in spite of the haze the sun had never shone so brightly on the terraced steeple of the meeting-house. He leaped out of the cab almost before the engine had stopped, and beamed upon everybody on the platform, — even upon Mr. Dodd, who chanced to be there. In a twinkling the young man is in Mr. Sherman's hack, and Mr. Sherman galloping his horse down Brampton Street, the young man with his head out of the window, smiling ; grinning would be a better word. Here are the iron mastiffs, and they seem to be grinning, too. The young man flings open the carriage door and leaps out, and the door is almost broken from its hinges by the maple tree. He rushes up the steps and through the hall, and into the library, where the first citizen and his seneschal are sitting.

"Hello, Father, you see I didn't waste any time," he cried, grasping his father's hand in a grip that made Mr. Worthington wince. "Well, you are a trump, after all. We're both a little hot-headed, I guess, and do things we're sorry for, — but that's all over now, isn't it? I'm sorry. I might have known you'd come round when you found out for yourself what kind of a girl Cynthia was. Did you ever see anybody like her ? "

Mr. Flint turned his back, and started to walk out of the room.

"Don't go, Flint, old boy," Bob called out, seizing Mr. Flint's hand, too. "I can't stay but a minute, now. How are you ? "

"All right, Bob," answered Mr. Flint, with a curious, kindly look in his eyes that was not often there. "I'm glad to see you home. I have to go to the bank."

"Well, Father," said Bob, "school must be out, and I imagine you know where I'm going. I just thought I'd stop in to — to thank you, and get a benediction."

"I am very happy to have you back, Robert," replied Mr. Worthington, and it was true. It would have been strange indeed if some tremor of sentiment had not been in his voice and some gleam of pride in his eye as he looked upon his son.

"So you saw her, and couldn't resist her," said Bob. "Wasn't that how it happened ? "

Mr. Worthington sat down again at the desk, and his hand began to stray among the papers. He was thinking of Mr. Flint's exit.

"I do not arrive at my decisions quite in that way, Robert," he answered.

"But you have seen her?"

"Yes, I have seen her."

There was a hesitation, an uneasiness in his father's tone for which Bob could not account, and which he attributed to emotion. He did not guess that this hour of supreme joy could hold for Isaac Worthington another sensation.

"Isn't she the finest girl in the world?" he demanded. "How does she seem? How does she look?"

"She looks extremely well," said Mr. Worthington, who had now schooled his voice. "In fact, I am quite ready to admit that Cynthia Wetherell possesses the qualifications necessary for your wife. If she had not, I should never have written you."

Bob walked to the window.

"Father," he said, speaking with a little difficulty, "I can't tell you how much I appreciate your — your coming round. I wanted to do the right thing, but I just couldn't give up such a girl as that."

"We shall let bygones be bygones, Robert," answered Mr. Worthington, clearing his throat.

"She never would have me without your consent. By the way," he cried, turning suddenly, "did she say she'd have me now?"

"I believe," said Mr. Worthington, clearing his throat again, "I believe she reserved her decision."

"I must be off," said Bob, "she goes to Coniston on Fridays. I'll drive her out. Good-by, Father."

He flew out of the room, ran against Mrs. Holden, whom he astonished by saluting on the cheek, and astonished even more by asking her to tell Silas to drive his black horses to Gabriel Post's house — as the cottage was still known in Brampton. And having hastily removed some of the cinders, he flew out of the door and reached the parklike space in the middle of Brampton Street. Then he tried to walk decorously, but it was hard work. What if she should not be in?

The door and windows of the little house were open that balmy afternoon, and the bees were buzzing among the flowers which Cynthia had planted on either side of the step. Bob went up the path, and caught a glimpse of her through the entry standing in the sitting room. She was, indeed, waiting for the Coniston stage, and she did not see him. Shall I destroy the mental image of the reader who has known her so long by trying to tell what she looked like ? Some heroines grow thin and worn by the troubles which they are forced to go through. Cynthia was not this kind of a heroine. She was neither tall nor short, and the dark blue gown which she wore set off (so Bob thought) the curves of her figure to perfection. Her face had become a little more grave, — yes, and more noble ; and the eyes and mouth had an indescribable, womanly sweetness.

He stood for a moment outside the doorway gazing at her ; hesitating to desecrate that revery, which seemed to him to have a touch of sadness in it. And then she turned her head, slowly, and saw him, and her lips parted, and a startled look came into her eyes, but she did not move. He came quickly into the room and stopped again, quivering from head to foot with the passion which the sight of her never failed to unloose within him. Still she did not speak, but her lip trembled, and the love leaping in his eyes kindled a yearning in hers, — a yearning she was powerless to resist. He may by that strange power have drawn her toward him — he never knew. Neither of them could have given evidence on that marvellous instant when the current bridged the space between them. He could not say whether this woman whom he had seized by force before had shown a like vitality in her surrender. He only knew that her arms were woven about his neck, and that the kiss of which he had dreamed was again on his lips, and that he felt once more her wonderful, supple body pressed against his, and her heart beating, and her breast heaving. And he knew that the strength of the love in her which he had gained was beyond estimation.

Thus for a time they swung together in ethereal space, breathless with the motion of their flight. The duration of such moments is — in words — limitless. Now he held her against him, and again he held her away that his eyes might feast upon hers until she dropped her lashes and the crimson tide flooded into her face and she hid it again in the refuge she had longed for, — murmuring his name. But at last, startled by some sound without and so brought back to earth, she led him gently to the window at the side and looked up at him searchingly. He was tanned no longer.

"I was afraid you had been working too hard," she said.

"So you do love me?" was Bob's answer to this remark.

Cynthia smiled at him with her eyes: gravely, if such a thing may be said of a smile.

"Bob, how can you ask?"

"Oh, Cynthia," he cried, "if you knew what I have been through, you wouldn't have held out, I know it. I began to think I should never have you."

"But you have me now," she said, and was silent.

"Why do you look like that?" he asked.

She smiled up at him again.

"I, too, have suffered, Bob," she said. "And I have thought of you night and day."

"God bless you, sweetheart," he cried, and kissed her again, — many times. "It's all right now, isn't it? I knew my father would give his consent when he found out what you were."

The expression of pain which had troubled him crossed her face again, and she put her hand on his shoulder.

"Listen, dearest," she said, "I love *you*. I am doing this for *you*. You must understand that."

"Why, yes, Cynthia, I understand it — of course I do," he answered, perplexed. "I understand it, but I don't deserve it."

"I want you to know," she continued in a low voice, "that I should have married you anyway. I — I could not have helped it."

"Cynthia!"

"If you were to go back to the locomotive works to-morrow, I would marry you."

"On ninety dollars a month?" exclaimed Bob.

"If you wanted me," she said.

"Wanted you! I could live in a log cabin with you the rest of my life."

She drew down his face to hers, and kissed him.

"But I wished you to be reconciled with your father," she said; "I could not bear to come between you. You — you are reconciled, aren't you?"

"Indeed, we are," he said.

"I am glad, Bob," she answered simply. "I should not have been happy if I had driven you away from the place where you should be, which is your home."

"Wherever you are will be my home, sweetheart," he said, and pressed her to him once more.

At length, looking past his shoulder into the street, she saw Lem Hallowell pulling up the Brampton stage before the door.

"Bob," she said, "I must go to Coniston and see Uncle Jethro. I promised him."

Bob's answer was to walk into the entry, where he stood waving the most joyous of greetings at the surprised stage driver.

"I guess you won't get anybody here, Lem," he called out.

"But, Bob," protested Cynthia, from within, afraid to show her face just then, "I have to go, I promised. And — and I want to go," she added when he turned.

"I'm running a stage to Coniston to-day myself, Lem," said he "and I'm going to steal your best passenger."

Lemuel immediately flung down his reins and jumped out of the stage and came up the path and into the entry, where he stood confronting Cynthia.

"Hev you took him, Cynthy?" he demanded.

"Yes, Lem," she answered, "won't you congratulate me?"

The warm-hearted stage driver did congratulate her in a most unmistakable manner.

"I think a sight of her, Bob," he said after he had shaken both of Bob's hands and brushed his own eyes with his coat sleeve. "I've knowed her so long —" Whereupon utterance failed him, and he ran down the path and jumped into his stage again and drove off.

And then Cynthia sent Bob on an errand — not a very long one, and while he was gone, she sat down at the table and tried to realize her happiness, and failed. In less than ten minutes Bob had come back with Cousin Ephraim, as fast as he could hobble. He flung his arms around her, stick and all, and he was crying. It is a fact that old soldiers sometimes cry. But his tears did not choke his utterance.

"Great Tecumseh!" said Cousin Ephraim, "so you've went and done it, Cynthy. Siege got a little mite too hot. I callated she'd capitulate in the end, but she held out uncommon long."

"That she did," exclaimed Bob, feelingly.

"I was tellin' Bob I hain't got nothin' against him," continued Ephraim.

"Oh, Cousin Eph," said Cynthia, laughing in spite of herself, and glancing at Bob, "is that all you can say?"

"Cousin Eph's all right," said Bob, laughing too. "We understand each other."

"Callate we do," answered Ephraim. "I'll go so far as to say there hain't nobody I'd ruther see you marry. Guess I'll hev to go back to the kit, now. What's to become of the old pensioner, Cynthy?"

"The old pensioner needn't worry," said Cynthia.

Then drove up Silas the Silent, with Bob's buggy and his black trotters. All of Brampton might see them now, and all of Brampton did see them. Silas got out, — his presence not being required, — and Cynthia was helped in, and Bob got in beside her, and away they went, leaving Ephraim waving his stick after them from the door-step.

It is recorded against the black trotters that they made very poor time to Coniston that day, though I cannot discover that either of them was lame. Lem Hallowell, who was there nearly an hour ahead of them, declares that the off horse had a bunch of branches in his mouth. Perhaps Bob held them in on account of the scenery that September afternoon. Incomparable scenery! I doubt if two lovers of the renaissance ever wandered through a more wondrous realm of pleasance — to quote the words of the poet. Spots in it are like a park, laid out by that peerless landscape gardener, nature: dark, symmetrical pine trees on the sward, and maples in the fulness of their leaf, and great oaks on the hillsides, and coppices; and beyond, the mountain, the evergreens massed like cloud-shadows on its slopes; and all — trees and coppice and mountain — flattened by the haze until they seemed woven in the softest of blues and blue greens into one exquisite picture of an ancient tapestry. I, myself, have seen these pictures in that country, and marvelled.

So they drove on through that realm, which was to be their realm, and came all too soon to Coniston green. Lem Hallowell had spread the well-nigh incredible news, that Cynthia Wetherell was to marry the son of the mill-owner and railroad president of Brampton, and it seemed to Cynthia that every man and woman and child of the village was gathered at the store. Although she loved them, every one, she whispered something to Bob when she caught sight of that group on the platform, and he spoke to the trotters. Thus it happened that they flew by, and were at the tannery house before they knew it; and Cynthia, all unaided, sprang out of the buggy and ran in, alone. She found Jethro sitting outside of the kitchen door with a volume on his knee, and she saw that the print of it was large, and she knew that the book was "Robinson Crusoe."

Cynthia knelt down on the grass beside him and caught his hands in hers.

"Uncle Jethro," she said, "I am going to marry Bob Worthington."

"Yes, Cynthy," he answered. And taking the initiative for the first time in his life, he stooped down and kissed her.

" I knew — you would be happy — in my happiness,"
she said, the tears brimming in her eyes.

" N-never have been so happy, Cynthy, — never have."

" Uncle Jethro, I never will desert you. I shall always
take care of you."

" R-read to me sometimes, Cynthy — r-read to me ? "

But she could not answer him. She was sobbing on the
pages of that book he had given her — long ago.

*　　　*　　　*　　　*　　　*　　　*　　　*

I like to dwell on happiness, and I am reluctant to leave
these people whom I have grown to love. Jethro Bass
lived to take Cynthia's children down by the brook and to
show them the pictures, at least, in that wonderful edition
of " Robinson Crusoe." He would never depart from the
tannery house, but Cynthia went to him there, many times
a week. There is a spot not far from the Coniston road,
and five miles distant alike from Brampton and Coniston,
where Bob Worthington built his house, and where he and
Cynthia dwelt many years; and they go there to this
day, in the summer-time. It stands in the midst of broad
lands, and the ground in front of it slopes down to Coniston Water, artificially widened here by a stone dam into a
little lake. From the balcony of the summer-house which
overhangs the lake there is a wonderful view of Coniston
Mountain, and Cynthia Worthington often sits there with
her sewing or her book, listening to the laughter of her
children, and thinking, sometimes, of bygone days.

AFTERWORD

THE reality of the foregoing pages has to the author, at least, become so vivid that he regrets the necessity of having to add an afterword. Every novel is, to some extent, a compound of truth and fiction, and he has done his best to picture conditions as they were, and to make the spirit of his book true. Certain people who were living in St. Louis during the Civil War have been mentioned as the originals of characters in "The Crisis," and there are houses in that city which have been pointed out as fitting descriptions in that novel. An author has, frequently, people, houses, and localities in mind when he writes; but he changes them, sometimes very materially, in the process of literary construction.

It is inevitable, perhaps, that many people of a certain New England state will recognize Jethro Bass. There are different opinions extant concerning the remarkable original of this character; ardent defenders and detractors of his are still living, but all agree that he was a strange man of great power. The author disclaims any intention of writing a biography of him. Some of the things set down in this book he did, and others he did not do. Some of the anecdotes here related concerning him are, in the main, true, and for this material the author acknowledges his indebtedness particularly to Colonel Thomas B. Cheney of Ashland, New Hampshire, and to other friends who have helped him. Jethro Bass was typical of his Era, and it is of the Era that this book attempts to treat.

Concerning the locality where Jethro Bass was born and lived, it will and will not be recognized. It would have been the extreme of bad taste to have put into these pages any portraits which might have offended families or individuals, and in order that it may be known that the author has not done so he has written this Afterword. Nor has he particularly chosen for the field of this novel a state of which he is a citizen, and for which he has a sincere affection. The conditions here depicted, while retaining the characteristics of the locality, he believes to be typical of the Era over a large part of the United States.

Many of the Puritans who came to New England were impelled to emigrate from the old country, no doubt, by an aversion to pulling the forelock as well as by religious principles, and the spirit of these men prevailed for a certain time after the Revolution was fought. Such men lived and ruled in Coniston before the rise of Jethro Bass.

Self-examination is necessary for the moral health of nations as well as men, and it is the most hopeful of signs that in the United States we are to-day going through a period of self-examination.

We shall do well to ascertain the causes which have led us gradually to stray from the political principles laid down by our forefathers for all the world to see. Some of us do not even know what those principles were. I have met many intelligent men, in different states of the Union, who could not even repeat the names of the senators who sat for them in Congress. Macaulay said, in 1852, " We now know, by the clearest of all proof, that universal suffrage, even united with secret voting, is no security against the establishment of arbitrary power." To quote James Russell Lowell, writing a little later: " We have begun obscurely to recognize that . . . popular government is not in itself a panacea, is no better than any other form except as the virtue and wisdom of the people make it so."

As Americans, we cannot but believe that our political creed goes down in its foundations to the solid rock of truth. One of the best reasons for our belief lies in the fact that, since 1776, government after government has imitated our example. We have, by our very existence and rise to power, made any decided retrogression from these doctrines impossible. So many people have tried to rule themselves, and are still trying, that one begins to believe that the time is not far distant when the United

States, once the most radical, will become the most conservative of nations.

Thus the duty rests to-day, more heavily than ever, upon each American citizen to make good to the world those principles upon which his government was built. To use a figure suggested by the calamity which has lately befallen one of the most beloved of our cities, there is a theory that earthquakes are caused by a necessary movement on the part of the globe to regain its axis. Whether or not the theory be true, it has its political application. In America to-day we are trying — whatever the cost — to regain the true axis established for us by the founders of our Republic.

HARLAKENDEN HOUSE, May 7, 1906.